SECOND EDITION

Version Control with Git

Jon Loeliger and Matthew McCullough

Beijing · Cambridge · Farnham · Köln · Sebastopol · Tokyo

Version Control with Git, Second Edition
by Jon Loeliger and Matthew McCullough

Copyright © 2012 Jon Loeliger. All rights reserved.
Printed in the United States of America.

Published by O'Reilly Media, Inc., 1005 Gravenstein Highway North, Sebastopol, CA 95472.

O'Reilly books may be purchased for educational, business, or sales promotional use. Online editions are also available for most titles (*http://my.safaribooksonline.com*). For more information, contact our corporate/institutional sales department: 800-998-9938 or *corporate@oreilly.com*.

Editor: Andy Oram	**Indexer:** Nancy Guenther on behalf of Potomac Indexing, LLC
Production Editor: Iris Febres	
Copyeditor: Absolute Service, Inc.	**Cover Designer:** Karen Montgomery
Proofreader: Absolute Service, Inc.	**Interior Designer:** David Futato
	Illustrators: Robert Romano and Rebecca Demarest

May 2009:   First Edition.
August 2012:   Second Edition.

Revision History for the Second Edition:
    2012-08-03   First release
See *http://oreilly.com/catalog/errata.csp?isbn=9781449316389* for release details.

ISBN: 978-1-449-31638-9

[LSI]

1344026292

Table of Contents

Preface

Audience

Although some familiarity with revision control systems will be good background material, a reader who is not familiar with any other system will still be able to learn enough about basic Git operations to be productive in a short while. More advanced readers should be able to gain insight into some of Git's internal design and thus master some of its more powerful techniques.

The main intended audience of this book should be familiar and comfortable with the Unix shell, basic shell commands, and general programming concepts.

Assumed Framework

Almost all examples and discussions in this book assume the reader has a Unix-like system with a command-line interface. The author developed these examples on Debian and Ubuntu Linux environments. The examples should work under other environments, such as Mac OS X or Solaris, but the reader can expect slight variations.

A few examples require root access on machines where system operations are needed. Naturally, in such situations, you should have a clear understanding of the responsibilities of root access.

Book Layout and Omissions

This book is organized as a progressive series of topics, each designed to build upon concepts introduced earlier. The first 11 chapters focus on concepts and operations that pertain to one repository. They form the foundation for more complex operations on multiple repositories covered in the final 10 chapters.

If you already have Git installed or have even used it briefly, then you may not need the introductory and installation information in the first two chapters, nor even the quick tour presented in the third chapter.

The concepts covered in Chapter 4 are essential for a firm grasp on Git's object model. They set the stage and prepare the reader for a clearer understanding of many of Git's more complex operations.

Chapters 5 through 11 cover various topics in more detail. Chapter 5 describes the index and file management. Chapters 6 and 10 discuss the fundamentals of making commits and working with them to form a solid line of development. Chapter 7 introduces branches so that you may manipulate several different lines of development from your one local repository. Chapter 8 explains how Git derives and presents "diffs."

Git provides a rich and powerful ability to join different branches of development. The basics of branch merging and resolving merge conflicts are covered in Chapter 9. A key insight into Git's model is to realize that all merging performed by Git happens in your local repository in the context of your current working directory. Chapters 10 and 11 expose some operations for altering, storing, tracking, and recovering daily development within your development repository.

The fundamentals of naming and exchanging data with another, remote repository are covered in Chapter 12. Once the basics of merging have been mastered, interacting with multiple repositories is shown to be a simple combination of an exchange step plus a merge step. The exchange step is the new concept covered in this chapter and the merge step is covered in Chapter 9.

Chapter 13 provides a more philosophical and abstract coverage of repository management "in the large." It also establishes a context for Chapter 14 to cover patch handling when direct exchange of repository information isn't possible using Git's native transfer protocols.

The next four chapters cover advanced topics of interest: the use of hooks (Chapter 15), combining projects and multiple repositories into a superproject (Chapter 16), and interacting with Subversion repositories (Chapter 17).

Chapters 19 and 20 provide some advanced examples and clever tips, tricks, and techniques that may help transform you into a true Git guru.

Finally, Chapter 21 introduces GitHub and explains how Git has enabled a creative, social development process around version control.

Git is still evolving rapidly because there is an active developer base. It's not that Git is so immature that you cannot use it for development; rather, ongoing refinements and user interface issues are being enhanced regularly. Even as this book was being written, Git evolved. Apologies if I was unable to keep up accurately.

I do not give the command `gitk` the complete coverage that it deserves. If you like graphical representations of the history within a repository, you should explore `gitk`. Other history visualization tools exist as well, but they are not covered here either. Nor am I able to cover a rapidly evolving and growing host of other Git-related tools. I'm not even able to cover all of Git's own core commands and options thoroughly in this book. Again, my apologies.

Perhaps, though, enough pointers, tips, and direction can be found here to inspire readers to do some of their own research and exploration!

Conventions Used in This Book

The following typographical conventions are used in this book:

Italic

Indicates new terms, URLs, email addresses, filenames, and file extensions.

`Constant width`

Used for program listings as well as within paragraphs to refer to program elements such as variable or function names, databases, data types, environment variables, statements, and keywords.

`Constant width bold`

Shows commands or other text that should be typed literally by the user.

`Constant width italic`

Shows text that should be replaced with user-supplied values or by values determined by context.

 This icon signifies a useful hint or a tip.

 This icon indicates a warning or caution.

 This icon indicates a general note.

Furthermore, you should be familiar with basic shell commands to manipulate files and directories. Many examples will contain commands such as these to add or remove directories, copy files, or create simple files:

```
$ cp file.txt copy-of-file.txt
$ mkdir newdirectory
$ rm file
$ rmdir somedir
$ echo "Test line" > file
$ echo "Another line" >> file
```

Commands that need to be executed with root permissions appear as a sudo operation:

```
# Install the Git core package
```

```
$ sudo apt-get install git-core
```

How you edit files or effect changes within your working directory is pretty much up to you. You should be familiar with a text editor. In this book, I'll denote the process of editing a file by either a direct comment or a pseudocommand:

```
# edit file.c to have some new text
```

```
$ edit index.html
```

Using Code Examples

This book is here to help you get your job done. In general, you may use the code in this book in your programs and documentation. You do not need to contact us for permission unless you're reproducing a significant portion of the code. For example, writing a program that uses several chunks of code from this book does not require permission. Selling or distributing a CD-ROM of examples from O'Reilly books does require permission. Answering a question by citing this book and quoting example code does not require permission. Incorporating a significant amount of example code from this book into your product's documentation does require permission.

We appreciate, but do not require, attribution. An attribution usually includes the title, author, publisher, and ISBN. For example: "*Version Control with Git* by Jon Loeliger and Matthew McCullough. Copyright 2012 Jon Loeliger, 978-1-449-31638-9."

If you feel your use of code examples falls outside fair use or the permission given previously, feel free to contact us at *permissions@oreilly.com*.

Safari® Books Online

Safari Books Online (*www.safaribooksonline.com*) is an on-demand digital library that delivers expert content in both book and video form from the world's leading authors in technology and business.

Technology professionals, software developers, web designers, and business and creative professionals use Safari Books Online as their primary resource for research, problem solving, learning, and certification training.

Safari Books Online offers a range of product mixes and pricing programs for organizations, government agencies, and individuals. Subscribers have access to thousands of books, training videos, and prepublication manuscripts in one fully searchable database from publishers like O'Reilly Media, Prentice Hall Professional, Addison-Wesley Professional, Microsoft Press, Sams, Que, Peachpit Press, Focal Press, Cisco Press, John Wiley & Sons, Syngress, Morgan Kaufmann, IBM Redbooks, Packt, Adobe

Press, FT Press, Apress, Manning, New Riders, McGraw-Hill, Jones & Bartlett, Course Technology, and dozens more. For more information about Safari Books Online, please visit us online.

How to Contact Us

Please address comments and questions concerning this book to the publisher:

O'Reilly Media, Inc.
1005 Gravenstein Highway North
Sebastopol, CA 95472
800-998-9938 (in the United States or Canada)
707-829-0515 (international or local)
707-829-0104 (fax)

We have a web page for this book, where we list errata, examples, and any additional information. You can access this page at:

http://oreil.ly/VCWG2e

To comment or ask technical questions about this book, send email to:

bookquestions@oreilly.com

For more information about our books, courses, conferences, and news, see our website at *http://www.oreilly.com.*

Find us on Facebook: *http://facebook.com/oreilly*

Follow us on Twitter: *http://twitter.com/oreillymedia*

Watch us on YouTube: *http://www.youtube.com/oreillymedia*

Acknowledgments

This work would not have been possible without the help of many other people. I'd like to thank Avery Pennarun for contributing substantial material to Chapters 15, 16, and 18. He also contributed some material to Chapters 4 and 9. His help was appreciated. I'd like to thank Matthew McCullough for the material in Chapters 17 and 21, assorted suggestions, and general advice. Martin Langhoff is paraphrased with permission for some repository publishing advice in Chapter 13, and Bart Massey's tip on keeping a file without tracking is also used with permission. I'd like to publicly thank those who took time to review the book at various stages: Robert P. J. Day, Alan Hasty, Paul Jimenez, Barton Massey, Tom Rix, Jamey Sharp, Sarah Sharp, Larry Streepy, Andy Wilcox, and Andy Wingo. Robert P. J. Day, thankfully, took the time to review both editions of the book front to back.

Also, I'd like to thank my wife Rhonda, and daughters Brandi and Heather, who provided moral support, gentle nudging, Pinot Noir, and the occasional grammar tip. And thanks to Mylo, my long-haired dachshund who spent the entire writing process curled up lovingly in my lap. I'd like to add a special thanks to K. C. Dignan, who supplied enough moral support and double-stick butt-tape to keep my behind in my chair long enough to finish this book!

Finally, I would like to thank the staff at O'Reilly as well as my editors, Andy Oram and Martin Streicher.

Attributions

Linux® is the registered trademark of Linus Torvalds in the United States and other countries.

PowerPC® is a trademark of International Business Machines Corporation in the United States, other countries, or both.

UNIX is a registered trademark of The Open Group in the United States and other countries.

## CHAPTER 1

Introduction

Background

No cautious, creative person starts a project nowadays without a back-up strategy. Because data is ephemeral and can be lost easily—through an errant code change or a catastrophic disk crash, say—it is wise to maintain a living archive of all work.

For text and code projects, the back-up strategy typically includes version control, or tracking and managing revisions. Each developer can make several revisions per day, and the ever increasing corpus serves simultaneously as repository, project narrative, communication medium, and team and product management tool. Given its pivotal role, version control is most effective when tailored to the working habits and goals of the project team.

A tool that manages and tracks different versions of software or other content is referred to generically as a version control system (VCS), a source code manager (SCM), a revision control system (RCS), and several other permutations of the words "revision," "version," "code," "content," "control," "management," and "system." Although the authors and users of each tool might debate esoterics, each system addresses the same issue: develop and maintain a repository of content, provide access to historical editions of each datum, and record all changes in a log. In this book, the term *version control system* (VCS) is used to refer generically to any form of revision control system.

This book covers Git, a particularly powerful, flexible, and low-overhead version control tool that makes collaborative development a pleasure. Git was invented by Linus Torvalds to support the development of the Linux®[1] kernel, but it has since proven valuable to a wide range of projects.

---

1. Linux® is the registered trademark of Linus Torvalds in the United States and other countries.

The Birth of Git

Often, when there is discord between a tool and a project, the developers simply create a new tool. Indeed, in the world of software, the temptation to create new tools can be deceptively easy and inviting. In the face of many existing version control systems, the decision to create another shouldn't be made casually. However, given a critical need, a bit of insight, and a healthy dose of motivation, forging a new tool can be exactly the right course.

Git, affectionately termed "the information manager from hell" by its creator (Linus is known for both his irascibility and his dry wit), is such a tool. Although the precise circumstances and timing of its genesis are shrouded in political wrangling within the Linux kernel community, there is no doubt that what came from that fire is a well-engineered version control system capable of supporting the worldwide development of software on a large scale.

Prior to Git, the Linux kernel was developed using the commercial BitKeeper VCS, which provided sophisticated operations not available in then-current, free software VCSs such as RCS and the concurrent version system (CVS). However, when the company that owned BitKeeper placed additional restrictions on its "free as in beer" version in the spring of 2005, the Linux community realized that BitKeeper was no longer a viable solution.

Linus looked for alternatives. Eschewing commercial solutions, he studied the free software packages but found the same limitations and flaws that led him to reject them previously. What was wrong with the existing VCSs? What were the elusive missing features or characteristics that Linus wanted and couldn't find?

Facilitate Distributed Development
There are many facets to "distributed development," and Linus wanted a new VCS that would cover most of them. It had to allow parallel as well as independent and simultaneous development in private repositories without the need for constant synchronization with a central repository, which could form a development bottleneck. It had to allow multiple developers in multiple locations even if some of them were offline temporarily.

Scale to Handle Thousands of Developers
It isn't enough just to have a distributed development model. Linus knew that thousands of developers contribute to each Linux release. So any new VCS had to handle a very large number of developers whether they were working on the same or different parts of a common project. And the new VCS had to be able to integrate all of their work reliably.

Perform Quickly and Efficiently
Linus was determined to ensure that a new VCS was fast and efficient. In order to support the sheer volume of update operations that would be made on the Linux kernel alone, he knew that both individual update operations and network transfer

operations would have to be very fast. To save space and thus transfer time, compression and "delta" techniques would be needed. Using a distributed model instead of a centralized model also ensured that network latency would not hinder daily development.

Maintain Integrity and Trust

Because Git is a distributed revision control system, it is vital to obtain absolute assurance that data integrity is maintained and is not somehow being altered. How do you know the data hasn't been altered in transition from one developer to the next? Or from one repository to the next? Or, for that matter, that the data in a Git repository is even what it purports to be?

Git uses a common cryptographic hash function, called *Secure Hash Function* (SHA1), to name and identify objects within its database. Though perhaps not absolute, in practice it has proven to be solid enough to ensure integrity and trust for all Git's distributed repositories.

Enforce Accountability

One of the key aspects of a version control system is knowing who changed files and, if at all possible, why. Git enforces a change log on every commit that changes a file. The information stored in that change log is left up to the developer, project requirements, management, convention, and so on. Git ensures that changes will not happen mysteriously to files under version control because there is an accountability trail for all changes.

Immutability

Git's repository database contains data objects that are *immutable*. That is, once they have been created and placed in the database, they cannot be modified. They can be recreated differently, of course, but the original data cannot be altered without consequences. The design of the Git database means that the entire history stored within the version control database is also immutable. Using immutable objects has several advantages, including quick comparison for equality.

Atomic Transactions

With atomic transactions, a number of different but related changes are performed either all together or not at all. This property ensures that the version control database is not left in a partially changed or corrupted state while an update or commit is happening. Git implements atomic transactions by recording complete, discrete repository states that cannot be broken down into individual or smaller state changes.

Support and Encourage Branched Development

Almost all VCSs can name different genealogies of development within a single project. For instance, one sequence of code changes could be called "development" while another is referred to as "test." Each version control system can also split a single line of development into multiple lines and then unify, or merge, the disparate threads. As with most VCSs, Git calls a line of development a *branch* and assigns each branch a name.

Along with branching comes merging. Just as Linus wanted easy branching to foster alternate lines of development, he also wanted to facilitate easy merging of those branches. Because branch merging has often been a painful and difficult operation in version control systems, it would be essential to support clean, fast, easy merging.

Complete Repositories

So that individual developers needn't query a centralized repository server for historical revision information, it was essential that each repository have a complete copy of all historical revisions of every file.

A Clean Internal Design

Even though end users might not be concerned about a clean internal design, it was important to Linus and ultimately to other Git developers as well. Git's object model has simple structures that capture fundamental concepts for raw data, directory structure, recording changes, and so forth. Coupling the object model with a globally unique identifier technique allowed a very clean data model that could be managed in a distributed development environment.

Be Free, as in Freedom

'Nuff said.

Given a clean slate to create a new VCS, many talented software engineers collaborated and Git was born. Necessity was the mother of invention again!

Precedents

The complete history of VCSs is beyond the scope of this book. However, there are several landmark, innovative systems that set the stage for or directly led to the development of Git. (This section is selective, hoping to record when new features were introduced or became popular within the free software community.)

The Source Code Control System (SCCS) was one of the original systems on Unix®[2] and was developed by M. J. Rochkind in the very early 1970s. ["The Source Code Control System," *IEEE Transactions on Software Engineering* 1(4) (1975): 364-370.] This is arguably the first VCS available on any Unix system.

The central store that SCCS provided was called a repository, and that fundamental concept remains pertinent to this day. SCCS also provided a simple locking model to serialize development. If a developer needed files to run and test a program, he or she would check them out unlocked. However, in order to edit a file, he or she had to check it out with a lock (a convention enforced through the Unix file system). When finished, he or she would check the file back into the repository and unlock it.

---

2. UNIX is a registered trademark of The Open Group in the United States and other countries.

The Revision Control System (RCS) was introduced by Walter F. Tichy in the early 1980s. ["RCS: A System for Version Control," *Software Practice and Experience* 15(7) (1985): 637-654.] RCS introduced both forward and reverse delta concepts for the efficient storage of different file revisions.

The Concurrent Version System (CVS), designed and originally implemented by Dick Grune in 1986 and then crafted anew some four years later by Berliner and colleagues extended and modified the RCS model with great success. CVS became very popular and was the de facto standard within the open source (*http://www.opensource.org*) community for many years. CVS provided several advances over RCS, including distributed development and repository-wide change sets for entire "modules."

Furthermore, CVS introduced a new paradigm for the lock. Whereas earlier systems required a developer to lock each file before changing it and thus forced one developer to wait for another in serial fashion, CVS gave each developer write permission in his or her private working copy. Thus, changes by different developers could be merged automatically by CVS unless two developers tried to change the same line. In that case, the conflict was flagged and the developers were left to work out the solution. The new rules for the lock allowed different developers to write code concurrently.

As often occurs, perceived shortcomings and faults in CVS eventually led to a new VCS. Subversion (SVN), introduced in 2001, quickly became popular within the free software community. Unlike CVS, SVN committed changes atomically and had significantly better support for branches.

BitKeeper and Mercurial were radical departures from all the aforementioned solutions. Each eliminated the central repository; instead, the store was distributed, providing each developer with his own shareable copy. Git is derived from this peer-to-peer model.

Finally, Mercurial and Monotone contrived a hash fingerprint to uniquely identify a file's content. The name assigned to the file is a moniker and a convenient handle for the user and nothing more. Git features this notion as well. Internally, the Git identifier is based on the file's contents, a concept known as a content-addressable file store. The concept is not new. [See "The Venti Filesystem," (Plan 9), Bell Labs, *http://www.usenix .org/events/fast02/quinlan/quinlan_html/index.html*.] Git immediately borrowed the idea from Monotone, according to Linus.[3] Mercurial was implementing the concept simultaneously with Git.

3. Private email.

Timeline

With the stage set, a bit of external impetus, and a dire VCS crisis imminent, Git sprang to life in April 2005.

Git became self-hosted on April 7 with this commit:

```
commit e83c5163316f89bfbde7d9ab23ca2e25604af29
Author: Linus Torvalds <torvalds@ppc970.osdl.org>
Date:   Thu Apr 7 15:13:13 2005 -0700

Initial revision of "git", the information manager from hell
```

Shortly thereafter, the first Linux commit was made:

```
commit 1da177e4c3f41524e886b7f1b8a0c1fc7321cac2
Author: Linus Torvalds <torvalds@ppc970.osdl.org>
Date:   Sat Apr 16 15:20:36 2005 -0700

Linux-2.6.12-rc2

Initial git repository build. I'm not bothering with the full history,
even though we have it. We can create a separate "historical" git
archive of that later if we want to, and in the meantime it's about
3.2GB when imported into git - space that would just make the early
git days unnecessarily complicated, when we don't have a lot of good
infrastructure for it.

Let it rip!
```

That one commit introduced the bulk of the entire Linux Kernel into a Git repository.[4] It consisted of

```
17291 files changed, 6718755 insertions(+), 0 deletions(-)
```

Yes, that's an introduction of 6.7 million lines of code!

It was just three minutes later when the first patch using Git was applied to the kernel. Convinced that it was working, Linus announced it on April 20, 2005, to the Linux Kernel Mailing List.

Knowing full well that he wanted to return to the task of developing the kernel, Linus handed the maintenance of the Git source code to Junio Hamano on July 25, 2005, announcing that "Junio was the obvious choice."

About two months later, Version 2.6.12 of the Linux Kernel was released using Git.

---

4. See *http://kerneltrap.org/node/13996* for a starting point on how the old BitKeeper logs were imported into a Git repository for older history (pre-2.5).

What's in a Name?

Linus himself rationalizes the name "Git" by claiming "I'm an egotistical bastard, and I name all my projects after myself. First Linux, now git."[5] Granted, the name "Linux" for the kernel was sort of a hybrid of Linus and Minix. The irony of using a British term for a silly or worthless person was not missed, either.

Since then, others had suggested some alternative and perhaps more palatable interpretations: the Global Information Tracker seems to be the most popular.

5. See *http://www.infoworld.com/article/05/04/19/HNtorvaldswork_1.html*.

## CHAPTER 2

Installing Git

At the time of this writing, Git is (seemingly) not installed by default on any GNU/ Linux distribution or any other operating system. So, before you can use Git, you must install it. The steps to install Git depend greatly on the vendor and version of your operating system. This chapter describes how to install Git on Linux and Microsoft Windows and within Cygwin.

Using Linux Binary Distributions

Many Linux vendors provide precompiled, binary packages to make the installation of new applications, tools, and utilities easy. Each package specifies its dependencies, and the distribution's package manager typically installs the prerequisites and the desired package in one (well-orchestrated and automated) fell swoop.

Debian/Ubuntu

On most Debian and Ubuntu systems, Git is offered as a collection of packages, where each package can be installed independently depending on your needs. Prior to the 12.04 release, the primary Git package was called *git-core*. As of the 12.04 release, it is simply called *git*, and the documentation is available in *git-doc*. There are other packages to consider, too.

git-arch
git-cvs
git-svn
> If you need to transfer a project from Arch, CVS, or SVN to Git or vice versa, install one or more of these packages.

git-gui
gitk
gitweb

>   If you prefer to browse repositories in a graphical application or your web browser, install these as appropriate. *git-gui* is a Tcl/Tk-based graphical user interface for Git; *gitk* is another Git browser written in Tcl/Tk but focuses more on visualizing project history. *gitweb* is written in Perl and displays a Git repository in a browser window.

git-email

>   This is an essential component if you want to send Git patches through electronic mail, which is a common practice in some projects.

git-daemon-run

>   To share your repository, install this package. It creates a daemon service that allows you to share your repositories through anonymous download requests.

Because distributions vary greatly, it's best to search your distribution's package depot for a complete list of Git-related packages. *git-doc* and *git-email* are strongly recommended.

 Debian and Ubuntu provide a package named *git*, but it isn't a part of the Git version control system discussed in this book. *git* is a completely different program called GNU Interactive Tools. Be careful not to install the wrong package by accident!

This command installs the important Git packages by running `apt-get` as root.

```
$ sudo apt-get install git git-doc gitweb \
    git-gui gitk git-email git-svn
```

Other Binary Distributions

To install Git on other Linux distributions, find the appropriate package or packages and use the distribution's native package manager to install the software.

For example, on Gentoo systems, use `emerge`.

```
$ sudo emerge dev-util/git
```

On Fedora, use `yum`.

```
$ sudo yum install git
```

The Fedora *git* is roughly equivalent to Debian's *git*. Other `i386` Fedora packages include:

git.i386 :

>   The core Git tools

git-all.i386 :
> A meta-package for pulling in all Git tools

git-arch.i386 :
> Git tools for importing Arch repositories

git-cvs.i386 :
> Git tools for importing CVS repositories

git-daemon.i386 :
> The Git protocol daemon

git-debuginfo.i386 :
> Debug information for package *git*

git-email.i386 :
> Git tools for sending email

git-gui.i386 :
> Git GUI tool

git-svn.i386 :
> Git tools for importing SVN repositories

gitk.i386 :
> Git revision tree visualizer

Again, be mindful that, like Debian, some distributions may split the Git release among many different packages. If your system lacks a particular Git command, you may need to install an additional package.

Be sure to verify that your distribution's Git packages are sufficiently up-to-date. After Git is installed on your system, run `git --version`. If your collaborators use a more modern version of Git, you may have to replace your distribution's precompiled Git packages with a build of your own. Consult your package manager documentation to learn how to remove previously installed packages; proceed to the next section to learn how to build Git from source.

Obtaining a Source Release

If you prefer to download the Git code from its canonical source or if you want the latest version of Git, visit Git's master repository. As of this writing, the master repository for Git sources is *http://git.kernel.org* in the *pub/software/scm* directory.

The version of Git described in this book is roughly 1.7.9, but you might want to download the latest revision of the source. You can find a list of all the available versions at *http://code.google.com/p/git-core/downloads/list*.

To begin the build, download the source code for version 1.7.9 (or later) and unpack it.

```
$ wget http://git-core.googlecode.com/files/git-1.7.9.tar.gz
$ tar xzf git-1.7.9.tar.gz
$ cd git-1.7.9
```

Building and Installing

Git is similar to other pieces of open source software. Just configure it, type `make`, and install it. Small matter of software, right? Perhaps.

If your system has the proper libraries and a robust build environment and if you do not need to customize Git, then building the code can be a snap. On the other hand, if your machine lacks a compiler or a suite of server and software development libraries, or if you've never built a complex application from source, then you should consider building Git from scratch only as a last resort. Git is highly configurable, and building it shouldn't be taken lightly.

To continue the build, consult the *INSTALL* file in the Git source bundle. The file lists several external dependencies, including the *zlib*, *openssl*, and *libcurl* libraries.

Some of the requisite libraries and packages are a bit obscure or belong to larger packages. Here are three tips for a Debian stable distribution.

- *curl-config*, a small tool to extract information about the local *curl* install, can be found in the *libcurl4-openssl-dev* package.
- The header file *expat.h* comes from the *libexpat1-dev* package.
- The *msgfmt* utility belongs to the *gettext* package.

Because compiling from sources is considered "development" work, the normal binary versions of installed libraries are not sufficient. Instead, you need the *-dev* versions, because the development variants also supply header files required during compilation.

If you are unable to locate some of these packages or cannot find a necessary library on your system, the *Makefile* and configuration options offer alternatives. For example, if you lack the *expat* library, you can set the `NO_EXPAT` option in the *Makefile*. However, your build will lack some features, as noted in the *Makefile*. For example, you will not be able to push changes to a remote repository using the HTTP and HTTPS transports.

Other *Makefile* configuration options support ports to various platforms and distributions. For instance, several flags pertain to Mac OS X's Darwin operating system. Either hand-modify and select the appropriate options or find what parameters are set automatically in the top-level *INSTALL* file.

Once your system and build options are ready, the rest is easy. By default, Git is installed in your home directory in subdirectories *~/bin/*, *~/lib/*, and *~/share/*. In general, this default is useful only if you're using Git personally and don't need to share it with other users.

These commands build and install Git in your home directory.

```
$ cd git-1.7.9
$ ./configure
$ make all
$ make install
```

If you want to install Git into an alternate location, such as */usr/local/* to provide general access, add `--prefix=/usr/local` to the `./configure` command. To continue, run `make` as a normal user, but run `make install` as root.

```
$ cd git-1.7.9
$ ./configure --prefix=/usr/local
$ make all
$ sudo make install
```

To install the Git documentation, add the `doc` and `install-doc` targets to the `make` and `make install` commands, respectively.

```
$ cd git-1.7.9
$ make all doc
$ sudo make install install-doc
```

Several more libraries are needed to do a complete build of the documentation. As an alternative, prebuilt manpages and HTML pages are available and can be installed separately as well; just be careful to avoid version mismatch problems if you choose to go this route.

A build from source includes all the Git subpackages and commands, such as *git-email* and `gitk`. There is no need to build or install those utilities independently.

Installing Git on Windows

There are two competing Git packages for Windows: a Cygwin-based Git and a "native" version called *msysGit*.

Originally, only the Cygwin version was supported and *msysGit* was experimental and unstable. But as this book went to press, both versions work well and support an almost identical set of features. The most important exception, as of Git 1.6.0, is that *msysGit* does not yet properly support `git-svn`. If you need interoperability between Git and SVN, then you must use the Cygwin version of Git. Otherwise, the version you choose is a matter of personal preference.

If you aren't sure which one you want, here are some rules of thumb.

- If you use Cygwin already on Windows, use Cygwin's Git because it interoperates better with your Cygwin setup. For example, all your Cygwin-style filenames will work in Git, and redirecting program input and output will always work exactly as expected.
- If you don't use Cygwin, it's easier to install *msysGit* because it has its own stand-alone installer.
- If you want Git integration with the Windows Explorer shell (for example, the ability to right-click on a folder and pick "Git GUI Here" or "Git Bash Here"), then install *msysGit*. If you want this feature but prefer to use Cygwin, you can install both packages without harm.

If you're still in doubt about which package to use, install *msysGit*. Make sure you obtain the latest version (1.7.10 or higher) because the quality of Git's Windows support steadily improves in successive versions.

Installing the Cygwin Git Package

The Cygwin Git package, as the name implies, is a package inside the Cygwin system itself. To install it, run Cygwin's `setup.exe` program, which you can download from *http://cygwin.com*.

After `setup.exe` launches, use the default settings for most options until you get to the list of packages to install. The Git packages are in the *devel* category, as shown in Figure 2-1.

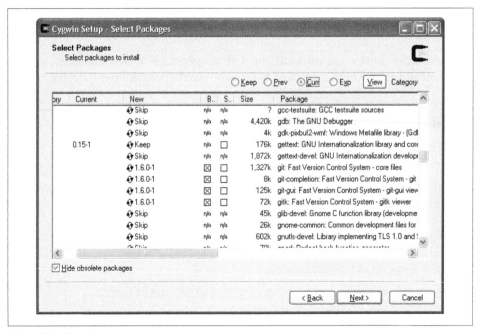

Figure 2-1. Cygwin setup

After choosing the packages you want to install, click Next a few more times until the Cygwin installation finishes. You can then start the Cygwin Bash Shell from your Start menu, which should now include the `git` command (Figure 2-2).

As an alternative, if your Cygwin configuration includes the various compiler tools like `gcc` and `make`, then you can build your own copy of Git from source code on Windows under Cygwin by following the same instructions as on Linux.

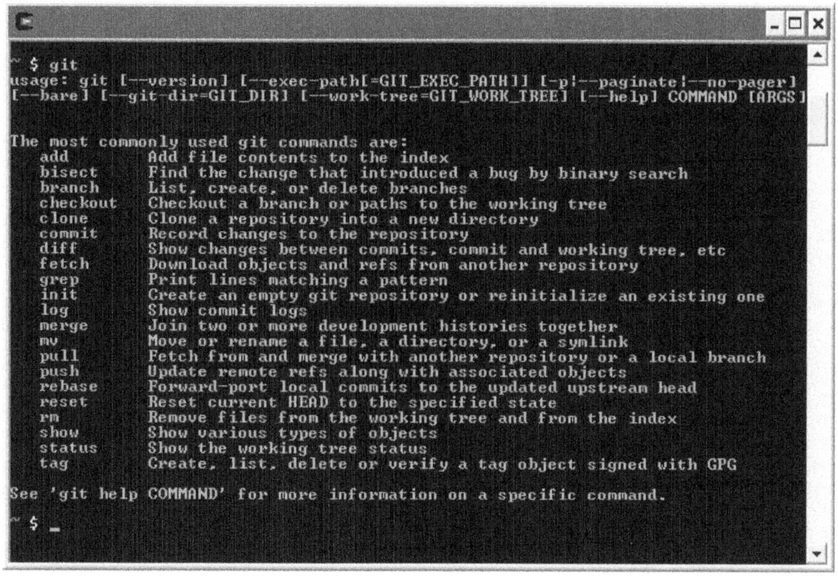

Figure 2-2. Cygwin shell

Installing Standalone Git (msysGit)

The *msysGit* package is easy to install on a Windows system because the package includes all its dependencies. It even has Secure Shell (SSH) commands to generate the keys that repository maintainers require to control access. *msysGit* is designed to integrate well with Windows-style native applications (such as the Windows Explorer shell).

First, download the latest version of the installer from its home at *http://code.google .com/p/msysgit*. The file to collect is usually called something like *Git-1.5.6.1-pre-view20080701.exe*.

After the download completes, run the installer. You should see a screen that looks something like Figure 2-3.

Depending on the actual version being installed, you may or may not need to click Next through a compatibility notice, as shown in Figure 2-4. This notice concerns incompatibilities between Windows-style and Unix-style line endings, called CRLF and LF, respectively.

Click Next a few more times until you see the screen shown in Figure 2-5. The best way to run *msysGit* on a daily basis is via Windows Explorer, so check the two pertinent boxes as shown.

Figure 2-3. msysGit setup

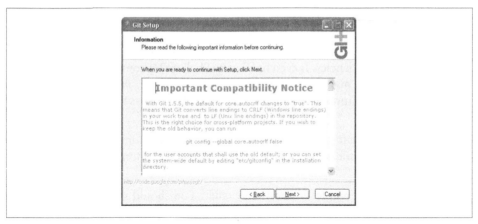

Figure 2-4. msysGit notice

In addition, an icon to start Git Bash (a command prompt that makes the git commands available) is installed in the Start menu in the section called Git. Because most of the examples in this book use the command line, use Git Bash to get started.

All the examples in this book work equally well on Linux and Windows, with one caveat: *msysGit* for Windows uses the older Git command names mentioned in "The Git Command Line" on page 19 of Chapter 3. To follow the examples with *msys-Git*, enter git-add for git add.

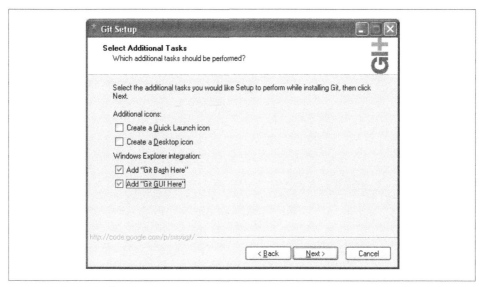

Figure 2-5. msysGit choices

Getting Started

Git manages change. Given that intent, Git shares much with other version control systems. Many tenets—the notion of a commit, the change log, the repository—are the same, and workflow is conceptually similar among the corpus of tools. However, Git offers many novelties, too. The notions and practices of other version control systems may work differently in Git or may not apply at all. Yet no matter what your experience, this book explains how Git works and teaches mastery.

Let's get started.

The Git Command Line

Git is simple to use. Just type `git`. Without any arguments, Git lists its options and the most common subcommands.

```
$ git

git [--version] [--exec-path[=GIT_EXEC_PATH]]
    [-p|--paginate|--no-pager] [--bare] [--git-dir=GIT_DIR]
    [--work-tree=GIT_WORK_TREE] [--help] COMMAND [ARGS]

The most commonly used git commands are:
   add        Add file contents to the index
   bisect     Find the change that introduced a bug by binary search
   branch     List, create, or delete branches
   checkout   Checkout and switch to a branch
   clone      Clone a repository into a new directory
   commit     Record changes to the repository
   diff       Show changes between commits, the commit and working trees, etc
   fetch      Download objects and refs from another repository
   grep       Print lines matching a pattern
   init       Create an empty git repository or reinitialize an existing one
   log        Show commit logs
   merge      Join two or more development histories
   mv         Move or rename a file, a directory, or a symlink
   pull       Fetch from and merge with another repository or a local branch
   push       Update remote refs along with associated objects
```

```
rebase      Forward-port local commits to the updated upstream head
reset       Reset current HEAD to the specified state
rm          Remove files from the working tree and from the index
show        Show various types of objects
status      Show the working tree status
tag         Create, list, delete, or verify a tag object signed with GPG
```

For a complete (and somewhat daunting) list of git subcommands, type git help --all.

As you can see from the usage hint, a small handful of options apply to git. Most options, shown as [ARGS] in the hint, apply to specific subcommands.

For example, the option --version affects the git command and produces a version number.

```
$ git --version
git version 1.6.0
```

In contrast , --amend is an example of an option specific to the git subcommand commit.

```
$ git commit --amend
```

Some invocations require both forms of options. (Here, the extra spaces in the command line merely serve to visually separate the subcommand from the base command and are not required.)

```
$ git --git-dir=project.git    repack -d
```

For convenience, documentation for each git subcommand is available using **git help** *subcommand*, **git --help** *subcommand* or **git** *subcommand* **--help**.

Historically, Git was provided as a suite of many simple, distinct, standalone commands developed according to the "Unix toolkit" philosophy: build small, interoperable tools. Each command sported a hyphenated name, such as git-commit and git-log. However, the current trend among developers is to use the single git executable and affix a subcommand. That being said, the forms git commit and git-commit are identical.

 You can visit *http://www.kernel.org/pub/software/scm/git/docs/* to read the complete Git documentation online.

Git commands understand both "short" and "long" options. For example, the git commit command treats the following examples as equivalents.

```
$ git commit -m "Fixed a typo."
$ git commit --message="Fixed a typo."
```

The short form, -m, uses a single hyphen, whereas the long form, --message, uses two. (This is consistent with the GNU long options extension.) Some options exist only in one form.

Finally, you can separate options from a list of arguments via the "bare double dash" convention. For instance, use the double dash to contrast the control portion of the command line from a list of operands, such as filenames.

```
$ git diff -w master origin -- tools/Makefile
```

You may need to use the double dash to separate and explicitly identify filenames if they might otherwise be mistaken for another part of the command. For example, if you happened to have both a file and a tag named *main.c*, then you will get different behavior:

```
# Checkout the tag named "main.c"
$ git checkout main.c

# Checkout the file named "main.c"
$ git checkout -- main.c
```

Quick Introduction to Using Git

To see git in action, let's create a new repository, add some content, and manage a few revisions.

There are two fundamental techniques for establishing a Git repository. You can either create it from scratch, populating it with an existing body of work, or you can copy, or *clone*, an existing repository. It's simpler to start with an empty repository, so let's start there.

Creating an Initial Repository

To model a typical situation, let's create a repository for your personal website from the directory *~/public_html* and place it in a Git repository.

If you don't have content for your personal website in *~/public_html*, create the directory and place some simple content in a file called *index.html*:

```
$ mkdir ~/public_html
$ cd ~/public_html
$ echo 'My website is alive!' > index.html
```

To turn *~/public_html* or any directory into a Git repository, run git init:

```
$ git init

Initialized empty Git repository in .git/
```

Git doesn't care whether you start with a completely empty directory or if you start with a directory full of files. In either case, the process of converting the directory into a Git repository is the same.

To signify that your directory is a Git repository, the `git init` command creates a hidden directory, called *.git*, at the top level of your project. Whereas CVS and SVN place revision information in *CVS* and *.svn* subdirectories within each of your project's directories, Git places all its revision information in this one, top-level *.git* directory. The contents and purpose of the data files are discussed in more detail in "Inside the .git Directory" on page 39 of Chapter 4.

Everything in your *~/public_html* directory remains untouched. Git considers it your project's *working directory*, or the directory where you alter your files. In contrast, the repository hidden within *.git* is maintained by Git.

Adding a File to Your Repository

The command `git init` creates a new Git repository. Initially, each Git repository is empty. To manage content, you must explicitly deposit it in the repository. Such a conscious step separates scratch files from important files.

Use `git add` *file* to add *file* to the repository:

```
$ git add index.html
```

 If you have a directory populated with several files, let Git add all the files in the directory and all subdirectories with `git add .`. (The argument `.`, the single period or "dot" in Unix parlance, is shorthand for the current directory.)

After an add, Git knows that the file, *index.html*, is to remain in the repository. However, so far, Git has merely *staged* the file, an interim step before committal. Git separates the add and commit steps to avoid volatility. Imagine how disruptive, confusing, and time-consuming it would be to update the repository each time you add, remove, or change a file. Instead, multiple provisional and related steps, such as an add, can be "batched," keeping the repository in a stable, consistent state.

Running `git status` reveals this in-between state of *index.html*:

```
$ git status
# On branch master
#
# Initial commit
#
# Changes to be committed:
#   (use "git rm --cached <file>..." to unstage)
#
#       new file: index.html
```

The command reports that the new file *index.html* will be added to the repository during the next commit.

In addition to actual changes to the directory and to file contents, Git records several other pieces of metadata with each commit, including a log message and the author of the change. A fully qualified `git commit` command supplies a log message and an author:

```
$ git commit -m "Initial contents of public_html" \
             --author="Jon Loeliger <jdl@example.com>"

Created initial commit 9da581d: Initial contents of public_html
 1 files changed, 1 insertions(+), 0 deletions(-)
 create mode 100644 index.html
```

You can provide a log message on the command line, but it's more typical to create the message during an interactive editor session. This gives you an opportunity to compose a complete and detailed log message in your favorite editor. To configure Git to open your favorite editor during a `git commit`, set your `GIT_EDITOR` environment variable.

```
# In tcsh
$ setenv GIT_EDITOR emacs

# In bash
$ export GIT_EDITOR=vim
```

After you commit the addition of the new file into the repository, `git status` indicates that there are no outstanding, staged changes to be committed.

```
$ git status

# On branch master
nothing to commit (working directory clean)
```

Git also takes the time to tell you that your working directory is *clean*, which means the working directory has no unknown or modified files that differ from what is in the repository.

Obscure Error Messages

Git tries hard to determine the author of each commit. If you haven't set up your name and email address in a way that Git can find it, you may encounter some odd warnings.

But there is no need to have an existential crisis if you see a cryptic error message like one of these:

```
You don't exist. Go away!
Your parents must have hated you!
Your sysadmin must hate you!
```

The error indicates that Git is unable to determine your real name, likely due to a problem (existence, readability, length) with your Unix "gecos" information. The problem can be fixed by setting your name and email configuration information as described in "Configuring the Commit Author" on page 24.

Quick Introduction to Using Git | 23

Configuring the Commit Author

Before making many commits to a repository, you should establish some basic environment and configuration options. At a bare minimum, Git must know your name and email address. You may specify your identity on every commit command line, as shown previously, but that is the hard way and quickly becomes tedious.

Instead, save your identity in a configuration file using the `git config` command.

```
$ git config user.name "Jon Loeliger"
$ git config user.email "jdl@example.com"
```

You can also tell Git your name and email address using the `GIT_AUTHOR_NAME` and `GIT_AUTHOR_EMAIL` environment variables. If set, these variables override all configuration settings.

Making Another Commit

To show a few more features of Git, let's make some modifications and create a complex history of changes within the repository.

Let's commit an alteration to the *index.html* file. Open the file, convert it to HTML, and save the file.

```
$ cd ~/public_html

# edit the index.html file

$ cat index.html
<html>
<body>
My web site is alive!
</body>
</html>

$ git commit index.html
```

If you are already somewhat familiar with Git, you may be tempted to think "Aha! You need to `git add index.html` before you can `commit` that file!" But that isn't true. Because the file was already added to the repository (in "Adding a File to Your Repository" on page 22), there's no need to tell the index about the file; it already knows. Furthermore, file changes are captured when directly committing a file named on the command line! Using a generic `git commit` without naming the file would not have worked in this case.

When your editor comes up, enter a commit log entry such as "Convert to HTML" and exit the editor. There are now two versions of *index.html* in the repository.

Viewing Your Commits

Once you have one or more commits in the repository, you can inspect them in a variety of ways. Some Git commands show the sequence of individual commits, others show the summary of an individual commit, and still others show the full details of any commit in the repository.

The command `git log` yields a sequential history of the individual commits within the repository:

```
$ git log

commit ec232cddfb94e0dfd5b5855af8ded7f5eb5c90d6
Author: Jon Loeliger <jdl@example.com>
Date:   Wed Apr 2 16:47:42 2008 -0500

Convert to HTML

commit 9da581d910c9c4ac93557ca4859e767f5caf5169
Author: Jon Loeliger <jdl@example.com>
Date:   Thu Mar 13 22:38:13 2008 -0500

Initial contents of public_html
```

The entries are listed, in order, from most recent to oldest[1] (the original file); each entry shows the commit author's name and email address, the date of the commit, the log message for the change, and the internal identification number of the commit. The commit ID number is explained in "Content-Addressable Names" on page 33 of Chapter 4, and commits are discussed in Chapter 6.

To see more detail about a particular commit, use `git show` with a commit number:

```
$ git show 9da581d910c9c4ac93557ca4859e767f5caf5169

commit 9da581d910c9c4ac93557ca4859e767f5caf5169
Author: Jon Loeliger <jdl@example.com>
Date:   Thu Mar 13 22:38:13 2008 -0500

Initial contents of public_html

diff --git a/index.html b/index.html
new file mode 100644
index 0000000..34217e9
--- /dev/null
+++ b/index.html
@@ -0,0 +1 @@
+My web site is alive!
```

If you run `git show` without an explicit commit number, it simply shows the details of the most recent commit.

---

1. Strictly speaking, they are not in *chronological* order but rather are a *topological* sort of the commits.

Another view, `show-branch`, provides concise, one-line summaries for the current development branch:

```
$ git show-branch --more=10

[master] Convert to HTML
[master^] Initial contents of public_html
```

The phrase `--more=10` reveals up to an additional 10 more versions, but only two exist so far and so both are shown. (The default in this case would list only the most recent commit.) The name `master` is the default branch name.

Branches are covered extensively in Chapter 7. "Viewing Branches" on page 94 describes the `git show-branch` command in more detail.

Viewing Commit Differences

To see the differences between the two revisions of *index.html*, recall both full commit ID names and run `git diff`:

```
$ git diff 9da581d910c9c4ac93557ca4859e767f5caf5169 \
           ec232cddfb94e0dfd5b5855af8ded7f5eb5c90d6

diff --git a/index.html b/index.html
index 34217e9..8638631 100644
--- a/index.html
+++ b/index.html
@@ -1 +1,5 @@
+<html>
+<body>
 My web site is alive!
+</body>
+</html>
```

This output should look familiar: It resembles what the `diff` program produces. As is the convention, the first revision named, `9da581d910c9c4ac93557ca4859e767f5caf5169`, is the earlier version of the content and the second revision, named `ec232cddfb94e0dfd5b5855af8ded7f5eb5c90d6` is the newer one. Thus, a plus sign (+) precedes each line of new content.

Scared yet? Don't worry about those intimidating hex numbers. Thankfully, Git provides many shorter, easier ways to do commands like this without having to produce large complicated numbers.

Removing and Renaming Files in Your Repository

Removing a file from a repository is analogous to adding a file but uses `git rm`. Suppose you have the file *poem.html* in your website content and it's no longer needed.

```
$ cd ~/public_html
$ ls
index.html  poem.html
```

```
$ git rm poem.html
rm 'poem.html'

$ git commit -m "Remove a poem"
Created commit 364a708: Remove a poem
 0 files changed, 0 insertions(+), 0 deletions(-)
 delete mode 100644 poem.html
```

As with an addition, a deletion requires two steps: `git rm` expresses your intent to remove the file and stages the change, and then `git commit` realizes the change in the repository. Again, you can omit the -m option and type a log message such as "Remove a poem" interactively in your favorite text editor.

You can rename a file indirectly by using a combination of `git rm` and `git add`, or you can rename it more quickly and directly with `git mv`. Here's an example of the former:

```
$ mv foo.html bar.html
$ git rm foo.html
rm 'foo.html'
$ git add bar.html
```

In this sequence, you must execute `mv foo.html bar.html` at the onset lest `git rm` permanently delete the *foo.html* file from the filesystem.

Here's the same operation performed with `git mv`.

```
$ git mv foo.html bar.html
```

In either case, the staged changes must be committed subsequently:

```
$ git commit -m "Moved foo to bar"
Created commit 8805821: Moved foo to bar
 1 files changed, 0 insertions(+), 0 deletions(-)
 rename foo.html => bar.html (100%)
```

Git handles file move operations differently than most akin systems, employing a mechanism based on the similarity of the content between two file versions. The specifics are described in Chapter 5.

Making a Copy of Your Repository

If you followed the previous steps and made an initial repository in your *~/public_html* directory, then you can now create a complete copy, or *clone*, of that repository using the `git clone` command. This is how people around the world use Git to pursue pet projects on the same files and keep in sync with other repositories.

For the purposes of this tutorial, let's just make a copy in your home directory and call it *my_website*:

```
$ cd ~
$ git clone public_html my_website
```

Although these two Git repositories now contain exactly the same objects, files, and directories, there are some subtle differences. You may want to explore those differences with commands such as:

```
$ ls -lsa public_html my_website
$ diff -r public_html my_website
```

On a local filesystem like this, using `git clone` to make a copy of a repository is quite similar to `cp -a` or `rsync`. However, Git supports a richer set of repository sources, including network names, for naming the repository to be cloned. These forms and usage are explained in Chapter 12.

Once you clone a repository, you are able to modify the cloned version, make new commits, inspect its logs and history, and so on. It is a complete repository with full history.

Configuration Files

Git's configuration files are all simple text files in the style of *.ini* files. They record various choices and settings used by many Git commands. Some settings represent purely personal preferences (should a `color.pager` be used?); others are vital to a repository functioning correctly (`core.repositoryformatversion`); and still others tweak command behavior a bit (`gc.auto`).

Like many tools, Git supports a hierarchy of configuration files. In decreasing precedence they are:

.git/config
> Repository-specific configuration settings manipulated with the `--file` option or by default. These settings have the highest precedence.

~/.gitconfig
> User-specific configuration settings manipulated with the `--global` option.

/etc/gitconfig
> System-wide configuration settings manipulated with the `--system` option if you have proper Unix file write permissions on it. These settings have the lowest precedence. Depending on your actual installation, the system settings file might be somewhere else (perhaps in */usr/local/etc/gitconfig*), or may be entirely absent.

For example, to establish an author name and email address that will be used on all the commits you make for all of your repositories, configure values for `user.name` and `user.email` in your *$HOME/.gitconfig* file using `git config --global`:

```
$ git config --global user.name "Jon Loeliger"
$ git config --global user.email "jdl@example.com"
```

Or, to set a repository-specific name and email address that would override a
--global setting, simply omit the --global flag:

```
$ git config user.name "Jon Loeliger"
$ git config user.email "jdl@special-project.example.org"
```

Use git config -l to list the settings of all the variables collectively found in the
complete set of configuration files:

```
# Make a brand new empty repository
$ mkdir /tmp/new
$ cd /tmp/new
$ git init

# Set some config values
$ git config --global user.name "Jon Loeliger"
$ git config --global user.email "jdl@example.com"
$ git config user.email "jdl@special-project.example.org"

$ git config -l
user.name=Jon Loeliger
user.email=jdl@example.com
core.repositoryformatversion=0
core.filemode=true
core.bare=false
core.logallrefupdates=true
user.email=jdl@special-project.example.org
```

Because the configuration files are simple text files, you can view their contents with
cat and edit them with your favorite text editor, too.

```
# Look at just the repository specific settings

$ cat .git/config
[core]
    repositoryformatversion = 0
    filemode = true
    bare = false
    logallrefupdates = true
[user]
    email = jdl@special-project.example.org
```

Oh, and, if you use a Pacific Northwest-based OS, you may see some differences here.
Maybe something like this:

```
[core]
        repositoryformatversion = 0
        filemode = true
        bare = true
        logallrefupdates = true
        symlinks = false
        ignorecase = true
        hideDotFiles = dotGitOnly
```

Many of these differences allow for different file system characteristics.

Use the `--unset` option to remove a setting:

```
$ git config --unset --global user.email
```

The behavior of the `git config` command changed between versions 1.6.2 and 1.6.3. Earlier versions required option `--unset` to follow option `--global`; newer versions allow either order.

Multiple configuration options and environment variables frequently exist for the same purpose. For example, the editor to be used when composing a commit log message follows these steps, in order:

- `GIT_EDITOR` environment variable
- `core.editor` configuration option
- `VISUAL` environment variable
- `EDITOR` environment variable
- the `vi` command

There are more than a few hundred configuration parameters. I'm not going to bore you with them, but I will point out important ones as we go along. A more extensive (yet still incomplete) list can be found on the `git config` manual page.

Configuring an Alias

For starters, here is a tip for setting up command aliases. If there is a common but complex Git command that you type frequently, consider setting up a simple Git alias for it.

```
$ git config --global alias.show-graph \
        'log --graph --abbrev-commit --pretty=oneline'
```

In this example, I've made up the `show-graph` alias and made it available for use in any repository I make. Now when I use the command `git show-graph`, it is just like I had typed that long `git log` command with all those options.

Inquiry

You will surely have a lot of unanswered questions about how Git works, even after the actions performed so far. For instance, how does Git store each version of a file? What really makes up a commit? Where did those funny commit numbers come from? Why the name `master`? And is a "branch" what I *think* it is? Good questions.

The next chapter defines some terminology, introduces some Git concepts, and establishes a foundation for the lessons found in the rest of the book.

## CHAPTER 4

Basic Git Concepts

Basic Concepts

The previous chapter presented a typical application of Git—and probably sparked a good number of questions. Does Git store the entire file at every commit? What's the purpose of the *.git* directory? Why does a commit ID resemble gibberish? Should I take note of it?

If you've used another VCS, such as SVN or CVS, the commands in the last chapter likely seemed familiar. Indeed, Git serves the same function and provides all the operations you expect from a modern VCS. However, Git differs in some fundamental and surprising ways.

In this chapter, we explore why and how Git differs by examining the key components of its architecture and some important concepts. Here we focus on the basics and demonstrate how to interact with one repository; Chapter 12 explains how to work with many, interconnected repositories. Keeping track of multiple repositories may seem like a daunting prospect, but the fundamentals you learn in this chapter apply just the same.

Repositories

A Git *repository* is simply a database containing all the information needed to retain and manage the revisions and history of a project. In Git, as with most version control systems, a repository retains a complete copy of the entire project throughout its lifetime. However, unlike most other VCSs, the Git repository not only provides a complete working copy of all the files in the repository, but also a copy of the repository itself with which to work.

Git maintains a set of configuration values within each repository. You saw some of these, such as the repository user's name and email address, in the previous chapter. Unlike file data and other repository metadata, configuration settings are not propagated from one repository to another during a *clone*, or duplicating, operation. Instead,

Git manages and inspects configuration and setup information on a per-site, per-user, and per-repository basis.

Within a repository, Git maintains two primary data structures, the *object store* and the *index*. All of this repository data is stored at the root of your working directory in a hidden subdirectory named *.git*.

The object store is designed to be efficiently copied during a clone operation as part of the mechanism that supports a fully distributed VCS. The index is transitory information, is private to a repository, and can be created or modified on demand as needed.

The next two sections describe the object store and index in more detail.

Git Object Types

At the heart of Git's repository implementation is the object store. It contains your original data files and all the log messages, author information, dates, and other information required to rebuild any version or branch of the project.

Git places only four types of objects in the object store: the *blobs*, *trees*, *commits*, and *tags*. These four atomic objects form the foundation of Git's higher level data structures.

Blobs
    Each version of a file is represented as a *blob*. Blob, a contraction of "binary large object," is a term that's commonly used in computing to refer to some variable or file that can contain any data and whose internal structure is ignored by the program. A blob is treated as being opaque. A blob holds a file's data but does not contain any metadata about the file or even its name.

Trees
    A *tree* object represents one level of directory information. It records blob identifiers, path names, and a bit of metadata for all the files in one directory. It can also recursively reference other (sub)tree objects and thus build a complete hierarchy of files and subdirectories.

Commits
    A *commit* object holds metadata for each change introduced into the repository, including the author, committer, commit date, and log message. Each commit points to a tree object that captures, in one complete snapshot, the state of the repository at the time the commit was performed. The initial commit, or *root commit*, has no parent. Most commits have one commit parent, although later in the book (Chapter 9) we explain how a commit can reference more than one parent.

Tags
    A *tag* object assigns an arbitrary yet presumably human readable name to a specific object, usually a commit. Although `9da581d910c9c4ac93557ca4859e767f5caf5169`

refs to an exact and well-defined commit, a more familiar tag name like `Ver-1.0-Alpha` might make more sense!

Over time, all the information in the object store changes and grows, tracking and modeling your project edits, additions, and deletions. To use disk space and network bandwidth efficiently, Git compresses and stores the objects in *pack files*, which are also placed in the object store.

Index

The index is a temporary and dynamic binary file that describes the directory structure of the entire repository. More specifically, the index captures a version of the project's overall structure at some moment in time. The project's state could be represented by a commit and a tree from any point in the project's history, or it could be a future state toward which you are actively developing.

One of the key, distinguishing features of Git is that it enables you to alter the contents of the index in methodical, well-defined steps. The index allows a separation between incremental development steps and the committal of those changes.

Here's how it works. As the developer, you execute Git commands to *stage* changes in the index. Changes usually add, delete, or edit some file or set of files. The index records and retains those changes, keeping them safe until you are ready to *commit* them. You can also remove or replace changes in the index. Thus, the index allows a gradual transition, usually guided by you, from one complex repository state to another, presumably better state.

As you'll see in Chapter 9, the index plays an important role in *merges*, allowing multiple versions of the same file to be managed, inspected, and manipulated simultaneously.

Content-Addressable Names

The Git object store is organized and implemented as a content-addressable storage system. Specifically, each object in the object store has a unique name produced by applying SHA1 to the contents of the object, yielding an SHA1 hash value. Because the complete contents of an object contribute to the hash value and the hash value is believed to be effectively unique to that particular content, the SHA1 hash is a sufficient index or name for that object in the object database. Any tiny change to a file causes the SHA1 hash to change, causing the new version of the file to be indexed separately.

SHA1 values are 160-bit values that are usually represented as a 40-digit hexadecimal number, such as `9da581d910c9c4ac93557ca4859e767f5caf5169`. Sometimes, during display, SHA1 values are abbreviated to a smaller, unique prefix. Git users speak of *SHA1*, *hash code*, and sometimes *object ID* interchangeably.

Git Tracks Content

It's important to see Git as something more than a VCS: Git is a *content tracking system*. This distinction, however subtle, guides much of the design of Git and is perhaps the key reason it can perform internal data manipulations with relative ease. Yet, this is also perhaps one of the most difficult concepts for new users of Git to grasp, so some exposition is worthwhile.

Git's content tracking is manifested in two critical ways that differ fundamentally from almost all other[1] revision control systems.

First, Git's object store is based on the hashed computation of the *contents* of its objects, not on the file or directory names from the user's original file layout. Thus, when Git places a file into the object store, it does so based on the hash of the data and not on the name of the file. In fact, Git does not track file or directory names, which are associated with files in secondary ways. Again, Git tracks content instead of files.

If two separate files have exactly the same content, whether in the same or different directories, Git stores a single copy of that content as a blob within the object store. Git computes the hash code of each file according solely to its content, determines that the files have the same SHA1 values and thus the same content, and places the blob object in the object store indexed by that SHA1 value. Both files in the project, regardless of where they are located in the user's directory structure, use that same object for content.

If one of those files changes, Git computes a new SHA1 for it, determines that it is now a different blob object, and adds the new blob to the object store. The original blob remains in the object store for the unchanged file to use.

Second, Git's internal database efficiently stores every version of every file—not their differences—as files go from one revision to the next. Because Git uses the hash of a file's complete content as the name for that file, it must operate on each complete copy

---

1. Monotone, Mercurial, OpenCMS, and Venti are notable exceptions here.

of the file. It cannot base its work or its object store entries on only part of the file's content nor on the differences between two revisions of that file.

The typical user view of a file—that it has revisions and appears to progress from one revision to another revision—is simply an artifact. Git computes this history as a set of changes between different blobs with varying hashes, rather than storing a file name and set of differences directly. It may seem odd, but this feature allows Git to perform certain tasks with ease.

Pathname Versus Content

As with many other VCSs, Git needs to maintain an explicit list of files that form the content of the repository. However, this need not require that Git's manifest be based on file names. Indeed, Git treats the name of a file as a piece of data that is distinct from the contents of that file. In this way, it separates index from data in the traditional database sense. It may help to look at Table 4-1, which roughly compares Git to other familiar systems.

Table 4-1. Database comparison

System	Index mechanism	Data store
Traditional database	Indexed Sequential Access Method (ISAM)	Data records
Unix file system	Directories (*/path/to/file*)	Blocks of data
Git	*.git/objects/hash*, tree object contents	Blob objects, tree objects

The names of files and directories come from the underlying filesystem, but Git does not really care about the names. Git merely records each pathname and makes sure it can accurately reproduce the files and directories from its content, which is indexed by a hash value.

Git's physical data layout isn't modeled after the user's file directory structure. Instead, it has a completely different structure that can, nonetheless, reproduce the user's original layout. Git's internal structure is a more efficient data structure for its own internal operations and storage considerations.

When Git needs to create a working directory, it says to the filesystem: "Hey! I have this big blob of data that is supposed to be placed at pathname *path/to/directory/file*. Does that make sense to you?" The filesystem is responsible for saying "Ah, yes, I recognize that string as a set of subdirectory names, and I know where to place your blob of data! Thanks!"

Pack Files

An astute reader my have formed a lingering question about Git's data model and its storage of individual files: Isn't it incredibly inefficient to store the complete content of every version of every file directly? Even if it is compressed, isn't it inefficient to have the complete content of different versions of the same file? What if you only add, say, one line to a file, doesn't Git store the complete content of both versions?

Luckily, the answer is "No, not really!"

Instead, Git uses a more efficient storage mechanism called a *pack file*. To create a packed file, Git first locates files whose content is very similar and stores the complete content for one of them. It then computes the differences, or deltas, between similar files and stores just the differences. For example, if you were to just change or add one line to a file, Git might store the complete, newer version and then take note of the one line change as a delta and store that in the pack too.

Storing a complete version of a file and the deltas needed to construct other versions of similar files is not a new trick. It is essentially the same mechanism that other VCSs such as RCS have used for decades.

Git does the file packing very cleverly, though. Since Git is driven by *content* it doesn't really care if the deltas it computes between two files actually pertain to two versions of the same file or not. That is, Git can take any two files from anywhere within the repository and compute deltas between them if it thinks they might be similar enough to yield good data compression. Thus, Git has a fairly elaborate algorithm to locate and match up potential delta candidates globally within a repository. Furthermore, Git is able to construct a series of deltas from one version of a file to a second, to a third, etc.

Git also maintains the knowledge of the original blob SHA1 for each complete file (either the complete content or as a reconstruction after deltas are applied) within the packed representation. This provides the basis for an index mechanism to locate objects within a pack.

Packed files are stored in the object store alongside the other objects. They are also used for efficient data transfer of repositories across a network.

Object Store Pictures

Let's look at how Git's objects fit and work together to form the complete system.

The blob object is at the "bottom" of the data structure; it references nothing and is referenced only by tree objects. In the figures that follow, each blob is represented by a rectangle.

Tree objects point to blobs and possibly to other trees as well. Any given tree object might be pointed at by many different commit objects. Each tree is represented by a triangle.

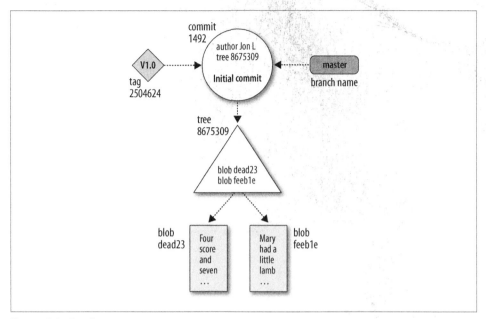

Figure 4-1. Git objects

A circle represents a commit. A commit points to one particular tree that is introduced into the repository by the commit.

Each tag is represented by a parallelogram. Each tag can point to, at most, one commit.

The branch is not a fundamental Git object, yet it plays a crucial role in naming commits. Each branch is pictured as a rounded rectangle.

Figure 4-1 captures how all the pieces fit together. This diagram shows the state of a repository after a single, initial commit added two files. Both files are in the top-level directory. Both the `master` branch and a tag named `V1.0` point to the commit with ID `1492`.

Now, let's make things a bit more complicated. Let's leave the original two files as is, adding a new subdirectory with one file in it. The resulting object store looks like Figure 4-2.

As in the previous picture, the new commit has added one associated tree object to represent the total state of directory and file structure. In this case, it is the tree object with ID `cafed00d`.

Because the top-level directory is changed by the addition of the new subdirectory, the *content* of the top-level tree object has changed as well, so Git introduces a new tree, `cafed00d`.

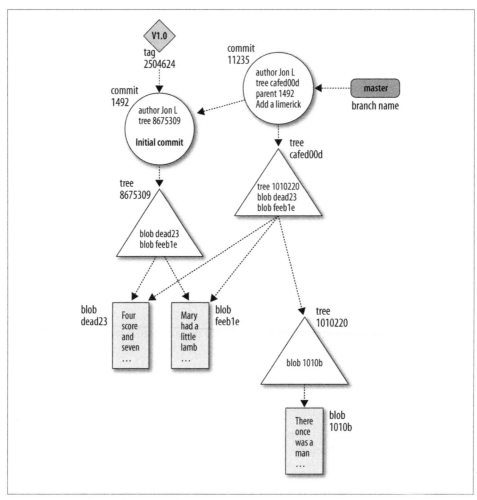

Figure 4-2. Git objects after a second commit

However, the blobs `dead23` and `feeb1e` didn't change from the first commit to the second. Git realizes that the IDs haven't changed and thus can be directly referenced and shared by the new `cafed00d` tree.

Pay attention to the direction of the arrows between commits. The parent commit or commits come earlier in time. Therefore, in Git's implementation, each commit points back to its parent or parents. Many people get confused because the state of a repository is conventionally portrayed in the opposite direction: as a dataflow *from* the parent commit *to* child commits.

In Chapter 6, we extend these pictures to show how the history of a repository is built up and manipulated by various commands.

Git Concepts at Work

With some tenets out of the way, let's see how all these concepts and components fit together in the repository itself. Let's create a new repository and inspect the internal files and object store in much greater detail.

Inside the .git Directory

To begin, initialize an empty repository using `git init` and then run `find` to reveal what's created.

```
$ mkdir /tmp/hello
$ cd /tmp/hello
$ git init
Initialized empty Git repository in /tmp/hello/.git/

# List all the files in the current directory
$ find .
.
./.git
./.git/hooks
./.git/hooks/commit-msg.sample
./.git/hooks/applypatch-msg.sample
./.git/hooks/pre-applypatch.sample
./.git/hooks/post-commit.sample
./.git/hooks/pre-rebase.sample
./.git/hooks/post-receive.sample
./.git/hooks/prepare-commit-msg.sample
./.git/hooks/post-update.sample
./.git/hooks/pre-commit.sample
./.git/hooks/update.sample
./.git/refs
./.git/refs/heads
./.git/refs/tags
./.git/config
./.git/objects
./.git/objects/pack
./.git/objects/info
./.git/description
./.git/HEAD
./.git/branches
./.git/info
./.git/info/exclude
```

As you can see, *.git* contains a lot of stuff. The files are displayed based on a template directory that you can adjust if desired. Depending on the version of Git you are using, your actual manifest may look a little different. For example, older versions of Git do not use a *.sample* suffix on the *.git/hooks* files.

In general, you don't have to view or manipulate the files in *.git*. These "hidden" files are considered part of Git's *plumbing* or configuration. Git has a small set of plumbing commands to manipulate these hidden files, but you will rarely use them.

Initially, the *.git/objects* directory (the directory for all of Git's objects) is empty, except for a few placeholders.

```
$ find .git/objects

.git/objects
.git/objects/pack
.git/objects/info
```

Let's now carefully create a simple object:

```
$ echo "hello world" > hello.txt
$ git add hello.txt
```

If you typed "hello world" exactly as it appears here (with no changes to spacing or capitalization), then your objects directory should now look like this:

```
$ find .git/objects
.git/objects
.git/objects/pack
.git/objects/3b
.git/objects/3b/18e512dba79e4c8300dd08aeb37f8e728b8dad
.git/objects/info
```

All this looks pretty mysterious. But it's not, as the following sections explain.

Objects, Hashes, and Blobs

When it creates an object for *hello.txt*, Git doesn't care that the filename is *hello.txt*. Git cares only about what's inside the file: the sequence of 12 bytes that represent "hello world" and the terminating newline (the same blob created earlier). Git performs a few operations on this blob, calculates its SHA1 hash, and enters it into the object store as a file named after the hexadecimal representation of the hash.

How Do We Know a SHA1 Hash Is Unique?

There is an extremely slim chance that two different blobs yield the same SHA1 hash. When this happens, it is called a *collision*. However, a SHA1 collision is so unlikely that you can safely bank on it never interfering with our use of Git.

SHA1 is a "cryptographically secure hash." Until recently, there was no known way (better than blind luck) for a user to cause a collision on purpose. But could a collision happen at random? Let's see.

With 160 bits, you have 2^{160} or about 10^{48} (1 with 48 zeroes after it) possible SHA1 hashes. That number is just incomprehensibly huge. Even if you hired a trillion people to produce a trillion new unique blobs per second for a trillion years, you would still only have about 10^{43} blobs.

If you hashed 2^{80} random blobs, you might find a collision.

Don't trust us. Go read Bruce Schneier.

The hash in this case is 3b18e512dba79e4c8300dd08aeb37f8e728b8dad. The 160 bits of an SHA1 hash correspond to 20 bytes, which takes 40 bytes of hexadecimal to display, so the content is stored as *.git/objects/3b/18e512dba79e4c8300dd08aeb37f8e728b8dad*. Git inserts a / after the first two digits to improve filesystem efficiency. (Some filesystems slow down if you put too many files in the same directory; making the first byte of the SHA1 into a directory is an easy way to create a fixed, 256-way partitioning of the namespace for all possible objects with an even distribution.)

To show that Git really hasn't done very much with the content in the file (it's still the same comforting "hello world"), you can use the hash to pull it back out of the object store any time you want:

```
$ git cat-file -p 3b18e512dba79e4c8300dd08aeb37f8e728b8dad
hello world
```

 Git also knows that 40 characters is a bit chancy to type by hand, so it provides a command to look up objects by a unique prefix of the object hash:

```
$ git rev-parse 3b18e512d
3b18e512dba79e4c8300dd08aeb37f8e728b8dad
```

Files and Trees

Now that the "hello world" blob is safely ensconced in the object store, what happened to its filename? Git wouldn't be very useful if it couldn't find files by name.

As mentioned before, Git tracks the pathnames of files through another kind of object called a *tree*. When you use `git add`, Git creates an object for the contents of each file you add, but it doesn't create an object for your tree right away. Instead, it updates the *index*. The index is found in *.git/index* and keeps track of file pathnames and corresponding blobs. Each time you run commands such as `git add`, `git rm`, or `git mv`, Git updates the index with the new pathname and blob information.

Whenever you want, you can create a tree object from your current index by capturing a snapshot of its current information with the low-level `git write-tree` command.

At the moment, the index contains exactly one file, *hello.txt*.

```
$ git ls-files -s
100644 3b18e512dba79e4c8300dd08aeb37f8e728b8dad 0       hello.txt
```

Here you can see the association of the file, *hello.txt*, and the 3b18e5... blob.

Next, let's capture the index state and save it to a tree object:

```
$ git write-tree
68aba62e560c0ebc3396e8ae9335232cd93a3f60

$ find .git/objects
.git/objects
.git/objects/68
```

```
.git/objects/68/aba62e560c0ebc3396e8ae9335232cd93a3f60
.git/objects/pack
.git/objects/3b
.git/objects/3b/18e512dba79e4c8300dd08aeb37f8e728b8dad
.git/objects/info
```

Now there are two objects: the "hello world" object at 3b18e5 and a new one, the tree object, at 68aba6. As you can see, the SHA1 object name corresponds exactly to the subdirectory and filename in *.git/objects*.

But what does a tree look like? Because it's an object, just like the blob, you can use the same low-level command to view it.

```
$ git cat-file -p 68aba6
100644 blob 3b18e512dba79e4c8300dd08aeb37f8e728b8dad    hello.txt
```

The contents of the object should be easy to interpret. The first number, 100644, represents the file attributes of the object in octal, which should be familiar to anyone who has used the Unix chmod command. Here, 3b18e5 is the object name of the *hello world* blob, and *hello.txt* is the name associated with that blob.

It is now easy to see that the tree object has captured the information that was in the index when you ran git ls-files -s.

A Note on Git's Use of SHA1

Before peering at the contents of the tree object in more detail, let's check out an important feature of SHA1 hashes:

```
$ git write-tree
68aba62e560c0ebc3396e8ae9335232cd93a3f60

$ git write-tree
68aba62e560c0ebc3396e8ae9335232cd93a3f60

$ git write-tree
68aba62e560c0ebc3396e8ae9335232cd93a3f60
```

Every time you compute another tree object for the same index, the SHA1 hash remains exactly the same. Git doesn't need to recreate a new tree object. If you're following these steps at the computer, you should be seeing *exactly the same SHA1 hashes* as the ones published in this book.

In this sense, the hash function is a true function in the mathematical sense: For a given input, it always produces the same output. Such a hash function is sometimes called a *digest* to emphasize that it serves as a sort of summary of the hashed object. Of course, any hash function, even the lowly parity bit, has this property.

That's extremely important. For example, if you create the exact same content as another developer, regardless of where or when or how both of you work, an identical hash is proof enough that the full content is identical, too. In fact, Git treats them as identical.

But hold on a second—aren't SHA1 hashes unique? What happened to the trillions of people with trillions of blobs per second who never produce a single collision? This is a common source of confusion among new Git users. So read on carefully, because if you can understand this distinction, then everything else in this chapter is easy.

Identical SHA1 hashes in this case *do not count as a collision*. It would be a collision only if two *different* objects produced the same hash. Here, you created two separate instances of the very same content, and the same content always has the same hash.

Git depends on another consequence of the SHA1 hash function: it doesn't matter *how* you got a tree called 68aba62e560c0ebc3396e8ae9335232cd93a3f60. If you have it, you can be extremely confident it is the same tree object that, say, another reader of this book has. Bob might have created the tree by combining commits A and B from Jennie and commit C from Sergey, whereas you got commit A from Sue and an update from Lakshmi that combines commits B and C. The results are the same, and this facilitates distributed development.

If you are asked to look for object 68aba62e560c0ebc3396e8ae9335232cd93a3f60 and can find such an object, then, because SHA1 is a cryptographic hash, you can be confident that you are looking at precisely the same data from which the hash was created.

The converse is also true: If you don't find an object with a specific hash in your object store, then you can be confident that you do not hold a copy of that exact object. In sum, you can determine whether your object store does or does not have a particular object even though you know nothing about its (potentially very large) contents. The hash thus serves as a reliable label or name for the object.

But Git also relies on something stronger than that conclusion, too. Consider the most recent commit (or its associated tree object). Because it contains, as part of its content, the hash of its parent commits and of its tree and *that* in turn contains the hash of all of its subtrees and blobs recursively through the whole data structure, it follows by induction that the hash of the original commit uniquely identifies the state of the whole data structure rooted at that commit.

Finally, the implications of our claim in the previous paragraph lead to a powerful use of the hash function: It provides an efficient way of comparing two objects, even two very large and complex data structures,[2] without transmitting either in full.

Tree Hierarchies

It's nice to have information regarding a single file, as was shown in the previous section, but projects contain complex, deeply nested directories that are refactored and moved around over time. Let's see how Git handles this by creating a new subdirectory that contains an identical copy of the *hello.txt* file:

---

2. This data structure is covered in more detail in "Commit Graphs" on page 74 of Chapter 6.

```
$ pwd
/tmp/hello
$ mkdir subdir
$ cp hello.txt subdir/
$ git add subdir/hello.txt
$ git write-tree
492413269336d21fac079d4a4672e55d5d2147ac

$ git cat-file -p 4924132693
100644 blob 3b18e512dba79e4c8300dd08aeb37f8e728b8dad    hello.txt
040000 tree 68aba62e560c0ebc3396e8ae9335232cd93a3f60    subdir
```

The new top-level tree contains two items: the original *hello.txt* file as well as the new *subdir* directory, which is of type *tree* instead of *blob*.

Notice anything unusual? Look closer at the object name of *subdir*. It's your old friend, 68aba62e560c0ebc3396e8ae9335232cd93a3f60!

What just happened? The new tree for *subdir* contains only one file, *hello.txt*, and that file contains the same old "hello world" content. So the **subdir** tree is exactly the same as the older, top-level tree! And of course it has the same SHA1 object name as before.

Let's look at the *.git/objects* directory and see what this most recent change affected:

```
$ find .git/objects
.git/objects
.git/objects/49
.git/objects/49/2413269336d21fac079d4a4672e55d5d2147ac
.git/objects/68
.git/objects/68/aba62e560c0ebc3396e8ae9335232cd93a3f60
.git/objects/pack
.git/objects/3b
.git/objects/3b/18e512dba79e4c8300dd08aeb37f8e728b8dad
.git/objects/info
```

There are still only three *unique* objects: a blob containing "hello world"; a tree containing *hello.txt*, which contains the text "hello world" plus a new line; and a second tree that contains *another* reference to *hello.txt* along with the first tree.

Commits

The next object to discuss is the *commit*. Now that *hello.txt* has been added with git add and the tree object has been produced with git write-tree, you can create a commit object using low-level commands like this:

```
$ echo -n "Commit a file that says hello\n" \
    | git commit-tree 492413269336d21fac079d4a4672e55d5d2147ac
3ede4622cc241bcb09683af36360e7413b9ddf6c
```

The result will look something like this:

```
$ git cat-file -p 3ede462
tree 492413269336d21fac079d4a4672e55d5d2147ac
author Jon Loeliger <jdl@example.com> 1220233277 -0500
```

```
committer Jon Loeliger <jdl@example.com> 1220233277 -0500

Commit a file that says hello
```

If you're following along on your computer, you probably found that the commit object you generated does *not* have the same name as the one in this book. If you've understood everything so far, the reason for that should be obvious: it's not the same commit. The commit contains your name and the time you made the commit, so of course it is different, however subtly. On the other hand, your commit does have the same *tree*. This is why commit objects are separate from their tree objects: different commits often refer to exactly the same tree. When that happens, Git is smart enough to transfer around only the new commit object, which is tiny, instead of the tree and blob objects, which are probably much larger.

In real life, you can (and should!) pass over the low-level `git write-tree` and `git commit-tree` steps, and just use the `git commit` command. You don't need to remember all those plumbing commands to be a perfectly happy Git user.

A basic commit object is fairly simple, and it's the last ingredient required for a real RCS. The commit object just shown is the simplest possible one, containing:

- The name of a tree object that actually identifies the associated files
- The name of the person who composed the new version (the author) and the time when it was composed
- The name of the person who placed the new version into the repository (the committer) and the time when it was committed
- A description of the reason for this revision (the commit message)

By default, the author and committer are the same; there are a few situations where they're different.

 You can use the command `git show --pretty=fuller` to see additional details about a given commit.

Commit objects are also stored in a graph structure, although it's completely different from the structures used by tree objects. When you make a new commit, you can give it one or more *parent* commits. By following back through the chain of parents, you can discover the history of your project. More details about commits and the commit graph are given in Chapter 6.

Tags

Finally, the last object Git manages is the tag. Although Git implements only one kind of tag object, there are two basic tag types, usually called *lightweight* and *annotated*.

Lightweight tags are simply references to a commit object and are usually considered private to a repository. These tags do not create a permanent object in the object store. An annotated tag is more substantial and creates an object. It contains a message, supplied by you, and can be digitally signed using a GnuPG key according to RFC4880.

Git treats both lightweight and annotated tag names equivalently for the purposes of naming a commit. However, by default, many Git commands work only on annotated tags, because they are considered "permanent" objects.

You create an annotated, unsigned tag with a message on a commit using the `git tag` command:

```
$ git tag -m "Tag version 1.0" V1.0 3ede462
```

You can see the tag object via the `git cat-file -p` command, but what is the SHA1 of the tag object? To find it, use the *Tip* from "Objects, Hashes, and Blobs" on page 40:

```
$ git rev-parse V1.0
6b608c1093943939ae78348117dd18b1ba151c6a

$ git cat-file -p 6b608c
object 3ede4622cc241bcb09683af36360e7413b9ddf6c
type commit
tag V1.0
tagger Jon Loeliger <jdl@example.com> Sun Oct 26 17:07:15 2008 -0500

Tag version 1.0
```

In addition to the log message and author information, the tag refers to the commit object 3ede462. Usually, Git tags a particular commit as named by some branch. Note that this behavior is notably different from that of other VCSs.

Git usually tags a commit object, which points to a tree object, which encompasses the total state of the entire hierarchy of files and directories within your repository.

Recall from Figure 4-1 that the V1.0 tag points to the commit named 1492, which in turn points to a tree (8675309) that spans multiple files. Thus, the tag simultaneously applies to all files of that tree.

This is unlike CVS, for example, which will apply a tag to each individual file and then rely on the collection of all those tagged files to reconstitute a whole tagged revision. And whereas CVS lets you move the tag on an individual file, Git requires a new commit, encompassing the file state change, onto which the tag will be moved.

## CHAPTER 5

File Management and the Index

When your project is under the care of a VCS, you edit in your working directory and commit your changes to your repository for safekeeping. Git works similarly but inserts another layer, the *index*, between the working directory and the repository to *stage*, or collect, alterations. When you manage your code with Git, you edit in your working directory, accumulate changes in your index, and commit whatever has amassed in the index as a single changeset.

You can think of Git's index as a set of intended or prospective modifications. You add, remove, move, or repeatedly edit files right up to the culminating commit, which actualizes the accumulated changes in the repository. Most of the critical work actually precedes the commit step.

Remember, a commit is a two-step process: stage your changes and commit the changes. An alteration found in the working directory but not in the index isn't staged and thus can't be committed.

For convenience, Git allows you to combine the two steps when you add or change a file:

```
$ git commit index.html
```

But if you move or remove a file, you don't have that luxury. The two steps must then be separate:

```
$ git rm index.html
$ git commit
```

This chapter[1] explains how to manage the index and your corpus of files. It describes how to add and remove a file from your repository, how to rename a file, and how to catalog the state of the index. The finale of this chapter shows how to make Git ignore temporary and other irrelevant files that need not be tracked by version control.

---

1. I have it on good authority that this chapter should, in fact, be titled "Things Bart Massey Hates About Git."

It's All About the Index

Linus Torvalds argued on the Git mailing list that you can't grasp and fully appreciate the power of Git without first understanding the purpose of the index.

Git's index doesn't contain any file content; it simply tracks what you want to commit. When you run `git commit`, Git checks the index rather than your working directory to discover what to commit. (Commits are covered fully in Chapter 6.)

Although many of Git's "porcelain" (higher level) commands are designed to hide the details of the index from you and make your job easier, it is still important to keep the index and its state in mind.

You can query the state of the index at any time with the command `git status`. It explicitly calls out what files Git considers staged. You can also peer into the internal state of Git with "plumbing" commands such as `git ls-files`.

You'll also likely find the `git diff` command useful during staging. (Diffs are discussed extensively in Chapter 8.) This command can display two different sets of changes: `git diff` displays the changes that remain in your working directory and are not staged; `git diff --cached` shows changes that are staged and will therefore contribute to your next commit.

You can use both variations of `git diff` to guide you through the process of staging changes. Initially, `git diff` is a large set of all modifications, and `--cached` is empty. As you stage, the former set will shrink and the latter set will grow. If all your working changes are staged and ready for a commit, the `--cached` will be full and `git diff` will show nothing.

File Classifications in Git

Git classifies your files into three groups: tracked, ignored, and untracked.

Tracked
> A tracked file is any file already in the repository or any file that is staged in the index. To add a new file *somefile* to this group, run `git add` *somefile*.

Ignored
> An ignored file must be explicitly declared invisible or ignored in the repository even though it may be present within your working directory. A software project tends to have a good number of ignored files. Common ignored files include temporary and scratch files, personal notes, compiler output, and most files generated automatically during a build. Git maintains a default list of files to ignore, and you can configure your repository to recognize others. Ignored files are discussed in detail later in this chapter (see "The .gitignore File" on page 58).

Untracked

An untracked file is any file not found in either of the previous two categories. Git considers the entire set of files in your working directory and subtracts both the tracked files and the ignored files to yield what is untracked.

Let's explore the different categories of files by creating a brand new working directory and repository and then working with some files.

```
$ cd /tmp/my_stuff
$ git init

$ git status
# On branch master
#
# Initial commit
#
nothing to commit (create/copy files and use "git add" to track)

$ echo "New data" > data

$ git status
# On branch master
#
# Initial commit
#
# Untracked files:
#   (use "git add <file>..." to include in what will be committed)
#
#       data
nothing added to commit but untracked files present (use "git add" to track)
```

Initially, there are no files and the tracked, ignored, and therefore untracked sets are empty. Once you create *data*, git status reports a single, untracked file.

Editors and build environments often leave temporary or transient files among your source code. Such files usually shouldn't be tracked as source files in a repository. To have Git ignore a file within a directory, simply add that file's name to the special file *.gitignore*:

```
# Manually create an example junk file
$ touch main.o

$ git status
# On branch master
#
# Initial commit
#
# Untracked files:
#   (use "git add <file>..." to include in what will be committed)
#
#       data
#       main.o

$ echo main.o > .gitignore
```

```
$ git status
# On branch master
#
# Initial commit
#
# Untracked files:
#   (use "git add <file>..." to include in what will be committed)
#
#       .gitignore
#       data
```

Thus *main.o* is ignored, but `git status` now shows a new, untracked file called *.gitignore*. Although the *.gitignore* file has special meaning to Git, it is managed just like any other normal file within your repository. Until *.gitignore* is added, Git considers it untracked.

The next few sections demonstrate different ways to change the tracked status of a file as well as how to add or remove it from the index.

Using git add

The command `git add` stages a file. In terms of Git's file classifications, if a file is untracked, then `git add` converts that file's status to tracked. When `git add` is used on a directory name, all of the files and subdirectories beneath it are staged recursively.

Let's continue the example from the previous section.

```
$ git status
# On branch master
#
# Initial commit
#
# Untracked files:
#   (use "git add <file>..." to include in what will be committed)
#
#       .gitignore
#       data

# Track both new files.
$ git add data .gitignore

$ git status
# On branch master
#
# Initial commit
#
# Changes to be committed:
#   (use "git rm --cached <file>..." to unstage)
#
#       new file: .gitignore
#       new file: data
#
```

The first `git status` shows you that two files are untracked and reminds you that to make a file tracked, you simply need to use `git add`. After `git add`, both *data* and *.gitignore* are staged and tracked, and ready to be added to the repository on the next commit.

In terms of Git's object model, the entirety of each file at the moment you issued `git add` was copied into the object store and indexed by its resulting SHA1 name. Staging a file is also called *caching a file*[2] or "putting a file in the index."

You can use `git ls-files` to peer under the object model hood and find the SHA1 values for those staged files:

```
$ git ls-files --stage
100644 0487f44090ad950f61955271cf0a2d6c6a83ad9a 0       .gitignore
100644 534469f67ae5ce72a7a274faf30dee3c2ea1746d 0       data
```

Most of the day-to-day changes within your repository will likely be simple edits. After any edit and before you commit your changes, run `git add` to update the index with the absolute latest and greatest version of your file. If you don't, you'll have two different versions of the file: one captured in the object store and referenced from the index, and the other in your working directory.

To continue the example, let's change the file *data* so it's different from the one in the index and use the arcane `git hash-object file` command (which you'll hardly ever invoke directly) to directly compute and print the SHA1 hash for the new version.

```
$ git ls-files --stage
100644 0487f44090ad950f61955271cf0a2d6c6a83ad9a 0       .gitignore
100644 534469f67ae5ce72a7a274faf30dee3c2ea1746d 0       data

# edit "data" to contain...
$ cat data
New data
And some more data now

$ git hash-object data
e476983f39f6e4f453f0fe4a859410f63b58b500
```

After the file is amended, the previous version of the file in the object store and index has SHA1 `534469f67ae5ce72a7a274faf30dee3c2ea1746d`. However, the updated version of the file has SHA1 `e476983f39f6e4f453f0fe4a859410f63b58b500`. Let's update the index to contain the new version of the file:

```
$ git add data
$ git ls-files --stage
100644 0487f44090ad950f61955271cf0a2d6c6a83ad9a 0       .gitignore
100644 e476983f39f6e4f453f0fe4a859410f63b58b500 0       data
```

2. You did see the `--cached` in the `git status` output, didn't you?

The index now has the updated version of the file. Again, "the file *data* has been *staged*," or speaking loosely, "the file *data* is *in the index*." The latter phrase is less accurate because the file is actually in the object store and the index merely refers to it.

The seemingly idle play with SHA1 hashes and the index brings home a key point: Think of `git add` not as "add this file," but more as "add this content."

In any event, the important thing to remember is that the version of a file in your working directory can be out of sync with the version staged in the index. When it comes time to make a commit, Git uses the version in the index.

 The `--interactive` option to either `git add` or `git commit` can be a useful way to explore which files you would like to stage for a commit.

Some Notes on Using git commit

Using git commit --all

The `-a` or `--all` option to `git commit` causes it to automatically stage all unstaged, tracked file changes—including removals of tracked files from the working copy— before it performs the commit.

Let's see how this works by setting up a few files with different staging characteristics:

```
# Setup test repository
$ mkdir /tmp/commit-all-example
$ cd /tmp/commit-all-example
$ git init
Initialized empty Git repository in /tmp/commit-all-example/.git/

$ echo something >> ready
$ echo somthing else >> notyet
$ git add ready notyet
$ git commit -m "Setup"
[master (root-commit) 71774a1] Setup
 2 files changed, 2 insertions(+), 0 deletions(-)
 create mode 100644 notyet
 create mode 100644 ready

# Modify file "ready" and "git add" it to the index
# edit ready
$ git add ready

# Modify file "notyet", leaving it unstaged
# edit notyet

# Add a new file in a subdirectory, but don't add it
$ mkdir subdir
$ echo Nope >> subdir/new
```

Use `git status` to see what a regular commit (without command line options) would do:

```
$ git status
# On branch master
# Changes to be committed:
#   (use "git reset HEAD <file>..." to unstage)
#
#       modified:   ready
#
# Changed but not updated:
#   (use "git add <file>..." to update what will be committed)
#
#       modified:   notyet
#
# Untracked files:
#   (use "git add <file>..." to include in what will be committed)
#
#       subdir/
```

Here, the index is prepared to commit just the one file named *ready*, because it's the only file that's been staged.

However, if you run `git commit --all`, Git recursively traverses the entire repository; stages all known, modified files and commits those. In this case, when your editor presents the commit message template, it should indicate that the modified and known file *notyet* will, in fact, be committed as well:

```
# Please enter the commit message for your changes.
# (Comment lines starting with '#' will not be included)
# On branch master
# Changes to be committed:
#   (use "git reset HEAD <file>..." to unstage)
#
#       modified:   notyet
#       modified:   ready
#
# Untracked files:
#   (use "git add <file>..." to include in what will be committed)
#
#       subdir/
```

Finally, because the directory named `subdir/` is new and no file name or path within it is tracked, not even the `--all` option causes it to be committed:

```
Created commit db7de5f: Some --all thing.
 2 files changed, 2 insertions(+), 0 deletions(-)
```

While Git recursively traverses the repository looking for modified and removed files, the completely new file *subdir/* directory and all of its files do not become part of the commit.

Writing Commit Log Messages

If you do not directly supply a log message on the command line, Git runs an editor and prompts you to write one. The editor chosen is selected from your configuration as described in "Configuration Files" on page 28 of Chapter 3.

If you are in the editor writing a commit log message and for some reason decide to abort the operation, simply exit the editor without saving; this results in an empty log message. If it's too late for that because you've already saved, just delete the entire log message and save again. Git will not process an empty (no text) commit.

Using git rm

The command `git rm` is, naturally the inverse of `git add`. It removes a file from both the repository and the working directory. However, because removing a file tends to be more problematic (if something goes wrong) than adding a file, Git treats the removal of a file with a bit more care.

Git will remove a file only from the index or from the index and working directory simultaneously. Git will not remove a file just from the working directory; the regular `rm` command may be used for that purpose.

Removing a file from your directory and the index does not remove the file's existing history from the repository. Any versions of the file that are part of its history already committed in the repository remain in the object store and retain that history.

Continuing the example, let's introduce an "accidental" additional file that shouldn't be staged and see how to remove it.

```
$ echo "Random stuff" > oops

# Can't "git rm" files Git considers "other"
# This should be just "rm oops"
$ git rm oops
fatal: pathspec 'oops' did not match any files
```

Because `git rm` is also an operation on the index, the command won't work on a file that hasn't been previously added to the repository or index; Git must first be aware of a file. So let's accidentally stage the *oops* file:

```
# Accidentally stage "oops" file
$ git add oops

$ git status
# On branch master
#
# Initial commit
#
# Changes to be committed:
#   (use "git rm --cached <file>..." to unstage)
#
```

```
#       new file: .gitignore
#       new file: data
#       new file: oops
#
```

To convert a file from staged to unstaged, use `git rm --cached`:

```
$ git ls-files --stage
100644 0487f44090ad950f61955271cf0a2d6c6a83ad9a 0       .gitignore
100644 e476983f39f6e4f453f0fe4a859410f63b58b500 0       data
100644 fcd87b055f261557434fa9956e6ce29433a5cd1c 0       oops

$ git rm --cached oops
rm 'oops'

$ git ls-files --stage
100644 0487f44090ad950f61955271cf0a2d6c6a83ad9a 0       .gitignore
100644 e476983f39f6e4f453f0fe4a859410f63b58b500 0       data
```

Whereas `git rm --cached` removes the file from the index and leaves it in the working directory, `git rm` removes the file from both the index and the working directory.

 Using `git rm --cached` to make a file untracked while leaving a copy in the working directory is dangerous, because you may forget that it is no longer being tracked. Using this approach also overrides Git's check that the working file's contents are current. Be careful.

If you want to remove a file once it's been committed, just stage the request through a simple `git rm` *filename*:

```
$ git commit -m "Add some files"
Created initial commit 5b22108: Add some files
 2 files changed, 3 insertions(+), 0 deletions(-)
 create mode 100644 .gitignore
 create mode 100644 data

$ git rm data
rm 'data'

$ git status
# On branch master
# Changes to be committed:
#   (use "git reset HEAD <file>..." to unstage)
#
#       deleted:    data
#
```

Before Git removes a file, it checks to make sure the version of the file in the working directory matches the latest version in the current branch (the version that Git commands call the `HEAD`). This verification precludes the accidental loss of any changes (due to your editing) that may have been made to the file.

Use `git rm -f` to *force* the removal of your file. Force is an explicit mandate and removes the file even if you have altered it since your last commit.

And in case you *really* meant to keep a file that you accidentally removed, simply add it back:

```
$ git add data
fatal: pathspec 'data' did not match any files
```

Darn! Git removed the working copy, too! But don't worry. VCSs are good at recovering old versions of files:

```
$ git checkout HEAD -- data
$ cat data
New data
And some more data now

$ git status
# On branch master
nothing to commit (working directory clean)
```

Using git mv

Suppose you need to move or rename a file. You may use a combination of `git rm` on the old file and `git add` on the new file, or you may use `git mv` directly. Given a repository with a file named *stuff* that you want to rename *newstuff*, the following sequences of commands are equivalent Git operations:

```
$ mv stuff newstuff
$ git rm stuff
$ git add newstuff
```

and

```
$ git mv stuff newstuff
```

In both cases, Git removes the pathname *stuff* from the index, adds a new pathname *newstuff*, keeps the original content for *stuff* in the object store, and reassociates that content with the pathname *newstuff*.

With *data* back in the example repository, let's rename it and commit the change:

```
$ git mv data mydata

$ git status
# On branch master
# Changes to be committed:
#   (use "git reset HEAD <file>..." to unstage)
#
#        renamed:    data -> mydata
#
```

```
$ git commit -m "Moved data to mydata"
Created commit ec7d888: Moved data to mydata
 1 files changed, 0 insertions(+), 0 deletions(-)
 rename data => mydata (100%)
```

If you happen to check the history of the file, you may be a bit disturbed to see that Git has apparently lost the history of the original *data* file and remembers only that it renamed *data* to the current name:

```
$ git log mydata
commit ec7d888b6492370a8ef43f56162a2a4686aea3b4
Author: Jon Loeliger <jdl@example.com>
Date:   Sun Nov 2 19:01:20 2008 -0600

    Moved data to mydata
```

Git does still remember the whole history, but the display is limited to the particular filename you specified in the command. The `--follow` option asks Git to trace back through the log and find the whole history associated with the content:

```
$ git log --follow mydata
commit ec7d888b6492370a8ef43f56162a2a4686aea3b4
Author: Jon Loeliger <jdl@example.com>
Date:   Sun Nov 2 19:01:20 2008 -0600

    Moved data to mydata

commit 5b22108820b6638a86bf57145a136f3a7ab71818
Author: Jon Loeliger <jdl@example.com>
Date:   Sun Nov 2 18:38:28 2008 -0600

    Add some files
```

One of the classic problems with VCSs is that renaming a file can cause them to lose track of a file's history. Git preserves this information even after a rename.

A Note on Tracking Renames

Let's talk a bit more about how Git keeps track of file renames.

SVN, as an example of traditional revision control, does a lot of work tracking when a file is renamed and moved around because it keeps track only of diffs between files. If you move a file, it's essentially the same as deleting all the lines from the old file and adding them to the new one. But it would be inefficient to transfer and store all the contents of the file again whenever you do a simple rename; imagine renaming a whole subdirectory that contains thousands of files.

To alleviate this situation, SVN tracks each rename explicitly. If you want to rename *hello.txt* to *subdir/hello.txt*, you must use `svn mv` instead of `svn rm` and `svn add` on the files. Otherwise, SVN has no way to see that it's a rename and must go through the inefficient delete/add sequence just described.

Next, given this exceptional feature of tracking a rename, the SVN server needs a special protocol to tell its clients, "please move *hello.txt* into *subdir/hello.txt*." Furthermore, each SVN client must ensure that it performs this (relatively rare) operation correctly.

Git, on the other hand, doesn't keep track of a rename. You can move or copy *hello.txt* anywhere you want, but doing so affects only tree objects. (Remember that tree objects store the relationships between content, whereas the content itself is stored in blobs.) A look at the differences between two trees makes it obvious that the blob named `3b18e5...` has moved to a new place. And even if you don't explicitly examine the differences, every part of the system knows it already has that blob, so every part knows it doesn't need another copy of it.

In this situation, as in many other places, Git's simple hash-based storage system simplifies a lot of things that baffle or elude other RCS.

Problems with Tracking a Rename

Tracking the renaming of a file engenders a perennial debate among developers of VCSs.

A simple rename is fodder enough for dissension. The argument becomes even more heated when the file's name changes and then its content changes. Then the scenarios turn the parley from practical to philosophical: Is that "new" file really a rename, or is it merely similar to the old one? How similar should the new file be before it's considered the same file? If you apply someone's patch that deletes a file and recreates a similar one elsewhere, how is that managed? What happens if a file is renamed in two different ways on two different branches? Is it less error prone to automatically detect renames in such a situation, as Git does, or to require the user to explicitly identify renames, as SVN does?

In real life use, it seems that Git's system for handling file renames is superior, because there are just too many ways for a file to be renamed and humans are simply not smart enough to make sure SVN knows about them all. But there is no perfect system for handling renames ... yet.

The .gitignore File

Earlier in this chapter you saw how to use the *.gitignore* file to pass over *main.o*, an irrelevant file. As in that example, you can skip any file by adding its name to *.gitignore* in the same directory. Additionally, you can ignore the file everywhere by adding it to the *.gitignore* file in the topmost directory of your repository.

But Git also supports a much richer mechanism. A *.gitignore* file can contain a list of filename *patterns* that specify what files to ignore. The format of *.gitignore* is as follows:

- Blank lines are ignored, and lines starting with a pound sign (#) can be used for comments. However, the # does not represent a comment if it follows other text on the line.

- A simple, literal filename matches a file in any directory with that name.

- A directory name is marked by a trailing slash character (/). This matches the named directory and any subdirectory but does not match a file or a symbolic link.

- A pattern containing shell globbing characters, such as an asterisk (*), is expanded as a shell glob pattern. Just as in standard shell globbing, the match cannot extend across directories and so an asterisk can match only a single file or directory name. But an asterisk can still be part of a pattern that includes slashes to specify directory names (e.g., *debug/32bit/*.o*).

- An initial exclamation point (!) inverts the sense of the pattern on the rest of the line. Additionally, any file excluded by an earlier pattern but matching an inversion rule is included. An inverted pattern overrides lower precedence rules.

Furthermore, Git allows you to have a *.gitignore* file in any directory within your repository. Each file affects its directory and all subdirectories. The *.gitignore* rules also cascade: you can override the rules in a higher directory by including an inverted pattern (using the initial !) in one of the subdirectories.

To resolve a hierarchy with multiple *.gitignore* directories, and to allow command-line addenda to the list of ignored files, Git honors the following precedence, from highest to lowest:

- Patterns specified on the command line.

- Patterns read from *.gitignore* in the same directory.

- Patterns in parent directories, proceeding upward. Hence, the current directory's patterns overrule the parents' patterns, and the parents close to the current directory take precedence over higher parents.

- Patterns from the *.git/info/exclude* file.

- Patterns from the file specified by the configuration variable `core.excludefile`.

Because a *.gitignore* is treated as a regular file within your repository, it is copied during clone operations and applies to all copies of your repository. In general, you should place entries into your version controlled *.gitignore* files only if the patterns apply to *all* derived repositories universally.

If the exclusion pattern is somehow specific to your one repository and should not (or might not) be applicable to anyone else's clone of your repository, then the patterns should instead go into the *.git/info/exclude* file, because it is not propagated during clone operations. Its pattern format and treatment is the same as *.gitignore* files.

Here's another scenario. It's typical to exclude *.o* files, which are generated from source by the compiler. To ignore *.o* files, place **.o* in your top level *.gitignore*. But what if you also had a particular **.o* file that was, say, supplied by someone else and for which you couldn't generate a replacement yourself? You'd likely want to explicitly track that particular file. You might then have a configuration like this:

```
$ cd my_package
$ cat .gitignore
*.o

$ cd my_package/vendor_files
$ cat .gitignore
!driver.o
```

The combination of rules means that Git will ignore all *.o* files within the repository but will track one exception, the file *driver.o* within the *vendor_files* subdirectory.

A Detailed View of Git's Object Model and Files

By now, you should have the basic skills to manage files. Nonetheless, keeping track of what file is where—working directory, index, and repository—can be confusing. Let's follow a series of four pictures to visualize the progress of a single file named *file1* as it is edited, staged in the index, and finally committed. Each picture simultaneously shows your working directory, the index, and the object store. For simplicity, let's stick to just the master branch.

The initial state is shown in Figure 5-1. Here, the working directory contains two files named *file1* and *file2*, with contents "foo" and "bar," respectively.

In addition to *file1* and *file2* in the working directory, the master branch has a commit that records a tree with exactly the same "foo" and "bar," contents for files *file1* and *file2*. Furthermore, the index records SHA1 values a23bf and 9d3a2 (respectively) for exactly those same file contents. The working directory, the index, and the object store are all synchronized and in agreement. Nothing is dirty.

Figure 5-2 shows the changes after editing *file1* in the working directory so that its contents now consist of "quux." Nothing in the index nor in the object store has changed, but the working directory is now considered dirty.

Some interesting changes take place when you use the command `git add file1` to stage the edit of *file1*.

As Figure 5-3 shows, Git first takes the version of *file1* from the working directory, computes a SHA1 hash ID (bd71363) for its contents, and places that ID in the object store. Next, Git records in the index that the pathname file1 has been updated to the new bd71363 SHA1.

Because the contents of *file2* haven't changed and no `git add` staged *file2*, the index continues to reference the original blob object for it.

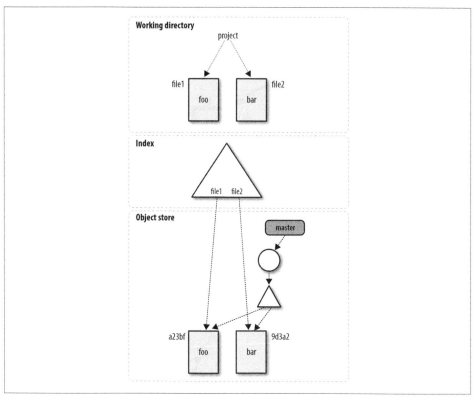

Figure 5-1. Initial files and objects

At this point, you have staged *file1* in the index, and the working directory and index agree. However, the index is considered dirty with respect to HEAD because it differs from the tree recorded in the object store for the HEAD commit of the master branch.[3]

Finally, after all changes have been staged in the index, a commit applies them to the repository. The effects of git commit are depicted in Figure 5-4.

As Figure 5-4 shows, the commit initiates three steps. First, the virtual tree object that is the index gets converted into a real tree object and placed into the object store under its SHA1 name. Second, a new commit object is created with your log message. The new commit points to the newly created tree object and also to the previous or parent commit. Third, the master branch ref is moved from the most recent commit to the newly created commit object, becoming the new master HEAD.

---

3. You can get a dirty index in the other direction, too, irrespective of the working directory state. By reading a non-HEAD commit out of the object store into the index and *not* checking out the corresponding files into the working directory, you create the situation where the index and working directory are not in agreement and where the index is still dirty with respect to the HEAD.

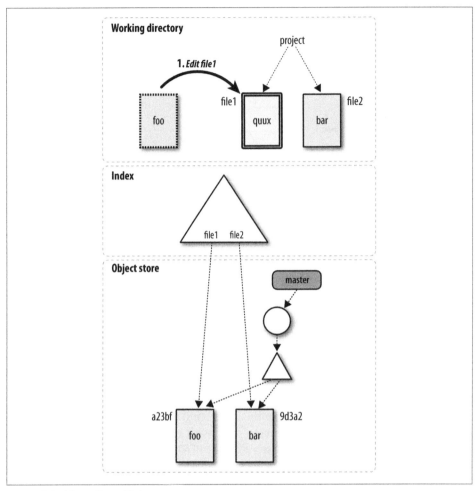

Figure 5-2. After editing file1

An interesting detail is that the working directory, index, and object store (represented by the HEAD of master) are once again all synchronized and in agreement, just as they were in Figure 5-1.

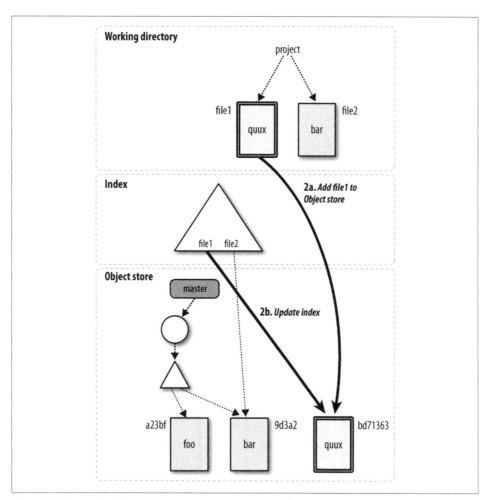

Figure 5-3. After git add

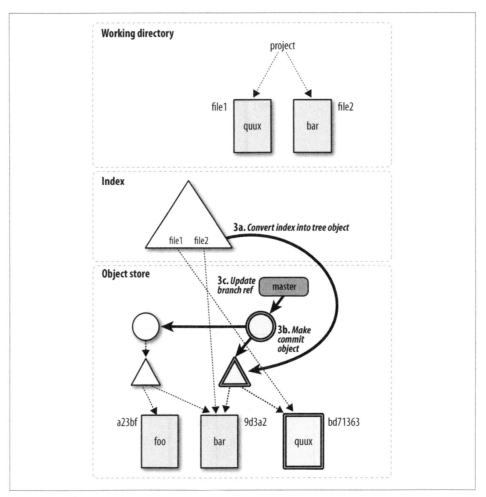

Figure 5-4. After git commit

## CHAPTER 6

Commits

In Git, a *commit* is used to record changes to a repository.

At face value, a Git commit seems no different from a commit or check in found in other VCS. Under the hood, however, a Git commit operates in a unique way.

When a commit occurs, Git records a *snapshot* of the index and places that snapshot in the object store. (Preparing the index for a commit is covered in Chapter 5.) This snapshot does *not* contain a copy of every file and directory in the index, because such a strategy would require enormous and prohibitive amounts of storage. Instead, Git compares the current state of the index to the previous snapshot and so derives a list of affected files and directories. Git creates new blobs for any file that has changed and new trees for any directory that has changed, and it reuses any blob or tree object that has not changed.

Commit snapshots are chained together, with each new snapshot pointing to its predecessor. Over time, a sequences of changes is represented as a series of commits.

It may seem expensive to compare the entire index to some prior state, yet the whole process is remarkably fast because every Git object has an SHA1 hash. If two objects, even two subtrees, have the same SHA1 hash, the objects are identical. Git can avoid swaths of recursive comparisons by pruning subtrees that have the same content.

There is a one-to-one correspondence between a set of changes in the repository and a commit: A commit is the only method of introducing changes to a repository, and any change in the repository must be introduced by a commit. This mandate provides accountability. Under no circumstance should repository data change without a record of the change! Just imagine the chaos if, somehow, content in the master repository changed and there was no record of how it happened, who did it, or why.

Although commits are most often introduced explicitly by a developer, Git itself can introduce commits. As you'll see in Chapter 9, a merge operation causes a commit in the repository in addition to any commits made by users before the merge.

How you decide when to commit is pretty much up to you and your preferences or development style. In general, you should perform a commit at well-defined points in time when your development is at a quiescent stage, such as when a test suite passes, when everyone goes home for the day, or any number of other reasons.

However, don't hesitate to introduce commits! Git is wellsuited to frequent commits and provides a rich set of commands for manipulating them. Later, you'll see how several commits—each with small, well-defined changes—can also lead to better organization of changes and easier manipulation of patch sets.

Atomic Changesets

Every Git commit represents a single, *atomic changeset* with respect to the previous state. Regardless of the number of directories, files, lines, or bytes that change with a commit,[1] either all changes apply or none do.

In terms of the underlying object model, atomicity just makes sense: A commit snapshot represents the total set of modified files and directories. It must represent one tree state or the other, and a changeset *between* two state snapshots represents a complete tree-to-tree transformation. (You can read about derived differences between commits in Chapter 8.)

Consider the workflow of moving a function from one file to another. If you perform the removal with one commit and then follow with a second commit to add it back, there remains a small "semantic gap" in the history of your repository during which time the function is gone. Two commits in the other order is problematic, too. In either case, before the first commit and after the second your code is semantically consistent, but after the first commit, the code is faulty.

However, with an atomic commit that simultaneously deletes and adds the function, no such semantic gap appears in the history. You can learn how best to construct and organize your commits in Chapter 10.

Git doesn't care *why* files are changing. That is, the content of the changes doesn't matter. As the developer, you might move a function from here to there and expect this to be handled as one unitary move. But you could, alternatively, commit the removal and then later commit the addition. Git doesn't care. It has nothing to do with the semantics of what is in the files.

But this does bring up one of the key reasons why Git implements atomicity: It allows you to structure your commits more appropriately by following some best practice advice.

Ultimately, you can rest assured that Git has not left your repository in some transitory state between one commit snapshot and the next.

---

1. Git also records a mode flag indicating the executability of each file. Changes in this flag are also part of a changeset.

Identifying Commits

Whether you code individually or with a team, identifying individual commits is an essential task. For example, to create a branch, you must choose a commit from which to diverge; to compare code variations, you must specify two commits; and to edit the commit history, you must provide a collection of commits. In Git, you can refer to every commit via an explicit or an implied reference.

You've already seen explicit references and a few implied references. The unique, 40-hexadecimal-digit SHA1 commit ID is an explicit reference, whereas HEAD, which always points to the most recent commit, is an implied reference. At times, though, neither reference is convenient. Fortunately, Git provides many different mechanisms for naming a commit, each with advantages and some more useful than others, depending on the context.

For example, when discussing a particular commit with a colleague working on the same data but in a distributed environment, it's best to use a commit name guaranteed to be the same in both repositories. On the other hand, if you're working within your own repository and need to refer to the state a few commits back on a branch, a simple relative name works perfectly.

Absolute Commit Names

The most rigorous name for a commit is its hash identifier. The hash ID is an absolute name, meaning it can only refer to exactly one commit. It doesn't matter where the commit is among the entire repository's history; the hash ID always identifies the same commit.

Each commit ID is *globally* unique, not just for one repository but for any and all repositories. For example, if a developer writes you with reference to a particular commit ID in his repository and if you find the same commit in your repository, then you can be certain that you both have the same commit with the same content. Furthermore, because the data that contribute to a commit ID contain the state of the whole repository tree as well as the prior commit state, by an inductive argument, an even stronger claim can be made: You can be certain that both of you are discussing the same complete line of development leading up to and including the commit.

Because a 40-hexadecimal-digit SHA1 number makes for a tedious and error-prone entry, Git allows you to shorten this number to a unique prefix within a repository's object database. Here is an example from Git's own repository.

```
$ git log -1 --pretty=oneline HEAD
1fbb58b4153e90eda08c2b022ee32d90729582e6 Merge git://repo.or.cz/git-gui

$ git log -1 --pretty=oneline 1fbb
error: short SHA1 1fbb is ambiguous.
fatal: ambiguous argument '1fbb': unknown revision or path
    not in the working tree.
```

```
Use '--' to separate paths from revisions
```

```
$ git log -1 --pretty=oneline 1fbb58
1fbb58b4153e90eda08c2b022ee32d90729582e6 Merge git://repo.or.cz/git-gui
```

Although a tag name isn't a globally unique name, it is absolute in that it points to a unique commit and doesn't change over time (unless you explicitly change it, of course).

refs and symrefs

A *ref* is an SHA1 hash ID that refers to an object within the Git object store. Although a ref may refer to any Git object, it usually refers to a commit object. A *symbolic reference*, or *symref*, is a name that indirectly points to a Git object. It is still just a ref.

Local topic branch names, remote tracking branch names, and tag names are all refs.

Each symbolic ref has an explicit, full name that begins with refs/ and each is stored hierarchically within the repository in the *.git/refs/* directory. There are basically three different namespaces represented in refs/: refs/heads/*ref* for your local branches, refs/remotes/*ref* for your remote tracking branches, and refs/tags/*ref* for your tags. (Branches are covered in more detail in Chapter 7 and in Chapter 12.)

For example, a local topic branch named dev is really a short form of refs/heads/dev. Remote tracking branches are in the refs/remotes/ namespace, so origin/master really names refs/remotes/origin/master. And finally, a tag such as v2.6.23 is short for refs/tags/v2.6.23.

You can use either a full ref name or its abbreviation, but if you have a branch and a tag with the same name, Git applies a disambiguation heuristic and uses the first match according to this list from the git rev-parse manpage:

```
.git/ref
.git/refs/ref
.git/refs/tags/ref
.git/refs/heads/ref
.git/refs/remotes/ref
.git/refs/remotes/ref/HEAD
```

The first rule is usually just for a few refs described later: HEAD, ORIG_HEAD, FETCH_HEAD, CHERRY_PICK_HEAD, and MERGE_HEAD.

 Technically, the name of the Git directory, *.git*, can be changed. Thus, Git's internal documentation uses the variable $GIT_DIR instead of the literal *.git*.

Git maintains several special symrefs automatically for particular purposes. They can be used anywhere a commit is used.

HEAD

> HEAD always refers to the most recent commit on the current branch. When you change branches, HEAD is updated to refer to the new branch's latest commit.

ORIG_HEAD

> Certain operations, such as merge and reset, record the previous version of HEAD in ORIG_HEAD just prior to adjusting it to a new value. You can use ORIG_HEAD to recover or revert to the previous state or to make a comparison.

FETCH_HEAD

> When remote repositories are used, git fetch records the heads of all branches fetched in the file *.git/FETCH_HEAD*. FETCH_HEAD is a shorthand for the head of the last branch fetched and is valid only immediately after a fetch operation. Using this symref, you can find the HEAD of commits from git fetch even if an anonymous fetch that doesn't specifically name a branch is used. The fetch operation is covered in Chapter 12.

MERGE_HEAD

> When a merge is in progress, the tip of the *other* branch is temporarily recorded in the symref MERGE_HEAD. In other words, MERGE_HEAD is the commit that is being merged into HEAD.

All of these symbolic references are managed by the plumbing command git symbolic-ref.

 Although it is possible to create your own branch with one of these special symbolic names (e.g., HEAD), it isn't a good idea.

There are a whole raft of special character variants for ref names. The two most common, the caret (^) and tilde (~), are described in the next section. In another twist on refs, colons can be used to refer to alternate versions of a common file involved in a merge conflict. This procedure is described in Chapter 9.

Relative Commit Names

Git also provides mechanisms for identifying a commit relative to another reference, commonly the tip of a branch.

You've seen some of these names already, such as master and master^, where master^ always refers to the penultimate commit on the master branch. There are others as well: you can use master^^, master~2, and even a complex name like master~10^2~2^2.

Except for the first *root commit*,[2] each commit is derived from at least one earlier commit and possibly many, where direct ancestors are called *parent commits*. For a commit to have multiple parent commits, it must be the result of a merge operation. As a result, there will be a parent commit for each branch contributing to a merge commit.

Within a single generation, the caret is used to select a different parent. Given a commit C, C^1 is the first parent, C^2 is the second parent, C^3 is the third parent, and so on, as shown in Figure 6-1.

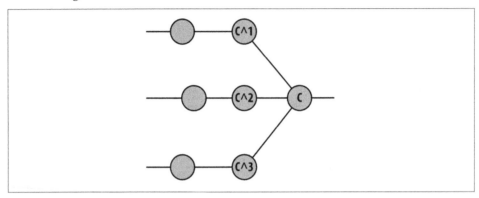

Figure 6-1. Multiple parent names

The tilde is used to go back before an ancestral parent and select a preceding generation. Again, given the commit C, C~1 is the first parent, C~2 is the first grandparent, and C~3 is the first great-grandparent. When there are multiple parents in a generation, the first parent of the first parent is followed. You might also notice that both C^1 and C~1 refer to the first parent; either name is correct, and is shown in Figure 6-2.

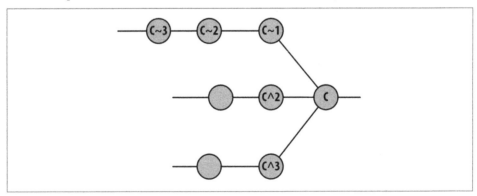

Figure 6-2. Multiple parent names

---

2. Yes, you can actually introduce multiple root commits into a single repository. This happens, for example, when two different projects and both entire repositories are brought together and merged into one.

Git supports other abbreviations and combinations as well. The abbreviated forms C^ and C~ are the same as C^1 and C~1, respectively. Also, C^^ is the same as C^1^1 and, because that means the "first parent of the first parent of commit C," it refers to the same commit as C~2.

By combining a *ref* and instances of caret and tilde, arbitrary commits may be selected from the ancestral commit graph of *ref*. Remember, though, that these names are relative to the *current* value of *ref*. If a new commit is made on top of *ref*, the commit graph is amended with a new generation and each "parent" name shifts further back in the history and graph.

Here's an example from Git's own history when Git's master branch was at commit 1fbb58b4153e90eda08c2b022ee32d90729582e6. Using the command:

```
git show-branch --more=35
```

and limiting the output to the final 10 lines, you can inspect the graph history and examine a complex branch merge structure:

```
$ git rev-parse master
1fbb58b4153e90eda08c2b022ee32d90729582e6

$ git show-branch --more=35 | tail -10
-- [master~15] Merge branch 'maint'
-- [master~3^2^] Merge branch 'maint-1.5.4' into maint
+* [master~3^2^2^] wt-status.h: declare global variables as extern
-- [master~3^2~2] Merge branch 'maint-1.5.4' into maint
-- [master~16] Merge branch 'lt/core-optim'
+* [master~16^2] Optimize symlink/directory detection
+* [master~17] rev-parse --verify: do not output anything on error
+* [master~18] rev-parse: fix using "--default" with "--verify"
+* [master~19] rev-parse: add test script for "--verify"
+* [master~20] Add svn-compatible "blame" output format to git-svn

$ git rev-parse master~3^2^2^
32efcd91c6505ae28f87c0e9a3e2b3c0115017d8
```

Between master~15 and master~16, a merge took place that introduced a couple of other merges as well as a simple commit named master~3^2^2^. That happens to be commit 32efcd91c6505ae28f87c0e9a3e2b3c0115017d8.

The command git rev-parse is the final authority on translating any form of commit name—tag, relative, shortened, or absolute—into an actual, absolute commit hash ID within the object database.

Commit History

Viewing Old Commits

The primary command to show the history of commits is `git log`. It has more options, parameters, bells, whistles, colorizers, selectors, formatters, and doodads than the fabled `ls`. But don't worry. Just as with `ls`, you don't need to learn all the details right away.

In its parameterless form, `git log` acts like `git log HEAD`, printing the log message associated with every commit in your history that is reachable from `HEAD`. Changes are shown starting with the `HEAD` commit and work back through the graph. They are likely to be in *roughly* reverse chronological order, but recall Git adheres to the commit graph, not time, when traveling back over the history.

If you supply a commit à la `git log` *commit*, the log starts at the named commit and works backward. This form of the command is useful for viewing the history of a branch:

```
$ git log master

commit 1fbb58b4153e90eda08c2b022ee32d90729582e6
Merge: 58949bb... 76bb40c...
Author: Junio C Hamano <gitster@pobox.com>
Date:   Thu May 15 01:31:15 2008 -0700

    Merge git://repo.or.cz/git-gui

    * git://repo.or.cz/git-gui:
      git-gui: Delete branches with 'git branch -D' to clear config
      git-gui: Setup branch.remote,merge for shorthand git-pull
      git-gui: Update German translation
      git-gui: Don't use '$$cr master' with aspell earlier than 0.60
      git-gui: Report less precise object estimates for database compression

commit 58949bb18a1610d109e64e997c41696e0dfe97c3
Author: Chris Frey <cdfrey@foursquare.net>
Date:   Wed May 14 19:22:18 2008 -0400

    Documentation/git-prune.txt: document unpacked logic

    Clarifies the git-prune manpage, documenting that it only
    prunes unpacked objects.

    Signed-off-by: Chris Frey <cdfrey@foursquare.net>
    Signed-off-by: Junio C Hamano <gitster@pobox.com>

commit c7ea453618e41e05a06f05e3ab63d555d0ddd7d9

...
```

The logs are authoritative, but rolling back through the entire commit history of your repository is likely not very practical or meaningful. Typically, a limited history is more informative. One technique to constrain history is to specify a commit *range* using the form *since..until*. Given a range, `git log` shows all commits following *since* running through *until*. Here's an example.

```
$ git log --pretty=short --abbrev-commit master~12..master~10

commit 6d9878c...
Author: Jeff King <peff@peff.net>

clone: bsd shell portability fix

commit 30684df...
Author: Jeff King <peff@peff.net>

t5000: tar portability fix
```

Here, `git log` shows the commits between `master~12` and `master~10`, or the 10th and 11th prior commits on the master branch. You'll see more about ranges in "Commit Ranges" on page 78 later in this chapter.

The previous example also introduces two formatting options, `--pretty=short` and `--abbrev-commit`. The former adjusts the amount of information about each commit and has several variations, including `oneline`, `short`, and `full`. The latter simply requests that hash IDs be abbreviated.

Use the `-p` option to print the patch, or changes, introduced by the commit.

```
$ git log -1 -p 4fe86488

commit 4fe86488e1a550aa058c081c7e67644dd0f7c98e
Author: Jon Loeliger <jdl@freescale.com>
Date:   Wed Apr 23 16:14:30 2008 -0500

Add otherwise missing --strict option to unpack-objects summary.

Signed-off-by: Jon Loeliger <jdl@freescale.com>
Signed-off-by: Junio C Hamano <gitster@pobox.com>

diff --git a/Documentation/git-unpack-objects.txt b/Documentation/git-unpack-objects.txt
index 3697896..50947c5 100644
--- a/Documentation/git-unpack-objects.txt
+++ b/Documentation/git-unpack-objects.txt
@@ -8,7 +8,7 @@ git-unpack-objects - Unpack objects from a packed archive

 SYNOPSIS
 --------
-'git-unpack-objects' [-n] [-q] [-r] <pack-file>
+'git-unpack-objects' [-n] [-q] [-r] [--strict] <pack-file>
```

Notice the `-1` option as well: it restricts the output to a single commit. You can also type `-n` to limit the output to at most *n* commits.

The `--stat` option enumerates the files changed in a commit and tallies how many lines were modified in each file.

```
$ git log --pretty=short --stat master~12..master~10

commit 6d9878cc60ba97fc99aa92f40535644938cad907
Author: Jeff King <peff@peff.net>

    clone: bsd shell portability fix

 git-clone.sh |    3 +--
 1 files changed, 1 insertions(+), 2 deletions(-)

commit 30684dfaf8cf96e5afc01668acc01acc0ade59db
Author: Jeff King <peff@peff.net>

    t5000: tar portability fix

 t/t5000-tar-tree.sh |    8 ++++----
 1 files changed, 4 insertions(+), 4 deletions(-)
```

 Compare the output of `git log --stat` with the output of `git diff --stat`. There is a fundamental difference in their displays. The former produces a summary for each individual commit named in the range, whereas the latter prints a single summary of the total difference between two repository states named on the command line.

Another command to display objects from the object store is `git show`. You can use it to see a commit:

```
$ git show HEAD~2
```

or to see a specific blob object:

```
$ git show origin/master:Makefile
```

In the latter display, the blob shown is the *Makefile* from the branch named origin/master.

Commit Graphs

In Chapter 4, "Object Store Pictures" on page 36 introduced some figures to help visualize the layout and connectivity of objects in Git's data model. Such sketches are illuminating, especially if you are new to Git; however, even a small repository with just a handful of commits, merges, and patches becomes unwieldy to render in the same detail. For example, Figure 6-3 shows a more complete but still somewhat simplified commit graph. Imagine how it would appear if all commits and all data structures were rendered.

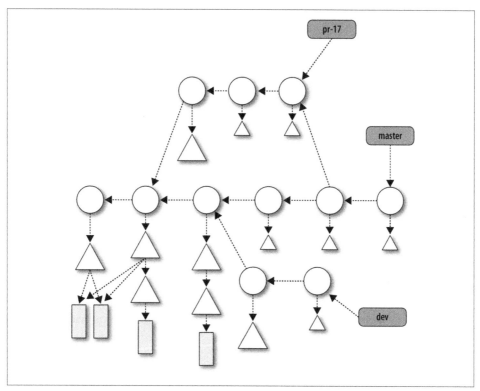

Figure 6-3. Full commit graph

Yet one observation about commits can simplify the blueprint tremendously: Each commit introduces a tree object that represents the entire repository. Therefore, a commit can be pictured as just a name.

Figure 6-4 shows the same commit graph as Figure 6-3 but without depicting the tree and blob objects. Usually for the purpose of discussion or reference, branch names are also shown in the commit graphs.

In the field of computer science, a *graph* is a collection of nodes and a set of edges between the nodes. There are several types of graphs with different properties. Git makes use of a special graph called a *directed acyclic graph* (DAG). A DAG has two important properties. First, the edges within the graph are all directed from one node to another. Second, starting at any node in the graph, there is no path along the directed edges that leads back to the starting node.

Git implements the history of commits within a repository as a DAG. In the *commit graph*, each node is a single commit, and all edges are directed from one *descendant* node to another parent node, forming an ancestor relationship. The graphs you saw in Figure 6-3 and Figure 6-4 are both DAGs. When speaking of the history of commits

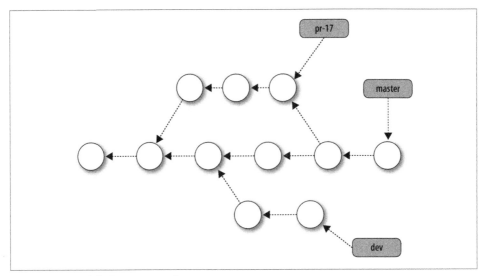

Figure 6-4. Simplified commit graph

and discussing the relationship between commits in a graph, the individual commit nodes are often labeled as shown in Figure 6-5.

In these diagrams, time is roughly left to right. A is the initial commit because it has no parent, and B occurred after A. Both E and C occurred after B, but no claim can be made about the relative timing between C and E; either could have occurred before the other. In fact, Git doesn't really care about the time or timing (absolute or relative) of commits. The actual "wall clock" time of a commit can be misleading because a computer's clock can be set incorrectly or inconsistently. Within a distributed development environment, the problem is exacerbated. Time stamps can't be trusted. What is certain, though, is that if commit Y points to parent X, then X captures the repository state prior to the repository state of commit Y, regardless of what time stamps might be on the commits.

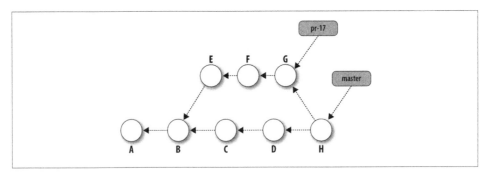

Figure 6-5. Labeled commit graph

The commits E and C share a common parent, B. Thus, B is the origin of a *branch*. The master branch begins with commits A, B, C, and D. Meanwhile, the sequence of commits A, B, E, F, and G form the branch named pr-17. The branch pr-17 points to commit G. (You can read more about branches in Chapter 7.)

The commit H is a *merge commit*, where the pr-17 branch has been merged into the master branch. Because it's a merge, H has more than one commit parent—in this case, D and G. After this commit is made, master will be updated to refer to the new commit H, but pr-17 will continue to refer to G. (The merge operation is discussed in more detail in Chapter 9.)

In practice, the fine points of intervening commits are considered unimportant. Also, the implementation detail of a commit pointing back to its parent is often elided, as shown in Figure 6-6.

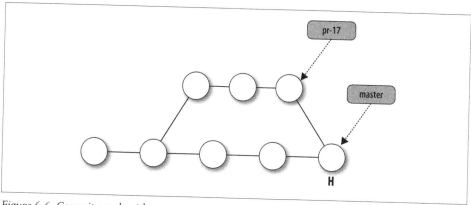

Figure 6-6. Commit graph without arrows

Time is still vaguely left to right, there are two branches shown, and there is one identified merge commit (H), but the actual directed edges are simplified because they are implicitly understood.

This kind of commit graph is often used to talk about the operation of certain Git commands and how each might modify the commit history. The graphs are a fairly abstract representation of the actual commit history, in contrast to tools (e.g., gitk and git show-branch) that provide concrete representations of commit history graphs. With these tools, though, time is usually represented from bottom to top, oldest to most recent. Conceptually, it is the same information.

Using gitk to View the Commit Graph

The purpose of a graph is to help you visualize a complicated structure and relationship. The gitk command[3] can draw a picture of a repository DAG whenever you want.

Let's look at our example website:

```
$ cd public_html
$ gitk
```

The `gitk` program can do a lot of things, but let's just focus on the DAG for now. The graph output looks something like Figure 6-7.

Figure 6-7. Merge viewed with gitk

Here's what you must know to understand the DAG of commits. First of all, each commit can have zero or more *parents*, as follows:

- Normal commits have exactly one parent, which is the previous commit in the history. When you make a change, your change is the difference between your new commit and its parent.
- There is usually only one commit with zero parents: the *initial commit*, which appears at the bottom of the graph.
- A *merge commit*, such as the one at the top of the graph, has more than one parent.

A commit with more than one *child* is the place where history began to diverge and formed a branch. In Figure 6-7, the commit `Remove my poem` is the branch point.

 There is no permanent record of branch start points, but Git can algorithmically determine them via the `git merge-base` command.

Commit Ranges

Many Git commands allow you to specify a *commit range*. In its simplest instantiation, a commit range is a shorthand for a series of commits. More complex forms allow you to include and exclude commits.

A range is denoted with a double-period (`..`), as in *start..end*, where *start* and *end* may be specified as described in "Identifying Commits" on page 67. Typically, a range is used to examine a branch or part of a branch.

---

3. Yes, this is one of the few Git commands that is not considered a subcommand; thus, it is given as `gitk` and not `git gitk`.

In "Viewing Old Commits" on page 72, you saw how to use a commit range with git log. The example used the range master~12..master~10 to specify the 11th and 10th prior commits on the master branch. To visualize the range, consider the commit graph of Figure 6-8. Branch M is shown over a portion of its commit history that is linear:

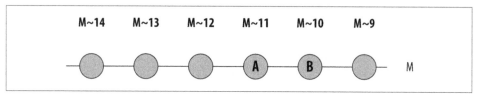

Figure 6-8. Linear commit history

Recall that time flows left to right, so M~14 is the oldest commit shown, M~9 is the most recent commit shown, and A is the 11th prior commit.

The range M~12..M~10 represents two commits, the 11th and 10th oldest commits, which are labeled A and B. The range does not include M~12. Why? It's a matter of definition. A *commit range*, *start..end*, is defined as the set of commits reachable from *end* that are not reachable from *start*. In other words, "the commit *end* is *included*" whereas "the commit *start* is *excluded*." Usually this is simplified to just the phrase "in *end* but not *start*."

Reachability in Graphs

In graph theory, a node X is said to be *reachable* from another node A if you can start at A, travel along the arcs of the graph according to the rules, and arrive at X. The *set of reachable nodes* for a node A is the collection of all nodes reachable from A.

In a Git commit graph, the set of reachable commits are those you can reach from a given commit by traversing the directed parent links. Conceptually and in terms of dataflow, the set of reachable commits is the set of ancestor commits that flow into and contribute to a given starting commit.

When you specify a commit Y, to git log, you are actually requesting Git to show the log for all commits that are reachable from Y. You can exclude a specific commit X and all commits reachable from X with the expression ^X.

Combining the two forms, git log ^X Y is the same as git log X..Y and might be paraphrased as "give me all commits that are reachable from Y and don't give me any commit leading up to and including X."

The commit range X..Y is mathematically equivalent to ^X Y. You can also think of it as a set subtraction: Use everything leading up to Y minus everything leading up to and including X.

Returning to the commit series from the earlier example, here's how M~12..M~10 specifies just two commits, A and B. Begin with everything leading up to M~10 as shown in the first line of Figure 6-9. Find everything leading up to and including M~12, as shown in the second line of the figure. And finally, subtract M~12 from M~10 to get the commits shown in the third line of the figure.

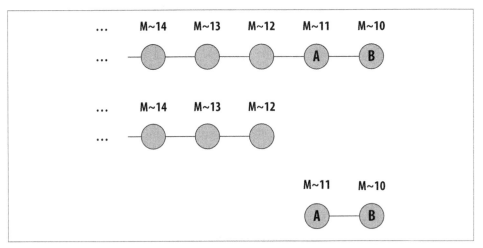

Figure 6-9. Interpreting ranges as set subtraction

When your repository history is a simple linear series of commits, it's fairly easy to understand how a range works. But when branches or merges are involved in the graph, things can become a bit tricky and so it's important to understand the rigorous definition.

Let's look at a few more examples. In the case of a `master` branch with a linear history, as shown in Figure 6-10, the set B..E, the set ^B E, and the set of C, D, and E are equivalent.

Figure 6-10. Simple linear history

In Figure 6-11, the `master` branch at commit V was merged into the `topic` branch at B.

The range `topic..master` represents those commits in `master`, but not in `topic`. Because each commit on the `master` branch prior to and including V (i.e., the set {..., T, U, V}) contributes to `topic`, those commits are excluded, leaving W, X, Y, and Z.

The inverse of the previous example is shown in Figure 6-12. Here, `topic` has been merged into `master`.

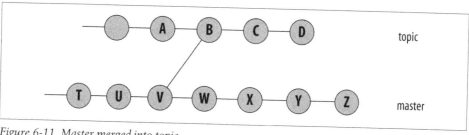

Figure 6-11. Master merged into topic

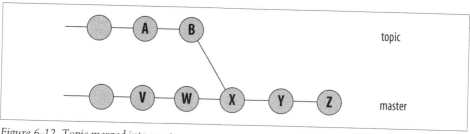

Figure 6-12. Topic merged into master

In this example, the range topic..master, again representing those commits in master but not in topic, is the set of commits on the master branch leading up to and including V, W, X, Y, and Z.

However, we have to be a little careful and consider the full history of the topic branch. Consider the case where it originally started as a branch of master and then merged again as shown in Figure 6-13.

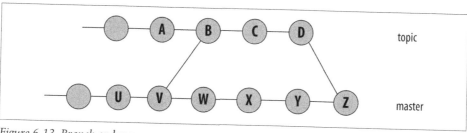

Figure 6-13. Branch and merge

In this case, topic..master, contains only the commits W, X, Y, and Z. Remember, the range will exclude *all* commits that are reachable (going back or left over the graph) from topic (i.e., the commits D, C, B, A, and earlier), as well as V, U, and earlier from the other parent of B. The result is just W through Z.

There are two other range permutations. If you leave either the *start* or *end* commits out of range, HEAD is assumed. Thus, *..end* is equivalent to HEAD..*end* and *start*.. is equivalent to *start*..HEAD.

Finally, just as *start..end* can be thought of as representing a set subtraction operation, the notation *A...B* (using three periods) represents the *symmetric difference* between A and B, or the set of commits that are reachable from either A or B but not from both. Because of the function's symmetry, neither commit can really be considered a start or end. In this sense A and B are equal.

More formally, the set of revisions in the symmetric difference between A and B, *A...B*, is given by

```
$ git rev-list A B --not $(git merge-base --all A B)
```

Let's look at the example in Figure 6-14.

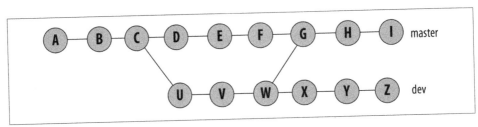

Figure 6-14. Symmetric difference

We can compute each piece of the symmetric difference definition:

```
master...dev = (master OR dev) AND NOT (merge-base --all master dev)
```

The commits that contribute to `master` are (I, H, . . . , B, A, W, V, U). The commits that contribute to `dev` are (Z, Y, . . . , U, C, B, A).

The union of those two sets is (A, . . . , I, U, . . . , Z). The merge base between `master` and `dev` is commit W. In more complex cases, there might be multiple merge bases, but here we have only one. The commits that contribute to W are (W, V, U, C, B, and A); those are also the commits that are common to both `master` and `dev`, so they need to be removed to form the symmetric difference: (I, H, Z, Y, X, G, F, E, D).

It may be helpful to think of the symmetric difference between two branches, A and B, as "show everything in branch A or in branch B, but only back to the point where the two branches diverged."

Now that we've described what commit ranges are, how to write them, and how they work, it's important to reveal that Git doesn't actually support a true range operator. It is purely a notational convenience that A..B represents the underlying ^A B form. Git actually allows much more powerful commit set manipulation on its command line. Commands that accept a range are actually accepting an arbitrary sequence of included and excluded commits. For example, you could use:

```
$ git log ^dev ^topic ^bugfix master
```

to select those commits in `master` but not in either of the `dev`, `topic`, or `bugfix` branches.

All of these example may be a bit abstract, but the power of the range representation really comes to fruition when you consider that any branch name can be used as part of the range. As described in "Tracking Branches" on page 199 of Chapter 12, if one of your branches represents the commits from another repository, then you can quickly discover the set of commits that are in *your* repository that are not in another repository!

Finding Commits

Part of a good RCS is the support it provides for "archaeology" and investigating a repository. Git provides several mechanisms to help you locate commits that meet certain criteria within your repository.

Using git bisect

The `git bisect` command is a powerful tool for isolating a particular, faulty commit based on essentially arbitrary search criteria. It is well-suited to those times when you discover that something "wrong" or "bad" is affecting your repository and you know the code had been fine. For example, let's say you are working on the Linux kernel and a test boot fails, but you're positive the boot worked sometime earlier, perhaps last week or at a previous release tag. In this case, your repository has transitioned from a known "good" state to a known "bad" state.

But when? Which commit caused it to break? That is precisely the question `git bisect` is designed to help you answer.

The only real search requirement is that, given a checked-out state of your repository, you are able to determine if it does or does not meet your search requirement. In this case, you have to be able to answer the question: "Does the version of the kernel checked out build and boot?" You also have to know a good and a bad version or commit before starting so that the search will be bounded.

The `git bisect` command is often used to isolate a particular commit that introduced some regression or bug into the repository. For example, if you were working on the Linux kernel, `git bisect` could help you find issues and bugs such as fails to compile, fails to boot, boots but can't perform some task, or no longer has a desired performance characteristic. In all of these cases, `git bisect` can help you isolate and determine the exact commit that caused the problem.

The `git bisect` command systematically chooses a new commit in an ever decreasing range bounded by good behavior at one end and by bad behavior at the other. Eventually, the narrowing range will pinpoint the one commit that introduced the faulty behavior.

There is no need for you to do anything more than provide an initial good and bad commit and then repeatedly answer the question "Does this version work?"

To start, you first need to identify a good commit and a bad commit. In practice, the bad version is often your current `HEAD`, because that's where you are working when you suddenly noticed something wrong or were assigned a bug to fix.

Finding an initial good version can be a bit difficult, because it's usually buried in your history somewhere. You can probably name or guess some version back in the history of the repository that you know works correctly. This may be a tagged release like `v2.6.25` or some commit 100 revisions ago, `master~100`, on your master branch. Ideally, it is close to your bad commit (`master~25` is better than `master~100`) and not buried too far in the past. In any event, you need to know or be able to verify that it is, in fact, a good commit.

It is essential that you start the `git bisect` process from a clean working directory. The process necessarily adjusts your working directory to contain various different versions of your repository. Starting with a dirty work space is asking for trouble; your working directory could easily be lost.

Using a clone of the Linux kernel in our example, let's tell Git to begin a search:

```
$ cd linux-2.6
$ git bisect start
```

After initiating a bisection search, Git enters a bisect mode, setting up some state information for itself. Git employs a *detached HEAD* to manage the current checked-out version of the repository. This detached `HEAD` is essentially an anonymous branch that can be used to bounce around within the repository and point to different revisions as needed.

Once started, tell Git which commit is bad. Again, because this is typically your current version, you can simply default the revision to your current `HEAD`.[4]

```
# Tell git the HEAD version is broken
$ git bisect bad
```

Similarly, tell Git which version works:

```
$ git bisect good v2.6.27
Bisecting: 3857 revisions left to test after this
[cf2fa66055d718ae13e62451bb546505f63906a2] Merge branch 'for_linus'
    of git://git.kernel.org/pub/scm/linux/kernel/git/mchehab/linux-2.6
```

Identifying a good and bad version delineates a range of commits over which a good to bad transition occurs. At each step along the way, Git will tell you how many revisions are in that range. Git also modifies your working directory by checking out a revision that is roughly midway between the good and bad end points. It is now up to you to answer the question: "Is this version good or bad?" Each time you answer this question, Git narrows the search space in half, identifies a new revision, checks it out, and repeats the "good or bad?" question.

---

4. For the curious reader who would like to duplicate this example, `HEAD` is commit `49fdf6785fd660e18a1eb4588928f47e9fa29a9a` here.

Suppose this version is good:

```
$ git bisect good
Bisecting: 1939 revisions left to test after this
[2be508d847392e431759e370d21cea9412848758] Merge git://git.infradead.org/mtd-2.6
```

Notice that 3,857 revisions have been narrowed down to 1,939. Let's do a few more:

```
$ git bisect good
Bisecting: 939 revisions left to test after this
[b80de369aa5c7c8ce7ff7a691e86e1dcc89accc6] 8250: Add more OxSemi devices
```

```
$ git bisect bad
Bisecting: 508 revisions left to test after this
[9301975ec251bab1ad7cfcb84a688b26187e4e4a] Merge branch 'genirq-v28-for-linus'
    of git://git.kernel.org/pub/scm/linux/kernel/git/tip/linux-2.6-tip
```

In a perfect bisection run, it takes $\log_2$ of the original number of revision steps to narrow down to just one commit.

After another good and bad answer:

```
$ git bisect good
Bisecting: 220 revisions left to test after this
[7cf5244ce4a0ab3f043f2e9593e07516b0df5715] mfd: check for
    platform_get_irq() return value in sm501
```

```
$ git bisect bad
Bisecting: 104 revisions left to test after this
[e4c2ce82ca2710e17cb4df8eb2b249fa2eb5af30] ring_buffer: allocate
    buffer page pointer
```

Throughout the bisection process, Git maintains a log of your answers along with their commit IDs.

```
$ git bisect log
git bisect start
# bad: [49fdf6785fd660e18a1eb4588928f47e9fa29a9a] Merge branch
    'for-linus' of git://git.kernel.dk/linux-2.6-block
git bisect bad 49fdf6785fd660e18a1eb4588928f47e9fa29a9a
# good: [3fa8749e584b55f1180411ab1b51117190bac1e5] Linux 2.6.27
git bisect good 3fa8749e584b55f1180411ab1b51117190bac1e5
# good: [cf2fa66055d718ae13e62451bb546505f63906a2] Merge branch 'for_linus'
    of git://git.kernel.org/pub/scm/linux/kernel/git/mchehab/linux-2.6
git bisect good cf2fa66055d718ae13e62451bb546505f63906a2
# good: [2be508d847392e431759e370d21cea9412848758] Merge
    git://git.infradead.org/mtd-2.6
git bisect good 2be508d847392e431759e370d21cea9412848758
# bad: [b80de369aa5c7c8ce7ff7a691e86e1dcc89accc6] 8250: Add more
    OxSemi devices
git bisect bad b80de369aa5c7c8ce7ff7a691e86e1dcc89accc6
# good: [9301975ec251bab1ad7cfcb84a688b26187e4e4a] Merge branch
    'genirq-v28-for-linus' of
git://git.kernel.org/pub/scm/linux/kernel/git/tip/linux-2.6-tip
git bisect good 9301975ec251bab1ad7cfcb84a688b26187e4e4a
# bad: [7cf5244ce4a0ab3f043f2e9593e07516b0df5715] mfd: check for
```

```
            platform_get_irq() return value in sm501
git bisect bad 7cf5244ce4a0ab3f043f2e9593e07516b0df5715
```

If you get lost during the process, or if you just want to start over for any reason, type the git bisect replay command using the log file as input. If needed, this is an excellent mechanism to back up one step in the process and explore a different path.

Let's narrow down the defect with five more "bad" answers:

```
$ git bisect bad
Bisecting: 51 revisions left to test after this
[d3ee6d992821f471193a7ee7a00af9ebb4bf5d01] ftrace: make it
    depend on DEBUG_KERNEL

$ git bisect bad
Bisecting: 25 revisions left to test after this
[3f5a54e371ca20b119b73704f6c01b71295c1714] ftrace: dump out
    ftrace buffers to console on panic

$ git bisect bad
Bisecting: 12 revisions left to test after this
[8da3821ba5634497da63d58a69e24a97697c4a2b] ftrace: create
    _mcount_loc section

$ git bisect bad
Bisecting: 6 revisions left to test after this
[fa340d9c050e78fb21a142b617304214ae5e0c2d] tracing: disable
    tracepoints by default

$ git bisect bad
Bisecting: 2 revisions left to test after this
[4a0897526bbc5c6ac0df80b16b8c60339e717ae2] tracing: tracepoints, samples
```

You may use the git bisect visualize to visually inspect the set of commits still within the range of consideration. Git uses the graphical tool gitk if the DISPLAY environment variable is set. If not, then Git will use git log instead. In that case, --pretty=oneline might be useful, too.

```
$ git bisect visualize --pretty=oneline

fa340d9c050e78fb21a142b617304214ae5e0c2d tracing: disable tracepoints
    by default
b07c3f193a8074aa4afe43cfa8ae38ec4c7ccfa9 ftrace: port to tracepoints
0a16b6075843325dc402edf80c1662838b929aff tracing, sched: LTTng
    instrumentation - scheduler
4a0897526bbc5c6ac0df80b16b8c60339e717ae2 tracing: tracepoints, samples
24b8d831d56aac7907752d22d2aba5d8127db6f6 tracing: tracepoints,
    documentation
97e1c18e8d17bd87e1e383b2e9d9fc740332c8e2 tracing: Kernel Tracepoints
```

The current revision under consideration is roughly in the middle of the range.

```
$ git bisect good
Bisecting: 1 revisions left to test after this
[b07c3f193a8074aa4afe43cfa8ae38ec4c7ccfa9] ftrace: port to tracepoints
```

When you finally test the last revision and Git has isolated the one revision that introduced the problem,[5] it's displayed:

```
$ git bisect good
fa340d9c050e78fb21a142b617304214ae5e0c2d is first bad commit
commit fa340d9c050e78fb21a142b617304214ae5e0c2d
Author: Ingo Molnar <mingo@elte.hu>
Date:   Wed Jul 23 13:38:00 2008 +0200

    tracing: disable tracepoints by default

    while it's arguably low overhead, we dont enable new features by default.

    Signed-off-by: Ingo Molnar <mingo@elte.hu>

:040000 040000 4bf5c05869a67e184670315c181d76605c973931
    fd15e1c4adbd37b819299a9f0d4a6ff589721f6c M  init
```

Finally, when your bisection run is complete and you are finished with the bisection log and the saved state, it is vital that you tell Git that you have finished. As you may recall, the whole bisection process is performed on a detached HEAD:

```
$ git branch
* (no branch)
  master

$ git bisect reset
Switched to branch "master"

$ git branch
* master
```

Running git bisect reset places you back on your original branch.

Using git blame

Another tool you can use to help identify a particular commit is git blame. This command tells you who last modified each line of a file and which commit made the change.

```
$ git blame -L 35, init/version.c

4865ecf1 (Serge E. Hallyn 2006-10-02 02:18:14 -0700 35)          },
^1da177e (Linus Torvalds  2005-04-16 15:20:36 -0700 36) };
4865ecf1 (Serge E. Hallyn 2006-10-02 02:18:14 -0700 37) EXPORT_SYMBOL_GPL(init_uts_ns);
3eb3c740 (Roman Zippel    2007-01-10 14:45:28 +0100 38)
c71551ad (Linus Torvalds  2007-01-11 18:18:04 -0800 39) /* FIXED STRINGS!
                                                           Don't touch! */
c71551ad (Linus Torvalds  2007-01-11 18:18:04 -0800 40) const char linux_banner[] =
3eb3c740 (Roman Zippel    2007-01-10 14:45:28 +0100 41)     "Linux version "
                                                           UTS_RELEASE "
3eb3c740 (Roman Zippel    2007-01-10 14:45:28 +0100 42)     (" LINUX_COMPILE_BY "@"
```

---

5. No, this commit did not necessarily introduce a problem. The "good" and "bad" answers were fabricated and landed here.

```
3eb3c740 (Roman Zippel    2007-01-10 14:45:28 +0100 43)        LINUX_COMPILE_HOST ")
3eb3c740 (Roman Zippel    2007-01-10 14:45:28 +0100 44)        (" LINUX_COMPILER ")
3eb3c740 (Roman Zippel    2007-01-10 14:45:28 +0100 45)        " UTS_VERSION "\n";
3eb3c740 (Roman Zippel    2007-01-10 14:45:28 +0100 46)
3eb3c740 (Roman Zippel    2007-01-10 14:45:28 +0100 47) const char linux_proc_banner[] =
3eb3c740 (Roman Zippel    2007-01-10 14:45:28 +0100 48)        "%s version %s"
3eb3c740 (Roman Zippel    2007-01-10 14:45:28 +0100 49)        " (" LINUX_COMPILE_BY
                                                               "@"
3eb3c740 (Roman Zippel    2007-01-10 14:45:28 +0100 50)        LINUX_COMPILE_HOST ")"
3eb3c740 (Roman Zippel    2007-01-10 14:45:28 +0100 51)        " (" LINUX_COMPILER ")
                                                               %s\n";
```

Using Pickaxe

87-88 Wheareas `git blame` tells you about the current state of a file, `git log -S`*string* searches back through the history of a file's diffs for the given *string*. By searching the actual diffs between revisions, this command can find commits that perform a *change* in both additions and deletions.

```
$ git log -Sinclude --pretty=oneline --abbrev-commit init/version.c
cd354f1... [PATCH] remove many unneeded #includes of sched.h
4865ecf... [PATCH] namespaces: utsname: implement utsname namespaces
63104ee... kbuild: introduce utsrelease.h
1da177e... Linux-2.6.12-rc2
```

Each of the commits listed on the left (`cd354f1`, etc.) will either add or delete lines that contain the word `include`. Be careful, though. If a commit both adds and subtracts exactly the same number of instances of lines with your key phrase, that won't be shown. The commit must have a *change* in the number of additions and deletions in order to count.

The `-S` option to `git log` is called *pickaxe*. That's brute force archeology for you.

## CHAPTER 7

Branches

A *branch* is the fundamental means of launching a separate line of development within a software project. A branch is a split from a kind of unified, primal state, allowing development to continue in multiple directions simultaneously and, potentially, to produce different versions of the project. Often, a branch is reconciled and merged with other branches to reunite disparate efforts.

Git allows many branches and thus many different lines of development within a repository. Git's branching system is lightweight and simple. Moreover, Git has first-rate support for merges. As a result, most Git users make routine use of branches.

This chapter shows you how to select, create, view, and remove branches. It also provides some best practices, so your branches don't twist into something akin to a manzanita.[1]

Reasons for Using Branches

A branch can be created for a countless number of technical, philosophical, managerial, and even social reasons. Here is just a smattering of common rationales.

- A branch often represents an individual customer release. If you want to start version 1.1 of your project but you know that some of your customers want to stick with version 1.0, then keep the old version alive as a separate branch.

- A branch can encapsulate a development phase, such as the prototype, beta, stable, or bleeding-edge release. You can think of the version 1.1 release as a separate phase, too; the maintenance release.

- A branch can isolate the development of a single feature or research into a particularly complex bug. For example, you can introduce a branch for a well-defined and conceptually isolated task or to facilitate a merge of several branches prior to a release.

---

1. OK, OK. It's a small, bushy tree, a highly branched shrub thing. Perhaps a better analogy is a banyan tree.

It may seem like overkill to create a new branch just to fix one bug, but Git's branching system encourages such small-scale use.

- An individual branch can represent the work of an individual contributor. Another branch—the "integration" branch—can be used specifically to unify efforts.

Git refers to a branch like those just listed as a *topic branch* or a *development branch*. The word "topic" simply indicates that each branch in the repository has a particular purpose.

Git also has the notion of a *tracking branch*, or a branch to keep clones of a repository in sync. Chapter 12 explains how to use a tracking branch.

Branch or Tag?

90 A branch and a tag seem similar, perhaps even interchangeable. So when should you use a tag name and when should you use a branch name?

A tag and a branch serve different purposes. A tag is meant to be a static name that does not change or move over time. Once applied, you should leave it alone. It serves as a stake in the ground and reference point. On the other hand, a branch is dynamic and moves with each commit you make. The branch name is designed to follow your continuing development.

Curiously, you can name a branch and a tag with the same name. If you do, you will have to use their full ref names to distinguish them. For example, you could use `refs/tags/v1.0` and `refs/heads/v1.0`. You may want to use the same name as a branch name during development and then convert it to a tag name at the conclusion of your development.

Naming branches and tags is ultimately up to you and your project policies. However, you should consider the key differentiating characteristic: is this name static and immutable, or is it dynamic for development? The former should be a tag and the latter a branch.

Finally, unless you have a compelling reason to do so, you should simply avoid using the same name for both a branch and a tag.

Branch Names

The name you assign to a branch is essentially arbitrary, though there are some limitations. The default branch in a repository is named `master` and most developers keep the repository's most robust and dependable line of development on that branch. There is nothing magic about the name `master`, except that Git introduces it during the initialization of a repository. If you prefer, you can rename or even delete the `master` branch, although it's probably best practice to leave it alone.

To support scalability and categorical organization, you can create a hierarchical branch name that resembles a Unix pathname. For example, suppose you are part of a development team that fixes a multitude of bugs. It may be useful to place the development of each repair in a hierarchical structure, under the branch name bug, on separate branches named something like bug/pr-1023 and bug/pr-17. If you find you have many branches or are just terminally overorganized, you can use this slash syntax to introduce some structure to your branch names.

 One reason to use hierarchical branch names is that Git, just like the Unix shell, supports wildcards. For instance, given the naming scheme bug/pr-1023 and bug/pr-17, you can select all bug branches at once with a clever and familiar shorthand.

```
git show-branch 'bug/*'
```

Dos and Don'ts in Branch Names

Branch names must conform to a few simple rules.

- You can use the forward slash (/) to create a hierarchical name scheme. However, the name cannot end with a slash.

- The name cannot start with a minus sign (-).

- No slash-separated component can begin with a dot (.). A branch name such as feature/.new is invalid.

- The name cannot contain two consecutive dots (..) anywhere.

- Further, the name cannot contain:
    — Any space or other whitespace character
    — A character that has special meaning to Git, including the tilde (~), caret (^), colon (:), question mark (?), asterisk (*), and open bracket ([)
    — An ASCII control character, which is any byte with a value lower than \040 octal, or the DEL character (\177 octal)

These branch name rules are enforced by the `git check-ref-format` plumbing command, and they are designed to ensure that each branch name is both easily typed and usable as a filename within the *.git* directory and scripts.

Using Branches

There may be many different branches within a repository at any given time, but there is at most one active or current branch. The active branch determines which files are checked out in the working directory. Furthermore, the current branch is often an implicit operand in Git commands, such as the target of the merge operation. By default, master is the active branch, but you can make any branch the current branch.

In Chapter 6, we presented commit graph diagrams containing several branches. Keep this graph structure in mind when you manipulate branches because it reinforces your understanding of the elegant and simple object model underlying Git's branches.

A branch allows the content of the repository to diverge in many directions, one per branch. Once a repository forks at least one branch, each commit is applied to one branch or the other, whichever is active.

Each branch in a specific repository must have a unique name, and the name always refers to the most recent revision committed on that branch. The most recent commit on a branch is called the *tip* or *head* of the branch.

Git doesn't keep information about where a branch originated. Instead, the branch name moves incrementally forward as new commits are made on the branch. Older commits must therefore be named by their hash or via a relative name such as dev~5. If you want to keep track of a particular commit—because it represents a stable point in the project, say, or is a version you want to test—you can explicitly assign it a lightweight tag name.

Because the original commit from which a branch was started is not explicitly identified, that commit (or its equivalent) can be found algorithmically using the name of the original branch from which the new branch forked:

```
$ git merge-base original-branch new-branch
```

A merge is the complement of a branch. When you merge, the content of one or more branches is joined with an implicit target branch. However, a merge does not eliminate any of the source branches or those branches' names. The rather complex process of merging branches is the focus of Chapter 9.

You can think of a branch name as a pointer to a particular (albeit evolving) commit. A branch includes the commits sufficient to rebuild the entire history of the project along the branch from which it came, all the way back to the very beginning of the project.

In Figure 7-1, the dev branch name points to the head commit, Z. If you wanted to rebuild the repository state at Z, then all the commits reachable from Z back to the original commit, A, are needed. The reachable portion of the graph is highlighted with wide lines and covers every commit except (S, G, H, J, K, L).

Each of your branch names, as well as the committed content on each branch, is local to your repository. However, when making your repository available to others, you can *publish* or elect to make one or any number of branches and the associated commits available, too. Publishing a branch must be done explicitly. Also, if your repository is cloned, your branch names and the development on those branches will all be part of the newly cloned repository copy.

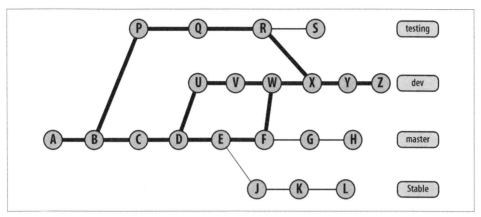

Figure 7-1. Commits reachable from dev

Creating Branches

A new branch is based upon an existing commit within the repository. It is entirely up to you to determine and specify which commit to use as the start of the new branch. Git supports an arbitrarily complex branching structure, including branching branches and forking multiple branches from the same commit.

The lifetime of a branch is, again, your decision. A branch may be short lived or long lived. A given branch name may be added and deleted multiple times over the lifetime of the repository.

Once you have identified the commit from which a branch should start, simply use the `git branch` command. Thus, to create a new branch off the HEAD of your current branch for the purposes of fixing Problem Report #1138, you might use:

```
$ git branch prs/pr-1138
```

The basic form of the command is

```
git branch branch [starting-commit]
```

When no *starting-commit* is specified, the default is the revision committed most recently on the current branch. In other words, the default is to start a new branch at the point where you're working right now.

Note that the `git branch` command merely introduces the name of a branch into the repository. It does not change your working directory to *use* the new branch. No working directory files change, no implicit branch context changes, and no new commits are made. The command simply creates a named branch at the given commit. You can't actually start work on the branch until you switch to it, as we show shortly in "Checking out Branches" on page 97.

Sometimes you want to specify a different commit as the start of a branch. For instance, suppose that your project creates a new branch for each reported bug and you hear about a bug in a certain release. It may be convenient to use the *starting-commit* parameter as an alternative to switching your working directory to the branch that represents the release.

Normally, your project establishes conventions that let you specify a starting commit with certainty. For instance, to make a bug fix on the Version 2.3 release of your software, you might specify a branch named `rel-2.3` as the starting commit:

```
$ git branch prs/pr-1138 rel-2.3
```

 The only commit name guaranteed to be unique is the hash ID. If you know a hash ID, you can use it directly:

```
$ git branch prs/pr-1138 db7de5feebef8bcd18c5356cb47c337236b50c13
```

Listing Branch Names

The `git branch` command lists branch names found in the repository.

```
$ git branch
  bug/pr-1
  dev
* master
```

In this example, three topic branches are shown. The branch currently checked out into your working tree is identified by the asterisk. This example also shows two other branches, `bug/pr-1` and `dev`.

Without additional parameters, only topic branches in the repository are listed. As you'll see in Chapter 12, there may be additional remote tracking branches in your repository. You can list those with the `-r` option. You can list both topic and remote branches with `-a`.

Viewing Branches

The `git show-branch` command provides more detailed output than `git branch`, listing the commits that contribute to one or more branches in roughly reverse chronological order. As with `git branch`, no options list the topic branches, `-r` shows remote tracking branches, and `-a` shows all branches.

Let's look at an example.

```
$ git show-branch
! [bug/pr-1] Fix Problem Report 1
 * [dev] Improve the new development
  ! [master] Added Bob's fixes.
---
 *  [dev] Improve the new development
 *  [dev^] Start some new development.
```

```
+   [bug/pr-1] Fix Problem Report 1
+*+ [master] Added Bob's fixes.
```

The `git show-branch` output is broken down into two sections separated by a line of dashes. The section above the separator lists the names of branches enclosed in square brackets, one per line. Each branch name is associated with a single column of output, identified by either an exclamation mark or—if it is also the current branch—an asterisk. In the example just shown, commits within the branch `bug/pr-1` start in the first column, commits within the current branch `dev` start in the second column, and commits in the third branch `master` start in the third column. For quick reference, each branch in the upper section is also listed with the first line of the log message from the most recent commit on that branch.

The lower section of output is a matrix stating which commits are present in each branch. Again, each commit is listed with the first log message line from that commit. A commit is present in a branch if there a plus (+), an asterisk (*), or a minus (-) in that branch's column. The plus sign indicates the commit is in a branch; the asterisk just highlights the commit as being present on the active branch. The minus sign denotes a merge commit.

For example, both of the following commits are identified by asterisks and are present in the `dev` branch:

```
* [dev] Improve the new development
* [dev^] Start some new development.
```

These two commits are not present in any other branch. They are listed in reverse chronological order: The most recent commit is at the top and the oldest commit at the bottom.

Enclosed within square brackets on each commit line, Git also shows you a name for that commit. As already mentioned, Git assigns the branch name to the most recent commit. Previous commits have the same name with trailing caret (^) characters. In Chapter 6, you saw `master` as the name for the most recent commit and `master^` as the name for the penultimate commit. Similarly, `dev` and `dev^` are the two most recent commits on the branch `dev`.

Although the commits within a branch are ordered, branches themselves are listed in an arbitrary order. This is because all branches have equal status; there is no rule stating that one branch is more important than another.

If the same commit is present in multiple branches, then it will have a plus sign or an asterisk indicator for each branch. Thus, the last commit shown in the previous output is present in all three branches:

```
+*+ [master] Added Bob's fixes.
```

The first plus sign means that the commit is in `bug/pr-1`, the asterisk means the same commit is in the active branch `dev`, and the final plus sign means the commit is also in the `master` branch.

When invoked, `git show-branch` traverses through all the commits on all branches being shown, stopping the listing on the most recent common commit present on all of them. In this case, Git listed four commits before it found one common to all three branches (`Added Bob's fixes.`), at which point it stopped.

Stopping at the first common commit is the default heuristic for reasonable behavior. It is presumed that reaching such a common point yields sufficient context to understand how the branches relate to each other. If for some reason you actually want more commit history, use the `--more=num` option, specifying the number of additional commits you want to see going back in time along the common branch.

The `git show-branch` command accepts a set of branch names as parameters, allowing you to limit the history shown to those branches. For example, if new branch named `bug/pr-2` is added starting at the `master` commit, it would look like this:

```
$ git branch bug/pr-2 master
$ git show-branch
! [bug/pr-1] Fix Problem Report 1
 ! [bug/pr-2] Added Bob's fixes.
  * [dev] Improve the new development
   ! [master] Added Bob's fixes.
----
  * [dev] Improve the new development
  * [dev^] Start some new development.
 +  [bug/pr-1] Fix Problem Report 1
++*+ [bug/pr-2] Added Bob's fixes.
```

If you wanted to see the commit history for just the `bug/pr-1` and `bug/pr-2` branches, you could use

```
$ git show-branch bug/pr-1 bug/pr-2
```

Although that might be fine for a few branches, if there were many such branches, then naming them all would be quite tedious. Fortunately, Git allows wildcard matching of branch names as well. The same results can be achieved using the simpler `bug/*` branch wildcard name:

```
$ git show-branch bug/pr-1 bug/pr-2
! [bug/pr-1] Fix Problem Report 1
 ! [bug/pr-2] Added Bob's fixes.
--
 + [bug/pr-1] Fix Problem Report 1
++ [bug/pr-2] Added Bob's fixes.

$ git show-branch bug/*
! [bug/pr-1] Fix Problem Report 1
 ! [bug/pr-2] Added Bob's fixes.
--
 + [bug/pr-1] Fix Problem Report 1
++ [bug/pr-2] Added Bob's fixes.
```

Checking out Branches

As mentioned earlier in this chapter, your working directory can reflect only one branch at a time. To start working on a different branch, issue the `git checkout` command. Given a branch name, `git checkout` makes the branch the new, current working branch. It changes your working tree file and directory structure to match the state of the given branch. However, as you'll see, Git builds in safeguards to keep you from losing data you haven't yet committed.

In addition, `git checkout` gives you access to all states of the repository going back from the tip of the branch to the beginning of the project. This is because, as you may recall from Chapter 6, each commit captures a snapshot of the complete repository state at a given moment in time.

A Basic Example of Checking out a Branch

Suppose you wanted to shift gears from the `dev` branch in the previous section's example and instead devote your attention to fixing the problem associated with the `bug/pr-1` branch. Let's look at the state of the working directory before and after `git checkout`:

```
$ git branch
  bug/pr-1
  bug/pr-2
* dev
  master

$ git checkout bug/pr-1
Switched to branch "bug/pr-1"

$ git branch
* bug/pr-1
  bug/pr-2
  dev
  master
```

The files and directory structure of your working tree have been updated to reflect the state and contents of the new branch, `bug/pr-1`. However, in order to see that the files your working directory have changed to match the state at the tip of that branch, you must use a regular Unix command such as `ls`.

Selecting a new current branch might have dramatic effects on your working tree files and directory structure. Naturally, the extent of that change depends on the differences between your current branch and the new, target branch that you would like to check out. The effects of changing branches are:

- Files and directories present in the branch being checked out but not in the current branch are checked out of the object store and placed into your working tree.
- Files and directories present in your current branch but absent in the branch being checked out will be removed from your working tree.

- Files common to both branches are modified to reflect the content present in the checked out branch.

Don't be alarmed if it looks like the checkout appears to happen almost instantaneously. A common newbie mistake is to think that the checkout didn't work because it returned instantly after supposedly making huge changes. This is one of the features of Git that truly and strongly differentiates it from many other VCSs. Git is good at determining the minimum set of files and directories that actually need to change during a checkout.

Checking out When You Have Uncommitted Changes

Git precludes the accidental removal or modification of data in your local working tree without your explicit request. Files and directories in your working directory that are not being tracked are always left alone; Git won't remove or modify them. However, if you have local modifications to a file that are different from changes that are present on the new branch, Git issues an error message such as the following and refuses to check out the target branch:

```
$ git branch
  bug/pr-1
  bug/pr-2
  dev
* master

$ git checkout dev
error: Your local changes to the following files would be overwritten by checkout:
    NewStuff
Please, commit your changes or stash them before you can switch branches.
Aborting
```

In this case, a message warns that something has caused Git to stop the checkout request. But what? You can find out by inspecting the contents of the file *NewStuff*, as it is locally modified in the current working directory, and the target **dev** branch:

```
# Show what NewStuff looks like in the working directory
$ cat NewStuff
Something
Something else

# Show that the local version of the file has an extra line that
# is not committed in the working directory's current branch (master)
$ git diff NewStuff
diff --git a/NewStuff b/NewStuff
index 0f2416e..5e79566 100644
--- a/NewStuff
+++ b/NewStuff
@@ -1 +1,2 @@
 Something
+Something else

# Show what the file looks like in the dev branch
```

```
$ git show dev:NewStuff
Something
A Change
```

If Git brashly honored the request to check out the dev branch, your local modifications to *NewStuff* in your working directory would be overwritten by the version from dev. By default, Git detects this potential loss and prevents it from happening.

 If you really don't care about losing changes in your working directory and are willing to throw them away, you can force Git to perform the checkout by using the -f option.

Seeing the error message might suggest that you update the file within the index and then proceed with the checkout. However, this isn't quite sufficient. Using, say, git add to update the new contents of *NewStuff* into the index only places the contents of that file in the index; it won't commit it to any branch. Git still can't check out the new branch without losing your change, so it fails again.

```
$ git add NewStuff
$ git checkout dev
error: Your local changes to the following files would be overwritten by checkout:
    NewStuff
Please, commit your changes or stash them before you can switch branches.
Aborting
```

Indeed, it would still be overwritten. Clearly, just adding it to the index isn't sufficient.

You could just issue git commit at this point to commit your change into your current branch (master). But suppose you want the change to be made in the new dev branch instead. You seem to be stuck: You can't put your change into the dev branch until you check it out, and Git won't let you check it out because your change is present.

Luckily, there are ways out of this catch-22. One approach uses the *stash* and is described in Chapter 11. Another approach is described in the next section, "Merging Changes into a Different Branch" on page 99.

Merging Changes into a Different Branch

In the previous section, the current state of your working directory conflicted with that of the branch you wanted to switch to. What's needed is a merge: The changes in your working directory must be merged with the files being checked out.

If possible or if specifically requested with the -m option, Git attempts to carry your local change into the new working directory by performing a merge operation between your local modifications and the target branch.

```
$ git checkout -m dev
M       NewStuff
Switched to branch "dev"
```

Here, Git has modified the file *NewStuff* and checked out the `dev` branch successfully.

This merge operation occurs entirely in your working directory. It does not introduce a merge commit on any branch. It is somewhat analogous to the `cvs update` command in that your local changes are merged with the target branch and are left in your working directory.

You must be careful in these scenarios, however. Although it may look like the merge was performed cleanly and all is well, Git has simply modified the file and left the merge conflict indicators within it. You must still resolve any conflicts that are present:

```
$ cat NewStuff
Something
<<<<<<< dev:NewStuff
A Change
=======
Something else
>>>>>>> local:NewStuff
```

See Chapter 9 to learn more about merges and helpful techniques to resolve merge conflicts.

If Git can check out a branch, change to it, and merge your local modifications cleanly without any merge conflicts, then the checkout request succeeds.

Suppose you're on the `master` branch in your development repository and you've made some changes to the *NewStuff* file. Moreover, you realize that the changes you made really should be made on another branch, perhaps because they fix Problem Report #1 and should be committed on the `bug/pr-1` branch.

Here is the setup. Start on the `master` branch. Make some changes to some files, which are represented here by adding the text `Some bug fix` to the file *NewStuff*.

```
$ git show-branch
! [bug/pr-1] Fix Problem Report 1
 ! [bug/pr-2] Added Bob's fixes.
  ! [dev] Started developing NewStuff
   * [master] Added Bob's fixes.
----
   + [dev] Started developing NewStuff
   + [dev^] Improve the new development
   + [dev~2] Start some new development.
   +    [bug/pr-1] Fix Problem Report 1
+++* [bug/pr-2] Added Bob's fixes.

$ echo "Some bug fix" >> NewStuff

$ cat NewStuff
Something
Some bug fix
```

At this point, you realize that all this work should be committed on the bug/pr-1 branch and not the master branch. For reference, here is what the *NewStuff* file looks like in the bug/pr-1 branch prior to the checkout in the next step:

```
$ git show bug/pr-1:NewStuff
Something
```

To carry your changes into the desired branch, simply attempt to check it out:

```
$ git checkout bug/pr-1
M       NewStuff
Switched to branch "bug/pr-1"

$ cat NewStuff
Something
Some bug fix
```

Here, Git was able to correctly merge the changes from your working directories and the target branch and leave them in your new working directory structure. You might want to verify that the merge went according to your expectations by using git diff:

```
$ git diff
diff --git a/NewStuff b/NewStuff
index 0f2416e..b4d8596 100644
--- a/NewStuff
+++ b/NewStuff
@@ -1 +1,2 @@
 Something
+Some bug fix
```

That one line addition is correct.

Creating and Checking out a New Branch

Another fairly common scenario happens when you want to both create a new branch and simultaneously switch to it as well. Git provides a shortcut for this with the -b *new-branch* option.

Let's start with the same setup as the previous example, except now you must start a new branch instead of checking changes into an existing branch. In other words, you are in the master branch, editing files, and suddenly realize that you would like all of the changes to be committed on an entirely new branch named bug/pr-3. The sequence is as follows:

```
$ git branch
  bug/pr-1
  bug/pr-2
  dev
* master

$ git checkout -b bug/pr-3
M       NewStuff
Switched to a new branch "bug/pr-3"
```

```
$ git show-branch
! [bug/pr-1] Fix Problem Report 1
 ! [bug/pr-2] Added Bob's fixes.
  * [bug/pr-3] Added Bob's fixes.
   ! [dev] Started developing NewStuff
! [master] Added Bob's fixes.
-----
    + [dev] Started developing NewStuff
    + [dev^] Improve the new development
    + [dev~2] Start some new development.
+     [bug/pr-1] Fix Problem Report 1
++*++ [bug/pr-2] Added Bob's fixes.
```

Unless some problem prevents a checkout command from completing, the command:

```
$ git checkout -b new-branch start-point
```

is exactly the same as the two-command sequence:

```
$ git branch new-branch start-point
$ git checkout new-branch
```

Detached HEAD Branches

Normally, it's advisable to check out only the tip of a branch by naming the branch directly. Thus, by default, git checkout changes to the tip of a desired branch.

However, you can check out any commit. In such an instance, Git creates a sort of anonymous branch for you called a *detached HEAD*. Git creates a detached HEAD when you:

- Check out a commit that is not the head of a branch.
- Check out a tracking branch. You might do this to explore changes recently brought into your repository from a remote repository.
- Check out the commit referenced by a tag. You might do this to put together a release based on tagged versions of files.
- Start a git bisect operation, described in "Using git bisect" on page 83 of Chapter 6.
- Use the git submodule update command.

In these cases, Git tells you that you have moved to a detached HEAD:

```
# I have a copy of the Git sources handy!
$ cd git.git

$ git checkout v1.6.0
Note: moving to "v1.6.0" which isn't a local branch
If you want to create a new branch from this checkout, you may do so
(now or later) by using -b with the checkout command again. Example:
  git checkout -b <new_branch_name>
HEAD is now at ea02eef... GIT 1.6.0
```

If, after finding yourself on a detached HEAD, you later decide that you need to make new commits at that point and keep them, you must first create a new branch:

```
$ git checkout -b new_branch
```

This will give you a new, proper branch based on the commit where the detached HEAD was. You can then continue with normal development. Essentially, you named the branch that was previously anonymous.

To find out if you are on a detached HEAD, just ask:

```
$ git branch
* (no branch)
  master
```

On the other hand, if you are finished with the detached HEAD and want to simply abandon that state, you can convert to a named branch by simply entering git checkout *branch*.

```
$ git checkout master
Previous HEAD position was ea02eef... GIT 1.6.0
Checking out files: 100% (608/608), done.
Switched to branch "master"

$ git branch
* master
```

Deleting Branches

The command git branch -d *branch* removes the named branch from a repository. Git prevents you from removing the current branch:

```
$ git branch -d bug/pr-3
error: Cannot delete the branch 'bug/pr-3' which you are currently on.
```

Removing the current branch would leave Git unable to determine what the resulting working directory tree should look like. Instead, you must always name a noncurrent branch.

But there is another subtle issue. Git won't allow you to delete a branch that contains commits that are not also present on the current branch. That is, Git prevents you from accidentally removing development in commits that will be lost if the branch were to be deleted.

```
$ git checkout master
Switched to branch "master"

$ git branch -d bug/pr-3
error: The branch 'bug/pr-3' is not an ancestor of your current HEAD.
If you are sure you want to delete it, run 'git branch -D bug/pr-3'.
```

In this `git show-branch` output, the commit "Added a bug fix for pr-3" is found only on the `bug/pr-3` branch. If that branch were to be deleted, there would no longer be a way to access that commit.

By stating that the `bug/pr-3` branch is not an ancestor of your current `HEAD`, Git is telling you that the line of development represented by the `bug/pr-3` branch does not contribute to the development of the current branch, `master`.

Git is not mandating that all branches be merged into the `master` branch before they can be deleted. Remember, a branch is simply a name or pointer to a commit that has actual content. Instead, Git is keeping you from accidentally losing content from the branch to be deleted that is not merged into your *current* branch.

If the content from the deleted branch is already present on another branch, checking *that* branch out and then requesting the branch deletion from that context would work. Another approach is to merge the content from the branch you want to delete into your current branch (see Chapter 9). Then the other branch can be safely deleted.

```
$ git merge bug/pr-3
Updating 7933438..401b78d
Fast forward
 NewStuff |    1 +
 1 files changed, 1 insertions(+), 0 deletions(-)

$ git show-branch
! [bug/pr-1] Fix Problem Report 1
 ! [bug/pr-2] Added Bob's fixes.
  ! [bug/pr-3] Added a bug fix for pr-3.
   ! [dev] Started developing NewStuff
* [master] Added a bug fix for pr-3.
-----
  + * [bug/pr-3] Added a bug fix for pr-3.
  +   [dev] Started developing NewStuff
  +   [dev^] Improve the new development
  +   [dev~2] Start some new development.
  +     [bug/pr-1] Fix Problem Report 1
++++* [bug/pr-2] Added Bob's fixes.

$ git branch -d bug/pr-3
Deleted branch bug/pr-3.

$ git show-branch
! [bug/pr-1] Fix Problem Report 1
 ! [bug/pr-2] Added Bob's fixes.
  ! [dev] Started developing NewStuff
   * [master] Added a bug fix for pr-3.
----
   * [master] Added a bug fix for pr-3.
  + [dev] Started developing NewStuff
  + [dev^] Improve the new development
  + [dev~2] Start some new development.
  +   [bug/pr-1] Fix Problem Report 1
+++* [bug/pr-2] Added Bob's fixes.
```

Finally, as the error message suggests, you can override Git's safety check by using -D instead of -d. Do this if you are certain you don't want the extra content in that branch.

Git does not maintain any form of historical record of branch *names* being created, moved, manipulated, merged, or deleted. Once a branch name has been removed, it is gone.

The commit history on that branch, however, is a separate question. Git will eventually prune away commits that are no longer referenced and reachable from some named ref such as a branch or tag name. If you want to keep those commits, you must either merge them into a different branch, make a branch for them, or point a tag reference to them. Otherwise, without a reference to them, commits and blobs are unreachable and will eventually be collected as garbage by the `git gc` tool.

 After accidentally removing a branch or other ref, you can recover it by using the `git reflog` command. Other commands such as `git fsck` and configuration options such as `gc.reflogExpire` and `gc.pruneExpire` can also help recover lost commits, files, and branch heads.

## CHAPTER 8

Diffs

A *diff* is a compact summary of the differences (hence the name "diff") between two items. For example, given two files, the Unix and Linux `diff` command compares the files line by line and summarizes the deviations in a diff, as shown in Example 8-1. In the example, *initial* is one version of some prose and *rewrite* is a subsequent revision. The -u option produces a *unified diff*, a standardized format used widely to share modifications.

Example 8-1. Simple Unix diff

```
$ cat initial               $ cat rewrite
Now is the time             Today is the time
For all good men            For all good men
To come to the aid          And women
Of their country.           To come to the aid
                            Of their country.


$ diff -u initial rewrite
--- initial     1867-01-02 11:22:33.000000000 -0500
+++ rewrite     2000-01-02 11:23:45.000000000 -0500
@@ -1,4 +1,5 @@
-Now is the time
+Today is the time
 For all good men
+And women
 To come to the aid
 Of their country.
```

Let's look at the diff in detail. In the header, the original file is denoted by - - - and the new file by +++. The @@ line provides line number context for both file versions. A line prefixed with a minus sign (-) must be removed from the original file to produce the new file. Conversely, a line with a leading plus sign (+) must be added to the original file to produce the new file. A line that begins with a space is the same in both files and is provided by the -u option as context.

By itself, a diff offers no reason or rationale for a change, nor does it justify the initial or final state. However, a diff offers more than just a digest of how files differ. It provides a formal description of how to transform one file to the other. (You'll find such instructions useful when applying or reverting changes.) In addition, `diff` can be extended to show differences among multiple files and entire directory hierarchies.

The Unix `diff` command can compute the differences of all pairs of files found in two directory hierarchies. The command `diff -r` traverses each hierarchy in tandem, twins files by pathname (say, *original/src/main.c* and *new/src/main.c*), and summarizes the differences between each pair. Using `diff -r -u` produces a set of unified diffs comparing two hierarchies.

Git has its own diff facility and can likewise produce a digest of differences. The command `git diff` can compare files much akin to Unix's `diff` command. Moreover, like `diff -r`, Git can traverse two *tree* objects and generate a representation of the variances. But `git diff` also has its own nuances and powerful features tailored to the particular needs of Git users.

 Technically, a tree object represents only one directory level in the repository. It contains information on the directory's immediate files and immediate subdirectories, but it does not catalog the complete contents of all subdirectories. However, because a tree object references the tree objects for each subdirectory, the tree object at the root of the project effectively represents the entire project at a moment in time. Hence, we can paraphrase and say `git diff` traverses "two" trees.

In this chapter, we'll cover some of the basics of `git diff` and some of its special capabilities. You will learn how to use Git to show editorial changes in your working directory as well as arbitrary changes between any two commits within your project history. You will see how Git's diff can help you make well-structured commits during your normal development process and you will also learn how to produce Git patches, which are described in detail in Chapter 14.

Forms of the git diff Command

If you pick two different root-level tree objects for comparison, `git diff` yields all deviations between the two project states. That's powerful. You could use such a diff to convert wholesale from one project state to another. For example, if you and a co-worker are developing code for the same project, a root-level diff could effectively sync the repositories at any time.

There are three basic sources for tree or treelike objects to use with `git diff`:

- Any tree object anywhere within the entire commit graph
- Your working directory
- The index

Typically, the trees compared in a `git diff` command are named via commits, branch names, or tags, but any commit name discussed in "Identifying Commits" on page 67 of Chapter 6 suffices. Also, both the file and directory hierarchy of your working directory, as well as the complete hierarchy of files staged in the index, can be treated as trees.

The `git diff` command can perform four fundamental comparisons using various combinations of those three sources.

`git diff`

> `git diff` shows the difference between your working directory and the index. It exposes what is *dirty* in your working directory and is thus a candidate to *stage* for your next commit. This command does not reveal differences between what's in your index and what's permanently stored in the repository (not to mention remote repositories you might be working with).

`git diff` *commit*

> This form summarizes the differences between your working directory and the given *commit*. Common variants of this command name HEAD or a particular branch name as the *commit*.

`git diff --cached` *commit*

> This command shows the differences between the staged changes in the index and the given *commit*. A common commit for the comparison—and the default if no commit is specified—is HEAD. With HEAD, this command shows you how your next commit will alter the current branch.
>
> If the option `--cached` doesn't make sense to you, perhaps the synonym `--staged` will. It is available in Git version 1.6.1 and later.

`git diff` *commit1 commit2*

> If you specify two arbitrary commits, the command displays the differences between the two. This command ignores the index and working directory, and it is the workhorse for arbitrary comparisons between two trees that are already in your object store.

The number of parameters on the command line determines what fundamental form is used and what is compared. You can compare any two commits or trees. What's being compared need not have a direct or even an indirect parent–child relationship. If you don't supply a tree object or two, then `git diff` compares implied sources, such as your index or working directory.

Let's examine how these different forms apply to Git's object model. The example in Figure 8-1 shows a project directory with two files. The file *file1* has been modified in the working directory, changing its content from "foo" to "quux." That change has been staged in the index using `git add file1`, but it is not yet committed.

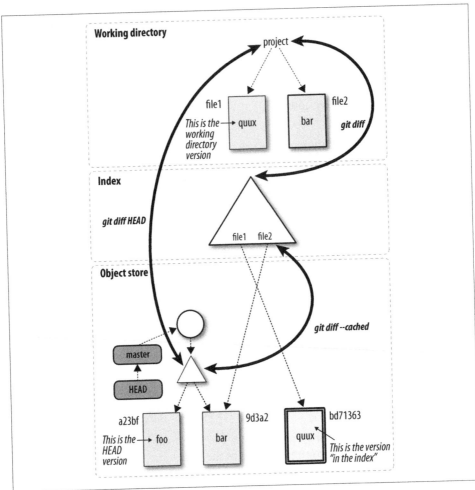

Figure 8-1. Various file versions that can be compared

A version of the file *file1* from each of your working directory, the index, and the HEAD have been identified. Even though the version of *file1* that is in the index, bd71363, is actually stored as a blob object in the object store, it is indirectly referenced through the virtual tree object that is the index. Similarly, the HEAD version of the file, a23bf, is also indirectly referenced through several steps.

This example nominally demonstrates the changes within *file1*. The bold arrows in the figure point to the tree or virtual tree objects to remind you that the comparison is actually based on complete trees and not just on individual files.

From Figure 8-1, you can see how using git diff without arguments is a good technique for verifying the readiness of your next commit. As long as that command emits output, you have edits or changes in your working directory that are not yet staged. Check the edits on each file. If you are satisfied with your work, use `git add` to stage the file. Once you stage a changed file, the next `git diff` no longer yields diff output for that file. In this way, you can step progressively through each dirty file in your working directory until the differences disappear, meaning that all files are staged in your index. Don't forget to check for new or deleted files, too. At any time during the staging process, the command `git diff --cached` shows the complementary changes, or those changes already staged in the index that will be present in your next commit. When you're finished, `git commit` captures all changes in your index into a new commit.

You are not required to stage all the changes from your working directory for a single commit. In fact, if you find you have conceptually different changes in your working directory that should be made in different commits, you can stage one set at a time, leaving the other edits in your working directory. A commit captures only your staged changes. Repeat the process, staging the next set of files appropriate for a subsequent commit.

The astute reader might have noticed that, although there are four fundamental forms of the `git diff` command, only three are highlighted with bold arrows in Figure 8-1. So, what is the fourth? There is only one tree object represented by your working directory, and there is only one tree object represented by the index. In the example, there is one commit in the object store along with its tree. However, the object store is likely to have many commits named by different branches and tags, all of which have trees that can be compared with `git diff`. Thus, the fourth form of `git diff` simply compares any two arbitrary commits (trees) already stored within the object store.

In addition to the four basic forms of `git diff`, there are myriad options as well. Here are a few of the more useful ones.

`--M`

The `--M` option detects renames and generates a simplified output that simply records the file rename rather than the complete removal and subsequent addition of the source file. If the rename is not a pure rename but also has some additional content changes, Git calls those out.

`-w` *or* `--ignore-all-space`

Both `-w` and `--ignore-all-space` compare lines without considering changes in whitespace as significant.

`--stat`

The `--stat` option adds statistics about the difference between any two tree states. It reports in a compact syntax how many lines changed, how many were added, and how many were elided.

`--color`

The `--color` option colorizes the output; a unique color represents each of the different types of changes present in the diff.

Finally, the `git diff` may be limited to show diffs for a specific set of files or directories.

The -a option for git diff does nothing even remotely like the -a option for git commit. To get both staged and unstaged changes, use git diff HEAD. The lack of symmetry is unfortunate and counterintuitive.

Simple git diff Example

Here we construct the scenario presented in Figure 8-1, run through the scenario, and watch the various forms of git diff in action. First, let's set up a simple repository with two files in it.

```
$ mkdir /tmp/diff_example
$ cd /tmp/diff_example

$ git init
Initialized empty Git repository in /tmp/diff_example/.git/

$ echo "foo" > file1
$ echo "bar" > file2

$ git add file1 file2

$ git commit -m "Add file1 and file2"
[master (root-commit)]: created fec5ba5: "Add file1 and file2"
 2 files changed, 2 insertions(+), 0 deletions(-)
 create mode 100644 file1
 create mode 100644 file2
```

Next, let's edit *file1* by replacing the word "foo" with "quux."

```
$ echo "quux" > file1
```

The *file1* has been modified in the working directory but has not been staged. This state is not yet the situation depicted in Figure 8-1, but you can still make a comparison. You should expect output if you compare the working directory with the index or the existing HEAD versions. However, there should be no difference between the index and the HEAD because nothing has been staged. (In other words, what is staged *is* the current HEAD tree still.)

```
# working directory versus index
$ git diff
diff --git a/file1 b/file1
index 257cc56..d90bda0 100644
--- a/file1
+++ b/file1
@@ -1 +1 @@
-foo
+quux

# working directory versus HEAD
$ git diff HEAD
diff --git a/file1 b/file1
index 257cc56..d90bda0 100644
```

```
--- a/file1
+++ b/file1
@@ -1 +1 @@
-foo
+quux

# index vs HEAD, identical still
$ git diff --cached
$
```

Applying the maxim just given, git diff produced output and so *file1* could be staged.
Let's do this now.

```
$ git add file1

$ git status
# On branch master
# Changes to be committed:
#   (use "git reset HEAD <filed>..." to unstage)
#
#       modified:   file1
```

Here you have exactly duplicated the situation described by Figure 8-1. Because *file1* is now staged, the working directory and the index are synchronized and should not show any differences. However, there are now differences between the HEAD version and both the working directory and the staged version in the index.

```
# working directory versus index
$ git diff

# working directory versus HEAD
$ git diff HEAD
diff --git a/file1 b/file1
index 257cc56..d90bda0 100644
--- a/file1
+++ b/file1
@@ -1 +1 @@
-foo
+quux

# index vs HEAD
$ git diff --cached
diff --git a/file1 b/file1
index 257cc56..d90bda0 100644
--- a/file1
+++ b/file1
@@ -1 +1 @@
-foo
+quux
```

If you ran git commit now, the new commit would capture the staged changes shown by the last command, git diff --cached (which, as mentioned before, has the new synonym git diff --staged).

Now, to throw a monkey wrench in the works, what would happen if you edited *file1* before making a commit? Let's see!

```
$ echo "baz" > file1

# wd versus index
$ git diff
diff --git a/file1 b/file1
index d90bda0..7601807 100644
--- a/file1
+++ b/file1
@@ -1 +1 @@
-quux
+baz

# wd versus HEAD
$ git diff HEAD
diff --git a/file1 b/file1
index 257cc56..7601807 100644
--- a/file1
+++ b/file1
@@ -1 +1 @@
-foo
+baz

# index vs HEAD
$ git diff --cached
diff --git a/file1 b/file1
index 257cc56..d90bda0 100644
--- a/file1
+++ b/file1
@@ -1 +1 @@
-foo
+quux
```

All three diff operations show some form of difference now! But which version will be committed? Remember, `git commit` captures the state present in the index. And what's in the index? It's the content revealed by `git diff --cached` or `git diff --staged` command, or the version of *file1* that contains the word "quux"!

```
$ git commit -m "quux uber alles"
[master]: created f8ae1ec: "quux uber alles"
 1 files changed, 1 insertions(+), 1 deletions(-)
```

Now that the object store has two commits in it, let's try the general form of the `git diff` command.

```
# Previous HEAD version versus current HEAD
$ git diff HEAD^ HEAD
diff --git a/file1 b/file1
index 257cc56..d90bda0 100644
--- a/file1
+++ b/file1
@@ -1 +1 @@
```

```
-foo
+quux
```

This diff confirms that the previous commit changed *file1* by replacing "foo" with "quux."

So is everything synchronized now? No. The working directory copy of *file1* contains "baz."

```
$ git diff
diff --git a/file1 b/file1
index d90bda0..7601807 100644
--- a/file1
+++ b/file1
@@ -1 +1 @@
-quux
+baz
```

git diff and Commit Ranges

There are two additional forms of `git diff` that bear some explanation, especially in contrast to `git log`.

The `git diff` command supports a double-dot syntax to represent the difference between two commits. Thus, the following two commands are equivalent:

```
$ git diff master bug/pr-1
$ git diff master..bug/pr-1
```

Unfortunately, the double-dot syntax in `git diff` means something quite different from the same syntax in `git log`, which you learned about in Chapter 6. It's worth comparing `git diff` and `git log` in this regard because doing so highlights the relationship of these two commands to changes made in repositories. Some points to keep in mind for the following example:

- `git diff` doesn't care about the history of the files it compares or anything about branches
- `git log` is extremely conscious of how one file changed to become another—for example, when two branches diverged and what happened on each branch

The `log` and `diff` commands perform two fundamentally different operations. Whereas `log` operates on a set of commits, `diff` operates on two different end points.

Imagine the following sequence of events:

1. Someone creates a new branch off the `master` branch to fix bug `pr-1`, calling the new branch `bug/pr-1`.

2. The same developer adds the line "Fix Problem report 1" to a file in the `bug/pr-1` branch.

3. Meanwhile, another developer fixes bug pr-3 in the master branch, adding the line "Fix Problem report 3" to the same file in the master branch.

In short, one line was added to a file in each branch. If you look at the changes to branches at a high level, you can see when the bug/pr-1 branch was launched and when each change was made:

```
$ git show-branch master bug/pr-1
* [master] Added a bug fix for pr-3.
 ! [bug/pr-1] Fix Problem Report 1
--
*   [master] Added a bug fix for pr-3.
 + [bug/pr-1] Fix Problem Report 1
*+ [master^] Added Bob's fixes.
```

If you type git log -p master..bug/pr-1, you will see one commit, because the syntax master..bug/pr-1 represents all those commits in bug/pr-1 that are not also in master. The command traces back to the point where bug/pr-1 diverged from master, but it does not look at anything that happened to master since that point.

```
$ git log -p master..bug/pr-1
commit 8f4cf5757a3a83b0b3dbecd26244593c5fc820ea
Author: Jon Loeliger <jdl@example.com>
Date:   Wed May 14 17:53:54 2008 -0500

Fix Problem Report 1

diff --git a/ready b/ready
index f3b6f0e..abbf9c5 100644
--- a/ready
+++ b/ready
@@ -1,3 +1,4 @@
 stupid
 znill
 frot-less
+Fix Problem report 1
```

In contrast, git diff master..bug/pr-1 shows the total set of differences between the two trees represented by the heads of the master and bug/pr-1 branches. History doesn't matter; only the current state of the files does.

```
$ git diff master..bug/pr-1
diff --git a/ready b/ready
index f3b6f0e..abbf9c5 100644
--- a/ready
+++ b/ready
@@ -1,4 +1,4 @@
 stupid
 znill
 frot-less
-Fix Problem report 3
+Fix Problem report 1
```

To paraphrase the `git diff` output, you can change the file in the `master` branch to the version in the `bug/pr-1` branch by removing the line "Fix Problem report 3" and then adding the line "Fix Problem report 1" to the file.

As you can see, this diff includes commits from both branches. This may not seem crucial with this small example, but consider the example in Figure 8-2 with more expansive lines of development on two branches.

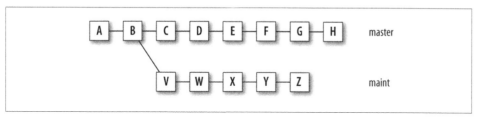

Figure 8-2. git diff larger history

In this case, `git log master..maint` represents the five individual commits V, W, ..., Z. On the other hand, `git diff master..maint` represents the differences in the trees at H and Z, an accumulated 11 commits: C, D, ..., H and V, ..., Z.

Similarly, both `git log` and `git diff` accept the form *commit1...commit2* to produce a *symmetrical difference*. As before, however, `git log` *commit1...commit2* and `git diff` *commit1...commit2* yield different results.

As discussed in "Commit Ranges" on page 78 of Chapter 6, the command `git log` *commit1...commit2* displays the commits reachable from either commit but not both. Thus, `git log master...maint` in the previous example would yield C, D, ..., H and V, ..., Z.

The symmetric difference in `git diff` shows the differences between a commit that is a common ancestor (or *merge base*) of *commit1* and *commit2*. Given the same genealogy in Figure 8-2, `git diff master...maint` combines the changes in the commits V, W, ..., Z.

git diff with Path Limiting

By default, the command `git diff` operates on the entire directory structure rooted at a given tree object. However, you can leverage the same *path limiting* technique employed by `git log` to limit the output of `git diff` to a subset of the repository.

For example, at one point[1] in the development of the Git's own repository, `git diff --stat` displayed this:

```
$ git diff --stat master~5 master
 Documentation/git-add.txt                  |    2 +-
```

---

1. d2b3691b61d516a0ad2bf700a2a5d9113ceff0b1

```
Documentation/git-cherry.txt             |   6 +++++
Documentation/git-commit-tree.txt        |   2 +-
Documentation/git-format-patch.txt       |   2 +-
Documentation/git-gc.txt                 |   2 +-
Documentation/git-gui.txt                |   4 +-
Documentation/git-ls-files.txt           |   2 +-
Documentation/git-pack-objects.txt       |   2 +-
Documentation/git-pack-redundant.txt     |   2 +-
Documentation/git-prune-packed.txt       |   2 +-
Documentation/git-prune.txt              |   2 +-
Documentation/git-read-tree.txt          |   2 +-
Documentation/git-remote.txt             |   2 +-
Documentation/git-repack.txt             |   2 +-
Documentation/git-rm.txt                 |   2 +-
Documentation/git-status.txt             |   2 +-
Documentation/git-update-index.txt       |   2 +-
Documentation/git-var.txt                |   2 +-
Documentation/gitk.txt                   |   2 +-
builtin-checkout.c                       |   7 ++++-
builtin-fetch.c                          |   6 ++--
git-bisect.sh                            |  29 ++++++++++++--------------
t/t5518-fetch-exit-status.sh             |  37 +++++++++++++++++++++++++++++++++++
23 files changed, 83 insertions(+), 40 deletions(-)
```

To limit the output to just *Documentation* changes, you could instead use
`git diff --stat master~5 master Documentation`:

```
$ git diff --stat master~5 master Documentation
Documentation/git-add.txt                |   2 +-
Documentation/git-cherry.txt             |   6 ++++++
Documentation/git-commit-tree.txt        |   2 +-
Documentation/git-format-patch.txt       |   2 +-
Documentation/git-gc.txt                 |   2 +-
Documentation/git-gui.txt                |   4 ++--
Documentation/git-ls-files.txt           |   2 +-
Documentation/git-pack-objects.txt       |   2 +-
Documentation/git-pack-redundant.txt     |   2 +-
Documentation/git-prune-packed.txt       |   2 +-
Documentation/git-prune.txt              |   2 +-
Documentation/git-read-tree.txt          |   2 +-
Documentation/git-remote.txt             |   2 +-
Documentation/git-repack.txt             |   2 +-
Documentation/git-rm.txt                 |   2 +-
Documentation/git-status.txt             |   2 +-
Documentation/git-update-index.txt       |   2 +-
Documentation/git-var.txt                |   2 +-
Documentation/gitk.txt                   |   2 +-
19 files changed, 25 insertions(+), 19 deletions(-)
```

Of course, you can view the diffs for a single file, too.

```
$ git diff master~5 master Documentation/git-add.txt
diff --git a/Documentation/git-add.txt b/Documentation/git-add.txt
index bb4abe2..1afd0c6 100644
--- a/Documentation/git-add.txt
+++ b/Documentation/git-add.txt
```

```
@@ -246,7 +246,7 @@ characters that need C-quoting. `core.quotepath` configuration can be
 used to work this limitation around to some degree, but backslash,
 double-quote and control characters will still have problems.

-See Also
+SEE ALSO
 --------
 linkgit:git-status[1]
 linkgit:git-rm[1]
```

In the following example, also taken from Git's own repository, the -S"*string*" searches
the past 50 commits to the `master` branch for changes containing *string*.

```
$ git diff -S"octopus" master~50
diff --git a/Documentation/RelNotes-1.5.5.3.txt b/Documentation/RelNotes-1.5.5.3.txt
new file mode 100644
index 0000000..f22f98b
--- /dev/null
+++ b/Documentation/RelNotes-1.5.5.3.txt
@@ -0,0 +1,12 @@
+GIT v1.5.5.3 Release Notes
+==========================
+
+Fixes since v1.5.5.2
+--------------------
+
+ * "git send-email --compose" did not notice that non-ascii contents
+   needed some MIME magic.
+
+ * "git fast-export" did not export octopus merges correctly.
+
+Also comes with various documentation updates.
```

Used with -S, often called the *pickaxe*, Git lists the diffs that contain a change in the
number of times the given *string* is used in the diff. Conceptually, you can think of
this as "Where is the given *string* either introduced or removed?" You can find an
example of the pickaxe used with `git log` in "Using Pickaxe" on page 88 of Chapter 6.

Comparing How Subversion and Git Derive diffs

Most systems, such as CVS or SVN, track a series of revisions and store just the changes
between each pair of files. This technique is meant to save storage space and overhead.

Internally, such systems spend a lot of time thinking about things like "the series of
changes between A and B." When you update your files from the central repository,
for example, SVN remembers that the last time you updated the file you were at revision
r1095, but now the repository is at revision r1123. Thus, the server must send you the
diff between r1095 and r1123. Once your SVN client has these diffs, it can incorporate
them into your working copy and produce r1123. (That's how SVN avoids sending you
all the contents of all files every time you update.)

To save disk space, SVN also stores its own repository as a series of diffs on the server. When you ask for the diffs between r1095 and r1123, it looks up all the individual diffs for each version between those two versions, merges them together into one large diff, and sends you the result. But Git doesn't work like that.

In Git, as you've seen, each commit contains a tree, which is a list of files contained by that commit. Each tree is independent of all other trees. Git users still talk about diffs and patches, of course, because these are still extremely useful. Yet, in Git, a diff and a patch are derived data, not the fundamental data they are in CVS or SVN. If you look in the *.git* directory, you won't find a single diff; if you look in a SVN repository, it consists mostly of diffs.

Just as SVN is able to derive the complete set of differences between r1095 and r1123, Git can retrieve and derive the differences between any two arbitrary states. But SVN must look at each version between r1095 and r1123, whereas Git doesn't care about the intermediate steps.

Each revision has its own tree, but Git doesn't require those to generate the diff; Git can operate directly on snapshots of the complete state at each of the two versions. This simple difference in storage systems is one of the most important reasons that Git is so much faster than other RCSs.

## CHAPTER 9

Merges

Git is a *distributed version control system* (DVCS). It allows, for example, a developer in Japan and another in New Jersey to make and record changes independently, and it permits the two developers to combine their changes at any time, all without a central repository. In this chapter, we'll learn how to combine two or more different lines of development.

A *merge* unifies two or more commit history branches. Most often, a merge unites just two branches, although Git supports a merge of three, four, or more branches at the same time.

In Git, a merge must occur within a single repository—that is, all the branches to be merged must be present in the same repository. How the branches come to be in the repository is not important. (As you will see in Chapter 12, Git provides mechanisms for referring to other repositories and for bringing remote branches into your current working repository.)

When modifications in one branch do not conflict with modifications found in another branch, Git computes a merge result and creates a new commit that represents the new, unified state. But when branches conflict, which occurs whenever changes compete to alter the same line of the same file, Git does not resolve the dispute. Instead, Git marks such contentious changes as "unmerged" in the index and leaves reconciliation up to you, the developer. When Git cannot merge automatically, it's also up to you to make the final commit once all conflicts are resolved.

Merge Examples

To merge other_branch into branch, you should check out the target branch and merge the other branches into it, like this:

```
$ git checkout branch
$ git merge other_branch
```

Let's work through a pair of example merges, one without conflicts and one with substantial overlaps. To simplify the examples in this chapter, we'll use multiple branches per the techniques presented in Chapter 7.

Preparing for a Merge

Before you begin a merge, it's best to tidy up your working directory. During a normal merge, Git creates new versions of files and places them in your working directory when it is finished. Furthermore, Git also uses the index to store temporary and intermediate versions of files during the operation.

If you have modified files in your working directory or if you've modified the index via `git add` or `git rm`, then your repository has a *dirty* working directory or index. If you start a merge in a dirty state, Git may be unable to combine the changes from all the branches *and* from those in your working directory or index in one pass.

 You don't *have* to start with a clean directory. Git performs the merge, for example, if the files affected by the merge operation and the dirty files in your working directory are disjoint. However, as a general rule, your Git life will be much easier if you start each merge with a clean working directory and index.

Merging Two Branches

For the simplest scenario, let's set up a repository with a single file, create two branches, and then merge the pair of branches together again.

```
$ git init
Initialized empty Git repository in /tmp/conflict/.git/
$ git config user.email "jdl@example.com"
$ git config user.name "Jon Loeliger"

$ cat > file
Line 1 stuff
Line 2 stuff
Line 3 stuff
^D
$ git add file
$ git commit -m "Initial 3 line file"
Created initial commit 8f4d2d5: Initial 3 line file
1 files changed, 3 insertions(+), 0 deletions(-)
create mode 100644 file
```

Let's create another commit on the master branch:

```
$ cat > other_file
Here is stuff on another file!
^D
$ git add other_file
$ git commit -m "Another file"
```

```
Created commit 761d917: Another file
 1 files changed, 1 insertions(+), 0 deletions(-)
 create mode 100644 other_file
```

So far, the repository has one branch with two commits, where each commit introduced a new file. Next, let's change to a different branch and modify the first file.

```
$ git checkout -b alternate master^
Switched to a new branch "alternate"

$ git show-branch
* [alternate] Initial 3 line file
 ! [master] Another file
--
 + [master] Another file
*+ [alternate] Initial 3 line file
```

Here, the alternate branch is initially forked from the master^ commit, one commit behind the current head.

Make a trivial change to the file so you have something to merge, and then commit it. Remember, it's best to commit outstanding changes and start a merge with a clean working directory.

```
$ cat >> file
Line 4 alternate stuff
^D
$ git commit -a -m "Add alternate's line 4"
Created commit b384721: Add alternate's line 4
 1 files changed, 1 insertions(+), 0 deletions(-)
```

Now there are two branches and each has different development work. A second file has been added to the master branch, and a modification has been made to alternate the branch. Because the two changes do not affect the same parts of a common file, a merge should proceed smoothly and without incident.

The git merge operation is context sensitive. Your current branch is always the target branch, and the other branch or branches are merged into the current branch. In this case, the alternate branch should be merged into the master branch, so the latter must be checked out before you continue:

```
$ git checkout master
Switched to branch "master"

$ git status
# On branch master
nothing to commit (working directory clean)

# Yep, ready for a merge!

$ git merge alternate
Merge made by recursive.
 file |    1 +
 1 files changed, 1 insertions(+), 0 deletions(-)
```

You can use another commit graph viewing tool, a part of `git log`, to see what what's been done:

```
$ git log --graph --pretty=oneline --abbrev-commit

*   1d51b93... Merge branch 'alternate'
|\
| * b384721... Add alternate's line 4
* | 761d917... Another file
|/
* 8f4d2d5... Initial 3 line file
```

That is conceptually the commit graph described earlier in the section "Commit Graphs" on page 74 (Chapter 6), except that this graph is turned sideways, with the most recent commits at the top rather than the right. The two branches have split at the initial commit, 8f4d2d5; each branch shows one commit each (761d917 and b384721); and the two branches merge again at commit 1d51b93.

 Using `git log --graph` is an excellent alternative to graphical tools such as `gitk`. The visualization provided by `git log --graph` is well-suited to dumb terminals.

Technically, Git performs each merge symmetrically to produce one identical, combined commit that is added to your current branch. The other branch is not affected by the merge. Because the merge commit is added only to your current branch, you can say, "I merged some other branch *into* this one."

A Merge with a Conflict

The merge operation is inherently problematic because it necessarily brings together potentially varying and conflicting changes from different lines of development. The changes on one branch may be similar to or radically different from the changes on a different branch. Modifications may alter the same files or a disjoint set of files. Git can handle all these varied possibilities, but often it requires guidance from you to resolve conflicts.

Let's work through a scenario in which a merge leads to a conflict. We begin with the results of the merge from the previous section and introduce independent and conflicting changes on the `master` and `alternate` branches. We then merge the `alternate` branch into the `master` branch, face the conflict, resolve it, and commit the final result.

On the `master` branch, create a new version of *file* with a few additional lines in it and then commit the changes:

```
$ git checkout master

$ cat >> file
Line 5 stuff
```

```
Line 6 stuff
^D

$ git commit -a -m "Add line 5 and 6"
Created commit 4d8b599: Add line 5 and 6
 1 files changed, 2 insertions(+), 0 deletions(-)
```

Now, on the `alternate` branch, modify the same file differently. Whereas you made new commits to the `master` branch, the `alternate` branch has not progressed yet.

```
$ git checkout alternate
Switched branch "alternate"

$ git show-branch
* [alternate] Add alternate's line 4
 ! [master] Add line 5 and 6
--
 + [master] Add line 5 and 6
*+ [alternate] Add alternate's line 4

# In this branch, "file" left off with "Line 4 alternate stuff"

$ cat >> file
Line 5 alternate stuff
Line 6 alternate stuff
^D

$ cat file
Line 1 stuff
Line 2 stuff
Line 3 stuff
Line 4 alternate stuff
Line 5 alternate stuff
Line 6 alternate stuff

$ git diff
diff --git a/file b/file
index a29c52b..802acf8 100644
--- a/file
+++ b/file
@@ -2,3 +2,5 @@ Line 1 stuff
 Line 2 stuff
 Line 3 stuff
 Line 4 alternate stuff
+Line 5 alternate stuff
+Line 6 alternate stuff

$ git commit -a -m "Add alternate line 5 and 6"
Created commit e306e1d: Add alternate line 5 and 6
 1 files changed, 2 insertions(+), 0 deletions(-)
```

Let's review the scenario. The current branch history looks like this:

```
$ git show-branch
* [alternate] Add alternate line 5 and 6
 ! [master] Add line 5 and 6
```

```
         --
      *  [alternate] Add alternate line 5 and 6
      +  [master] Add line 5 and 6
      *+ [alternate^] Add alternate's line 4
```

To continue, check out the `master` branch and try to perform the merge:

```
$ git checkout master
Switched to branch "master"

$ git merge alternate
Auto-merged file
CONFLICT (content): Merge conflict in file
Automatic merge failed; fix conflicts and then commit the result.
```

When a merge conflict like this occurs, you should almost invariably investigate the extent of the conflict using the `git diff` command. Here, the single file named *file* has a conflict in its content:

```
$ git diff
diff --cc file
index 4d77dd1,802acf8..0000000
--- a/file
+++ b/file
@@@ -2,5 -2,5 +2,10 @@@ Line 1 stuf
  Line 2 stuff
  Line 3 stuff
  Line 4 alternate stuff
++<<<<<<< HEAD:file
 +Line 5 stuff
 +Line 6 stuff
++=======
+ Line 5 alternate stuff
+ Line 6 alternate stuff
++>>>>>>> alternate:file
```

The `git diff` command shows the differences between the file in your working directory and the index. In the traditional `diff` command output style, the changed content is presented between <<<<<<< and =======, with an alternate between ======= and >>>>>>>. However, additional plus and minus signs are used in the *combined diff* format to indicate changes from multiple sources relative to the final resulting version.

The previous output shows that the conflict covers lines 5 and 6, where deliberately different changes were made in the two branches. It's then up to you to resolve the conflict. When resolving a merge conflict, you are free to choose any resolution you would like for the file. That includes picking lines from only one side or the other, or a mix from both sides, or even making up something completely new and different. Although that last option might be confusing, it is a valid choice.

In this case, I chose a line from each branch as the makeup of my resolved version. The edited file now has this content:

```
$ cat file
Line 1 stuff
```

```
Line 2 stuff
Line 3 stuff
Line 4 alternate stuff
Line 5 stuff
Line 6 alternate stuff
```

If you are happy with the conflict resolution, you should `git add` the file to the index and stage it for the merge commit:

```
$ git add file
```

After you have resolved conflicts and staged final versions of each file in the index using `git add`, it is finally time to commit the merge using `git commit`. Git places you in your favorite editor with a template message that looks like this:

```
Merge branch 'alternate'

Conflicts:
        file
#
# It looks like you may be committing a MERGE.
# If this is not correct, please remove the file
#       .git/MERGE_HEAD
# and try again.
#

# Please enter the commit message for your changes.
# (Comment lines starting with '#' will not be included)
# On branch master
# Changes to be committed:
#   (use "git reset HEAD <file>..." to unstage)
#
#       modified:   file
#
```

As usual, the lines beginning with the octothorp (#) are comments and meant solely for your information while you write a message. All comment lines are ultimately elided from the final commit log message. Feel free to alter or augment the commit message as you see fit, perhaps adding a note about how the conflict was resolved.

When you exit the editor, Git should indicate the successful creation of a new merge commit:

```
$ git commit

# Edit merge commit message

Created commit 7015896: Merge branch 'alternate'

$ git show-branch
! [alternate] Add alternate line 5 and 6
 * [master] Merge branch 'alternate'
--
 - [master] Merge branch 'alternate'
+* [alternate] Add alternate line 5 and 6
```

You can see the resulting merge commit using:

```
$ git log
```

Working with Merge Conflicts

As demonstrated by the previous example, there are instances when conflicting changes can't be merged automatically.

Let's create another scenario with a merge conflict to explore the tools Git provides to help resolve disparities. Starting with a common *hello* with just the contents "hello," let's create two different branches with two different variants of the file.

```
$ git init
Initialized empty Git repository in /tmp/conflict/.git/

$ echo hello > hello
$ git add hello
$ git commit -m "Initial hello file"
Created initial commit b8725ac: Initial hello file
 1 files changed, 1 insertions(+), 0 deletions(-)
 create mode 100644 hello

$ git checkout -b alt
Switched to a new branch "alt"
$ echo world >> hello
$ echo 'Yay!' >> hello
$ git commit -a -m "One world"
Created commit d03e77f: One world
 1 files changed, 2 insertions(+), 0 deletions(-)

$ git checkout master
$ echo worlds >> hello
$ echo 'Yay!' >> hello
$ git commit -a -m "All worlds"
Created commit eddcb7d: All worlds
 1 files changed, 2 insertions(+), 0 deletions(-)
```

One branch says world, whereas the other says worlds—a deliberate difference.

As in the earlier example, if you check out master and try to merge the alt branch into it, a conflict arises.

```
$ git merge alt
Auto-merged hello
CONFLICT (content): Merge conflict in hello
Automatic merge failed; fix conflicts and then commit the result.
```

As expected, Git warns you about the conflict found in the *hello* file.

Locating Conflicted Files

But what if Git's helpful directions scrolled off the screen or if there were many files with conflicts? Luckily, Git keeps track of problematic files by marking each one in the index as *conflicted*, or unmerged.

You can also use either the `git status` command or the `git ls-files -u` command to show the set of files that remain unmerged in your working tree.

```
$ git status
hello: needs merge
# On branch master
# Changed but not updated:
#   (use "git add <file>..." to update what will be committed)
#
#       unmerged:   hello
#
no changes added to commit (use "git add" and/or "git commit -a")

$ git ls-files -u
100644 ce013625030ba8dba906f756967f9e9ca394464a 1       hello
100644 e63164d9518b1e6caf28f455ac86c8246f78ab70 2       hello
100644 562080a4c6518e1bf67a9f58a32a67bff72d4f00 3       hello
```

You can use `git diff` to show what's not yet merged, but it will show all of the gory details, too!

Inspecting Conflicts

When a conflict appears, the working directory copy of each conflicted file is enhanced with three-way diff or merge markers. Continuing from where the example left off, the resulting conflicted file now looks like this:

```
$ cat hello
hello
<<<<<<< HEAD:hello
worlds
=======
world
>>>>>>> 6ab5ed10d942878015e38e4bab333daff614b46e:hello
Yay!
```

The merge markers delineate the two possible versions of the conflicting chunk of the file. In the first version, the chunk says "worlds"; in the other version, it says "world." You could simply choose one phrase or the other, remove the conflict markers, and then run `git add` and `git commit`, but let's explore some of the other features Git offers to help resolve conflicts.

The three-way merge marker lines (<<<<<<<, =======, and >>>>>>>) are automatically generated, but they're just meant to be read by you, not (necessarily) a program. You should delete them with your text editor once you resolve the conflict.

git diff with conflicts

Git has a special, merge-specific variant of git diff to display the changes made against *both* parents simultaneously. In the example, it looks like this:

```
$ git diff
diff --cc hello
index e63164d,562080a..0000000
--- a/hello
+++ b/hello
@@@ -1,3 -1,3 +1,7 @@@
  hello
++<<<<<<< HEAD:hello
 +worlds
++=======
+ world
++>>>>>>> alt:hello
  Yay!
```

What does it all mean? It's the simple combination of two diffs: one versus the first parent, called HEAD, and one against the second parent, or alt. (Don't be surprised if the second parent is an absolute SHA1 name representing some unnamed commit from some other repository!) To make things easier, Git also gives the second parent the special name MERGE_HEAD.

You can compare both the HEAD and MERGE_HEAD versions against the working directory ("merged") version:

```
$ git diff HEAD
diff --git a/hello b/hello
index e63164d..4e4bc4e 100644
--- a/hello
+++ b/hello
@@ -1,3 +1,7 @@
 hello
+<<<<<<< HEAD:hello
 worlds
+=======
+world
+>>>>>>> alt:hello
 Yay!
```

And then this:

```
$ git diff MERGE_HEAD
diff --git a/hello b/hello
index 562080a..4e4bc4e 100644
--- a/hello
+++ b/hello
```

```
@@ -1,3 +1,7 @@
 hello
+<<<<<<< HEAD:hello
+worlds
+=======
 world
+>>>>>>> alt:hello
 Yay!
```

 In newer versions of Git, `git diff --ours` is a synonym for `git diff HEAD`, because it shows the differences between "our" version and the merged version. Similarly, `git diff MERGE_HEAD` can be written as `git diff --theirs`. You can use `git diff --base` to see the combined set of changes since the merge base, which would otherwise be rather awkwardly written as:

$ **git diff $(git merge-base HEAD MERGE_HEAD)**

If you line up the two diffs side by side, all the text except the + columns are the same, so Git prints the main text only once and prints the + columns next to each other.

The conflict found by `git diff` has two columns of information prepended to each line of output. A plus sign in a column indicates a line addition, a minus sign indicates a line removal, and a blank indicates a line with no change. The first column shows what's changing versus your version, and the second column shows what's changing versus the other version. The conflict marker lines are new in both versions, so they get a ++. The `world` and `worlds` lines are new only in one version or the other, so they have just a single + in the corresponding column.

Suppose you edit the file to pick a third option, like this:

```
$ cat hello
hello
worldly ones
Yay!
```

Then the new `git diff` output is

```
$ git diff
diff --cc hello
index e63164d,562080a..0000000
--- a/hello
+++ b/hello
@@@ -1,3 -1,3 +1,3 @@@
  hello
- worlds
 -world
++worldly ones
  Yay!
```

Alternatively, you could choose one or the other original version, like this:

```
$ cat hello
hello
world
Yay!
```

The `git diff` output would then be:

```
$ git diff
diff --cc hello
index e63164d,562080a..0000000
--- a/hello
+++ b/hello
```

Wait! Something strange happened there. Where does it show where the `world` line was added to the base version? Where does it show that the `worlds` line was removed from the `HEAD` version? As you have resolved the conflict in favor of the `MERGE_HEAD` version, Git deliberately omits the diff because it thinks you probably don't care about that section anymore.

Running `git diff` on a conflicted file only shows you the sections that really have a conflict. In a large file with numerous changes scattered throughout, most of those changes don't have a conflict; either one side of the merge changed a particular section or the other side did. When you're trying to resolve a conflict, you rarely care about those sections, so `git diff` trims out uninteresting sections using a simple heuristic: if a section has changes versus only one side, that section isn't shown.

This optimization has a slightly confusing side effect: once you resolve something that *used* to be a conflict by simply picking one side or the other, it stops showing up. That's because you modified the section so that it only changes one side or the other (i.e., the side that you didn't choose), so to Git it looks just like a section that was never conflicted at all.

This is really more a side effect of the implementation than an intentional feature, but you might consider it useful anyway: `git diff` shows you only those sections of the file that are *still* conflicted, so you can use it to keep track of the conflicts you haven't fixed yet.

git log with conflicts

While you're in the process of resolving a conflict, you can use some special `git log` options to help you figure out exactly where the changes came from and why. Try this:

```
$ git log --merge --left-right -p

commit <eddcb7dfe63258ae4695eb38d2bc22e726791227
Author: Jon Loeliger <jdl@example.com>
Date:   Wed Oct 22 21:29:08 2008 -0500

    All worlds

diff --git a/hello b/hello
index ce01362..e63164d 100644
```

```
--- a/hello
+++ b/hello
@@ -1 +1,3 @@
 hello
+worlds
+Yay!

commit >d03e77f7183cde5659bbaeef4cb51281a9ecfc79
Author: Jon Loeliger <example@example.com>
Date:   Wed Oct 22 21:27:38 2008 -0500

    One world

diff --git a/hello b/hello
index ce01362..562080a 100644
--- a/hello
+++ b/hello
@@ -1 +1,3 @@
 hello
+world
+Yay!
```

This command shows all the commits in both parts of the history that affect conflicted files in your merge, along with the actual changes each commit introduced. If you wondered when, why, how, and by whom the line worlds came to be added to the file, you can see exactly which set of changes introduced it.

The options provided to git log are as follows:

- --merge shows only commits related to files that produced a conflict
- --left-right displays < if the commit was from the "left" side of the merge ("our" version, the one you started with), or > if the commit was from the "right" side of the merge ("their" version, the one you're merging in)
- -p shows the commit message and the patch associated with each commit

If your repository were more complicated and several files had conflicts, you could also provide the exact filename(s) you're interested in as a command line option, like this:

```
$ git log --merge --left-right -p hello
```

The examples here have been kept small for demonstration purposes. Of course, real-life situations are likely to be significantly larger and more complex. One technique to mitigate the pain of large merges with nasty, extended conflicts is to use several small commits with well-defined effects contained to individual concepts. Git handles small commits well, so there is no need to wait until the last minute to commit large, wide-spread changes. Smaller commits and more frequent merge cycles reduce the pain of conflict resolution.

How Git Keeps Track of Conflicts

How exactly does Git keep track of all the information about a conflicted merge? There are several parts:

- *.git/MERGE_HEAD* contains the SHA1 of the commit you're merging in. You don't really have to use the SHA1 yourself; Git knows to look in that file whenever you talk about `MERGE_HEAD`.

- *.git/MERGE_MSG* contains the default merge message used when you `git commit` after resolving the conflicts.

- The Git *index* contains three copies of each conflicted file: the merge base, "our" version, and "their" version. These three copies are assigned respective *stage numbers* 1, 2, and 3.

- The conflicted version (merge markers and all) is *not* stored in the index. Instead, it is stored in a file in your working directory. When you run `git diff` without any parameters, the comparison is always between what's in the index with what's in your working directory.

To see how the index entries are stored, you can use the `git ls-files` plumbing command as follows:

```
$ git ls-files -s
100644 ce013625030ba8dba906f756967f9e9ca394464a 1       hello
100644 e63164d9518b1e6caf28f455ac86c8246f78ab70 2       hello
100644 562080a4c6518e1bf67a9f58a32a67bff72d4f00 3       hello
```

The `-s` option to `git ls-files` shows *all* the files with *all* stages. If you want to see only the conflicted files, use the `-u` option instead.

In other words, the *hello* file is stored three times, and each has a different hash corresponding to the three different versions. You can look at a specific variant by using `git cat-file`:

```
$ git cat-file -p e63164d951
hello
worlds
Yay!
```

You can also use some special syntax with `git diff` to compare different versions of the file. For example, if you want to see what changed between the merge base and the version you're merging in, you can do this:

```
$ git diff :1:hello :3:hello
diff --git a/:1:hello b/:3:hello
index ce01362..562080a 100644
--- a/:1:hello
+++ b/:3:hello
@@ -1 +1,3 @@
 hello
+world
+Yay!
```

Starting with Git version 1.6.1, the `git checkout` command accepts the `--ours` or `--theirs` option as shorthand for simply checking out (a file from) one side or the other of a conflicted merge; your choice resolves the conflict. These two options can only be used during a conflict resolution.

Using the stage numbers to name a version is different from `git diff --theirs`, which shows the differences between their version and the resulting, merged (or still conflicted) version in your working directory. The merged version is not yet in the index, so it doesn't even have a number.

Because you fully edited and resolved the working copy version in favor of their version, there should be no difference now:

```
$ cat hello
hello
world
Yay!

$ git diff --theirs
* Unmerged path hello
```

All that remains is an unmerged path reminder to add it to the index.

Finishing Up a Conflict Resolution

Let's make one last change to the *hello* file before declaring it merged:

```
$ cat hello
hello
everyone
Yay!
```

Now that the file is fully merged and resolved, `git add` reduces the index to just a single copy of the *hello* file again:

```
$ git add hello
$ git ls-files -s
100644 ebc56522386c504db37db907882c9dbd0d05a0f0 0        hello
```

That lone 0 between the SHA1 and the path name tells you that the stage number for a nonconflicted file is zero.

You must work through all the conflicted files as recorded in the index. You cannot commit as long as there is an unresolved conflict. Therefore, as you fix the conflicts in a file, run `git add` (or `git rm`, `git update-index`, etc.) on the file to clear its conflict status.

Be careful not to `git add` files with lingering conflict markers. Although that will clear the conflict in the index and allow you to commit, your file won't be correct.

Finally, you can `git commit` the end result and use `git show` to see the *merge commit*:

```
$ cat .git/MERGE_MSG
Merge branch 'alt'

Conflicts:
        hello

$ git commit

$ git show

commit a274b3003fc705ad22445308bdfb172ff583f8ad
Merge: eddcb7d... d03e77f...
Author: Jon Loeliger <@example.com>
Date:   Wed Oct 22 23:04:18 2008 -0500

    Merge branch 'alt'

    Conflicts:
        hello

diff --cc hello
index e63164d,562080a..ebc5652
--- a/hello
+++ b/hello
@@@ -1,3 -1,3 +1,3 @@@
  hello
- worlds
 -world
++everyone
  Yay!
```

You should notice three interesting things when you look at a merge commit:

- There is a new, second line in the header that says `Merge:`. Normally there's no need to show the parent of a commit in `git log` or `git show`, since there is only one parent and it's typically the one that comes right after it in the log. But merge commits typically have two (and sometimes more) parents, and those parents are important to understanding the merge. Hence, `git log` and `git show` always print the SHA1 of each ancestor.

- The automatically generated commit log message helpfully notes the list of files that conflicted. This can be useful later if it turns out a particular problem was caused by your merge. Usually, problems caused by a merge are caused by the files that had to be merged by hand.

- The diff of a merge commit is not a normal diff. It is always in the *combined diff* or "conflicted merge" format. A successful merge in Git is considered to be no change at all; it is simply the combination of other changes that already appeared in the history. Thus, showing the contents of a merge commit shows *only* the parts that are different from one of the merged branches, not the entire set of changes.

Aborting or Restarting a Merge

If you start a merge operation but then decide for some reason that you don't want to complete it, Git provides an easy way to abort the operation. Prior to executing the final `git commit` on the merge commit, use:

```
$ git reset --hard HEAD
```

This command restores both your working directory and the index to the state immediately prior to the `git merge` command.

If you want to abort or discard the merge after it has finished (that is, after it's introduced a new merge commit), use the command:

```
$ git reset --hard ORIG_HEAD
```

Prior to beginning the merge operation, Git saves your original branch HEAD in the ORIG_HEAD ref for just this sort of purpose.

You should be very careful here, though. If you did not start the merge with a clean working directory and index, you could get in trouble and lose any uncommitted changes you have in your directory.

You can initiate a `git merge` request with a dirty working directory, but if you execute `git reset --hard` then your dirty state prior to the merge is not fully restored. Instead, the reset loses your dirty state in the working directory area. In other words, you requested a `--hard` reset to the HEAD state! (See "Using git reset" on page 154.)

Starting with Git version 1.6.1, you have another choice. If you have botched a conflict resolution and want to return to the original conflict state before trying to resolve it again, you can use the command `git checkout -m`.

Merge Strategies

So far, our examples have been easy to handle because there are only two branches. It might seem like Git's extra complexity of DAG-shaped history and long, hard-to-remember commit IDs isn't really worth it. And maybe it isn't for such a simple case. So, let's look at something a little more complicated.

Imagine that instead of just one person working on in your repository there are three. To keep things simple, suppose that each developer—Alice, Bob, and Cal—is able to contribute changes as commits on three separate eponymous branches within a shared repository.

Because the developers are all contributing to separate branches, let's leave it up to one person, Alice, to manage the integration of the various contributions. In the meantime, each developer is allowed to leverage the development of the others by directly incorporating or merging a coworker's branch, as needed.

Eventually, the coders develop a repository with a commit history as shown in Figure 9-1.

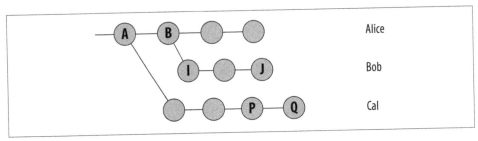

Figure 9-1. Criss-cross merge setup

Imagine that Cal started the project and Alice joined in. Alice worked on it for a while, then Bob joined in. In the meantime, Cal has been working away on his own version.

Eventually, Alice merged in Bob's changes, and Bob kept on working without merging Alice's changes back into his tree. There are now three different branch histories (Figure 9-2).

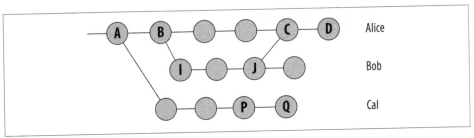

Figure 9-2. After Alice merges in Bob

Let's imagine that Bob wants to get Cal's latest changes. The diagram is looking pretty complicated now, but this part is still relatively easy. Trace up the tree from Bob, through Alice, until you reach the point where she first diverged from Cal. That's A, the merge base between Bob and Cal. To merge from Cal, Bob needs to take the set of changes between the merge base, A, and Cal's latest, Q, and three-way merge them into his own tree, yielding commit K. The result is the history shown in Figure 9-3.

 You can always find the *merge base* between two or more branches by using git merge-base. It is possible for there to be more than one equally valid merge base for a set of branches.

So far, so good.

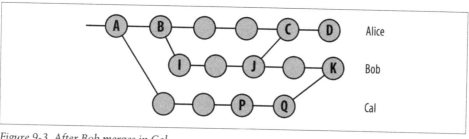

Figure 9-3. After Bob merges in Cal

Alice now decides that she, too, wants to get Cal's latest changes, but she doesn't realize Bob has already merged Cal's tree into his. So she just merges Cal's tree into hers. That's another easy operation because it's obvious where she diverged from Cal. The resulting history is shown in Figure 9-4.

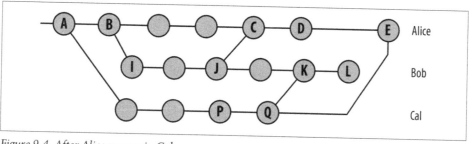

Figure 9-4. After Alice merges in Cal

Next, Alice realizes that Bob has done some more work, L, and wants to merge from him again. What's the merge base (between L and E) this time?

Unfortunately, the answer is ambiguous. If you trace all the way back up the tree, you might think the original revision from Cal is a good choice. But that doesn't really make sense: both Alice and Bob now have Cal's *newest* revision. If you ask for the differences from Cal's original revision to Bob's latest then it will also include Cal's newer changes, which Alice already has, which is likely to result in a merge conflict.

What if you use Cal's latest revision as the base? It's better, but still not quite right: if you take the diff from Cal's latest to Bob's latest, you get *all* Bob's changes. But Alice already has *some* of Bob's changes, so you'll probably get a merge conflict there, too.

And what if you use the version that Alice last merged from Bob, version J? Creating a diff from there to Bob's latest will include only the newest changes from Bob, which is what you want. But it also includes the changes from Cal, which Alice already has!

What to do?

This kind of situation is called a *criss-cross merge* because changes have been merged back and forth between branches. If changes moved in only one direction (e.g., from

Cal to Alice to Bob, but never from Bob to Alice or from Alice to Cal), then merging would be simple. Unfortunately, life isn't always that easy.

The Git developers originally wrote a straightforward mechanism to join two branches with a merge commit, but scenarios like the one just described soon led them to realize that a more clever approach was needed. Hence, the developers generalized, parameterized, and introduced alternate, configurable *merge strategies* to handle different scenarios.

Let's look at the various strategies and see how to apply each one.

Degenerate Merges

There are two common degenerate scenarios that lead to merges and are called *already up-to-date* and *fast-forward*. Because neither of these scenarios actually introduces a new merge commit after performing the git merge,[1] some might consider them not to be true merge strategies.

- *Already up-to-date.* When all the commits from the other branch (its HEAD) are already present in your target branch, even if it has advanced on its own, the target branch is said to be already up-to-date. As a result, no new commits are added to your branch.

  For example, if you perform a merge and immediately follow it with the exact same merge request, then you will be told that your branch is already up-to-date.

  ```
  # Show that alternate is already merged into master

  $ git show-branch
  ! [alternate] Add alternate line 5 and 6
   * [master] Merge branch 'alternate'
  --
   - [master] Merge branch 'alternate'
  +* [alternate] Add alternate line 5 and 6

  # Try to merge alternate into master again

  $ git merge alternate
  Already up-to-date.
  ```

- *Fast-forward.* A fast-forward merge happens when your branch HEAD is already fully present and represented in the other branch. This is the inverse of the *Already up-to-date* case.

  Because your HEAD is already present in the other branch (likely due to a common ancestor), Git simply tacks on to your HEAD the new commits from the other branch. Git then moves your branch HEAD to point to the final, new commit. Naturally, the

---

1. Yes, you can force Git to create one anyway by using the --no-ff option in the fast-forward case. However, you should fully understand why you want to do so.

index and your working directory are also adjusted accordingly to reflect the new, final commit state.

The *fast-forward* case is particularly common on tracking branches because they simply fetch and record the remote commits from other repositories. Your local tracking branch HEADs will always be fully present and represented, because that is where the branch HEAD was after the *previous* fetch operation. See Chapter 12 for more details.

It is important for Git to handle these cases without introducing actual commits. Imagine what would happen in the fast-forward case if Git created a commit. Merging branch A into B would first produce Figure 9-5. Then merging B into A would produce Figure 9-6, and merging back again would yield Figure 9-7.

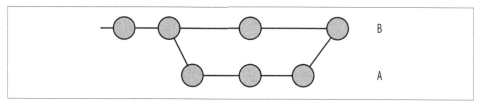

Figure 9-5. First nonconverging merge

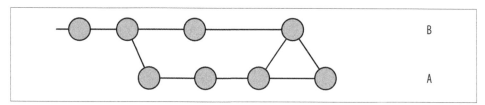

Figure 9-6. Second nonconverging merge

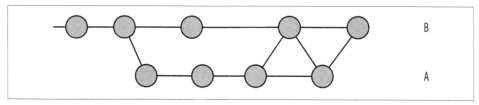

Figure 9-7. Third nonconverging merge

Each new merge is a new commit, so the sequence will never converge on a steady state and reveal that the two branches are identical.

Normal Merges

These merge strategies all produce a final commit, added to your current branch, that represents the combined state of the merge.

- *Resolve.* The *resolve* strategy operates on only two branches, locating the common ancestor as the merge basis and performing a direct *three-way merge* by applying the changes from the merge base to the tip of the other branch HEAD onto the current branch. This method makes intuitive sense.

- *Recursive.* The *recursive* strategy is similar to the *resolve* strategy in that it can only join two branches at once. However, it is designed to handle the scenario where there is more than one merge base between the two branches. In these cases, Git forms a temporary merge of all of the common merge bases and then uses *that* as the base from which to derive the resulting merge of the two given branches via a normal three-way merge algorithm.

    The temporary merge basis is thrown away, and the final merge state is committed on your target branch.

- *Octopus.* The *octopus* strategy is specifically designed to merge together more than two branches simultaneously. Conceptually, it is fairly simple; internally, it calls the *recursive* merge strategy multiple times, once for each branch you are merging.

    However, this strategy cannot handle a merge that requires any form of conflict resolution that would necessitate user interaction. In such a case, you are forced to do a series of normal merges, resolving the conflicts one step at a time.

Recursive merges

A simple criss-cross merge example is shown in Figure 9-8.

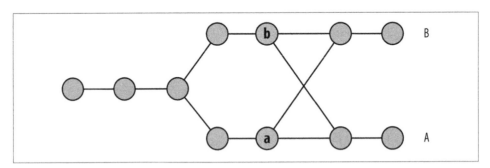

Figure 9-8. Simple criss-cross merge

The nodes a and b are both merge bases for a merge between A and B. Either one could be used as the merge base and yield reasonable results. In this case, the recursive strategy would merge a and b into a temporary merge base, using that as the merge base for A and B.

Because a and b could have the same problem, merging them could require another merge of still older commits. That is why this algorithm is called *recursive*.

Octopus merges

The main reasons why Git supports merging multiple branches together all at once are generality and design elegance. In Git, a commit can have no parents (the initial commit), one parent (a normal commit), or more than one parent (a merge commit). Once you have more than one parent, there is no particular reason to limit that number to only two, so Git data structures support multiple parents.[2] The octopus merge strategy is a natural consequence of the general design decision to allow a flexible list of commit parents.

Octopus merges look nice in diagrams, so Git users tend to use them as often as possible. You can just imagine the rush of endorphins a developer gets when merging six branches of a program into one. Besides looking pretty, octopus merges don't actually do anything extra. You could just as easily make multiple merge commits, one per branch, and accomplish exactly the same thing.

Specialty Merges

There are two special merge strategies that you should be aware of because they can sometimes help you solve strange problems. Feel free to skip this section if you don't have a strange problem. The two special strategies are *ours* and *subtree*.

These merge strategies each produce a final commit, added to your current branch, that represents the combined state of the merge.

- *Ours*. The *ours* strategy merges in any number of other branches, but it actually discards changes from those branches and uses only the files from the current branch. The result of an *ours* merge is identical to the current HEAD, but any other named branches are also recorded as commit parents.

  This is useful if you know you already have all the changes from the other branches but want to combine the two histories anyway. That is, it lets you record that you have somehow performed the merge, perhaps directly by hand, and that future Git operations shouldn't try to merge the histories again. Git can treat this as real merge no matter how it came to be.

- *Subtree*. The *subtree* strategy merges in another branch, but everything in that branch is merged into a particular subtree of the current tree. You don't specify which subtree; Git determines that automatically.

---

2. That's the "Zero, One, or Infinity Principle" at work.

Applying Merge Strategies

So how does Git know or determine which strategy to use? Or, if you don't like Git's choice, how do you specify a different one?

Git tries to keep the algorithms it uses as simple and inexpensive as possible, so it first tries using the `already up-to-date` and `fast-forward` to eliminate the trivial, easy scenarios if possible.

If you specify more than one other branch to be merged into your current branch, Git has no choice but trying the `octopus` strategy because that is the only one capable of joining more than two branches in a single merge.

Failing those special cases, Git must use a default strategy that works reliably in all other scenarios. Originally, `resolve` was the default merge strategy used by Git.

In criss-cross merge situations such as those described previously, where there is more than one possible merge basis, the *resolve* strategy works like this: pick one of the possible merge bases (either the last merge from Bob's branch or the last merge from Cal's branch) and hope for the best. This is actually not as bad as it sounds. It often turns out that Alice, Bob, and Cal have all been working on different parts of the code. In that case, Git detects that it's remerging some changes that are already in place and just skips duplicate changes, avoiding the conflict. Or, if there are slight changes that do cause a conflict, at least the conflicts should be fairly easy for a developer to handle.

Because `resolve` is no longer Git's default, if Alice wanted to use it then she would make an explicit request:

```
$ git merge -s resolve Bob
```

In 2005, Fredrik Kuivinen contributed the new *recursive* merge strategy, which has since become the default. It is more general than `resolve` and has been shown to result in fewer conflicts, without fault, on the Linux kernel. It also handles merges with renames quite well.

In the previous example, where Alice wants to merge all of Bob's work, the `recursive` strategy would work like this:

1. Start with the most recent revision from Cal that *both* Alice and Bob have. In this case, that's Cal's most recent revision, Q, which has been merged into both Bob's and Alice's branches.

2. Calculate the diff between that revision and the most recent revision that Alice merged from Bob, and patch that in.

3. Calculate the diff between that combined version and Bob's latest version, and patch that in.

This method is called "recursive" because there may be extra iterations, depending on how many levels of criss-crossing and merge bases Git encounters. And it works. Not only does the `recursive` method make intuitive sense, it has also been proven to result in fewer conflicts in real-life situations than the simpler resolve strategy. That's why recursive is now the default strategy for git merge.

Of course, no matter which strategy Alice chooses to use, the final history looks the same (Figure 9-9).

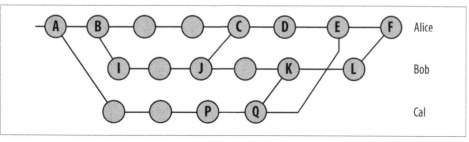

Figure 9-9. Final criss-cross merge history

Using ours and subtree

You can use these two merge strategies together. For example, once upon a time, the gitweb program (which is now part of git) was developed outside the main git.git repository. But at revision 0a8f4f, its entire history was merged into git.git under the gitweb subtree. If you wanted to do something similar, you could proceed as follows

1. Copy the current files from the gitweb.git project into the *gitweb* subdirectory of your project.

2. Commit them as usual.

3. Pull from the gitweb.git project using the ours strategy:

   ```
   $ git pull -s ours gitweb.git master
   ```

   You use ours here because you know that you already have the latest version of the files and you have already put them exactly where you want them (which is not where the normal *recursive* strategy would have put them).

4. In the future, you can continue to pull the latest changes from the gitweb.git project using the subtree strategy:

   ```
   $ git pull -s subtree gitweb.git master
   ```

   Because the files already exist in your repository, Git knows automatically which subtree you put them in and performs the updates without any conflicts.

Merge Drivers

Each of the merge strategies described in this chapter uses an underlying *merge driver* to resolve and merge each individual file. A merge diver accepts the names of three temporary files that represent the common ancestor, the target branch version, and the other branch version of a file. The driver modifies the target branch version to have the merged result.

The *text* merge driver leaves the usual three-way merge markers, (<<<<<<<<, ========, and >>>>>>>).

The *binary* merge driver simply keeps the target branch version of the file and leaves the file marked as a conflict in the index. Effectively, that forces you to handle binary files by hand.

The final built-in merge diver, *union*, simply leaves all the lines from both versions in the merged file.

Through Git's attribute mechanism, Git can tie specific files or file patterns to specific merge drivers. Most text files are handled by the `text` driver and most binary files by the `binary` driver. Yet, for special needs that warrant an application-specific merge operation, you can create and specify your own custom merge driver and tie it to your specific files.

 If you think you need custom merge drivers, you may want to investigate custom *diff drivers* as well!

How Git Thinks About Merges

At first, Git's automatic merging support seems nothing short of magical, especially compared to the more complicated and error-prone merging steps needed in other VCSs.

Let's take a look at what's going on behind the scenes to make it all possible.

Merges and Git's Object Model

In most VCSs, each commit has only one parent. On such a system, when you merge some_branch into my_branch, you create a new commit on my_branch with the changes from some_branch. Conversely, if you merge my_branch into some_branch then this creates a new commit on some_branch containing the changes from my_branch. Merging branch A into branch B and merging branch B into branch A are two different operations.

However, the Git designers noticed that each of these two operations results in the same set of files when you're done. The natural way to express either operation is simply to say, "Merge all the changes from some_branch and another_branch into a single branch."

In Git, the merge yields a new tree object with the merged files, but it also introduces a new commit object on only the target branch. After these commands:

```
$ git checkout my_branch
$ git merge some_branch
```

the object model looks like Figure 9-10.

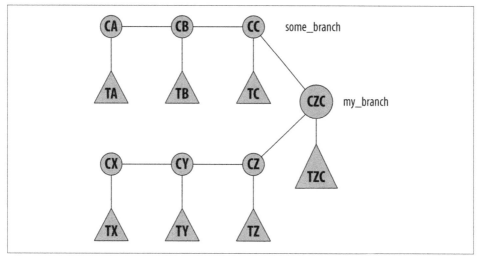

Figure 9-10. Object model after a merge

In Figure 9-10, each Cx is a commit object and each Tx represents the corresponding tree object. Notice how there is one common merged commit (CZC) that has both CC and CZ as commit parents, but it has only one resulting set of files represented in the TZC tree. The merged tree object symmetrically represents both source branches equally. But because my_branch was the checked out branch into which the merge happened, only my_branch has been updated to show the new commit on it; some_branch remains where it was.

This is not just a matter of semantics. It reflects Git's underlying philosophy that all branches are created equal.[3]

Squash Merges

Suppose some_branch had contained not just one new commit, but instead, 5 or 10 or even hundreds of commits. In most systems, merging some_branch into my_branch would involve producing a single diff, applying it as a single patch onto my_branch, and creating one new element in the history. This is called a *squash commit* because it "squashes" all the individual commits into one big change. As far as the history of my_branch is concerned, the history of some_branch would be lost.

---

3. And, by extension, so are all complete repository clones.

In Git, the two branches are treated as equal, so it's improper to squash one side or the other. Instead, the entire history of commits on both sides is retained. As users, you can see from Figure 9-10 that you pay for this complexity. If Git had made a squash commit, you wouldn't have to see (or think about) a diagram that diverges and then rejoins again. The history of my_branch could have been just a straight line.

> Git can make squash commits if desired. Just give the --squash option to git merge or git pull. Beware, however! Squashing commits will upset Git's history, and that will complicate future merges because the squashed comments alter the history of commits (see Chapter 10).

The added complexity might appear unfortunate, but it is actually quite worthwhile. For example, this feature means that the git blame and git bisect commands, discussed in Chapter 6, are much more powerful than equivalents in other systems. And as you saw with the recursive merge strategy, Git is able to automate very complicated merges as a result of this added complexity and the resulting detailed history.

> Although the merge operation itself treats both parents as equal, you can choose to treat the first parent as special when you go back through the history later. Some commands (e.g., git log and gitk) support the --first-parent option, which follows only the first parent of every merge. The resulting history looks much the same as if you had used --squash on all your merges.

Why Not Just Merge Each Change One by One?

You might ask wouldn't it be possible to have it both ways: a simple, linear history with every individual commit represented? Git could just take all the commits from some_branch and apply them, one by one, onto my_branch. But that wouldn't be the same thing at all.

An important observation about Git's commit histories is that each revision in the history is *real*. (You can read more about treating alternate histories as equal realities in Chapter 13.)

If you apply a *sequence* of someone else's patches on top of your version, you will create a series of entirely new versions with the union of their changes and yours. Presumably, you will test the final version as you always would. But what about all those new, intermediate versions? In reality, those versions never existed: nobody actually produced those commits, so nobody can say for sure whether they ever worked.

Git keeps a detailed history so that you can later revisit what your files were like at a particular moment in the past. If some of your merged commits reflect file versions that never really existed, then you've lost the reason for having a detailed history in the first place!

This is why Git merges don't work that way. If you were ask "What was it like five minutes before I did the merge?" then the answer would be ambiguous. Instead you must ask about either my_branch or some_branch specifically, because both were different five minutes ago and Git can give the true answer for each one.

Even though you almost always want the standard history merging behavior, Git can also apply a sequence of patches (see Chapter 14) as described here. This process is called *rebasing* and is discussed in Chapter 10. The implications of changing commit histories are discussed in "Changing Public History" on page 248 of Chapter 13.

Altering Commits

A commit records the history of your work and keeps your changes sacrosanct, but the commit itself isn't cast in stone. Git provides several tools and commands specifically designed to help you modify and improve the commit history cataloged within your repository.

There are many valid reasons why you might modify or rework a commit or your overall commit sequence.

- You can fix a problem before it becomes a legacy.
- You can decompose a large, sweeping change into a number of small, thematic commits. Conversely, you can combine individual changes into a larger commit.
- You can incorporate review feedback and suggestions.
- You can reorder commits into a sequence that doesn't break a build requirement.
- You can order commits into a more logical sequence.
- You can remove debug code committed accidentally.

As you'll see in Chapter 12, which explains how to share a repository, there are many more reasons to change commits prior to publishing your repository.

In general, you should feel empowered to alter a commit or a commit sequence if your effort makes it cleaner and more understandable. Of course, as with all of software development, there is a trade-off between repeated overrefinement and acceptance of something that is satisfactory. You should strive for clean, well-structured patches that have concise meaning for both you and your collaborators. However, there comes a time when good enough is good enough.

Philosophy of Altering History

When it comes to manipulating the development history, there are several schools of thought.

One philosophy might be termed realistic history: every commit is retained and nothing is altered.

One variant is a fine-grained realistic history, where you commit every change as soon as possible, ensuring that each and every step is saved for posterity. Another option is didactic realistic history, where you take your time and commit your best work only at convenient and suitable moments.

Given the opportunity to adjust the history—possibly cleaning up a bad intermediate design decision or rearranging commits into a more logical flow—you can create a more "idealistic" history.

As a developer, you may find value in the full, fine-grained realistic history, because it might provide archaeological details on how some good or bad idea developed. A complete narrative may provide insight into the introduction of a bug, or explicate a meticulous bug fix. In fact, an analysis of the history may even yield insight into how a developer or team of developers works and how the development process can be improved.

Many of those details might be lost if a revised history removes intermediate steps. Was a developer able to simply intuit such a good solution? Or did it take several iterations of refinement? What is the root cause of a bug? If the intermediate steps are not captured in the commit history, answers to those types of questions may be lost.

On the other hand, having a clean history showing well-defined steps, each with logical forward progress, can often be a joy to read and a pleasure to work with. There is, moreover, no need to worry about the vagaries of a possibly broken or suboptimal step in the repository history. Also, other developers reading the history may thereby learn a better development technique and style.

So is a detailed realistic history without information loss the best approach? Or is a clean history better? Perhaps an intermediate representation of the development is warranted. Or, with a clever use of Git branches, perhaps you could represent both a fine-grained realistic history and an idealized history in the same repository.

Git gives you the ability to clean up the actual history and turn it into a more idealized or cleaner one before it is published or committed to public record. Whether you choose to do so, to keep a detailed record without alteration, or to pick some middle ground is entirely up to you and your project policies.

Caution About Altering History

As a general guideline, you should feel free to alter and improve your repository commit history as long as no other developer[1] has obtained a copy of your repository. Or, to be more pedantic, you can alter a specific branch of your repository as long as no one has a copy of that branch. The notion to keep in mind is you shouldn't rewrite, alter, or change any part of a branch that's been made available and might be present in a different repository.

For example, let's say you've worked on your master branch and made commits A through D available to another developer, as shown in Figure 10-1. Once you make your development history available to another developer, that chronicle is known as a "published history."

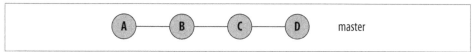

Figure 10-1. Your published history

Let's say you then do further development and produce new commits W through Z as unpublished history on the same branch. This is pictured in Figure 10-2.

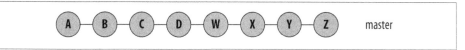

Figure 10-2. Your unpublished history

In this situation, you should be very careful to leave commits earlier than W alone. However, until you republish your master branch, there is no reason you can't modify the commits W through Z. This could include reordering, combining, and removing one or more commits or, obviously, adding even more commits as new development.

You might end up with a new and improved commit history, as depicted in Figure 10-3. In this example, commits X and Y have been combined into one new commit; commit W has been slightly altered to yield a new, similar commit W'; commit Z has been moved earlier in the history; and new commit P has been introduced.

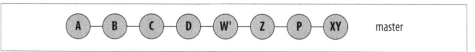

Figure 10-3. Your new history

This chapter explores techniques to help you alter and improve your commit history. It is for you to judge whether the new history is better, when the history is good enough, and when the history is ready to be published.

1. That includes you too!

Using git reset

The `git reset` command changes your repository and working directory to a known state. Specifically, `git reset` adjusts the HEAD ref to a given *commit* and, by default, updates the index to match that commit. If desired, `git reset` can also modify your working directory to mirror the revision of your project represented by the given commit.

You might construe `git reset` as "destructive" because it can overwrite and destroy changes in your working directory. Indeed, data can be lost. Even if you have a backup of your files, you might not be able to recover your work. However, the whole point of this command is to establish and recover known states for the HEAD, index, and working directory.

The `git reset` command has three main options: `--soft`, `--mixed`, and `--hard`.

`git reset --soft` *commit*

>The `--soft` changes the HEAD ref to point to the given *commit*. The contents of your index and working directory are left unchanged. This version of the command has the "least" effect, changing only the state of a symbolic reference so it points to a new commit.

`git reset --mixed` *commit*

>`--mixed` changes HEAD to point to the given *commit*. Your index contents are also modified to align with the tree structure named by *commit*, but your working directory contents are left unchanged. This version of the command leaves your index as if you had just staged all the changes represented by *commit*, and it tells you what remains modified in your working directory.

>Note that `--mixed` is the default mode for `git reset`.

`git reset --hard` *commit*

>This variant changes the HEAD ref to point to the given *commit*. The contents of your index are also modified to agree with the tree structure named by the named *commit*. Furthermore, your working directory contents are changed to reflect the state of the tree represented by the given *commit*.

>When changing your working directory, the complete directory structure is altered to correspond to the given *commit*. Modifications are lost and new files are removed. Files that are in the given *commit* but no longer exist in your working directory are reinstated.

These effects are summarized in Table 10-1.

Table 10-1. git reset option effects

Option	HEAD	Index	Working directory
--soft	Yes	No	No
--mixed	Yes	Yes	No

Option	HEAD	Index	Working directory
--hard	Yes	Yes	Yes

The git reset command also saves the original HEAD value in the ref ORIG_HEAD. This is useful, for example, if you wish to use that original HEAD's commit log message as the basis for some follow-up commit.

In terms of the object model, git reset moves the current branch HEAD within the commit graph to a specific commit. If you specify --hard, your working directory is transformed as well.

Let's look at some examples of how git reset operates.

In the following example, the file *foo.c* has been accidentally staged in the index. Using git status reveals that it will be committed:

```
$ git add foo.c
# Oops! Didn't mean to add foo.c!

$ git status
# On branch master
# Changes to be committed:
#   (use "git reset HEAD <file>..." to unstage)
#
#   new file:   foo.c
#
```

As suggested, to avoid committing the file, use git reset HEAD to unstage it:

```
$ git ls-files
foo.c
main.c

$ git reset HEAD foo.c

$ git ls-files
main.c
```

In the commit represented by HEAD, there is no pathname *foo.c* (or else git add foo.c would be superfluous). Here, git reset on HEAD for *foo.c* might be paraphrased as "With respect to file *foo.c*, make my index look like it did in HEAD, where it wasn't present." Or, in other words, "Remove foo.c from the index."

Another common use for git reset is to simply redo or eliminate the topmost commit on a branch. As an example, let's set up a branch with two commits on it.

```
$ git init
Initialized empty Git repository in /tmp/reset/.git/
$ echo foo >> master_file
$ git add master_file
$ git commit
Created initial commit e719b1f: Add master_file to master branch.
 1 files changed, 1 insertions(+), 0 deletions(-)
```

```
    create mode 100644 master_file

$ echo "more foo" >> master_file
$ git commit master_file
Created commit 0f61a54: Add more foo.
 1 files changed, 1 insertions(+), 0 deletions(-)

$ git show-branch --more=5
[master] Add more foo.
[master^] Add master_file to master branch.
```

Suppose you now realize that the second commit is wrong and you want to go back
and do it differently. This is a classic application of `git reset --mixed HEAD^`. Recall
(from "Identifying Commits" on page 67 of Chapter 6) that HEAD^ references the commit
parent of the current master HEAD and represents the state immediately prior to completing the second, faulty commit.

```
# --mixed is the default
$ git reset HEAD^
master_file: locally modified

$ git show-branch --more=5
[master] Add master_file to master branch.

$ cat master_file
foo
more foo
```

After `git reset HEAD^`, Git has left the new state of the *master_file* and the entire working
directory just as it was immediately prior to making the "Add more foo" commit.

Because the --mixed option resets the index, you must restage any changes you want
in the new commit. This gives you the opportunity to reedit *master_file*, add other files,
or perform other changes before making a new commit.

```
$ echo "even more foo" >> master_file
$ git commit master_file
Created commit 04289da: Updated foo.
 1 files changed, 2 insertions(+), 0 deletions(-)

$ git show-branch --more=5
[master] Updated foo.
[master^] Add master_file to master branch.
```

Now only two commits have been made on the master branch, not three.

Similarly, if you have no need to change the index (because everything was staged
correctly) but you want to adjust the commit message, then you can use --soft instead:

```
$ git reset --soft HEAD^
$ git commit
```

The `git reset --soft HEAD^` command moves you back to the prior place in the commit
graph but keeps the index exactly the same. Everything is staged just as it was prior to
the `git reset` command. You just get another shot at the commit message.

But now that you understand that command, don't use it. Instead, read about git commit --amend , which follows!

Suppose, however, that you want to eliminate the second commit entirely and don't care about its content. In this case, use the --hard option:

```
$ git reset --hard HEAD^
HEAD is now at e719b1f Add master_file to master branch.

$ git show-branch --more=5
[master] Add master_file to master branch.
```

Just as with --mixed, the --hard option has the effect of pulling the master branch back to its immediately prior state. It also modifies the working directory to mirror the prior (HEAD^) state as well. Specifically, the state of the *master_file* in your working directory is modified to again contain just the one, original line:

```
$ cat master_file
foo
```

Although the examples all use HEAD in some form, you can apply git reset to any commit in the repository. For example, to eliminate several commits on your current branch, you could use git reset --hard HEAD~3 or even git reset --hard master~3.

But be careful. Just because you can name other commits using a branch name, this is not the same as checking the branch out. Throughout the git reset operation, you remain on the same branch. You can alter your working directory to *look like* the head of a different branch, but you are still on your original branch.

To illustrate the use of git reset with other branches, let's add a second branch called dev and add a new file to it.

```
# Should already be on master, but be sure.
$ git checkout master
Already on "master"

$ git checkout -b dev
$ echo bar >> dev_file
$ git add dev_file
$ git commit
Created commit 7ecdc78: Add dev_file to dev branch
 1 files changed, 1 insertions(+), 0 deletions(-)
 create mode 100644 dev_file
```

Back on the master branch, there is only one file:

```
$ git checkout master
Switched to branch "master"

$ git rev-parse HEAD
e719b1fe81035c0bb5e1daaa6cd81c7350b73976
```

```
$ git rev-parse master
e719b1fe81035c0bb5e1daaa6cd81c7350b73976

$ ls
master_file
```

By using --soft, only the HEAD reference is changed.

```
# Change HEAD to point to the dev commit
$ git reset --soft dev

$ git rev-parse HEAD
7ecdc781c3eb9fbb9969b2fd18a7bd2324d08c2f

$ ls
master_file

$ git show-branch
! [dev] Add dev_file to dev branch
 * [master] Add dev_file to dev branch
--
+* [dev] Add dev_file to dev branch
```

It certainly seems as if the master branch and the dev branch are at the same commit. And, to a limited extent, they are—you're still on the master branch, and that's good —but doing this operation leaves things in a peculiar state. To wit, if you made a commit now, what would happen? The HEAD points to a commit that has the file *dev_file* in it, but that file isn't in the master branch.

```
$ echo "Funny" >> new
$ git add new
$ git commit -m "Which commit parent?"
Created commit f48bb36: Which commit parent?
 2 files changed, 1 insertions(+), 1 deletions(-)
 delete mode 100644 dev_file
 create mode 100644 new

$ git show-branch
! [dev] Add dev_file to dev branch
 * [master] Which commit parent?
--
 * [master] Which commit parent?
+* [dev] Add dev_file to dev branch
```

Git correctly added *new* and has evidently determined that *dev_file* isn't present in this commit. But why did Git *remove* this *dev_file*? Git is correct that *dev_file* isn't part of this commit, but it's misleading to say that it was removed because it was never there in the first place! So why did Git elect to remove the file? The answer is that Git uses the commit to which HEAD points at the time a new commit is made. Let's see what that was:

```
$ git cat-file -p HEAD
tree 948ed823483a0504756c2da81d2e6d8d3cd95059
parent 7ecdc781c3eb9fbb9969b2fd18a7bd2324d08c2f
author Jon Loeliger <jdl@example.com> 1229631494 -0600
```

```
committer Jon Loeliger <jdl@example.com> 1229631494 -0600

Which commit parent?
```

The parent of this commit is 7ecdc7, which you can see is the tip of the dev branch and not master. But this commit was made while on the master branch. The mix-up shouldn't come as a surprise, because master HEAD was changed to point at the dev HEAD!

At this point, you might conclude that the last commit is totally bogus and should be removed entirely. And well you should. It is a confused state that shouldn't be allowed to remain in the repository.

Just as the earlier example showed, this seems like an excellent opportunity for the git reset --hard HEAD^ command. But now things are in a bit of pickle.

The obvious approach to get to the previous version of the master HEAD is simply to use HEAD^, like this:

```
# Make sure we're on the master branch first
$ git checkout master

# BAD EXAMPLE!
# Reset back to master's prior state
$ git reset --hard HEAD^
```

So what's the problem? You just saw that HEAD's parent points to dev and *not* to the prior commit on the original master branch.

```
# Yep, HEAD^ points to the dev HEAD.  Darn.
$ git rev-parse HEAD^
7ecdc781c3eb9fbb9969b2fd18a7bd2324d08c2f
```

There are several ways of determining the commit to which the master branch should, in fact, be reset.

```
$ git log
commit f48bb36016e9709ccdd54488a0aae1487863b937
Author: Jon Loeliger <jdl@example.com>
Date:   Thu Dec 18 14:18:14 2008 -0600

Which commit parent?

commit 7ecdc781c3eb9fbb9969b2fd18a7bd2324d08c2f
Author: Jon Loeliger <jdl@example.com>
Date:   Thu Dec 18 13:05:08 2008 -0600

Add dev_file to dev branch

commit e719b1fe81035c0bb5e1daaa6cd81c7350b73976
Author: Jon Loeliger <jdl@example.com>
Date:   Thu Dec 18 11:44:45 2008 -0600

Add master_file to master branch.
```

The last commit (e719b1f) is the correct one.

Another method uses the *reflog*, which is a history of changes to refs within your repository.

```
$ git reflog
f48bb36... HEAD@{0}: commit: Which commit parent?
7ecdc78... HEAD@{1}: dev: updating HEAD
e719b1f... HEAD@{2}: checkout: moving from dev to master
7ecdc78... HEAD@{3}: commit: Add dev_file to dev branch
e719b1f... HEAD@{4}: checkout: moving from master to dev
e719b1f... HEAD@{5}: checkout: moving from master to master
e719b1f... HEAD@{6}: HEAD^: updating HEAD
04289da... HEAD@{7}: commit: Updated foo.
e719b1f... HEAD@{8}: HEAD^: updating HEAD
72c001c... HEAD@{9}: commit: Add more foo.
e719b1f... HEAD@{10}: HEAD^: updating HEAD
0f61a54... HEAD@{11}: commit: Add more foo.
```

Reading through this list, the third line down records a switch from the dev branch to the master branch. At that time, e719b1f was the master HEAD. So, once again, you could directly use e719b1f or you could use the symbolic name HEAD@{2}.

```
$ git rev-parse HEAD@{2}
e719b1fe81035c0bb5e1daaa6cd81c7350b73976
```

```
$ git reset --hard HEAD@{2}
HEAD is now at e719b1f Add master_file to master branch.
```

```
$ git show-branch
! [dev] Add dev_file to dev branch
 * [master] Add master_file to master branch.
--
+  [dev] Add dev_file to dev branch
+* [master] Add master_file to master branch.
```

As just shown, the reflog can frequently be used to help locate prior state information for refs such as branch names.

Similarly, it is wrong to try and change branches using git reset --hard.

```
$ git reset --hard dev
HEAD is now at 7ecdc78 Add dev_file to dev branch
```

```
$ ls
dev_file  master_file
```

Again, this *appears* to be correct. In this case, the working directory has even been populated with the correct files from the dev branch. But it didn't really work. The master branch remains current.

```
$ git branch
  dev
* master
```

Just as in the previous example, a commit at this point would cause the graph to be confused. And, as before, the proper action is to determine the correct state and reset to that:

```
$ git reset --hard e719b1f
```

Or, possibly, even:

```
$ git reset --soft e719b1f
```

Using --soft, the working directory is not modified, which means that your working directory now represents the total content (files and directories) present in the tip of the dev branch. Furthermore, because HEAD now correctly points to the original tip of the master branch as it used to, a commit at *this* point would yield a valid graph with the new master state identical to the tip of the dev branch.

That may or may not be what you want, of course. But you can do it.

Using git cherry-pick

The command git cherry-pick *commit* applies the changes introduced by the named *commit* on the current branch. It will introduce a new, distinct commit. Strictly speaking, using git cherry-pick doesn't *alter* the existing history within a repository; instead, it adds to the history.

As with other Git operations that introduce changes via the process of applying a diff, you may need to resolve conflicts to fully apply the changes from the given *commit*.

The command git cherry-pick is typically used to introduce particular commits from one branch within a repository onto a different branch. A common use is to forward- or back-port commits from a maintenance branch to a development branch.

In Figure 10-4, the dev branch has normal development, whereas the rel_2.3 contains commits for the maintenance of release 2.3.

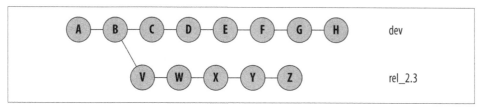

Figure 10-4. Before git cherry-pick of one commit

During the course of normal development, a bug is fixed on the development line with commit F. If that bug turns out to be present in the 2.3 release also, the bug fix, F, can be made to the rel_2.3 branch using git cherry-pick:

```
$ git checkout rel_2.3

$ git cherry-pick dev~2    # commit F, above
```

After `cherry-pick`, the graph resembles Figure 10-5.

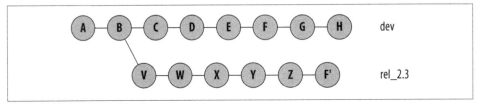

Figure 10-5. After git cherry-pick of one commit

In Figure 10-5, commit `F'` is substantially similar to commit F, but it is a new commit and will have to be adjusted—perhaps with conflict resolutions—to account for its application to commit Z rather than commit E. None of the commits following F are applied after `F'`; only the named commit is picked and applied.

Another common use for `cherry-pick` is to rebuild a series of commits by selectively picking a batch from one branch and introducing them onto a new branch.

Suppose you had a series of commits on your development branch, `my_dev`, as shown in Figure 10-6, and you wanted to introduce them onto the `master` branch but in a substantially different order.

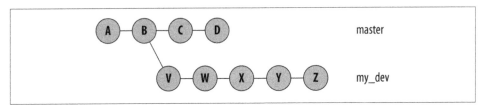

Figure 10-6. Before git cherry-pick shuffle

To apply them on the `master` branch in the order Y, W, X, Z, you could use the following commands.

```
$ git checkout master
$ git cherry-pick my_dev^       # Y
$ git cherry-pick my_dev~3      # W
$ git cherry-pick my_dev~2      # X
$ git cherry-pick my_dev        # Z
```

Afterward, your commit history would look something like Figure 10-7.

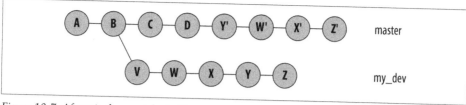

Figure 10-7. After git cherry-pick shuffle

In situations like this, where the order of commits undergoes fairly volatile changes, it is quite likely that you will have to resolve conflicts. It depends entirely on the relationship between the commits. If they are highly coupled and change overlapping lines, then you will have conflicts that need to be resolved. If they are highly independent, then you will be able to move them around quite readily.

Originally, the `git cherry-pick` command selected and reapplied one commit at a time. However, in later versions of Git, `git cherry-pick` allowed a range of commits to be selected and reapplied in a single command. For example, the following command:

```
# on branch master
$ git cherry-pick X..Z
```

would apply new commits `X'`, `Y'`, and `Z'` on the `master` branch. This is particularly handy in porting or moving a large sequence of commits from one line of development to another without necessarily using the entire source branch at one time.

Using git revert

The `git revert` *commit* command is substantially similar to the command `git cherry-pick` *commit* with one important difference: it applies the *inverse* of the given *commit*. Thus, this command is used to introduce a new commit that reverses the effects of a given commit.

Like `git cherry-pick`, the `revert` doesn't *alter* the existing history within a repository. Instead it adds a new commit to the history.

A common application for `git revert` is to "undo" the effects of a commit that is buried, perhaps deeply, in the history of a branch. In Figure 10-8, a history of changes have been built up on the master branch. For some reason, perhaps through testing, commit D has been deemed faulty.

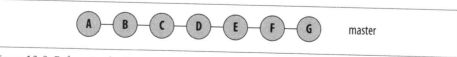

Figure 10-8. Before simple git revert

One way to fix the situation is to simply make edits to undo the effects of D and then commit the reversal directly. You might also note in your commit message that the purpose of this commit is to revert the changes that were caused by the earlier commit.

An easier approach is to simply run git revert:

```
$ git revert master~3    # commit D
```

The result look likes Figure 10-9, where commit D' is the inverse of commit D.

Figure 10-9. After simple git revert

reset, revert, and checkout

The three Git commands reset, revert, and checkout can be somewhat confusing, because all appear to perform similar operations. Another reason these three commands can be confusing is that other VCSs have different meanings for the words reset, revert, and checkout.

However, there are some good guidelines and rules for when each command should and should not be used.

If you want to change to a different branch, use git checkout. Your current branch and HEAD ref change to match the tip of the given branch.

The git reset command does not change your branch. However, if you supply the name of a branch, it will change the state of your current working directory to *look* like the tip of the named branch. In other words, git reset is intended to reset the current branch's HEAD reference.

Because git reset --hard is designed to recover to a known state, it is also capable of clearing out failed or stale merge efforts, whereas git checkout will not. Thus, if there were a pending merge commit and you attempted to recover using git checkout instead of git reset --hard, your next commit would erroneously be a merge commit.

The confusion with git checkout is due to its additional ability to extract a file from the object store and put it into your working directory, possibly replacing a version in your working directory in the process. Sometimes the version of that file is one corresponding to the current HEAD version and sometimes it is an earlier version.

```
# Checkout file.c from index
$ git checkout -- path/to/file.c

# Checkout file.c from rev v2.3
$ git checkout v2.3 -- some/file.c
```

Git calls this "checking out a path."

In the former case, obtaining the current version from the object store appears to be a form of a "reset" operation—that is, your local working directory edits of the file are discarded because the file is reset to its current, HEAD version. That is double-plus ungood Git thinking.

In the latter case, an earlier version of the file is pulled out of the object store and placed into your working directory. This has the appearance of being a "revert" operation on the file. That, too, is double-plus ungood Git thinking.

In both cases, it is improper to think of the operation as a Git reset or a revert. In both cases, the file is "checked out" from a particular commit: HEAD and v2.3, respectively.

The git revert command works on full commits, not on files.

If another developer has cloned your repository or fetched some of your commits, there are implications for changing the commit history. In this case, you probably should not use commands that *alter history* within your repository. Instead, use git revert; do not use git reset nor the git commit --amend command described in the next section.

Changing the Top Commit

One of the easiest ways to alter the most recent commit on your current branch is with git commit --amend. Typically, amend implies that the commit has fundamentally the same *content* but some aspect requires adjustment or tidying. The actual commit object that is introduced into the object store will, of course, be different.

A frequent use of git commit --amend is to fix typos immediately after a commit. This is not the only use, however as with any commit, this command can amend any file or files in the repository and, indeed, can add or delete a file as part of the new commit.

As with a normal git commit command, git commit --amend prompts you with an editor session in which you may also alter the commit message.

For example, suppose you are working on a speech and made the following recent commit:

```
$ git show
commit 0ba161a94e03ab1e2b27c2e65e4cbef476d04f5d
Author: Jon Loeliger <jdl@example.com>
Date:   Thu Jun 26 15:14:03 2008 -0500

Initial speech

diff --git a/speech.txt b/speech.txt
new file mode 100644
index 0000000..310bcf9
--- /dev/null
+++ b/speech.txt
@@ -0,0 +1,5 @@
+Three score and seven years ago
+our fathers brought forth on this continent,
```

```
+a new nation, conceived in Liberty,
+and dedicated to the proposition
+that all men are created equal.
```

At this point, the commit is stored in Git's object repository, albeit with small errors in the prose. To make corrections, you could simply edit the file again and make a second commit. That would leave a history like this:

```
$ git show-branch --more=5
[master] Fix timeline typo
[master^] Initial speech
```

However, if you wish to leave a slightly cleaner commit history in your repository, then you can alter this commit directly and replace it.

To do this, fix the file in your working directory. Correct the typos and add or remove files as needed. As with any commit, update the index with your changes using commands such as git add or git rm. Then issue the git commit --amend command.

```
# edit speech.txt as needed.

$ git diff
diff --git a/speech.txt b/speech.txt
index 310bcf9..7328a76 100644
--- a/speech.txt
+++ b/speech.txt
@@ -1,5 +1,5 @@
-Three score and seven years ago
+Four score and seven years ago
 our fathers brought forth on this continent,
 a new nation, conceived in Liberty,
 and dedicated to the proposition
-that all men are created equal.
+that all men and women are created equal.

$ git add speech.txt

$ git commit --amend

# Also edit the "Initial speech" commit message if desired
# In this example it was changed a bit...
```

With an amendment, anyone can see that the original commit has been modified and that it replaces the existing commit.

```
$ git show-branch --more=5
[master] Initial speech that sounds familiar.

$ git show
commit 47d849c61919f05da1acf983746f205d2cdb0055
Author: Jon Loeliger <jdl@example.com>
Date:   Thu Jun 26 15:14:03 2008 -0500

    Initial speech that sounds familiar.

diff --git a/speech.txt b/speech.txt
```

```
new file mode 100644
index 0000000..7328a76
--- /dev/null
+++ b/speech.txt
@@ -0,0 +1,5 @@
+Four score and seven years ago
+our fathers brought forth on this continent,
+a new nation, conceived in Liberty,
+and dedicated to the proposition
+that all men and women are created equal.
```

This command can edit the meta-information on a commit. For example, by specifying `--author` you can alter the author of the commit:

```
$ git commit --amend --author "Bob Miller <kbob@example.com>"
# ...just close the editor...

$ git log
commit 0e2a14f933a3aaff9edd848a862e783d986f149f
Author: Bob Miller <kbob@example.com>
Date:   Thu Jun 26 15:14:03 2008 -0500

Initial speech that sounds familiar.
```

Pictorially, altering the top commit using `git commit --amend` changes the commit graph from that shown in Figure 10-10 to that shown in Figure 10-11.

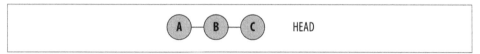

Figure 10-10. Commit graph before git commit --amend

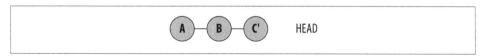

Figure 10-11. Commit graph after git commit --amend

Here, the substance of the `C` commit is still the same, but it has been altered to obtain `C'`. The `HEAD` ref has been changed from the old commit, `C`, so that it points to the replacement ref, `C'`.

Rebasing Commits

The `git rebase` command is used to alter where a sequence of commits is based. This command requires at least the name of the other branch onto which your commits will be relocated. By default, the commits from the current branch that are not already on the other branch are rebased.

A common use for `git rebase` is to keep a series of commits that you are developing up-to-date with respect to another branch, usually a `master` branch or a tracking branch from another repository.

In Figure 10-12, two branches have been developed. Originally, the `topic` branch started on the `master` branch when it was at commit B. In the meantime, it has progressed to commit E.

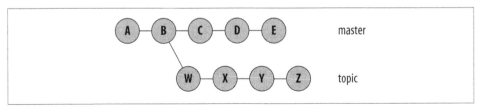

Figure 10-12. Before git rebase

You can keep your commit series up-to-date with respect to the `master` branch by writing the commits so that they are based on commit E rather than B. Because the `topic` branch needs to be the current branch, you can use either:

```
$ git checkout topic
$ git rebase master
```

or

```
$ git rebase master topic
```

After the rebase operation is complete, the new commit graph resembles Figure 10-13.

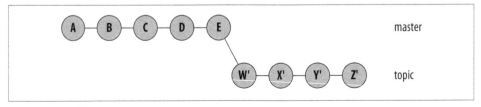

Figure 10-13. After git rebase

Using the `git rebase` command in situations like the one shown in Figure 10-12 is often called *forward porting*. In this example, the topic branch `topic` has been forward ported to the `master` branch.

There is no magic to a rebase being a forward or a backward port; both are possible using `git rebase`. The interpretation is usually left to a more fundamental understanding of what functionality is considered ahead of or behind another functionality.

In the context of a repository that you have cloned from somewhere else, it is common to forward port your development branch or branches onto the `origin/master` tracking branch like this using the `git rebase` operation. In Chapter 12, you will see how this operation is requested frequently by a repository maintainer using a phrase such as "Please rebase your patch to the tip-of-master."

The `git rebase` command may also be used to completely transplant a line of development from one branch to an entirely different branch using the `--onto` option.

For example, suppose you've developed a new feature on the `feature` branch with the commits P and Q, which were based on the `maint` branch as shown in Figure 10-14. To transplant the P and Q commits on the `feature` branch from the `maint` to the `master` branch, issue the command:

```
$ git rebase --onto master maint^ feature
```

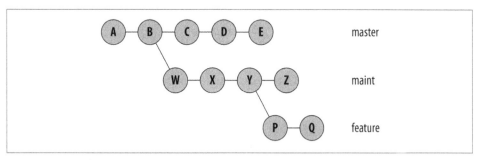

Figure 10-14. Before git rebase transplant

The resulting commit graph looks like Figure 10-15.

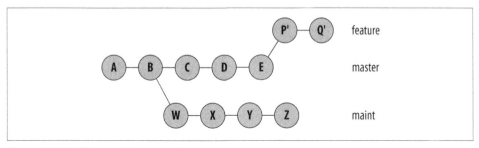

Figure 10-15. After git rebase transplant

The rebase operation relocates commits one at a time from each respective original commit location to a new commit base. As a result, each commit that is moved might have conflicts to resolve.

If a conflict is found, the `rebase` operation suspends its processing temporarily so you can resolve the conflict. Any conflict during the rebase process that needs to be resolved should be handled as described in "A Merge with a Conflict" on page 124 of Chapter 9.

Once all conflicts are resolved and the index has been updated with the results, the rebase operation can be resumed using the `git rebase --continue` command. The command resumes its operation by committing the resolved conflict and proceeding to the next commit in the series being rebased.

If, while inspecting a rebase conflict, you decide that this particular commit really isn't necessary, then you can also instruct the `git rebase` command to simply skip this commit and move to the next by using `git rebase --skip`. This may not be the correct thing to do, especially if subsequent commits in the series really depend on the changes introduced by this one. The problems are likely to snowball in this case, so it's better to truly resolve the conflict.

Finally, if the `rebase` operation turns out to be the totally wrong thing to do, `git rebase --abort` abandons the operation and restores the repository to the state prior to issuing the original `git rebase`.

Using git rebase -i

Suppose you start writing a haiku and manage to compose two full lines before checking it in:

```
$ git init
Initialized empty Git repository in .git/
$ git config user.email "jdl@example.com"

$ cat haiku
Talk about colour
No jealous behaviour here

$ git add haiku
$ git commit -m "Start my haiku"
Created initial commit a75f74e: Start my haiku
 1 files changed, 2 insertions(+), 0 deletions(-)
 create mode 100644 haiku
```

Your writing continues, but you decide you really should use the American spelling of color instead of the British. So, you make a commit to change it:

```
$ git diff
diff --git a/haiku b/haiku
index 088bea0..958aff0 100644
--- a/haiku
+++ b/haiku
@@ -1,2 +1,2 @@
-Talk about colour
+Talk about color
 No jealous behaviour here

$ git commit -a -m "Use color instead of colour"
Created commit 3d0f83b: Use color instead of colour
 1 files changed, 1 insertions(+), 1 deletions(-)
```

Finally, you develop the final line and commit it:

```
$ git diff
diff --git a/haiku b/haiku
index 958aff0..cdeddf9 100644
--- a/haiku
+++ b/haiku
@@ -1,2 +1,3 @@
 Talk about color
 No jealous behaviour here
+I favour red wine

$ git commit -a -m "Finish my colour haiku"
Created commit 799dba3: Finish my colour haiku
 1 files changed, 1 insertions(+), 0 deletions(-)
```

However, again you have spelling quandary and decide to change all British "ou" spellings to the American "o" spelling:

```
$ git diff
diff --git a/haiku b/haiku
index cdeddf9..064c1b5 100644
--- a/haiku
+++ b/haiku
@@ -1,3 +1,3 @@
 Talk about color
-No jealous behaviour here
-I favour red wine
+No jealous behavior here
+I favor red wine

$ git commit -a -m "Use American spellings"
Created commit b61b041: Use American spellings
 1 files changed, 2 insertions(+), 2 deletions(-)
```

At this point, you've accumulated a history of commits that looks like this:

```
$ git show-branch --more=4
[master] Use American spellings
[master^] Finish my colour haiku
[master~2] Use color instead of colour
[master~3] Start my haiku
```

After looking at the commit sequence or receiving review feedback, you decide that you prefer to complete the haiku before correcting it and want the following commit history:

```
[master] Use American spellings
[master^] Use color instead of colour
[master~2] Finish my colour haiku
[master~3] Start my haiku
```

But then you also notice that there's no good reason to have two similar commits that correct the spellings of different words. Thus, you would also like to master the *squash* and master^ into just one commit.

```
[master] Use American spellings
[master^] Finish my colour haiku
[master~2] Start my haiku
```

Reordering, editing, removing, squashing multiple commits into one, and splitting a commit into several are all easily performed by the `git rebase` command using the `-i` or `--interactive` option. This command allows you to modify the commits that make up a branch and place them back onto the same branch or onto a different branch.

A typical use, and one apropos for this example, modifies the same branch in place. In this case there are three changesets between four commits to be modified; `git rebase -i` needs to be told the name of the commit beyond which you actually intend to change.

```
$ git rebase -i master~3
```

You will be placed in an editor on a file that looks like this:

```
pick 3d0f83b Use color instead of colour
pick 799dba3 Finish my colour haiku
pick b61b041 Use American spellings

# Rebase a75f74e..b61b041 onto a75f74e
#
# Commands:
#  pick = use commit
#  edit = use commit, but stop for amending
#  squash = use commit, but meld into previous commit
#
# If you remove a line here THAT COMMIT WILL BE LOST.
# However, if you remove everything, the rebase will be aborted.
#
```

The first three lines list the commits within the editable commit range you specified on the command line. The commits are initially listed in order from oldest to most recent and have the *pick* verb on each one. If you were to leave the editor now, each commit would be *picked* (in order), applied to the target branch, and committed. The lines preceded by a # are helpful reminders and comments that are ignored by the program.

At this point, however, you are free to reorder the commits, squash commits together, change a commit, or delete one entirely. To follow the listed steps, simply reorder the commits in your editor as follows and exit it:

```
pick 799dba3 Finish my colour haiku
pick 3d0f83b Use color instead of colour
pick b61b041 Use American spellings
```

Recall that the very first commit for the rebase is the "Start my haiku" commit. The next commit will become "Finish my colour haiku," followed by the "Use color ..." and "Use American ..." commits.

```
$ git rebase -i master~3

# reorder the first two commits and exit your editor
```

```
Successfully rebased and updated refs/heads/master.

$ git show-branch --more=4
[master] Use American spellings
[master^] Use color instead of colour
[master~2] Finish my colour haiku
[master~3] Start my haiku
```

Here, the history of commits has been rewritten; the two spelling commits are together and the two writing commits are together.

Still following the outlined order, your next step is to *squash* the two spelling commits into just one commit. Again, issue the `git rebase -i master~3` command. This time, convert the commit list from

```
pick d83f7ed Finish my colour haiku
pick 1f7342b Use color instead of colour
pick 1915dae Use American spellings
```

to

```
pick d83f7ed Finish my colour haiku
pick 1f7342b Use color instead of colour
squash 1915dae Use American spellings
```

The third commit will be squashed into the immediately preceding commit, and the new commit log message template will be formed from the combination of the commits being squashed together.

In this example, the two commit log messages are joined and offered in an editor:

```
# This is a combination of two commits.
# The first commits message is:

Use color instead of colour

# This is the 2nd commit message:

Use American spellings
```

These messages can be edited down to just

```
Use American spellings
```

Again, all # lines are ignored.

Finally, the results of the rebase sequence can be seen:

```
$ git rebase -i master~3

# squash and rewrite the commit log message

Created commit cf27784: Use American spellings
 1 files changed, 3 insertions(+), 3 deletions(-)
Successfully rebased and updated refs/heads/master.
```

```
$ git show-branch --more=4
[master] Use American spellings
[master^] Finish my colour haiku
[master~2] Start my haiku
```

Although the reordering and squash steps demonstrated here occurred in two separate invocations of `git rebase -i master~3`, the two phases could have been performed in one. It is also perfectly valid to squash multiple sequential commits into one commit in a single step.

rebase Versus merge

In addition to the problem of simply altering history, the rebase operation has further ramifications of which you should be aware.

Rebasing a sequence of commits to the tip of a branch is similar to merging the two branches; in either case, the new head of that branch will have the combined effect of both branches represented.

You might ask yourself "Should I use merge or rebase on my sequence of commits?" In Chapter 12, this will become an important question—especially when multiple developers, repositories, and branches come into play.

The process of rebasing a sequence of commits causes Git to generate an entirely new sequences of commits. They have new SHA1 commit IDs, are based on a new initial state, and represent different diffs even though they involve changes that achieve the same ultimate state.

When faced with a situation like that of Figure 10-12, rebasing it into Figure 10-13 doesn't present a problem because no other commit relies on the branch being rebased. However, even within your own repository you might have additional branches based on the one you wish to rebase. Consider the graph shown in Figure 10-16.

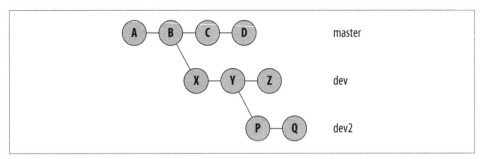

Figure 10-16. Before git rebase multibranch

You might think that executing the command:

```
# Move onto tip of master the dev branch
$ git rebase master dev
```

would yield the graph in Figure 10-17. But it does not. Your first clue that it didn't happen comes from the command's output.

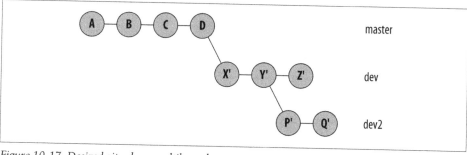

Figure 10-17. Desired git rebase multibranch

```
$ git rebase master dev
First, rewinding head to replay your work on top of it...
Applying: X
Applying: Y
Applying: Z
```

This says that Git applied the commits for X, Y, and Z only. Nothing was said about P or Q, and instead you obtain the graph in Figure 10-18.

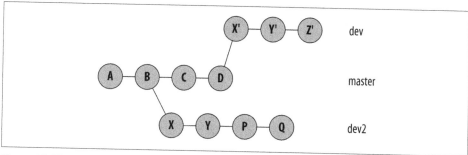

Figure 10-18. Actual git rebase multibranch

The commits X', Y', and Z' are the new versions of the old commits that stem from B. The old X and Y commits both still exist in the graph because they are still reachable from the dev2 branch. However, the original Z commit has been removed because it is no longer reachable. The branch name that *was* pointing to it has been moved to the new version of that commit.

The branch history now looks like it has duplicate commit messages in it, too:

```
$ git show-branch
* [dev] Z
 ! [dev2] Q
  ! [master] D
---
```

```
 *   [dev] Z
 *   [dev^] Y
 *   [dev~2] X
 * + [master] D
 * + [master^] C
   + [dev2] Q
   + [dev2^] P
   + [dev2~2] Y
   + [dev2~3] X
*++ [master~2] B
```

But remember, these are different commits that do essentially the same change. If you merge a branch with one of the new commits into another branch that has one of the old commits, Git has no way of knowing that you're applying the same change twice. The result is duplicate entries in `git log`, most likely a merge conflict, and general confusion. It's a situation that you should find a way to clean up.

If this resulting graph is actually what you want, then you're done. More likely, moving the entire branch (including subbranches) is what you really want. To achieve that graph, you will, in turn, need to rebase the **dev2** branch on the new Y' commit on the dev branch:

```
$ git rebase dev^ dev2
First, rewinding head to replay your work on top of it...
Applying: P
Applying: Q

$ git show-branch
! [dev] Z
 * [dev2] Q
  ! [master] D
---
 *   [dev2] Q
 *   [dev2^] P
 +   [dev] Z
+*   [dev2~2] Y
+*   [dev2~3] X
+*+ [master] D
```

And this is the graph shown in Figure 10-17.

Another situation that can be extremely confusing is rebasing a branch that has a merge on it. For example, suppose you had a branch structure like that shown in Figure 10-19.

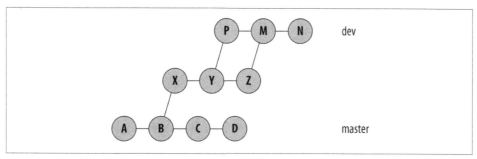

Figure 10-19. Before git rebase merge

If you want to move the entire dev branch structure from commit N down through to commit X off of B and onto D, as shown in Figure 10-20, then you might expect simply to use the command git rebase master dev.

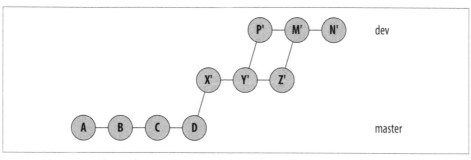

Figure 10-20. Desired git rebase merge

Again, however, that command yields some surprising results:

```
$ git rebase master dev
First, rewinding head to replay your work on top of it...
Applying: X
Applying: Y
Applying: Z
Applying: P
Applying: N
```

It *looks* like it did the right thing. After all, Git says that it applied all the (nonmerge) commit changes. But did it really get things right?

```
$ git show-branch
* [dev] N
 ! [master] D
--
*  [dev] N
*  [dev^] P
*  [dev~2] Z
*  [dev~3] Y
```

```
*  [dev~4] X
*+ [master] D
```

All those commits are now in one long string!

What happened here?

Git needs to move the portion of the graph reachable from dev back to the merge base at B, so it found the commits in the range master..dev. To list all those commits, Git performs a topological sort on that portion of the graph to produce a linearized sequence of all the commits in that range. Once that sequence has been determined, Git applies the commits one at a time starting on the target commit, D. Thus, we say that "Rebase has linearized the original branch history (with merges) onto the master branch," as shown in Figure 10-21.

Again, if that is what you wanted or if you don't care that the graph shape has been altered, then you are done. But if in such cases you want to explicitly preserve the branching and merging structure of the entire branch being rebased, then use the --preserve-merges option.

```
# This option is a version 1.6.1 feature

$ git rebase --preserve-merges master dev
Successfully rebased and updated refs/heads/dev.
```

Using my Git alias from "Configuring an Alias" on page 30 of Chapter 3, we can see that the resulting graph structure maintains the original merge structure.

```
$ git show-graph
* 061f9fd... N
*   f669404... Merge branch 'dev2' into dev
|\
| * c386cfc... Z
* | 38ab25e... P
|/
* b93ad42... Y
* 65be7f1... X
* e3b9e22... D
* f2b96c4... C
* 8619681... B
* d6fba18... A
```

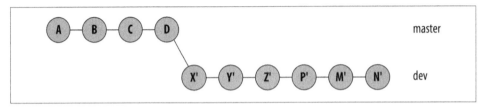

Figure 10-21. git rebase merge after linearization

And this looks like the graph in Figure 10-20.

Some of the principles for answering the rebase-versus-merge question apply equally to your own repository as they do to a distributed or multirepository scenario. In Chapter 13, you can read about the additional implications that affect developers using other repositories.

Depending on your development style and your ultimate intent, having the original branch development history linearized when it is rebased may or may not be acceptable. If you have already published or provided the commits on the branch that you wish to rebase, consider the negative ramifications on others.

If the rebase operation isn't the right choice and you still need the branch changes, then merging may be the correct choice.

The important concepts to remember are:

- Rebase rewrites commits as new commits.
- Old commits that are no longer reachable are gone.
- Any user of one of the old, pre-rebase commits might be stranded.
- If you have a branch that uses a pre-rebase commit, you might need to rebase it in turn.
- If there is a user of a pre-rebase commit in a different repository, he still has a copy of that commit even though it has moved in your repository; the user will now have to fix up his commit history, too.

## CHAPTER 11

The Stash and the Reflog

The Stash

Do you ever feel overwhelmed in your daily development cycle when the constant interruptions, demands for bug fixes, and requests from coworkers or managers all pile up and clutter the *real* work you are trying to do? If so, the *stash* was designed to help you!

The stash is a mechanism for capturing your work in progress, allowing you to save it and return to it later when convenient. Sure, you can already do that using the existing branch and commit mechanisms within Git, but the stash is a quick convenience mechanism that allows a complete and thorough capturing of your index and working directory in one simple command. It leaves your repository clean, uncluttered, and ready for an alternate development direction. Another single command restores that index and working directory state completely, allowing you to resume where you left off.

Let's see how the stash works with the canonical use case: the so-called "interrupted work flow."

In this scenario, you are happily working in your Git repository and have changed several files and maybe even staged a few in the index. Then, some interruption happens. Perhaps a critical bug is discovered and lands on your plate and must be fixed immediately. Perhaps your team lead has suddenly prioritized a new feature over everything else and insists you drop everything to work on it. Whatever the circumstance, you realize you must stash everything, clean your slate and work tree, and start afresh. This is a perfect opportunity for `git stash`!

```
$ cd the-git-project
# edit a lot, in the middle of something

# High-Priority Work-flow Interrupt!
# Must drop everything and do Something Else now!

$ git stash save
```

```
# edit high-priority change
$ git commit -a -m "Fixed High-Priority issue"

$ git stash pop
```

And resume where you were!

The default and optional operation to `git stash` is `save`. Git also supplies a default log message when saving a stash, but you can supply your own to better remind you what you were doing. Just supply it in the command after the then-required **save** argument:

```
$ git stash save "WIP: Doing real work on my stuff"
```

The acronym `WIP` is a common abbreviation used in these situations meaning "work in progress."

To achieve the same effect with other, more basic Git commands requires manual creation of a new branch on which you commit all of your modifications, re-establishing your previous branch to continue your work, and then later recovering your saved branch state on top of your new working directory. For the curious, that process is roughly this sequence:

```
# ... normal development process interrupted ...

# Create new branch on which current state is stored.
$ git checkout -b saved_state
$ git commit -a -m "Saved state"

# Back to previous branch for immediate update.
$ git checkout master

# edit emergency fix
$ git commit -a -m "Fix something."

# Recover saved state on top of working directory.
$ git checkout saved_state
$ git reset --soft HEAD^

# ... resume working where we left off above ...
```

That process is sensitive to completeness and attention to detail. All of your changes have to be captured when you save your state, and the restoration process can be disrupted if you forget to move your HEAD back as well.

The `git stash save` command will save your current index and working directory state and clear them out so that they again match the head of your current branch. Although this operation gives the appearance that your modified files and any files updated into the index using, for example, `git add` or `git rm`, have been lost, they have not. Instead, the contents of your index and working directory are actually stored as independent, regular commits and are accessible through the ref `refs/stash`.

```
$ git show-branch stash
[stash] WIP on master: 3889def Some initial files.
```

As you might surmise by the use of pop to restore your state, the two basic stash commands, git stash save and git stash pop, implement a stack of stash states. That allows your interrupted work flow to be interrupted yet again! Each stashed context on the stack can be managed independently of your regular commit process.

The git stash pop command restores the context saved by a previous save operation on top of your current working directory and index. And by restore here, I mean that the pop operation takes the stash content and *merges* those changes into the current state rather than just overwriting or replacing files. Nice, huh?

You can only git stash pop into a clean working directory. Even then, the command may or may not fully succeed in recreating the full state you originally had at the time it was saved. Because the application of the saved context can be performed on top of a different commit, merging may be required, complete with possible user resolution of any conflicts.

After a successful pop operation, Git will automatically remove your saved state from the stack of saved states. That is, once applied, the stash state will be "dropped." However, when conflict resolution is needed, Git will not automatically drop the state, just in case you want to try a different approach or want to restore it onto a different commit. Once you clear the merge conflicts and want to proceed, you should use the git stash drop to remove it from the stash stack. Otherwise, Git will maintain an ever growing[1] stack of contexts.

If you just want to recreate the context you have saved in a stash state without dropping it from the stack, use git stash apply. Thus, a pop command is a successful apply followed by a drop.

 In fact, you can use git stash apply to apply the same saved stashed context onto several different commits prior to dropping it from the stack.

However, you should consider carefully if you want to use git stash apply or git stash pop to regain the contents of a stash. Will you ever need it again? If not, pop it. Clean the stashed content and referents out of your object store.

The git stash list command lists the stack of saved contexts from most to least recent.

```
$ cd my-repo
$ ls
file1   file2

$ echo "some foo" >> file1

$ git status
```

---

1. Technically, not growing without bounds. The stash is subject to reflog expiration and garbage collection.

```
# On branch master
# Changes not staged for commit:
#   (use "git add <file>..." to update what will be committed)
#   (use "git checkout -- <file>..." to discard changes in working directory)
#
#    modified:   file1
#
no changes added to commit (use "git add" and/or "git commit -a")

$ git stash save "Tinkered file1"
Saved working directory and index state On master: Tinkered file1
HEAD is now at 3889def Add some files

$ git commit --dry-run
# On branch master
nothing to commit (working directory clean)

$ echo "some bar" >> file2

$ git stash save "Messed with file2"
Saved working directory and index state On master: Messed with file2
HEAD is now at 3889def Add some files

$ git stash list
stash@{0}: On master: Messed with file2
stash@{1}: On master: Tinkered file1
```

Git always numbers the stash entries with the most recent entry being zero. As entries get older, they increase in numerical order. And yes, the different stash entry names are stash@{0} and stash@{1}, as explained in "The Reflog" on page 189.

The git stash show command shows the index and file changes recorded for a given stash entry, relative to its parent commit.

```
$ git stash show
 file2 |   1 +
 1 files changed, 1 insertions(+), 0 deletions(-)
```

That summary may or may not be the extent of the information you sought. If not, adding -p to see the diffs might be more useful. Note that by default the git stash show command shows the most recent stash entry, stash@{0}.

Because the changes that contribute to making a stash state are relative to a particular commit, showing the state is a state-to-state comparison suitable for git diff, rather than a sequence of commit states suitable for git log. Thus, all the options for git diff may also be supplied to git stash show as well. As we saw previously, --stat is the default, but other options are valid, too. Here, -p is used to obtain the patch differences for a given stash state.

```
$ git stash show -p stash@{1}
diff --git a/file1 b/file1
index 257cc56..f9e62e5 100644
--- a/file1
+++ b/file1
```

```
@@ -1 +1,2 @@
 foo
+some foo
```

Another classic use case for git stash is the so-called "pull into a dirty tree" scenario.

Until you are familiar with the use of remote repositories and pulling changes (see "Getting Repository Updates" on page 212), this might not make sense yet. But it goes like this. You're developing in your local repository and have made several commits. You still have some modified files that haven't been committed yet, but you realize there are upstream changes that you want. If you have conflicting modifications, a simple git pull will fail, refusing to overwrite your local changes. One quick way to work around this problem uses git stash.

```
$ git pull
# ... pull fails due to merge conflicts ...

$ git stash save
$ git pull
$ git stash pop
```

At this point you may or may not need to resolve conflicts created by the pop.

In case you have new, uncommitted (and hence "untracked") files as part of your local development, it is possible that a git pull that would also introduce a file of the same name might fail, thus not wanting to overwrite your version of the new file. In this case, add the --include-untracked option on your git stash so that it *also* stashes your new, untracked files along with the rest of your modifications. That will ensure a completely clean working directory for the pull.

The --all option will gather up the untracked files as well as the explicitly ignored files from the *.gitignore* and *exclude* files.

Finally, for more complex stashing operations where you wish to selectively choose which hunks should be stashed, use the -p or --patch option.

In another similar scenario, git stash can be used when you want to move modified work out of the way, enabling a clean pull --rebase. This would happen typically just prior to pushing your local commits upstream.

```
# ... edit and commit ...
# ... more editing and working...

$ git commit --dry-run
# On branch master
# Your branch is ahead of 'origin/master' by 2 commits.
#
# Changed but not updated:
#   (use "git add <file>..." to update what will be committed)
#   (use "git checkout -- <file>..." to discard changes in working directory)
#
#       modified:   file1.h
#       modified:   file1.c
```

```
#
no changes added to commit (use "git add" and/or "git commit -a")
```

At this point you may decide the commits you have already made should go upstream, but you also want to leave the modified files here in your work directory. However, git refuses to pull:

```
$ git pull --rebase
file1.h: needs update
file1.c: needs update
refusing to pull with rebase: your working tree is not up-to-date
```

This scenario isn't as contrived as it might seem at first. For example, I frequently work in a repository where I want to have modifications to a *Makefile*, perhaps to enable debugging, or I need to modify some configuration options for a build. I don't want to commit those changes, and I don't want to lose them between updates from a remote repository. I just want them to linger here in my working directory.

Again, this is where `git stash` helps:

```
$ git stash save
Saved working directory and index state WIP on master: 5955d14 Some commit log.
HEAD is now at 5955d14 Some commit log.

$ git pull --rebase
remote: Counting objects: 63, done.
remote: Compressing objects: 100% (43/43), done.
remote: Total 43 (delta 36), reused 0 (delta 0)
Unpacking objects: 100% (43/43), done.
From ssh://git/var/git/my_repo
   871746b..6687d58  master      -> origin/master
First, rewinding head to replay your work on top of it...
Applying: A fix for a bug.
Applying: The fix for something else.
```

After you pull in upstream commits and rebase your local commits on top of them, your repository is in good shape to send your work upstream. If desired, you can readily push them now:

```
# Push upstream now if desired!
$ git push
```

or after restoring your previous working directory state:

```
$ git stash pop
Auto-merging file1.h
# On branch master
# Your branch is ahead of 'origin/master' by 2 commits.
#
# Changed but not updated:
#   (use "git add <file>..." to update what will be committed)
#   (use "git checkout -- <file>..." to discard changes in working directory)
#
#       modified:   file1.h
#       modified:   file1.c
#
```

```
no changes added to commit (use "git add" and/or "git commit -a")
Dropped refs/stash@{0} (7e2546f5808a95a2e6934fcffb5548651badf00d)

$ git push
```

If you decide to `git push` after popping your stash, remember that only completed, committed work will be pushed. There's no need to worry about pushing your partial, uncommitted work. There is also no need to worry about pushing your stashed content: the stash is purely a local notion.

Sometimes stashing your changes leads to a whole sequence of development on your branch and, ultimately, restoring your stashed state on top of all those changes may not make direct sense. In addition, merge conflicts might make popping hard to do. Nonetheless, you may still want to recover the work you stashed. In situations like this, git offers the `git stash branch` command to help you. This command converts the contents of a saved stash into a new branch based on the commit that was current at the time the stash entry was made.

Let's see how that works on a repository with a bit of history in it.

```
$ git log --pretty=one --abbrev-commit
d5ef6c9 Some commit.
efe990c Initial commit.
```

Now, some files are modified and subsequently stashed:

```
$ git stash
Saved working directory and index state WIP on master: d5ef6c9 Some commit.
HEAD is now at d5ef6c9 Some commit.
```

Note that the stash was made against commit d5ef6c9.

Due to other development reasons, more commits are made and the branch drifts away from the d5ef6c9 state.

```
$ git log --pretty=one --abbrev-commit
2c2af13 Another mod
1d1e905 Drifting file state.
d5ef6c9 Some commit.
efe990c Initial commit.

$ git show-branch -a
[master] Another mod
```

And although the stashed work is available, it doesn't apply cleanly to the current master branch.

```
$ git stash list
stash@{0}: WIP on master: d5ef6c9 Some commit.

$ git stash pop
Auto-merging foo
CONFLICT (content): Merge conflict in foo
Auto-merging bar
CONFLICT (content): Merge conflict in bar
```

Say it with me: "Ugh."

So reset some state and take a different approach, creating a new branch called mod that contains the stashed changes.

```
$ git reset --hard master
HEAD is now at 2c2af13 Another mod

$ git stash branch mod
Switched to a new branch 'mod'
# On branch mod
# Changes not staged for commit:
#   (use "git add <file>..." to update what will be committed)
#   (use "git checkout -- <file>..." to discard changes in working directory)
#
#       modified:   bar
#       modified:   foo
#
no changes added to commit (use "git add" and/or "git commit -a")
Dropped refs/stash@{0} (96e53da61f7e5031ef04d68bf60a34bd4f13bd9f)
```

There are several important points to notice here. First, notice that the branch is based on the original commit d5ef6c9, and not the current head commit 2c2af13.

```
$ git show-branch -a
! [master] Another mod
 * [mod] Some commit.
--
+  [master] Another mod
+  [master^] Drifting file state.
+* [mod] Some commit.
```

Second, because the stash is always reconstituted against the original commit, it will always succeed and hence will be dropped from the stash stack.

Finally, reconstituting the stash state doesn't automatically commit any of your changes onto the new branch. All the stashed file modifications (and index changes, if desired) are still left in your working directory on the newly created and checked out branch.

```
$ git commit --dry-run
# On branch mod
# Changes not staged for commit:
#   (use "git add <file>..." to update what will be committed)
#   (use "git checkout -- <file>..." to discard changes in working directory)
#
#       modified:   bar
#       modified:   foo
#
no changes added to commit (use "git add" and/or "git commit -a")
```

At this point you are of course welcome to commit the changes onto the new branch, presumably as a precursor to further development or merging as you deem necessary. No, this isn't a magic bullet to avoid resolving merge conflicts. If there were merge conflicts when you tried to pop the stash directly onto the master branch earlier, trying to merge the new branch with the `master` will yield the same effects and the same merge conflicts.

```
$ git commit -a -m "Stuff from the stash"
[mod 42c104f] Stuff from the stash
 2 files changed, 2 insertions(+), 0 deletions(-)

$ git show-branch
! [master] Another mod
 * [mod] Stuff from the stash
--
 * [mod] Stuff from the stash
 + [master] Another mod
 + [master^] Drifting file state.
+* [mod^] Some commit.

$ git checkout master
Switched to branch 'master'

$ git merge mod
Auto-merging foo
CONFLICT (content): Merge conflict in foo
Auto-merging bar
CONFLICT (content): Merge conflict in bar
Automatic merge failed; fix conflicts and then commit the result.
```

As some parting advice on the `git stash` command, let me leave you with this analogy: you name your pets and you number your livestock. So branches are named and stashes are numbered. The ability to create stashes might be appealing, but be careful not to overuse it and create too many stashes. And don't just convert them to named branches to make them linger!

The Reflog

OK, I confess: sometimes Git does something either mysterious or magical and causes one to wonder what just happened. Sometimes you simply want an answer to the question, "Wait, where was I? What just happened?" Other times, you do some operation and realize, "Uh oh, I shouldn't have done that!" But it is too late and you have already lost the top commit with a week's worth of awesome development.

Not to worry! Git's reflog has you covered in either case! By using the reflog, you can gain the assurance that operations happened as you expected on the branches you intended, and that you have the ability to recover lost commits just in case something goes astray.

The *reflog* is a record of changes to the tips of branches within nonbare repositories. Every time an update is made to any ref, including `HEAD`, the reflog is updated to record how that ref has changed. Think of the reflog as a trail of bread crumbs showing where you and your refs have been. With that analogy, you can also use the reflog to follow your trail of crumbs and trace back through your branch manipulations.

Some of the basic operations that record reflog updates include:

- Cloning
- Pushing
- Making new commits
- Changing or creating branches
- Rebase operations
- Reset operations

Note that some of the more esoteric and complex operations, such as `git filter-branch`, ultimately boil down to simple commits and are thus also logged. Fundamentally, any Git operation that modifies a ref or changes the tip of a branch is recorded.

By default, the reflog is enabled in nonbare repositories and disabled in bare repositories. Specifically, the reflog is controlled by the Boolean configuration option `core.logAllRefUpdates`. It may be enabled using the command `git config core.logAllRefUpdates true` or disabled with `false` as desired on a per-repository basis.

So what does the reflog look like?

```
$ git reflog show
a44d980 HEAD@{0}: reset: moving to master
79e881c HEAD@{1}: commit: last foo change
a44d980 HEAD@{2}: checkout: moving from master to fred
a44d980 HEAD@{3}: rebase -i (finish): returning to refs/heads/master
a44d980 HEAD@{4}: rebase -i (pick): Tinker bar
a777d4f HEAD@{5}: rebase -i (pick): Modify bar
e3c46b8 HEAD@{6}: rebase -i (squash): More foo and bar with additional stuff.
8a04ca4 HEAD@{7}: rebase -i (squash): updating HEAD
1a4be28 HEAD@{8}: checkout: moving from master to 1a4be28
ed6e906 HEAD@{9}: commit: Tinker bar
6195b3d HEAD@{10}: commit: Squash into 'more foo and bar'
488b893 HEAD@{11}: commit: Modify bar
1a4be28 HEAD@{12}: commit: More foo and bar
8a04ca4 HEAD@{13}: commit (initial): Initial foo and bar.
```

Although the reflog records transactions for all refs, `git reflog show` displays the transactions for only one ref at a time. The previous example shows the default ref, HEAD. If you recall that branch names are also refs, you will realize that you can also get the reflog for any branch as well. From the previous example, we can see that there is also a branch named `fred`, so we can display its changes in another command:

```
$ git reflog fred
a44d980 fred@{0}: reset: moving to master
79e881c fred@{1}: commit: last foo change
a44d980 fred@{2}: branch: Created from HEAD
```

Each line records an individual transaction from the history of the ref, starting with the most recent change and going back in time. The leftmost column contains the commit ID at the time the change was made. The entries like HEAD@{7} from the second column provide convenient names for the commit at each transaction. Thus, `HEAD@{0}` is the most recent entry, `HEAD@{1}` records where `HEAD` was just prior to that, etc. The oldest entry, here `HEAD@{13}`, is actually the very first commit in this repository. The rest of each line after the colon describes what transaction occurred. Finally, for each transaction there is a time stamp (not shown) recording when the event took place within your repository.

So what good is all that? Here's the interesting aspect of the reflog: each of the sequentially numbered names like `HEAD@{1}` may be used as symbolic names of commits for any Git command that takes a commit. For example:

```
$ git show HEAD@{10}
commit 6195b3dfd30e464ffb9238d89e3d15f2c1dc35b0
Author: Jon Loeliger <jdl@example.com>
Date:   Sat Oct 29 09:57:05 2011 -0500

    Squash into 'more foo and bar'

diff --git a/foo b/foo
index 740fd05..a941931 100644
--- a/foo
+++ b/foo
@@ -1,2 +1 @@
-Foo!
-more foo
+junk
```

That means that as you go about your development process, recording commits, moving to different branches, rebasing, and otherwise manipulating a branch, you can always use the reflog to reference where the branch was. The name `HEAD@{1}` always references the previous commit for the branch, `HEAD@{2}` names the `HEAD` commit just prior to that, etc. Keep in mind, though, that although the history names individual commits, transactions other than `git commit` are present also. Every time you move the tip of your branch to a different commit, it is logged. Thus, `HEAD@{3}` doesn't necessarily mean the third prior `git commit` operation. More accurately, it means the third prior visited or referenced commit.

 Botch a `git merge` and want try again? Use `git reset HEAD@{1}`. Add `--hard` if desired.

Git also supports more English-like qualifiers for the part of the reference within braces. Maybe you aren't sure exactly how many changes took place since something happened, but you know you want what it looked like yesterday or an hour ago.

```
$ git log 'HEAD@{last saturday}'
commit 1a4be2804f7382b2dd399891eef097eb10ddc1eb
Author: Jon Loeliger <jdl@example.com>
Date:   Sat Oct 29 09:55:52 2011 -0500
```

```
More foo and bar

commit 8a04ca4207e1cb74dd3a3e261d6be72e118ace9e
Author: Jon Loeliger <jdl@example.com>
Date:   Sat Oct 29 09:55:07 2011 -0500

    Initial foo and bar.
```

Git supports a fairly wide variety of date-based qualifiers for refs. These include words like yesterday, noon, midnight, tea,[2] weekdays, month names, A.M. and P.M. indicators, absolute times or dates, and relative phrases like last monday, 1 hour ago, 10 minutes ago, and combinations of these phrases such as 1 day 2 hours ago. And, finally, if you omit the actual ref name and just use the @{...} form, the current branch name is assumed. Thus, while on the bugfix branch, using just @{noon} refers to bug fix@{noon}.

 The Git tool responsible for understanding references is git rev-parse. Its manpage is extensive and details more than you would ever care to know about how refs are interpreted. Good luck!

Although these date-based qualifiers are fairly liberal, they are not perfect. Understand that Git uses a heuristic to interpret them and exercise some caution in referring to them. Also remember that the notion of time is local and relative to your repository: these time-qualified refs reference the value of a ref in your local repository only. Using the same phrase about time in a different repository will likely yield different results due to different reflogs. Thus, master@{2.days.ago} refers to the state of your local master branch two days ago. If you don't have reflog history to cover that time period, Git should warn you:

```
$ git log HEAD@{last-monday}
warning: Log for 'HEAD' only goes back to Sat, 29 Oct 2011 09:55:07 -0500.
commit 8a04ca4207e1cb74dd3a3e261d6be72e118ace9e
Author: Jon Loeliger <jdl@example.com>
Date:   Sat Oct 29 09:55:07 2011 -0500

    Initial foo and bar.
```

One last warning. Don't let the shell trick you. There is a significant difference between these two commands:

```
# Bad!
$ git log dev@{2 days ago}

# Likely correct for your shell
$ git log 'dev@{2 days ago}'
```

---

2. No, really. And yes, that is 5:00 P.M.!

The former, without single quotes, provides multiple command line arguments to your shell, whereas the latter, with quotes, passes the entire ref phrase as one command line argument. Git needs to see the ref as one word from the shell. To help simplify the word break issue, Git allows several variations:

```
# These should all be equivalent
$ git log 'dev@{2 days ago}'
$ git log dev@{2.days.ago}
$ git log dev@{2-days-ago}
```

One more concern to address. If Git is maintaining a transaction history of every operation performed on every ref in the repository, doesn't the reflog eventually become huge?

Luckily, no. Git automatically runs a garbage collection process occasionally. During this process, some of the older reflog entries are expired and dropped. Normally, a commit that is otherwise not referenced or reachable from some branch or ref will be expired after a default of 30 days, and commits that are reachable expire after a default of 90 days.

If that schedule isn't ideal, the configuration variables gc.reflogExpireUnreachable and gc.reflogExpire, respectively, can be set to alternate values in your repository. You can use the command git reflog delete to remove individual entries, or use the command git reflog expire to directly cause entries older than a specified time to be immediately removed. It can also be used to forcefully expire the reflog.

```
$ git reflog expire --expire=now --all
$ git gc
```

As you might have guessed by now, the stash and the reflog are intimately related. In fact, the stash is implemented as a reflog using the ref stash.

One last implementation detail: reflogs are stored under the *.git/logs* directory. The file *.git/logs/HEAD* contains the history of HEAD values, whereas the subdirectory *.git/logs/refs/* contains the history of all refs, including the stash. The sub-subdirectory *.git/logs/refs/heads* contains the history for branch heads.

All the information stored in the reflogs, specifically everything under the *.git/logs* directory, is ultimately transitory and expendable. Throwing away the *.git/logs* directory or turning the reflog off harms no Git-internal data structure; it simply means references like master@{4} can't be resolved.

Conversely, having the reflog enabled introduces references to commits that might otherwise be unreachable. If you are trying to clean up and shrink your repository size, removing the reflog may enable the removal of otherwise unreachable (i.e., irrelevant) commits.

## CHAPTER 12

Remote Repositories

So far, you've worked almost entirely within one local repository. Now it's time to explore the much lauded distributed features of Git and learn how to collaborate with other developers via shared repositories.

Working with multiple and remote repositories adds a few new terms to the Git vernacular.

A *clone* is a copy of a repository. A clone contains all the objects from the original; as a result, each clone is an independent and autonomous repository and a true, symmetric peer of the original. A clone allows each developer to work locally and independently without centralization, polls, or locks. Ultimately, it's cloning that allows Git to easily scale and permit many geographically separated contributors.

Essentially, separate repositories are useful whenever:

* Developers work autonomously.
* Developers are separated by a wide area network. A cluster of developers in the same location may share a local repository to amass localized changes.
* A project is expected to diverge significantly along separate development paths. Although the regular branching and merging mechanisms demonstrated in previous chapters can handle any amount of separate development, the resulting complexity may become more trouble than it's worth. Instead, separate development paths can use separate repositories to be merged again whenever appropriate.

Cloning a repository is just the first step in sharing code. You must also relate one repository to another to establish paths for data exchange. Git establishes these repository connections through *remotes*.

A *remote* is a reference, or handle, to another repository through a filesystem or network path. You use a remote as a shorthand name for an otherwise lengthy and complicated Git URL. You can define any number of remotes in a repository, thus creating terraced networks of repository sharing.

Once a remote is established, Git can transfer data from one repository to another using either a push or a pull model. For example, it's common practice to occasionally transfer commit data from an original repository to its clone in order to keep the clone in sync. You can also create a remote to transfer data from the clone to its original or configure the two to exchange information bidirectionally.

To keep track of data from other repositories, Git uses *remote-tracking branches*. Each remote-tracking branch in your repository is a branch that serves as a proxy for a specific branch in a remote repository. You may set up a *local-tracking branch* that forms the basis for integrating your local changes with the remote changes from a corresponding remote-tracking branch.

Finally, you can make your repository available to others. Git generally refers to this as *publishing a repository* and provides several techniques for doing so.

This chapter presents examples and techniques to share, track, and obtain data across multiple repositories.

Repository Concepts

Bare and Development Repositories

A Git repository is either a *bare* or a *development* (*nonbare*) repository.

A development repository is used for normal, daily development. It maintains the notion of a current branch and provides a checked out copy of the current branch in a working directory. All of the repositories mentioned in the book so far have been development repositories.

In contrast, a bare repository has no working directory and shouldn't be used for normal development. A bare repository has no notion of a checked out branch, either. Think of a bare repository as simply the contents of the *.git* directory. In other words, you shouldn't make commits in a bare repository.

A bare repository might seem to be of little use, but its role is crucial: to serve as an authoritative focal point for collaborative development. Other developers `clone` and `fetch` from the bare repository and `push` updates to it. We'll work through an example later in this chapter that shows how all this works together.

If you issue `git clone` with the `--bare` option, Git creates a bare repository; otherwise, a development repository is created.

Notice that we did not say that git clone --bare creates a new or empty repository. We said it creates a *bare* repository. And that newly cloned repository will contain a copy of the content from the upstream repository. The command git init creates a new and empty repository, and that new repository can come in both *development* and *bare* variants. Also, be aware of how the --bare flag affects the directory that is initialized:

```
$ cd /tmp
$ git init fluff2
Initialized empty Git repository in /tmp/fluff2/.git/
$ git init --bare fluff
Initialized empty Git repository in /tmp/fluff/
```

By default, Git enables a *reflog* (a record of changes to refs) on development repositories but not on bare repositories. This again anticipates that development will take place in the former and not in the latter. By the same reasoning, no remotes are created in a bare repository.

If you set up a repository into which developers push changes, it should be bare. In effect, this is a special case of the more general best practice that a published repository should be bare.

Repository Clones

The git clone command creates a new Git repository based on the original you specify via a filesystem or network address. Git doesn't have to copy all the information in the original to the clone. Instead, Git ignores information that is pertinent only to the original repository, such as remote-tracking branches.

In normal git clone use, the local, development branches of the original repository, stored within *refs/heads/*, become *remote-tracking branches* in the new clone under *refs/remotes/*. Remote-tracking branches within *refs/remotes/* in the original repository are not cloned. (The clone doesn't need to know what, if anything, the upstream repository is in turn tracking.)

Tags from the original repository are copied into the clone, as are all objects that are reachable from the copied refs. However, repository-specific information such as hooks (see Chapter 15), configuration files, the reflog, and the stash of the original repository are not reproduced in the clone.

In "Making a Copy of Your Repository" on page 27 of Chapter 3, we showed how git clone can be used to create a copy of your *public_html* repository:

```
$ git clone public_html my_website
```

Here, *public_html* is considered the original, "remote" repository. The new, resulting clone is *my_website*.

Similarly, git clone can be used to clone a copy of a repository from network sites:

```
# All on one line...
$ git clone \
    git://git.kernel.org/pub/scm/linux/kernel/git/torvalds/linux-2.6.git
```

By default, each new clone maintains a link back to its parent repository via a remote called *origin*. However, the original repository has no knowledge of—nor does it maintain a link to—any clone. It is purely a one-way relationship.[1]

The name "origin" isn't special in any way. If you don't want to use it, simply specify an alternate with the `--origin` *name* option during the clone operation.

Git also configures the default `origin` remote with a default `fetch` refspec:

```
fetch = +refs/heads/*:refs/remotes/origin/*
```

Establishing this refspec anticipates that you want to continue updating your local repository by fetching changes from the originating repository. In this case, the remote repository's branches are available in the clone on branch names prefixed with `origin/`, such as `origin/master`, `origin/dev`, or `origin/maint`.

Remotes

The repository you're currently working in is called the *local* or *current* repository, and the repository with which you exchange files is called the *remote repository*. But the latter term is a bit of a misnomer, because the repository may or may not be on a physically remote or even different machine; it could conceivably be just another repository on a local filesystem. In Chapter 13, I discuss how the term *upstream repository* is usually used to identify the remote repository from which your local repository is derived via a clone operation.

Git uses both the remote and the remote-tracking branch to reference and facilitate the connection to another repository. The remote provides a friendly name for the repository and can be used in place of the actual repository URL. A remote also forms part of the name basis for the remote-tracking branches for that repository.

Use the `git remote` command to create, remove, manipulate, and view a remote. All the remotes you introduce are recorded in the *.git/config* file and can be manipulated using `git config`.

In addition to `git clone`, other common Git commands that refer to remote repositories are:

git fetch
: Retrieves objects and their related metadata from a remote repository.

git pull
: Like `git fetch`, but also merges changes into a corresponding local branch.

---

1. Of course, a bidirectional remote relationship can be set up later using the `git remote` command.

git push
> Transfers objects and their related metadata to a remote repository.

git ls-remote
> Shows a list of references held by a given remote (on an upstream server). This command indirectly answers the question "Is an update available?"

Tracking Branches

Once you clone a repository, you can keep up with changes in the original source repository even as you make local commits and create local branches.

As Git itself has evolved, some terminology around branch names have also evolved and become more standard. To help clarify the purposes of the various branches, different namespaces have been created. Although any branch in your local repository is still considered a local branch, they can be further divided into different categories.

- *Remote-tracking branches* are associated with a remote and have the specific purpose of following the changes of each branch in that remote repository.

- A *local-tracking branch* is paired with a remote-tracking branch. It is a form of integration branch that collects both the changes from your local development and the changes from the remote-tracking branch.

- Any local, nontracking branch is usually generically called a *topic* or *development branch*.

- Finally, to complete the namespaces, a *remote branch* is a branch located in a non-local, remote repository. It is likely an upstream source for a remote-tracking branch.

During a clone operation, Git creates a remote-tracking branch in the clone for each topic branch in the upstream repository. The set of remote-tracking branches is introduced in a new, separate namespace within the local repository that is specific to the remote being cloned. They are not branches in a remote repository. The local repository uses its remote-tracking branches to follow or track changes made in the remote repository.

> You may recall from "refs and symrefs" on page 68 of Chapter 6 that a local topic branch that you call dev is really named refs/heads/dev. Similarly, remote-tracking branches are retained in the refs/remotes/ namespace. Thus, the remote-tracking branch origin/master is actually refs/remotes/origin/master.

Because remote-tracking branches are lumped into their own namespace, there is a clear separation between branches made in a repository by you (*topic branches*) and those branches that are actually based on another, remote repository (*remote-tracking branches*). In the early Git days, the separate namespaces were just convention and best practice, designed to help prevent you from making accidental conflicts. With later versions of Git, the separate namespaces are much more than convention: it is an integral part of how you are expected to use your branches to interact with your upstream repositories.

All the operations that you can perform on a regular topic branch can also be performed on a tracking branch. However, there are some restrictions and guidelines to observe.

Because remote-tracking branches are used exclusively to follow the changes from another repository, you should effectively treat them as read only. You shouldn't merge or make commits onto a remote-tracking branch. Doing so would cause your remote-tracking branch to become out of sync with the remote repository. Worse, each future update from the remote repository would likely require merging, making your clone increasingly more difficult to manage. The proper management of tracking branches is covered in more detail later in this chapter.

Referencing Other Repositories

To coordinate your repository with another repository, you define a *remote*, which here means a named entity stored in the config file of a repository. It consists of two different parts. The first part states the name of the other repository in the form of a URL. The second part, called a *refspec*, specifies how a ref (which usually represents a branch) should be mapped from the namespace of one repository into the namespace of the other repository.

Let's look at each of these components in turn.

Referring to Remote Repositories

Git supports several forms of *Uniform Resource Locators* (URLs) that can be used to name remote repositories. These forms specify both an access protocol and the location or address of the data.

Technically, Git's forms of URLs are neither true URLs nor Uniform Resource Identifiers (URIs), because none entirely conform to RFC 1738 or RFC 2396, respectively. However, because of their versatile utility in naming the location of Git repositories, Git's variants are usually referred to as *Git URLs*. Furthermore, the *.git/config* file uses the name url as well.

As you have seen, the simplest form of Git URL refers to a repository on a local filesystem, be it a true physical filesystem or a virtual filesystem mounted locally via the Network File System (NFS). There are two permutations:

```
/path/to/repo.git
file:///path/to/repo.git
```

Although these two formats are essentially identical, there is a subtle but important distinction between the two. The former uses hard links within the filesystem to directly share exactly the same objects between the current and remote repository; the latter copies the objects instead of sharing them directly. To avoid issues associated with shared repositories, the `file://` form is recommended.

The other forms of the Git URL refer to repositories on remote systems.

When you have a truly remote repository whose data must be retrieved across a network, the most efficient form of data transfer is often called the *Git native protocol*, which refers to the custom protocol used internally by Git to transfer data. Examples of a native protocol URL include:

```
git://example.com/path/to/repo.git
git://example.com/~user/path/to/repo.git
```

These forms are used by `git-daemon` to publish repositories for anonymous read. You can both clone and fetch using these URL forms.

The clients that use these formats are not authenticated, and no password will be requested. Hence, whereas a *~user* format can be employed to refer to a user's home directory, a bare ~ has no context for an expansion; there is no authenticated user whose home directory can be used. Furthermore, the *~user* form works only if the server side allows it with the `--user-path` option.

For secure, authenticated connections, the Git native protocol can be tunneled over Secure Shell(SSH) connection using the following URL templates:

```
ssh://[user@]example.com[:port]/path/to/repo.git
ssh://[user@]example.com/path/to/repo.git
ssh://[user@]example.com/~user2/path/to/repo.git
ssh://[user@]example.com/~/path/to/repo.git
```

The third form allows for the possibility of two different user names. The first is the user under whom the session is authenticated, and the second is the user whose home directory is accessed.

Git also supports a URL form with `scp`-like syntax. It's identical to the SSH forms, but there is no way to specify a port parameter:

```
[user@]example.com:/path/to/repo.git
[user@]example.com:~user/path/to/repo.git
[user@]example.com:path/to/repo.git
```

Although the HTTP and HTTPS URL variants have been fully supported since the early days of Git, they have undergone some important changes after Version 1.6.6.

```
http://example.com/path/to/repo.git
https://example.com/path/to/repo.git
```

Prior to Git Version 1.6.6, neither the HTTP nor the HTTPS protocols were as efficient as the Git native protocol. In Version 1.6.6, the HTTP protocols were improved dramatically and have become essentially as efficient as the native Git protocols. Git literature refers to this implementation as "smart" in contrast to the prior, so-called "dumb" implementation.

With the HTTP efficiency benefit realized now, the utility of the http:// and https:// URL forms will likely become more important and popular. Notably, most corporate firewalls allow the HTTP port 80 and HTTPS port 443 to remain open while the default Git port 9418 is typically blocked and would require an act of Congress to open it. Furthermore, these URL forms are being favored by popular Git hosting sites like GitHub.

Finally, the Rsync protocol can be specified:

```
rsync://example.com/path/to/repo.git
```

The use of Rsync is discouraged because it is inferior to the other options. If absolutely necessary, it should be used only for an initial clone, at which point the remote repository reference should be changed to one of the other mechanisms. Continuing to use the Rsync protocol for later updates may lead to the loss of locally created data.

The refspec

In "refs and symrefs" on page 68 of Chapter 6, I explained how the *ref*, or *reference*, names a particular commit within the history of the repository. Usually a ref is the name of a branch. A *refspec* maps branch names in the remote repository to branch names within your local repository.

Because a refspec must simultaneously name branches from the local repository and the remote repository, complete branch names are common in a refspec and are often required. In a *refspec*, you typically see the names of development branches with the *refs/heads/* prefix and the names of remote-tracking branches with the *refs/remotes/* prefix.

The syntax of a *refspec* is:

```
[+]source:destination
```

It consists primarily of a *source ref*, a colon (:), and a *destination ref*. The whole format may be prefixed with an optional plus sign (+). If present, the plus sign indicates that the normal fast-forward safety check will not be performed during the transfer. Furthermore, an asterisk (*) allows a limited form of wildcard matching on branch names.

In some uses, the *source* ref is optional; in others, the colon and *destination* ref are optional.

Refspecs are used by both git fetch and git push. The trick to using a refspec is to understand the data flow it specifies. The refspec itself is always *source:destination*, but the roles of *source* and *destination* depend on the Git operation being performed. This relationship is summarized in Table 12-1.

Table 12-1. Refspec data flow

Operation	Source	Destination
push	Local ref being pushed	Remote ref being updated
fetch	Remote ref being fetched	Local ref being updated

A typical `git fetch` command uses a refspec such as:

```
+refs/heads/*:refs/remotes/remote/*
```

This refspec might be paraphrased as follows:

All the source branches from a remote repository in namespace *refs/heads/* are (i) mapped into your local repository using a name constructed from the *remote* name and (ii) placed under the *refs/remotes/remote* namespace.

Because of the asterisks, this refspec applies to multiple branches as found in the remote's *refs/heads/*. It is *exactly* this specification that causes the remote's topic branches to be mapped into your repository's namespace as remote-tracking branches and separates them into subnames based on the remote name.

Although not mandatory, it is convention and common best practice to place the branches for a given *remote* under *refs/remotes/remote/*.

Use `git show-ref` to list the references within your current repository. Use `git ls-remote repository` to list the references in a remote repository.

Because `git pull`'s first step is `fetch`, the fetch refspecs apply equally to `git pull`.

You should not make commits or merges onto a remote-tracking branch identified on the righthand side of a `pull` or `fetch` refspec. Those refs will be used as remote-tracking branches.

During a `git push` operation, you typically want to provide and publish the changes you made on your local topic branches. To allow others to find your changes in the remote repository after you upload them, your changes must appear in that repository as topic branches. Thus, during a typical `git push` command, the source branches from your repository are sent to the remote repository using a refspec such as:

```
+refs/heads/*:refs/heads/*
```

This refspec can be paraphrased as follows:

From the local repository, take each branch name found under the source namespace `refs/heads/` and place it in a similarly named, matching branch under the destination namespace `refs/heads/` in the remote repository.

The first `refs/heads/` refers to your local repository (because you're executing a push), and the second refers to the remote repository. The asterisks ensure that all branches are replicated.

Multiple refspecs may be given on the `git fetch` and `git push` command lines. Within a remote definition, multiple fetch refspecs, multiple push refspecs, or a combination of both may be specified.

What if you don't specify a refspec at all on a `git push` command? How does Git know what to do or where to send data?

First, without an explicit remote given to the command, Git assumes you want to use `origin`. Without a refspec, `git push` will send your commits to the remote for all branches that are common between your repository and the upstream repository. Any local branch that is not already present in the upstream repository will not be sent upstream; branches must already exist and match names. Thus, new branches must be explicitly pushed by name. Later they can be defaulted with a simple `git push`. Thus, the default refspec makes the following two commands equivalent:

```
$ git push origin branch
$ git push origin branch:refs/heads/branch
```

For examples, see "Adding and Deleting Remote Branches" on page 231.

Example Using Remote Repositories

Now you have the basis for some sophisticated sharing via Git. Without a loss of generality and to make examples easy to run on your own system, this section shows multiple repositories on one physical machine. In real life, they'd probably be located on different hosts across the Internet. Other forms of remote URL specification may be used because the same mechanisms apply to repositories on physically disparate machines as well.

Let's explore a common use scenario for Git. For the sake of illustration, let's set up a repository that all developers consider authoritative, although technically it's no different from other repositories. In other words, authority lies in how everyone agrees to treat the repository, not in some technical or security measure.

This agreed on authoritative copy is often placed in a special directory known as a *depot*. (Avoid using the terms "master" or "repository" when referring to the depot, because those idioms mean something else in Git.)

There are often good reasons for setting up a depot. For instance, your organization may thereby reliably and professionally back up the filesystems of some large server. You want to encourage your coworkers to check everything into the main copy within the depot in order to avoid catastrophic losses. The depot will be the *remote origin* for all developers.

The following sections show how to place an initial repository in the depot, clone development repositories out of the depot, do development work within them, and then sync them with the depot.

To illustrate parallel development on this repository, a second developer will clone it, work with his repository, and then push his changes back into the depot for all to use.

Creating an Authoritative Repository

You can place your authoritative depot anywhere on your filesystem; for this example, let's use */tmp/Depot*. No actual development work should be done directly in the */tmp/Depot* directory or in any of its repositories. Instead, individual work should be performed in a local clone.

In practice, this authoritative upstream repository would likely already be hosted on some server, perhaps GitHub, `git.kernel.org`, or one of your private machines.

These steps, however, outline what is necessary to transform a repository into another bare clone repository capable of being the authoritative upstream source repository.

The first step is to populate */tmp/Depot* with an initial repository. Assuming you want to work on website content that is already established as a Git repository in *~/public_html*, make a copy of the *~/public_html* repository and place it in */tmp/Depot/public_html.git*.

```
# Assume that ~/public_html is already a Git repository

$ cd /tmp/Depot/
$ git clone --bare ~/public_html public_html.git
Initialized empty Git repository in /tmp/Depot/public_html.git/
```

This `clone` command copies the Git remote repository from *~/public_html* into the current working directory, */tmp/Depot*. The last argument gives the repository a new name, *public_html.git*. By convention, bare repositories are named with a *.git* suffix. This is not a requirement, but it is considered a best practice.

The original development repository has a full set of project files checked out at the top level, and the object store and all of the configuration files are located in the *.git* subdirectory:

```
$ cd ~/public_html/
$ ls -aF
./     fuzzy.txt   index.html   techinfo.txt
../    .git/       poem.html

$ ls -aF .git
./                config        hooks/    objects/
../               description   index     ORIG_HEAD
branches/         FETCH_HEAD    info/     packed-refs
COMMIT_EDITMSG    HEAD          logs/     refs/
```

Because a bare repository has no working directory, its files have a simpler layout:

```
$ cd /tmp/Depot/

$ ls -aF public_html.git
./     branches/  description  hooks/  objects/    refs/
../     config     HEAD         info/   packed-refs
```

You can now treat this bare */tmp/Depot/public_html.git* repository as the authoritative version.

Because you used the `--bare` option during this clone operation, Git did *not* introduce the normal, default `origin` remote.

Here's the configuration in the new, bare repository:

```
# In /tmp/Depot/public_html.git

$ cat config
[core]
        repositoryformatversion = 0
        filemode = true
        bare = true
```

Make Your Own Origin Remote

Right now, you have two repositories that are virtually identical, except the initial repository has a working directory and the bare clone does not.

Moreover, because the *~/public_html* repository in your home directory was created using `git init` and *not* via a clone, it lacks an `origin`. In fact, it has no remote configured at all.

It is easy enough to add one, though. And it's needed if the goal is to perform more development in your initial repository and then push that development to the newly established, authoritative repository in the depot. In a sense, you must manually convert your initial repository into a derived clone.

A developer who clones from the depot will have an `origin` remote created automatically. In fact, if you were to turn around now and clone off the depot, you would see it set up for you automatically, too.

The command for manipulating remotes is `git remote`. This operation introduces a few new settings in the *.git/config* file:

```
$ cd ~/public_html

$ cat .git/config
[core]
        repositoryformatversion = 0
        filemode = true
        bare = false
        logallrefupdates = true

$ git remote add origin /tmp/Depot/public_html
```

```
$ cat .git/config
[core]
        repositoryformatversion = 0
        filemode = true
        bare = false
        logallrefupdates = true
[remote "origin"]
        url = /tmp/Depot/public_html
        fetch = +refs/heads/*:refs/remotes/origin/*
```

Here, git remote added a new remote section called origin to our configuration. The name origin isn't magical or special. You could have used any other name, but the remote that points back to the basis repository is named origin by convention.

The remote establishes a link from your current repository to the remote repository found, in this case, at */tmp/Depot/public_html.git* as recorded in the url value. As a convenience, the *.git* suffix is not required; both */tmp/Depot/public_html* and */tmp/Depot/public_html.git* will work. Now, within this repository, the name ori gin can be used as a shorthand reference for the remote repository found in the depot. Note that a default fetch refspec that follows branch name mapping conventions has also been added.

The relationship between a repository that contains a remote reference (the referrer) and that remote repository (the referee) is asymmetric. A remote always points in one direction from referrer to referee. The referee has no idea that some other repository points to it. Another way to say this is as follows: a clone knows where its upstream repository is, but the upstream repository doesn't know where its clones are.

Let's complete the process of setting up the origin remote by establishing new remote-tracking branches in the original repository to represent the branches from the remote repository. First, you can see that there is only one branch, as expected, called master.

```
# List all branches

$ git branch -a
* master
```

Now, use git remote update:

```
$ git remote update
Updating origin
From /tmp/Depot/public_html
 * [new branch]      master     -> origin/master

$ git branch -a
* master
  origin/master
```

Depending on your version of Git,[2] the remote-tracking branch ref may be shown with or without the remotes/ prefix:

2. Version 1.6.3 appears to be the delineation here.

```
$ git branch -a
* master
  remotes/origin/master
```

Git introduced a new branch called `origin/master` into the repository. It is a *remote-tracking branch* within the `origin` remote. Nobody does development in this branch. Instead, its purpose is to hold and track the commits made in the remote `origin` repository's `master` branch. You could consider it your local repository's proxy for commits made in the remote; eventually you can use it to bring those commits into your repository.

The phrase `Updating origin`, produced by the `git remote update`, doesn't mean that the *remote* repository was updated. Rather, it means that the *local* repository's notion of the `origin` has been updated based on information brought in from the remote repository.

 The generic `git remote update` caused every remote within this repository to be updated by checking for and then fetching any new commits from each repository named in a remote. Rather than generically updating all remotes, you can restrict the operation to fetch updates from a single remote by supplying the desired remote name on the `git remote update` command:

> `$ git remote update remote_name`

Also, using the `-f` option when the remote is initially added causes an immediate fetch of from that remote repository:

> `$ git remote add -f origin repository`

Now you're done linking your repository to the remote repository in your depot.

Developing in Your Repository

Let's do some development work in the repository and add another poem, *fuzzy.txt*:

```
$ cd ~/public_html

$ git show-branch -a
[master] Merge branch 'master' of ../my_website

$ cat fuzzy.txt
Fuzzy Wuzzy was a bear
Fuzzy Wuzzy had no hair
Fuzzy Wuzzy wasn't very fuzzy,
Was he?

$ git add fuzzy.txt
$ git commit
Created commit 6f16880: Add a hairy poem.
 1 files changed, 4 insertions(+), 0 deletions(-)
```

```
    create mode 100644 fuzzy.txt
$ git show-branch -a
* [master] Add a hairy poem.
 ! [origin/master] Merge branch 'master' of ../my_website
--
*   [master] Add a hairy poem.
--  [origin/master] Merge branch 'master' of ../my_website
```

At this point, your repository has one more commit than the repository in */tmp/Depot*. Perhaps more interesting is that your repository has two branches, one (master) with the new commit on it, and the other (origin/master) that is tracking the remote repository.

Pushing Your Changes

Any change that you commit is completely local to your repository; it is not yet present in the remote repository. A convenient way to get your commits from your master branch into the origin remote repository is to use the git push command. Depending on your version of Git, the master parameter on this command was assumed.

```
$ git push origin master
Counting objects: 4, done.
Compressing objects: 100% (3/3), done.
Writing objects: 100% (3/3), 400 bytes, done.
Total 3 (delta 0), reused 0 (delta 0)
Unpacking objects: 100% (3/3), done.
To /tmp/Depot/public_html
   0d4ce8a..6f16880  master -> master
```

All that output means that Git has taken your master branch changes, bundled them up, and sent them to the remote repository named origin. Git has also performed one more step here: it has taken those same changes and added them to the origin/master branch in your repository as well. In effect, Git has caused the changes that were originally on your master branch to be sent to the remote repository and then has requested that they be brought back onto the origin/master remote-tracking branch as well.

Git doesn't actually round-trip the changes. After all, the commits are already in your repository. Git is smart enough to instead simply fast-forward the remote-tracking branch.

Now both local branches, master and origin/master, reflect the same commit within your repository:

```
$ git show-branch -a
* [master] Add a hairy poem.
 ! [origin/master] Add a hairy poem.
--
*+ [master] Add a hairy poem.
```

You can also probe the remote repository and verify that it, too, has been updated. If your remote repository is on a local filesystem, as it is here, then you can easily check by going to the depot directory:

```
$ cd /tmp/Depot/public_html.git
$ git show-branch
[master] Add a hairy poem.
```

When the remote repository is on a physically different machine, a plumbing command can be used to determine the branch information of the remote repository:

```
# Go to the actual remote repo and query it

$ git ls-remote origin
6f168803f6f1b987dffd5fff77531dcadf7f4b68          HEAD
6f168803f6f1b987dffd5fff77531dcadf7f4b68          refs/heads/master
```

You can then show that those commit IDs match your current, local branches using something like git rev-parse HEAD or git show *commit-id*.

Adding a New Developer

Once you have established an authoritative repository, it's easy to add a new developer to a project simply by letting him clone the repository and begin working.

Let's introduce Bob to the project by giving him his own cloned repository in which to work:

```
$ cd /tmp/bob
$ git clone /tmp/Depot/public_html.git
Initialized empty Git repository in /tmp/public_html/.git/

$ ls
public_html
$ cd public_html

$ ls
fuzzy.txt  index.html  poem.html  techinfo.txt

$ git branch
* master

$ git log -1
commit 6f168803f6f1b987dffd5fff77531dcadf7f4b68
Author: Jon Loeliger <jdl@example.com>
Date:   Sun Sep 14 21:04:44 2008 -0500

    Add a hairy poem.
```

Immediately, you can see from ls that the clone has a working directory populated with all the files under version control. That is, Bob's clone is a development repository, and not a bare repository. Good. Bob will be doing some development, too.

From the `git log` output, you can see that the most recent commit is available in Bob's repository. Additionally, because Bob's repository was cloned from a parent repository, it has a default remote called `origin`. Bob can find out more information about the origin remote within his repository:

```
$ git remote show origin
* remote origin
  URL: /tmp/Depot/public_html.git
  Remote branch merged with 'git pull' while on branch master
    master
  Tracked remote branch
    master
```

The complete contents of the configuration file after a default clone show how it contains the origin remote:

```
$ cat .git/config
[core]
        repositoryformatversion = 0
        filemode = true
        bare = false
        logallrefupdates = true
[remote "origin"]
        url = /tmp/Depot/public_html.git
        fetch = +refs/heads/*:refs/remotes/origin/*
[branch "master"]
        remote = origin
        merge = refs/heads/master
```

In addition to having the `origin` remote in his repository, Bob also has a few branches. He can list all of the branches in his repository by using `git branch -a`:

```
$ git branch -a
* master
  origin/HEAD
  origin/master
```

The `master` branch is Bob's main development branch. It is the normal, local topic branch. It is also a local-tracking branch associated with the correspondingly named `master` remote-tracking branch. The `origin/master` branch is a remote-tracking branch to follow the commits from the `master` branch of the `origin` repository. The `origin/HEAD` ref indicates which branch the remote considers the active branch, through a symbolic name. Finally, the asterisk next to the `master` branch name indicates that it is the current, checked-out branch in his repository.

Let's have Bob make a commit that alters the hairy poem and then push that to the main depot repository. Bob thinks the last line of the poem should be "Wuzzy?", makes this change, and commits it:

```
$ git diff

diff --git a/fuzzy.txt b/fuzzy.txt
index 0d601fa..608ab5b 100644
--- a/fuzzy.txt
```

```
+++ b/fuzzy.txt
@@ -1,4 +1,4 @@
 Fuzzy Wuzzy was a bear
 Fuzzy Wuzzy had no hair
 Fuzzy Wuzzy wasn't very fuzzy,
-Was he?
+Wuzzy?

$ git commit fuzzy.txt
Created commit 3958f68: Make the name pun complete!
 1 files changed, 1 insertions(+), 1 deletions(-)
```

To complete Bob's development cycle, he pushes his changes to the depot, using git push as before:

```
$ git push
Counting objects: 5, done.
Compressing objects: 100% (3/3), done.
Writing objects: 100% (3/3), 377 bytes, done.
Total 3 (delta 1), reused 0 (delta 0)
Unpacking objects: 100% (3/3), done.
To /tmp/Depot/public_html.git
   6f16880..3958f68  master -> master
```

Getting Repository Updates

Let's suppose that Bob goes on vacation and, in the meantime, you make further changes and push them to the depot repository. Let's assume you did this after getting Bob's latest changes.

Your commit looks like this:

```
$ cd ~/public_html
$ git diff
diff --git a/index.html b/index.html
index 40b00ff..063ac92 100644
--- a/index.html
+++ b/index.html
@@ -1,5 +1,7 @@
 <html>
 <body>
 My web site is alive!
+<br/>
+Read a <a href="fuzzy.txt">hairy</a> poem!
 </body>
 <html>

$ git commit -m "Add a hairy poem link." index.html
Created commit 55c15c8: Add a hairy poem link.
 1 files changed, 2 insertions(+), 0 deletions(-)
```

Using the default push refspec, push your commit upstream:

```
$ git push
Counting objects: 5, done.
```

```
Compressing objects: 100% (3/3), done.
Unpacking objects: 100% (3/3), done.
Writing objects: 100% (3/3), 348 bytes, done.
Total 3 (delta 1), reused 0 (delta 0)
To /tmp/Depot/public_html
   3958f68..55c15c8  master -> master
```

Now, when Bob returns he'll want to refresh his clone of the repository. The primary command for doing this is `git pull`:

```
$ git pull
remote: Counting objects: 5, done.
remote: Compressing objects: 100% (3/3), done.
remote: Total 3 (delta 1), reused 0 (delta 0)
Unpacking objects: 100% (3/3), done.
From /tmp/Depot/public_html
   3958f68..55c15c8  master     -> origin/master
Updating 3958f68..55c15c8
Fast forward
 index.html |    2 ++
 1 files changed, 2 insertions(+), 0 deletions(-)
```

The fully specified `git pull` command allows both the repository and multiple refspecs to be specified: `git pull options repository refspecs`.

If the repository is not specified on the command line, either as a Git URL or indirectly through a remote name, then the default remote `origin` is used. If you don't specify a refspec on the command line, the fetch refspec of the remote is used. If you specify a repository (directly or using a remote) but no refspec, Git fetches the `HEAD` ref of the remote.

The `git pull` operation is fundamentally two steps, each implemented by a separate Git command. Namely, `git pull` implies `git fetch` followed by either `git merge` or `git rebase`. By default, the second step is `merge` because this is almost always the desired behavior.

Because `pull` also performs the second `merge` or `rebase` step, `git push` and `git pull` are not considered opposites. Instead, `git push` and `git fetch` are considered opposites. Both `push` and `fetch` are responsible for transferring data between repositories, but in opposite directions.

Sometimes you may want to execute the `git fetch` and `git merge` as two separate operations. For example, you may want to fetch updates into your repository to inspect them but not necessarily merge immediately. In this case, you can simply perform the fetch, and then perform other operations on the remote-tracking branch such as `git log`, `git diff`, or even `gitk`. Later, when you are ready (if ever!), you may perform the merge at your convenience.

Even if you never separate the fetch and merge, you may do complex operations that require you to know what's happening at each step. So let's look at each one in detail.

The fetch step

In the first `fetch` step, Git locates the remote repository. Because the command line did not specify a direct repository URL or a direct remote name, it assumes the default remote name, `origin`. The information for that remote is in the configuration file:

```
[remote "origin"]
        url = /tmp/Depot/public_html.git
        fetch = +refs/heads/*:refs/remotes/origin/*
```

Git now knows to use the URL `/tmp/Depot/public_html` as the source repository. Furthermore, because the command line didn't specify a refspec, Git will use all of the `fetch` = lines from the `remote` entry. Thus, every `refs/heads/*` branch from the remote will be fetched.

Next, Git performs a negotiation protocol with the source repository to determine what new commits are in the remote repository and are absent from your repository, based on the desire to fetch all of the `refs/heads/*` refs as given in the fetch refspec.

 You don't have to fetch all of the topic branches from the remote repository using the `refs/heads/*` wildcard form. If you want only a particular branch or two, list them explicitly:

```
[remote "newdev"]
        url = /tmp/Depot/public_html.git
        fetch = +refs/heads/dev:refs/remotes/origin/dev
        fetch = +refs/heads/stable:refs/remotes/origin/stable
```

The pull output prefixed by `remote:` reflects the negotiation, compression, and transfer protocol, and it lets you know that new commits are coming into your repository.

```
remote: Counting objects: 5, done.
remote: Compressing objects: 100% (3/3), done.
remote: Total 3 (delta 1), reused 0 (delta 0)
```

Git places the new commits in your repository on an appropriate remote-tracking branch and then tells you what mapping it uses to determine where the new commits belong:

```
From /tmp/Depot/public_html
   3958f68..55c15c8  master      -> origin/master
```

Those lines indicate that Git looked at the remote repository `/tmp/Depot/public_html`, took *its* `master` branch, brought its contents back to your repository, and placed them on *your* `origin/master` branch. This process is the heart of branch *tracking*.

The corresponding commit IDs are also listed, just in case you want to inspect the changes directly. With that, the `fetch` step is finished.

The merge or rebase step

In the second step of the `pull` operation, Git performs a `merge` (the default), or a `rebase` operation. In this example, Git merges the contents of the remote-tracking branch, `origin/master`, into your local-tracking branch, `master`, using a special type of merge called a *fast-forward*.

But how did Git know to merge those particular branches? The answer comes from the configuration file:

```
[branch "master"]
        remote = origin
        merge = refs/heads/master
```

Paraphrased, this gives Git two key pieces of information:

> When `master` is the current, checked out branch, use `origin` as the default remote from which to fetch updates during a `fetch` (or `pull`). Further, during the `merge` step of `git pull`, use `refs/heads/master` from the remote as the default branch to merge into this, the `master` branch.

For readers paying close attention to detail, the first part of that paraphrase is the actual mechanism by which Git determines that `origin` should be the remote used during this parameterless `git pull` command.

The value of the `merge` field in the `branch` section of the configuration file (`refs/heads/master`) is treated like the remote part of a refspec, and it must match one of the *source* refs just fetched during the `git pull` command. It's a little convoluted, but think of this as a hint conveyed from the `fetch` step to the `merge` step of a `pull` command.

Because the `merge` configuration value applies only during `git pull`, a manual application of `git merge` at this point must name the merge source branch on the command line. The branch is likely a remote-tracking branch name, such as this:

```
# Or, fully specified: refs/remotes/origin/master

$ git merge origin/master
Updating 3958f68..55c15c8
Fast forward
 index.html |    2 ++
 1 files changed, 2 insertions(+), 0 deletions(-)
```

 There are slight semantic differences between the merging behavior of branches when multiple refspecs are given on the command line and when they are found in a remote entry. The former causes an octopus merge, wherein all branches are merged simultaneously in an n-way operation, whereas the latter does not. Read the `git pull` manual page carefully!

If you choose to rebase rather than merge, Git will instead forward port the changes on your local-tracking topic branch to the newly fetched HEAD of the corresponding remote-tracking branch. The operation is the same as that shown in Figure 10-12 and Figure 10-13 in Chapter 10.

The command `git pull --rebase` will cause Git to rebase (rather than merge) your local-tracking branch onto the remote-tracking branch during only this `pull`. To make `rebase` the normal operation for a branch, set the `branch.`*branch_name*`.rebase` configuration variable to `true`:

```
[branch "mydev"]
    remote = origin
    merge = refs/heads/master
    rebase = true
```

And with that, the `merge` (or `rebase`) step is also done.

Should you merge or rebase?

So, should you merge or rebase your changes during a `pull` operation? The short answer is "Do either as you wish." So, why would you choose to do one over the other? Here are some issues to consider.

By using merge, you will potentially incur an additional merge commit at each pull to record the updated changes simultaneously present in each branch. In a sense, it is a true reflection of the two paths of development that took place independently and were then, well, merged together. Conflicts will have to be resolved during the merge. Each sequence of commits on each branch will be based on exactly the commit on which it was originally written. When pushed upstream, any merge commits will continue to be present. Some consider these superfluous merges and would rather not see them cluttering up the history. Others consider these merges a more accurate portrayal of the development history and want to see them retained.

As a rebase fundamentally changes the notion of when and where a sequence of commits was developed, some aspects of the development history will be lost. Specifically, the original commit on which your development was originally based will be changed to be the newly pulled HEAD of the remote-tracking branch. That will make the development appear to happen later (in commit sequence) than it actually did. If that's OK with you, it's OK with me. It'll just be different and simpler than if the history was merged. Naturally, you will have to resolve conflicts during the rebase operation as needed still. As the changes that are being rebased are still strictly local within your repository and haven't been published yet, there's really no reason to fear the "don't change history" mantra with this rebase.

With both merge and rebase, you should consider that the new, final content is different from what was present on either development branch independently. As such, it might warrant some form of validation in its new form: perhaps a compilation and test cycle prior to being pushed to an upstream repository.

I tend to like to see simpler, linear histories. During most of my personal development, I'm usually not too concerned by a slight reordering of my changes with respect to those of my coworker's that came in on a remote-tracking branch fetch, so I am fond of using the rebase option.

If you really want to set up one consistent approach, consider setting config options branch.autosetupmerge or branch.autosetuprebase to true, false, or always as desired. There are also a few other options to handle behavior between purely local branches and not just between a local and a remote branch.

Remote Repository Development Cycle in Pictures

Integrating your local development with changes from an upstream repository is at the very core of the distributed development cycle in Git. Let's take a moment to visualize what happens to both your local repository and an upstream origin repository during clone and pull operations. A few pictures should also clarify the often confusing uses of the same name in different contexts.

Let's start with the simple repository shown in Figure 12-1 as the basis for discussion.

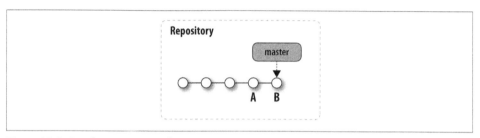

Figure 12-1. Simple repository with commits

As with all of our commit graphs, the sequence of commits flows from left to right and the master label points to the HEAD of the branch. The two most recent commits are labeled A and B. Let's follow these two commits, introduce a few more, and watch what occurs.

Cloning a Repository

A git clone command results in two separate repositories, as shown in Figure 12-2.

This picture illustrates some important results of the clone operation:

- All the commits from the original repository are copied to your clone; you could now easily retrieve earlier stages of the project from your own repository.
- The branch named master from the original repository is introduced into your clone on a new *remote-tracking* branch named origin/master.
- Within the new clone repository, the new origin/master branch is initialized to point to the master HEAD commit, which is B in the figure.

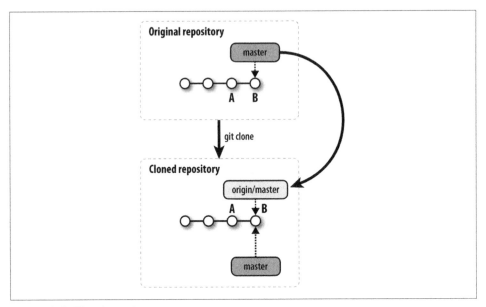

Figure 12-2. Cloned repository

- A new local-tracking branch called master is created in your clone.
- The new master branch is initialized to point to origin/HEAD, the original repository's active branch HEAD. That happens to be origin/master, so it also points to the exact same commit, B.

After cloning, Git selects the new master branch as the current branch and checks it out for you. Thus, unless you change branches, any changes you make after a clone will affect your master.

In all of these diagrams, development branches in both the original repository and the derived clone repository are distinguished by a dark shaded background, and remote-tracking branches by a lighter shaded background. It is important to understand that both the local-tracking development branches and remote-tracking branches are private and local to their respective repositories. In terms of Git's implementation, however, the dark shaded branch labels belong to the *refs/heads/* namespace whereas, the lighter ones belong to *refs/remotes/*.

Alternate Histories

Once you have cloned and obtained your development repository, two distinct paths of development may result. First, you may do development in your repository and make new commits on your master branch, as shown in Figure 12-3. In this picture, your development extends the master branch with two new commits, X and Y, which are based on B.

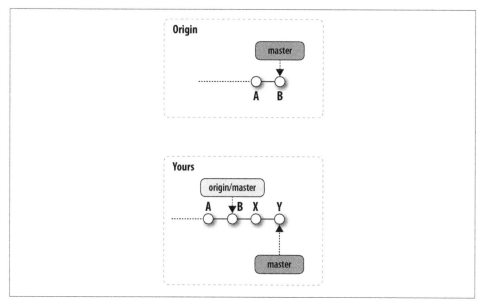

Figure 12-3. Commits in your repository

In the meantime, any other developer who has access to the original repository might have done further development and pushed her changes into that repository. Those changes are represented in Figure 12-4 by the addition of commits C and D.

In this situation, we say that the histories of the repositories have *diverged* or *forked* at commit B. In much the same way that local branching within one repository causes alternate histories to diverge at a commit, a repository and its clone can diverge into alternate histories as a result of separate actions by possibly different people. It is important to realize that this is perfectly fine and that neither history is more correct than the other.

In fact, the whole point of the merge operation is that these different histories may be brought back together and resolved again. Let's see how Git implements that!

Non–Fast-Forward Pushes

If you are developing in a repository model in which you have the ability to `git push` your changes into the `origin` repository, then you might attempt to push your changes at any time. This could create problems if some other developer has previously pushed commits.

This hazard is particularly common when you are using a shared repository development model in which all developers can push their own commits and updates into a common repository at any time.

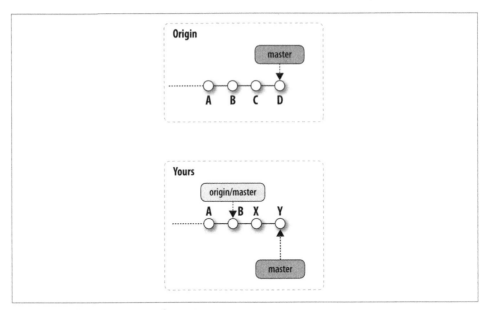

Figure 12-4. Commits in original repository

Let's look again at Figure 12-3, in which you have made new commits, X and Y, based on B.

If you wanted to push your X and Y commits upstream at this point, you could do so easily. Git would transfer your commits to the `origin` repository and add them on to the history at B. Git would then perform a special type of merge operation called a *fast-forward* on the `master` branch, putting in your edits and updating the ref to point to Y. A fast-forward is essentially a simple linear history advancement operation; it was introduced in "Degenerate Merges" on page 140 of Chapter 9.

On the other hand, suppose another developer had already pushed some commits to the origin repository and the picture was more like Figure 12-4 when you attempted to push *your* history up to the `origin` repository. In effect, you are attempting to cause your history to be sent to the shared repository when there is already a different history there. The `origin` history does not simply fast-forward from B. This situation is called the *non–fast-forward push problem*.

When you attempt your push, Git rejects it and tells you about the conflict with a message like this:

```
$ git push
To /tmp/Depot/public_html
 ! [rejected]        master -> master (non-fast forward)
error: failed to push some refs to '/tmp/Depot/public_html'
```

So what are you really trying to do? Do you want to overwrite the other developer's work, or do you want to incorporate both sets of histories?

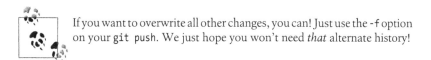

If you want to overwrite all other changes, you can! Just use the -f option on your git push. We just hope you won't need *that* alternate history!

More often, you are not trying to wipe out the existing `origin` history but just want your own changes to be added. In this case, you must perform a merge of the two histories in your repository before pushing.

Fetching the Alternate History

For Git to perform a merge between two alternate histories, both must be present within one repository on two different branches. Branches that are purely local development branches are a special (degenerate) case of their already being in the same repository.

However, if the alternate histories are in different repositories because of cloning, then the remote branch must be brought into your repository via a fetch operation. You can carry out the operation through a direct `git fetch` command or as part of a `git pull` command; it doesn't matter which. In either case, the fetch brings the remote's commits, here C and D, into your repository. The results are shown in Figure 12-5.

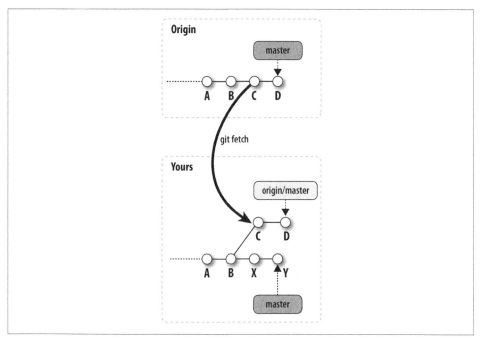

Figure 12-5. Fetching the alternate history

In no way does the introduction of the alternate history with commits C and D change the history represented by X and Y; the two alternate histories both now exist simultaneously in your repository and form a more complex graph. Your history is represented by your master branch, and the remote history is represented by the origin/master remote-tracking branch.

Merging Histories

Now that both histories are present in one repository, all that is needed to unify them is a merge of the origin/master branch into the master branch.

The merge operation can be initiated either with a direct git merge origin/master command or as the second step in a git pull request. In both cases, the techniques for the merge operation are exactly the same as those described in Chapter 9.

Figure 12-6 shows the commit graph in your repository after the merge has successfully assimilated the two histories from commit D and Y into a new merge commit, M. The ref for origin/master remains pointing at D because it hasn't changed, but master is updated to the merge commit, M, to indicate that the merge was into the master branch; this is where the new commit was made.

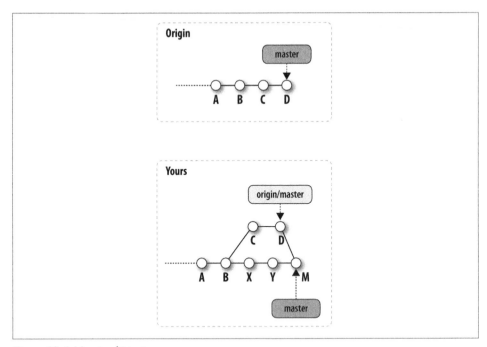

Figure 12-6. Merging histories

Merge Conflicts

Occasionally there will be merge conflicts between the alternate histories. Regardless of the outcome of the merge, the fetch still occurred. All the commits from the remote repository are still present in your repository on the tracking branch.

You may choose to resolve the merge normally, as described in Chapter 9, or you may choose to abort the merge and reset your `master` branch to its prior `ORIG_HEAD` state using the command `git reset --hard ORIG_HEAD`. Doing so in this example would move `master` to the *prior* `HEAD` value, `Y`, and change your working directory to match. It would also leave `origin/master` at commit `D`.

 You can brush up on the meaning of `ORIG_HEAD` by reviewing "refs and symrefs" on page 68 of Chapter 6; also see its use in the section "Aborting or Restarting a Merge" on page 137 (Chapter 9).

Pushing a Merged History

If you've performed all the steps shown, your repository has been updated to contain the latest changes from both the `origin` repository and your repository. But the converse is not true: the `origin` repository still doesn't have your changes.

If your objective is only to incorporate the latest updates from `origin` into your repository, then you are finished when your merge is resolved. On the other hand, a simple `git push` can return the unified and merged history from your `master` branch back to the `origin` repository. Figure 12-7 shows the results after you `git push`.

Finally, observe that the `origin` repository has been updated with your development even if it has undergone other changes that had to be merged first. Both your repository and the `origin` repository have been fully updated and are again synchronized.

Remote Configuration

Keeping track of all of the information about a remote repository reference by hand can become tedious and difficult: you have to remember the full URL for the repository; you must type and retype remote references and refspecs on the command line each time you want to fetch updates; you have to reconstruct the branch mappings; and so on. Repeating the information is also likely to be quite error prone.

You might also wonder how Git remembers the URL for the remote from the initial clone for use in subsequent fetch or push operations using `origin`.

Git provides three mechanisms for setting up and maintaining information about remotes: the `git remote` command, the `git config` command, and editing

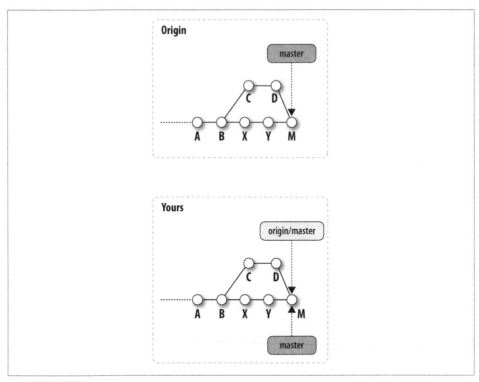

Figure 12-7. Merged histories after push

the *.git/config* file directly. All three mechanisms ultimately result in configuration information being recorded in the *.git/config* file.

Using git remote

The `git remote` command is a more specialized interface, specific to remotes, that manipulates the configuration file data and remote refs. It has several subcommands with fairly intuitive names. There is no help option, but you can circumvent that to display a message with subcommand names via the "unknown subcommand trick":

```
$ git remote xyzzy
error: Unknown subcommand: xyzzy
usage: git remote
   or: git remote add <name> <url>
   or: git remote rm <name>
   or: git remote show <name>
   or: git remote prune <name>
   or: git remote update [group]

    -v, --verbose         be verbose
```

You saw the `git remote add` and `update` commands in the section "Make Your Own Origin Remote" on page 206, earlier in this chapter, and you saw `show` in "Adding a New Developer" on page 210. You used `git remote add origin` to add a new remote named `origin` to the newly created parent repository in the depot, and you ran the `git remote show origin` command to extract all the information about the remote `origin`. Finally, you used the `git remote update` command to fetch all the updates available in the remote repository into your local repository.

The command `git remote rm` removes the given remote and all of its associated remote-tracking branches from your *local* repository. To remove just one remote-tracking branch from your local repository, use a command like this:

```
$ git branch -r -d origin/dev
```

But you shouldn't really do that unless the corresponding remote branch really has been removed from the upstream repository. Otherwise, your next fetch from the upstream repository is likely to recreate the branch again.

The remote repository may have branches deleted from it by the actions of other developers, even though your copies of those branches may linger in your repository. The `git remote prune` command may be used to remove the names of those stale (with respect to the actual remote repository) remote-tracking branches from your local repository.

To keep even more in sync with an upstream remote, use the command `git remote update --prune` *remote* to first get updates from the remote and then prune stale tracking branches all in one step.

To rename a remote and all of its refs, use `git remote rename` *old new*. After this command:

```
$ git remote rename jon jdl
```

any ref like `jon/bugfixes` will be renamed as `jdl/bugfixes`.

In addition to manipulations of the remote name and its refs, you can also update or change the URL of the remote:

```
$ git remote set-url origin git://repos.example.com/stuff.git
```

Using git config

The `git config` command can be used to manipulate the entries in your configuration file directly. This includes several config variables for remotes.

For example, to add a new remote named `publish` with a push refspec for all the branches you would like to publish, you might do something like this:

```
$ git config remote.publish.url 'ssh://git.example.org/pub/repo.git'
$ git config remote.publish.push '+refs/heads/*:refs/heads/*'
```

Each of the preceding commands adds a line to the *.git/config* file. If no `publish` remote section exists yet, then the first command you issue that refers to that remote creates a section in the file for it. As a result, your *.git/config* contains, in part, the following remote definition:

```
[remote "publish"]
        url = ssh://git.example.org/pub/repo.git
        push = +refs/heads/*:refs/heads/*
```

 Use the -l (lowercase L) option à la `git config -l` to list the contents of the configuration file with complete variable names:

```
# From a clone of git.git sources

$ git config -l
core.repositoryformatversion=0
core.filemode=true
core.bare=false
core.logallrefupdates=true
remote.origin.url=git://git.kernel.org/pub/scm/git/git.git
remote.origin.fetch=+refs/heads/*:refs/remotes/origin/*
branch.master.remote=origin
branch.master.merge=refs/heads/master
```

Using Manual Editing

Rather than wrestling with either the `git remote` or `git config` commands, directly editing the file with your favorite text editor may be easier or faster in some situations. There is nothing wrong with doing so, but it can be error prone and is usually done only by developers who are very familiar with Git's behavior and the configuration file. Yet having seen the parts of the file that influence various Git behaviors and the changes resulting from commands, you should have basis enough to understand and manipulate the configuration file.

Multiple Remote Repositories

Operations such as `git remote add` *remote repository-URL* can be executed multiple times to add several new remotes to your repository. With multiple remotes, you can subsequently fetch commits from multiple sources and combine them in your repository. This feature also allows you to establish several push destinations that might receive part or all of your repository.

In Chapter 13, we'll show you how to use multiple repositories in different scenarios during your development.

Working with Tracking Branches

Because the creation and manipulation of tracking branches is such a vital part of the Git development methodology, it is important to understand how and why Git creates the different tracking branches and how Git expects you to develop using them.

Creating Tracking Branches

In the same way that your master branch can be thought of as extending the development brought in on the origin/master branch, you can create a new branch based on any remote-tracking branch and use it to extend that line of development.

We've already seen that remote-tracking branches are introduced during a clone operation or when remotes are added to a repository. In later versions of Git, after about 1.6.6 or so, Git makes it very easy to create a local- and remote-tracking branch pair using a consistent ref name for them. A simple check out request using the name of a remote-tracking branch causes a new local-tracking branch to be created and associated with the remote-tracking branch. However, Git does this only if your branch name matches just one remote branch name from all of the repository remotes. And by the phrase "branch name matches," Git means the full branch name after the name of the remote in a refspec.

Let's use Git's source repository for some examples. By pulling both from GitHub and git.kernel.org, we'll create a repository that has a vast collection of branch names from two remotes, some of which are duplicates.

```
# Grab GitHub's repository
$ git clone git://github.com/gitster/git.git
Cloning into 'git'...
...

$ git remote add korg git://git.kernel.org/pub/scm/git/git.git

$ git remote update
Fetching origin
Fetching korg
remote: Counting objects: 3541, done.
remote: Compressing objects: 100% (1655/1655), done.
remote: Total 3541 (delta 1796), reused 3451 (delta 1747)
Receiving objects: 100% (3541/3541), 1.73 MiB | 344 KiB/s, done.
Resolving deltas: 100% (1796/1796), done.
From git://git.kernel.org/pub/scm/git/git
 * [new branch]      maint      -> korg/maint
 * [new branch]      master     -> korg/master
 * [new branch]      next       -> korg/next
 * [new branch]      pu         -> korg/pu
 * [new branch]      todo       -> korg/todo


# Find a uniquely name branch and check it out.
```

```
$ git branch -a | grep split-blob
  remotes/origin/jc/split-blob

$ git branch
* master

$ git checkout jc/split-blob
Branch jc/split-blob set up to track remote branch jc/split-blob from origin.
Switched to a new branch 'jc/split-blob'

$ git branch
* jc/split-blob
  master
```

Notice that we had to use the full branch name jc/split-blob and not simply split-blob.

In the case when the branch name is ambiguous, you can directly establish and set up the branch yourself.

```
$ git branch -a | egrep 'maint$'
  remotes/korg/maint
  remotes/origin/maint

$ git checkout maint
error: pathspec 'maint' did not match any file(s) known to git.

# Just select one of the maint branches.
$ git checkout --track korg/maint
Branch maint set up to track remote branch maint from korg.
Switched to a new branch 'maint'
```

It is likely that the two branches represent the same commit as found in two different repositories and you can simply choose one on which to base your local-tracking branch.

If for some reason you wish to use a different name for your local-tracking branch, use the -b option.

```
$ git checkout -b mypu --track korg/pu
Branch mypu set up to track remote branch pu from korg.
Switched to a new branch 'mypu'
```

Under the hood, Git automatically adds a branch entry to the *.git/config* to indicate that the remote-tracking branch should be merged into your new local-tracking branch. The collected changes from the previous series of commands yields the following config file:

```
$ cat .git/config
[core]
    repositoryformatversion = 0
    filemode = true
    bare = false
    logallrefupdates = true
[remote "origin"]
    fetch = +refs/heads/*:refs/remotes/origin/*
    url = git://github.com/gitster/git.git
```

```
[branch "master"]
    remote = origin
    merge = refs/heads/master
[remote "korg"]
    url = git://git.kernel.org/pub/scm/git/git.git
    fetch = +refs/heads/*:refs/remotes/korg/*
[branch "jc/split-blob"]
    remote = origin
    merge = refs/heads/jc/split-blob
[branch "maint"]
    remote = korg
    merge = refs/heads/maint
[branch "mypu"]
    remote = korg
    merge = refs/heads/pu
```

As usual, you may also use `git config` or a text editor to manipulate the branch entries in the configuration file.

 When you get lost in the tracking branch mire, use the command `git remote show` *remote* to help sort out all the remotes and branches.

At this point, it should be pretty clear that the default clone behavior introduces local-tracking branch `master` for the remote-tracking branch `origin/master` as a simplifying convenience just as if you had explicitly checked out the `master` branch yourself.

To reinforce the idea that making commits directly on a remote-tracking branch isn't good form, checking out a remote-tracking branch using early versions of Git (prior to about 1.6.6 or so) caused a detached `HEAD`. As mentioned in "Detached HEAD Branches" on page 102 of Chapter 7, a detached `HEAD` is essentially an anonymous branch name. Making commits on the detached `HEAD` is possible, but you shouldn't then update your remote-tracking branch `HEAD` with any local commits lest you suffer grief later when fetching new updates from that remote. (If you find you need to keep any such commits on a detached `HEAD`, use `git checkout -b` *my_branch* to create a new, local branch on which to further develop your changes.) Collectively, it isn't really a good, intuitive approach.

If you don't want to check out a local-tracking branch when you create it, you can instead use `git branch --track` *local-branch remote-branch* to create the local-tracking branch and record the local- and remote-branch association in the *.git/config* file for you:

```
$ git branch --track dev origin/dev
Branch dev set up to track remote branch dev from origin.
```

And, if you already have a topic branch that you decide should be associated with an upstream repository's remote-tracking branch, you can establish the relationship using the `--upstream` option. Typically, this is done after adding a new remote, like this:

```
$ git remote add upstreamrepo git://git.example.org/upstreamrepo.git

# Branch mydev already existed.
# Leave it alone, but associated it with upstreamrepo/dev.
$ git branch --set-upstream mydev upstreamrepo/dev
```

Ahead and Behind

With the establishment of a local- and remote-tracking branch pair, relative comparisons between the two branches can be made. In addition to the normal diff, log, and other content-based comparisons, Git offers a quick summary of the number of commits on each of the branches and states which branch it judges to be "ahead of" or "behind" the other branch.

If your local development introduces new commits on a local-tracking branch, it is considered to be ahead of the corresponding remote-tracking branch. Conversely, if you fetch new commits onto remote-tracking branches and they are not present on your local-tracking branch, Git considers your local-tracking branch to be behind the corresponding remote-tracking branch.

The git status usually reports this status:

```
$ git fetch
remote: Counting objects: 9, done.
remote: Compressing objects: 100% (6/6), done.
remote: Total 6 (delta 4), reused 0 (delta 0)
Unpacking objects: 100% (6/6), done.
From example.com:SomeRepo
   b1a68a8..b722324  ver2  -> origin/ver2

$ git status
# On branch ver2
# Your branch is behind 'origin/ver2' by 2 commits, and can be fast-forwarded.
```

To see which commits you have in master that are not in origin/master, use a command like this:

```
$ git log origin/master..master
```

Yes, it is possible to be both ahead and behind simultaneously!

```
# Make one local commit on top of previous example
$ git commit -m "Something" main.c
   ...

$ git status
# On branch ver2
# Your branch and 'origin/ver2' have diverged,
# and have 1 and 2 different commit(s) each, respectively.
```

And in this case, you probably want to use the symmetric difference to see the changes:

```
$ git log origin/master...master
```

Adding and Deleting Remote Branches

Any new development you create on branches in your local clone are not visible in the parent repository until you make a direct request to propagate it there. Similarly, a branch deletion in your repository remains a local change and is not removed from the parent repository until you request it to be removed from the remote as well.

In Chapter 7, you learned how to add new branches to and delete existing ones from your repository using the `git branch` command. But `git branch` operates only on a local repository.

To perform similar branch add and delete operations on a remote repository, you need to specify different forms of refspecs in a `git push` command. Recall that the syntax of a *refspec* is:

```
[+]source:destination
```

Pushes that use a refspec with just a *source* ref (i.e., with no *destination* ref) create a new branch in the remote repository:

```
$ cd ~/public_html

$ git checkout -b foo
Switched to a new branch "foo"

$ git push origin foo
Total 0 (delta 0), reused 0 (delta 0)
To /tmp/Depot/public_html
 * [new branch]      foo -> foo
```

A push that names only a source is just a shorthand for using the same name for both the source and destination ref name. A push that names both a source and a destination ref that are different can be used to create a new destination named *branch* or extend an existing destination remote branch with the content from the local source branch. That is, `git push origin mystuff:dev` will push the local branch `mystuff` to the upstream repository and either create or extend a branch named `dev`. Thus, due to a series of default behaviors, the following commands have the same effect:

```
$ git push upstream new_dev
$ git push upstream new_dev:new_dev
$ git push upstream new_dev:refs/heads/new_dev
```

Pushes that use a refspec with just a *destination* ref (i.e., no *source* ref) cause the *destination* ref to be deleted from the remote repository. To denote the ref as the *destination*, the colon separator must be specified:

```
$ git push origin :foo
To /tmp/Depot/public_html
 - [deleted]         foo
```

If that :*branch* form causes you heartache, you can use a syntactically equivalent form:

```
$ git push origin --delete foo
```

So what about renaming a remote branch? Unfortunately, there is not a simple solution. The short answer is create a new upstream branch with the new name and then delete the old branch. That's easy enough to do using the `git push` commands as shown previously.

```
# Create new name at exiting old commit
$ git branch new origin/old
$ git push origin new

# Remove the old name
$ git push origin :old
```

But that's the easy and obvious part. Now what are the distributed implications? Do you know who has a clone of the upstream repository that was just modified out from underneath them? If you do, they could all just `fetch` and `remote prune` to get their repositories updated. But if you don't, then all those other clones will suddenly have dangling tracking branches. And there's no real way to get them renamed in a distributed way.

Bottom line here: this is just a variant on the "Be careful how you rewrite history" theme.

Bare Repositories and git push

As a consequence of the peer-to-peer semantics of Git repositories, all repositories are of equal stature. You can push to and fetch from development and bare repositories equally, because there is no fundamental implementation distinction between them. This symmetric design is critically important to Git, but it also leads to some unexpected behavior if you try to treat bare and development repositories as exact equals.

Recall that the `git push` command does not check out files in the receiving repository. It simply transfers objects from the source repository to the receiving repository and then updates the corresponding refs on the receiving end.

In a bare repository, this behavior is all that can be expected, because there is no working directory that might be updated by checked out files. That's good. However, in a development repository that is the recipient of a push operation, it can later cause confusion to anyone using the development repository.

The push operation can update the repository state, including the HEAD commit. That is, even though the developer at the remote end has done nothing, the branch refs and HEAD might change, becoming out of sync with the checked out files and index.

A developer who is actively working in a repository into which an asynchronous push happens will not see the push. But a subsequent commit by that developer will occur on an unexpected HEAD, creating an odd history. A forced push will lose pushed commits from the other developer. The developer at that repository also may find herself unable to reconcile her history with either an upstream repository or a downstream clone because they are no longer simple fast-forwards as they should be. And she won't know why: the repository has silently changed out from underneath her. Cats and dogs will live together. It'll be bad.

As a result, you are encouraged to push only into a bare repository. This is not a hard-and-fast rule, but it's a good guide to the average developer and is considered a best practice. There are a few instances and use cases where you might want to push into a development repository, but you should fully understand its implications. When you *do* want to push into a development repository, you may want to follow one of two basic approaches.

In the first scenario, you really do want to have a working directory with a branch checked out in the receiving repository. You may know, for example, that no other developer will ever be doing active development there and therefore there is no one who might be blind sided by silent changes being pushed into his repository.

In this case, you may want to enable a hook in the receiving repository to perform a checkout of some branch, perhaps the one just pushed, into the working directory as well. To verify that the receiving repository is in a sane state prior to having an automatic checkout, the hook should ensure that the nonbare repository's working directory contains no edits or modified files and that its index has no files in the staged but uncommitted state when the push happens. When these conditions are not met, you run the risk of losing those edits or changes as the checkout overwrites them.

There is another scenario where pushing into a nonbare repository can work reasonably well. By agreement, each developer who pushes changes must push to a non–checked out branch that is considered simply a receiving branch. A developer never pushes to a branch that is expected to be checked out. It is up to some developer in particular to manage what branch is checked out and when. Perhaps that person is responsible for handling the receiving branches and merging them into a master branch before it is checked out.

## CHAPTER 13

Repository Management

This chapter describes how to publish Git repositories and then presents two approaches to managing and publishing repositories for cooperative development. One approach centralizes the repository; the other distributes the repository. Each solution has its place, and which is right for you and your project depends on your requirements and philosophy.

However, no matter which approach you adopt, Git implements a distributed development model. For example, even if your team centralizes the repository, each developer has a complete, private copy of that repository and can work independently. The work is distributed, yet it is coordinated through a central, shared repository. The repository model and the development model are orthogonal characteristics.

A Word About Servers

The word "server" gets used liberally and loosely for a variety of meanings. Neither Git nor this book will be an exception, so let's clarify some aspects of what a server may or may not be, might or might not do, and just how Git might use one.

Technically, Git doesn't need a server. In contrast to other VCSs, where a centralized server is often required, there is no need to hang onto the mindset that one is *required* to host Git repositories.

Having a server in the context of a Git repository is often little more than establishing a convenient, fixed, or known location from which repositories are obtained or updates are exchanged. The Git server might also provide some form of authentication or access control.

Git is happy to exchange files directly with a peer repository on the same machine without the need for some server to broker the deal, or with different machines via a variety of protocols none of which enforces a superior server to exist.

Instead, the word "server" here is more loose. On one hand, it may be just "some other computer willing to interact with us." On the other hand, it *could* be some rack-mounted, highly available, well-connected, centralized server with a lot of computational power. So, this whole notion of setting up a server needs to be understood in the context of "if that's how you want to do it." You be the judge of your requirements here.

Publishing Repositories

Whether you are setting up an open source development environment in which many people across the Internet might develop a project or establishing a project for internal development within a private group, the mechanics of collaboration are essentially the same. The main difference between the two scenarios is the location of the repository and access to it.

> The phrase "commit rights" is really sort of a misnomer in Git. Git doesn't try to manage access rights, leaving that issue to other tools, such as SSH, which are more suited to the task. You can always commit in any repository to which you have (Unix) access, either via SSH and cding to that repository, or to which you have direct rwx-mode access.
>
> The concept might better be paraphrased as "Can I update the published repository?" In that expression, you can see the issue is really the question, "Can I push changes to the published repository?"

Earlier, in "Referring to Remote Repositories" on page 200, you were cautioned about using the remote repository URL form /path/to/repo.git because it might exhibit problems characteristic of repositories that use shared files. On the other hand, setting up a common depot containing several similar repositories is a common situation where you would want to use a shared, underlying object store. In this case, you expect the repositories to be monotonically increasing in size without objects and refs being removed from them. This situation can benefit from large-scale sharing of the object store by many repositories, thus saving tremendous volumes of disk space. To achieve this space savings, consider using the --reference *repository*, the --local, or the --shared options during the initial bare repository clone setup step for your published repositories.

In any situation where you publish a repository, we strongly advise that you publish a bare one.

Repositories with Controlled Access

As mentioned earlier in the chapter, it might be sufficient for your project to publish a bare repository in a known location on a filesystem inside your organization that everyone can access.

Naturally, access in this context means that all developers can see the filesystem on their machines and have traditional Unix ownership and read/write permissions. In these scenarios, using a filename URL such as */path/to/Depot/project.git* or *file://path/to/Depot/project.git* might suffice. Although the performance might be less than ideal, an NFS-mounted filesystem can provide such sharing support.

Slightly more complex access is called for if multiple development machines are used. Within a corporation, for example, the IT department might provide a central server for the repository depot and keep it backed up. Each developer might then have a desktop machine for development. If direct filesystem access such as NFS is not available, you could use repositories named with SSH URLs, but this still requires each developer to have an account on the central server.

In the following example, the same repository published in */tmp/Depot/public_html.git* earlier in this chapter is accessed by a developer who has SSH access to the hosting machine:

```
desktop$ cd /tmp
desktop$ git clone ssh://example.com/tmp/Depot/public_html.git
Initialize public_html/.git
Initialized empty Git repository in /tmp/public_html/.git/
jdl@example.com's password:
remote: Counting objects: 27, done.
Receiving objects: 100% (27/27), done.objects:    3% (1/27)
Resolving deltas: 100% (7/7), done.
remote: Compressing objects: 100% (23/23), done.
remote: Total 27 (delremote: ta 7), reused 0 (delta 0)
```

When that clone is made, it records the source repository using the following URL: ssh://example.com/tmp/Depot/public_html.git.

Similarly, other commands such as git fetch and git push can now be used across the network:

```
desktop$ git push
jdl@example.com's password:
Counting objects: 5, done.
Compressing objects: 100% (3/3), done.
Writing objects: 100% (3/3), 385 bytes, done.
Total 3 (delta 1), reused 0 (delta 0)
To ssh://example.com/tmp/Depot/public_html.git
   55c15c8..451e41c  master -> master
```

In both of these examples, the password requested is the normal Unix login password for the remote hosting machine.

 If you need to provide network access with authenticated developers but are not willing to provide login access to the hosting server, check out the Gitolite project. Start here:

```
$ git clone git://github.com/sitaramc/gitolite
```

Again, depending on the desired scope of access, such SSH access to machines may be entirely within a group or corporate setting or may be available across the entire Internet.

Repositories with Anonymous Read Access

If you want to share code, then you'll probably want to set up a hosting server to publish repositories and allow others to clone them. Anonymous, read-only access is often all that developers need to clone or fetch from these repositories. A common and easy solution is to export them using `git-daemon` and also perhaps an HTTP daemon.

Again, the actual realm across which you can publish your repository is as limited or as broad as access to your HTTP pages or your `git-daemon`. That is, if you host these commands on a public-facing machine, then anyone can clone and fetch from your repositories. If you put it behind a corporate firewall, only those people inside the corporation will have access (in the absence of security breaches).

Publishing repositories using git-daemon

Setting up `git-daemon` allows you to export your repositories using the Git-native protocol.

You must mark repositories as "OK to be exported" in some way. Typically, this is done by creating the file *git-daemon-export-ok* in the top-level directory of the bare repository. This mechanism gives you fine-grained control over which repositories the daemon can export.

Instead of marking each repository individually, you can also run `git-daemon` with the `--export-all` option to publish all identifiable (by having both an *objects* and a *refs* subdirectory) repositories found in its list of *directories*. There are many `git-daemon` options that limit and configure which repositories will be exported.

One common way to set up the `git-daemon` on a server is to enable it as an `inetd` service. This involves ensuring that your */etc/services* has an entry for Git. The default port is 9418, though you may use any port you like. A typical entry might be:

```
git     9418/tcp     # Git Version Control System
```

Once you add that line to */etc/services*, you must set up an entry in your */etc/inetd.conf* to specify how the `git-daemon` should be invoked.

A typical entry might look like this:

```
# Place on one long line in /etc/inetd.conf

git stream tcp nowait nobody /usr/bin/git-daemon
        git-daemon --inetd --verbose --export-all
        --base-path=/pub/git
```

Using xinetd instead of inetd, place a similar configuration in the file */etc/xinetd.d/git-daemon*:

```
# description: The git server offers access to git repositories
service git
{
    disable          = no
    type             = UNLISTED
    port             = 9418
    socket_type      = stream
    wait             = no
    user             = nobody
    server           = /usr/bin/git-daemon
    server_args      = --inetd --export-all --base-path=/pub/git
    log_on_failure  += USERID
}
```

You can make it look as if repositories are located on separate hosts, even though they're just in separate directories on a single host, through a trick supported by git-daemon. The following example entry allows a server to provide multiple, virtually hosted Git daemons:

```
# Place on one long line in /etc/inetd.conf

git stream tcp nowait nobody /usr/bin/git-daemon
        git-daemon --inetd --verbose --export-all
        --interpolated-path=/pub/%H%D
```

In the command shown, git-daemon will fill in the %H with a fully qualified hostname and %D with the repository's directory path. Because %H can be a logical hostname, different sets of repositories can be offered by one physical server.

Typically, an additional level of directory structure, such as */software* or */scm*, is used to organize the advertised repositories. If you combine the --interpolated-path=/pub/ %H%D with a */software* repository directory path, then the bare repositories to be published will be physically present on the server, in directories such as:

```
/pub/git.example.com/software/
/pub/www.example.org/software/
```

You would then advertise the availability of your repositories at URLs such as:

```
git://git.example.com/software/repository.git
git://www.example.org/software/repository.git
```

Here, the %H is replaced by the host git.example.com or www.example.org and the %D is replaced by full repository names, such as /software/*repository.git*.

The important point of this example is that it shows how a single git-daemon can be used to maintain and publish multiple, separate collections of Git repositories that are physically hosted on one server but presented as logically separate hosts. Those repositories available from one host might be different from those offered by a different host.

Publishing repositories using an HTTP daemon

Sometimes, an easier way to publish repositories with anonymous read access is to simply make them available through an HTTP daemon. If you also set up `gitweb`, then visitors can load a URL into their web browsers, see an index listing of your repository, and negotiate using familiar clicks and the browser Back button. Visitors do not need to run Git in order to download files.

You will need to make one configuration adjustment to your bare Git repository before it can be properly served by an HTTP daemon: enable the *hooks/post-update* option as follows:

```
$ cd /path/to/bare/repo.git
$ mv hooks/post-update.sample hooks/post-update
```

Verify that the *post-update* script is executable, or use `chmod 755` on it just to be sure. Finally, copy that bare Git repository into a directory served by your HTTP daemon. You can now advertise that your project is available using a URL such as:

```
http://www.example.org/software/repository.git
```

If you see the error message such as:

```
... not found: did you run git update-server-info on the server?
```

or

```
Perhaps git-update-server-info needs to be run there?
```

then chances are good that you aren't running the `hooks/post-update` command properly on the server.

Publishing a repository using Smart HTTP

Publishing a repository via the newer, so-called Smart HTTP mechanism is pretty simple in principle, but you may want to consult the full online documentation for the process as found in the manual page of the `git-http-backend` command. What follows here is a simplified extraction of some of that material that should get you started.

First, this setup is really geared for use with Apache. Thus, the examples that follow show how to modify Apache configuration files. On a Ubuntu system, these are found in */etc/apache2*. Second, some mapping from your advertised repository names to the repository layout on the disk as made available to Apache needs to be defined. As with the `git-http-backend` documentation, the mapping here makes http://$hostname/git/foo/bar.git correspond to */var/www/git/foo/bar.git* under Apache's file view. Third, several Apache modules are required and must be enabled: `mod_cgi`, `mod_alias`, and `mod_env`.

Define some variables and a script alias that points to the `git-http-backend` command like this:

```
SetEnv GIT_PROJECT_ROOT /var/www/git
SetEnv GIT_HTTP_EXPORT_ALL
ScriptAlias /git/ /usr/libexec/git-core/git-http-backend/
```

The location of your `git-http-backend` may be different. For example, Ubuntu places it in *usr/lib/git-core/git-http-backend*.

Now you have a choice: you can allow anonymous read access but require authenticated write access to your repository, or you can require authentication for read and write.

For anonymous read access, set up a `LocationMatch` directive:

```
<LocationMatch "^/git/.*/git-receive-pack$">
    AuthType Basic
    AuthName "Git Access"
    Require group committers
    ...
</LocationMatch>
```

For authenticated read access, set up a `Location` directive for the repository or a parent directory of the repository:

```
<Location /git/private>
    AuthType Basic
    AuthName "Private Git Access"
    Require group committers
    ...
</Location>
```

Further recipes exist within the manual page to set up coordinated `gitweb` access, and show how to serve multiple repositories namespaces and configure accelerated access to static pages.

Publishing via Git and HTTP daemons

Although using a web server and browser is certainly convenient, think carefully about how much traffic you plan to handle on your server. Development projects can become large, and HTTP is less efficient than the native Git protocol.

You can provide both HTTP and Git daemon access, but it might take some adjusting and coordination between your Git daemon and your HTTP daemon. Specifically, it may require a mapping with the `--interpolated-path` option to `git-daemon` and an `Alias` option to Apache to provide seamless integration of the two views of the same data. Further details on the `--interpolated-path` are available in the `git daemon` manual page, whereas details about the Apache `Alias` option can be found in the Apache documentation or its configuration file, */etc/apache2/mods-available/alias.conf*.

Repositories with Anonymous Write Access

Technically, you may use the Git native protocol URL forms to allow anonymous write access into repositories served by git-daemon. To do so requires you to enable the receivepack option in the published repositories:

```
[daemon]
        receivepack = true
```

You might do this on a private LAN where every developer is trusted, but it is not considered best practice. Instead, you should consider tunneling your Git push needs over an SSH connection.

Publishing Your Repository to GitHub

We'll assume you have a repository with some commits and have already established a GitHub account. With these prerequisites established, the next step is creating a repository to accept your commits at GitHub.

Creating the GitHub Repository
> Sign in to GitHub and begin at your personal dashboard. You can access this personal dashboard at any time by clicking the GitHub logo. Next, click the "New repository" button.

Supplying the New Repository Name
> The only required field is the "Project Name" and it will be the last part of the URL at which you'll access your repository. For example, if your GitHub username was jonl, a Project Name of gitbook would appear at https://github.com/jonl/git book.

Choosing the Access Control Level
> There are two choices for access control at this juncture. One is to allow *anyone* to access the repository's contents. The other is to specify a *list of GitHub users* that are permitted to access it. GitHub, in its mission to foster more open source projects, allows for unlimited public repositories at no cost. Closed repositories, being more likely business focused, are charged on a monthly or annual subscription plan basis. Click "Create repository" to continue.

Initializing the Repository
> The repository has now been created, but doesn't yet have any contents. GitHub provides users with stepwise instructions from which we'll follow the "Existing Git Repo" process. At a shell prompt in your local existing Git repository, we'll add the GitHub remote and push the contents.

Adding the Remote
> First, type git remote add origin *githubrepoaddress*. This registers a remote destination to which Git can push contents. The specific *githubrepoaddress* and initialization instructions are repeatedly provided on the GitHub page for the project after creating the repository but before it has any contents.

Pushing the Contents

Second, type `git push -u origin master` if you wish to selectively publish your `master` branch. If you wish to publish all your local branches and tags, you can alternatively (one time only) issue the `git push --mirror origin` command. Subsequent invocations would less desirably push remote-tracking branches that are not intended to be pushed.

View the site

That's all there is to publishing a Git repository to GitHub. You can now refresh the project page and, in place of the initialization instructions, the project's *README* and directory and file structure will be shown in a web-navigable view.

Repository Publishing Advice

Before you go wildly setting up server machines and hosting services just to host Git repositories, consider what your needs really are and why you want to offer Git repositories. Perhaps your needs are already satisfied by existing companies, websites, or services.

For private code or even public code where you place a premium on the value of service, you might consider using a commerical Git hosting service.

If you are offering an open source repository and have minimal service needs or expectations, there are a multitude of Git hosting services available. Some offer upgrades to supported services as well.

The more complicated situations arise when you have private code that you want to keep in house and therefore must set up and maintain your own master depot for repository hosting. Oh, and don't forget your own backups!

In this case, the usual approach is to use the Git-over-SSH protocol and require all users of the repository to have SSH access to the hosting server. On the server itself, a semi-generic user account and group (e.g., `git` or `gituser`) are usually created. All repositories are group owned by this user and typically live in some filespace (e.g., */git*, */opt/git*, or */var/git*) set aside for this purpose. Here's the key: that directory must be owned by your `gituser` group, be writable by that group, and it must have the sticky group bit set.

Now, when you want to create a new, hosted repository called `newrepo.git` on your server, just `ssh` into the server and do this:

```
$ ssh git.my-host.example.com

$ cd /git
$ mkdir newrepo.git
$ cd newrepo.git
$ git init --shared --bare
```

Those last four commands can be simplified as follows:

```
$ git --git-dir /git/newrepo.git init --shared
```

At this point, the bare repository structure exists, but it remains empty. The important aspect of this repository, though, is that it is now receptive to a push of initial content from any user authorized to connect with the server.

```
# from some client
$ cd /path/to/existing/initial/repo.git
$ git push git+ssh://git.my-host.example.com/git/newrepo.git master
```

The whole process of executing that `git init` on the server in such a way that subsequent pushes will work is at the heart of the Git web hosting services. That command is essentially what happens when you click on the GitHub "New Repo" button.

Repository Structure

The Shared Repository Structure

Some VCSs use a centralized server to maintain a repository. In this model, every developer is a client of the server, which maintains the authoritative version of the repository. Given the server's jurisdiction, almost every versioning operation must contact the server to obtain or update repository information. Thus, for two developers to share data, all information must pass through the centralized server; no direct sharing of data between developers is possible.

With Git, in contrast, a shared, authoritative, and centralized repository is merely a convention. Each developer still has a clone of the depot's repository, so there's no need for every request or query to go to a centralized server. For instance, simple log history queries can be made privately and offline by each developer.

One of the reasons that some operations can be performed locally is that a checkout retrieves not just the particular version you ask for, the way most centralized VCSs operate, but the entire history. Hence, you can reconstruct any version of a file from the local repository.

Furthermore, nothing prevents a developer from either establishing an alternate repository and making it available on a peer-to-peer basis with other developers, or from sharing content in the form of patches and branches.

In summary, Git's notion of a shared, centralized repository model is purely one of social convention and agreement.

Distributed Repository Structure

Large projects often have a highly distributed development model consisting of a central, single, yet logically segmented repository. Although the repository still exists as one physical unit, logical portions are relegated to different people or teams that work largely or wholly independently.

When it's said that Git supports a distributed repository model, this doesn't mean that a single repository is broken up into separate pieces and spread around many hosts. Instead, the distributed repository is just a consequence of Git's distributed development model. Each developer has her own repository that is complete and self-contained. Each developer and her respective repository might be spread out and distributed around the network.

How the repository is partitioned or allocated to different maintainers is largely immaterial to Git. The repositories might have a deeply nested directory structure or they might be more broadly structured. For example, different development teams might be responsible for certain portions of a code base along submodule, library, or functional lines. Each team might raise a champion to be the *maintainer*, or steward, of its portion of the code base, and agree as a team to route all changes through this appointed maintainer.

The structure may even evolve over time as different people or groups become involved in the project. Furthermore, a team could likely form intermediate repositories that contain combinations of other repositories, with or without further development. There may be specific stable or release repositories, for instance, each with an attendant development team and a maintainer.

It may be a good idea to allow the large-scale repository iteration and dataflow to grow naturally and according to peer review and suggestion rather than impose a possibly artificial layout in advance. Git is flexible, so if development in one layout or flow doesn't seem to work, it is quite easy to change it to a better one.

How the repositories of a large project are organized, or how they coalesce and combine, is again largely immaterial to the workings of Git; Git supports any number of organizational models. Remember that the repository structure is not absolute. Moreover, the connection between any two repositories is not prescribed. Git repositories are peers.

So how is a repository structure maintained over time if no technical measures enforce the structure? In effect, the structure is a web of trust for the acceptance of changes. Repository organization and dataflow between repositories is guided by social or political agreements.

The question is, "Will the maintainer of a target repository allow your changes to be accepted?" Conversely, do you have enough trust in the source repository's data to fetch it into your own repository?

Repository Structure Examples

The Linux Kernel project is the canonical example of a highly distributed repository and development process. In each Linux Kernel release, there are roughly 1,000 to 1,300 individual contributors from approximately 200 companies. Over the last 20 kernel releases (2.6.24 through 3.3), the corp of developers averaged just over 10,000 commits per release. Releases were made on an average 82-day cycle. That's between four and six commits per hour, every development hour, somewhere on the planet. The rate-of-change trend is upward still.[1]

Although Linus Torvalds does maintain an official repository at the top of the heap that most people consider authoritative, there are still many, many derived second-tier repositories in use. For example, many of the Linux distribution vendors take Linus's official tagged release, test it, apply bug fixes, tweak it for their distribution, and publish it as *their* official release. (With any luck, bug fixes are sent back and applied to Linus's Linux repository so that all may benefit.)

During a kernel development cycle, hundreds of repositories are published and moderated by hundreds of maintainers and used by thousands of developers to gather changes for the release. The main kernel website, `http://kernel.org/`, alone publishes about 500 Linux Kernel–related repositories with roughly 150 individual maintainers.

There are certainly thousands, perhaps tens of thousands, of clones of these repositories around the world that form the basis of individual contributor patches or uses.

Short of some fancy snapshot technology and some statistical analysis, there isn't really a good way to tell how all these repositories interconnect. It is safe to say it is a mesh, or network, that is not strictly hierarchical at all.

Curiously, though, there is a sociological drive to get patches and changes into Linus's repository, thus effectively treating it like it *is* the top of the heap! If Linus himself had to accept each and every patch or change one at a time into his repository, there would simply be no way he could keep up. Linus, it is rumored, just doesn't scale up well. Remember, changes are collectively going into his tree at a rate of about one every 10 to 15 minutes throughout a release's entire development cycle.

It is only through the maintainers—who moderate, collect, and apply patches to sub-repositories—that Linus can keep up at all. It is as if the maintainers create a pyramid-like structure of repositories that funnel patches toward Linus's conventional master repository.

In fact, below the maintainers but still near the top of the Linux repository structure are many sub-maintainers and individual developers who act in the role of maintainer

---

1. Kernel statistics from the Linux Foundation Publications link `http://go.linuxfoundation.org/who-writes-linux-2012` for the Linux Foundation report by Jonathan Corbet, et al., titled "Linux Kernel Development."

and developer peer as well. The Linux Kernel effort is a large, multilayered mesh of cooperating people and repositories.

The point isn't that this is a phenomenally large code base that exceeds the grasp of a few individuals or teams. The point is that those many teams are scattered around the world and yet manage to coordinate, develop, and merge a common code base toward a fairly consistent long-term goal, all using Git's facilities for distributed development.

At the other end of the spectrum, Freedesktop.org development is done entirely using a shared, centralized repository model powered by Git. In this development model, each developer is trusted to push changes straight into a repository, as found on `git.freedesktop.org`.

The X.org project itself has roughly 350 X-related repositories available on `gitweb.free desktop.org`, with hundreds more for individual users. The majority of the X-related repositories are various submodules from the entire X project, representing a functional breakdown of applications, X servers, different fonts, and so on.

Individual developers are also encouraged to create branches for features that are not ready for a general release. These branches allow the changes (or proposed changes) to be made available for other developers to use, test, and improve. Eventually, when the new feature branches are ready for general use, they are merged into their respective mainline development branches.

A development model that allows individual developers to directly push changes into a repository runs some risk, though. Without any formal review process prior to a push, it is possible for bad changes to be quietly introduced into a repository and to go unnoticed for quite some time.

Mind you, there is no real fear of losing data or of being unable to recover a good state again because the complete repository history is still available. The issue is that it would take time to discover the problem and correct it.

As Keith Packard wrote:[2]

> We are slowly teaching people to post patches to the xorg mailing list for review, which happens sometimes. And, sometimes we just back stuff out. Git is robust enough that we never fear losing data, but the state of the top of the tree isn't always ideal.
>
> It's worked far better than using CVS in the same way....

2. Private email, March 23, 2008.

Living with Distributed Development

Changing Public History

Once you have published a repository from which others might make a clone, you should consider it static and refrain from rewriting the history of any branch. Although this is not an absolute guideline, avoiding rewinds and alterations of published history simplifies the life of anyone who clones your repository.

Let's say you publish a repository that has a branch with commits A, B, C, and D. Anyone who clones your repository gets those commits. Suppose Alice clones your repository and heads off to do some development based on your branch.

In the meantime you decide, for whatever reason, to fix something in commit C. Commits A and B remain the same, but starting with commit C, the branch's notion of commit history changes. You could slightly alter C or make some totally new commit, X. In either case, republishing the repository leaves the commits A and B as they were but will now offer, say, X and then Y instead of C and D.

Alice's work is now greatly affected. Alice cannot send you patches, make a pull request, or push her changes to your repository because her development is based on commit D.

Patches won't apply because they're based on commit D. Suppose Alice issues a pull request and you attempt to pull her changes; you may be able to fetch them into your repository (depending on your tracking branches for Alice's remote repository), but the merges will almost certainly have conflicts. The failure of this push is due to a non–fast-forward push problem.

In short, the basis for Alice's development has been altered. You have pulled the commit rug out from underneath her development feet.

The situation is not irrecoverable, though. Git can help Alice, especially if she uses the `git rebase --onto` command to relocate her changes onto your new branch after fetching the new branch into her repository.

Also, there are times when it is appropriate to have a branch with a dynamic history. For example, within the Git repository itself there is a so-called proposed updates branch, pu, which is specifically labeled and advertised as being rewound, rebased, or rewritten frequently. You, as a cloner, are welcome to use that branch as the basis for your development, but you must remain conscious of the branch's purpose and take special effort to use it effectively.

So why would anyone publish a branch with a dynamic commit history? One common reason is specifically to alert other developers about possible and fast-changing directions some other branch might take. You can also create such a branch for the sole purpose of making available, even temporarily, a published changeset that other developers can use.

Separate Commit and Publish Steps

One of the clear advantages of a distributed VCS is the separation of commit and publish. A commit just saves a state in your private repository; publishing through patches or push/pull makes the change public, which effectively freezes the repository history. Other VCSs, such as CVS or SVN, have no such conceptual separation. To make a commit, you must publish it simultaneously.

By making commit and publish separate steps, a developer is much more likely to make precise, mindful, small, and logical steps with patches. Indeed, any number of small changes can be made without affecting any other repository or developer. The commit operation is offline in the sense that it requires no network access to record positive, forward steps within your own repository.

Git also provides mechanisms for refining and improving commits into nice, clean sequences prior to making them public. Once you are ready, the commits can be made public in a separate operation.

No One True History

Development projects within a distributed environment have a few quirks that might not be obvious at first. And although these quirks might initially be confusing and their treatment often differs from other nondistributed VCSs, Git handles them in a clear and logical manner.

As development takes place in parallel among different developers of a project, each has created what he believes to be the correct history of commits. As a result, there is my repository and my commit history, your repository and your commit history, and possibly several others being developed, simultaneously or otherwise.

Each developer has a unique notion of history, and each history is correct. There is no one true history. You cannot point to one and say: "This is the *real* history."

Presumably, the different development histories have formed for a reason, and ultimately the various repositories and different commit histories will be merged into one common repository. After all, the intent is likely to be advancement toward a common goal.

When various branches from the different repositories are merged, all of the variations are present. The merged result states, effectively, "The merged history is better than any one independently."

Git expresses this history ambivalence toward branch variations when it traverses the commit DAG. So if Git, when trying to linearize the commit sequence, reaches a merge commit, then it must select one branch or the other first. What criteria would it use to favor or select one branch over another? The spelling of the author's last name? Perhaps the time stamp of a commit? That might be useful.

Even if you decide to use time stamps and agree to use Coordinated Universal Time (UTC) and extremely precise values, it doesn't help. Even that recipe turns out to be completely unreliable! (The clocks on a developer's computer can be wrong either intentionally or accidentally.)

Fundamentally, Git doesn't care what came first. The only real, reliable relationship that can be established between commits is the direct parent relationship recorded in the commit objects. At best, the time stamps offer a secondary clue, usually accompanied by various heuristics to allow for errors such as unset clocks.

In short, neither time nor space operates in well-defined ways, so Git must allow for the effects of quantum physics.

Git as Peer-to-Peer Backup

Linus Torvalds once said, "Only wimps use tape backup: *real* men just upload their important stuff on ftp, and let the rest of the world mirror it." The process of uploading files to the Internet and letting individuals make a copy was how the source code for the Linux kernel was "backed up" for years. And it worked!

In some ways, Git is just an extension of the same concept. Nowadays, when you download the source code to the Linux Kernel using Git, you're downloading not just the latest version but the entire history leading up to that version, making Linus's backups better than ever.

This concept has been leveraged by projects that allow system administrators to manage their /etc configuration directories with Git and even allow users to manage and back up their home directories. Remember, just because you use Git doesn't mean you are required to share your repositories; it does, however, make it easy to "version control" your repositories right onto your Network Attached Storage (NAS) box for a back-up copy.

Knowing Your Place

When participating in a distributed development project, it is important to know how you, your repository, and your development efforts fit into the larger picture. Besides the obvious potential for development efforts in different directions and the requirement for basic coordination, the mechanics of how you use Git and its features can greatly affect how smoothly your efforts align with other developers working on the project.

These issues can be especially problematic in a large-scale distributed development effort, as is often found in open source projects. By identifying your role in the overall effort and understanding who the consumers and producers of changes are, many of the issues can be easily managed.

Upstream and Downstream Flows

There isn't a strict relationship between two repositories that have been cloned one from the other. However, it's common to refer to the parent repository as being "upstream" from the new, cloned repository. Reflexively, the new, cloned repository is often described as being "downstream" from the original parent repository.

Furthermore, the upstream relationship extends "up" from the parent repository to any repository from which it might have been cloned. It also extends "down" past your repository to any that might be cloned from yours.

However, it is important to recognize that this notion of upstream and downstream is *not* directly related to the clone operation. Git supports a fully arbitrary network between repositories. New remote connections can be added and your original clone remote can be removed to create arbitrary new relationships between repositories.

If there is any established hierarchy, it is purely one of convention. Bob agrees to send his changes to you; in turn, you agree to send your changes on to someone further upstream; and so forth.

The important aspect of the repository relationship is how data is exchanged between them. That is, any repository to which you send changes is usually considered upstream of you. Similarly, any repository that relies on yours for its basis is usually considered downstream of yours.

It's purely subjective but conventional. Git itself doesn't care and doesn't track the stream notion in any way. Upstream and downstream simply help us visualize where patches are going.

Of course, it's possible for repositories to be true peers. If two developers exchange patches or push and fetch from each other's repositories, then neither is really upstream or downstream from the other.

The Maintainer and Developer Roles

Two common roles are the *maintainer* and the *developer*. The maintainer serves primarily as an integrator or moderator, and the developer primarily generates changes. The maintainer gathers and coordinates the changes from multiple developers and ensures that all are acceptable with respect to some standard. In turn, the maintainer makes the whole set of updates available again. That is, the maintainer is also the publisher.

The maintainer's goal should be to collect, moderate, accept or reject changes, and then ultimately publish branches that project developers can use. To ensure a smooth development model, maintainers should not alter a branch once it has been published. In turn, a maintainer expects to receive changes from developers that are relevant and that apply to published branches.

A developer's goal, beyond improving the project, is to get her changes accepted by the maintainer. After all, changes kept in a private repository do no one else any good. The changes need to be accepted by the maintainer and made available for others to use and exploit. Developers need to base their work on the published branches in the repositories that the maintainer offers.

In the context of a derived clone repository, the maintainer is usually considered to be upstream from developers.

Because Git is fully symmetric, there is nothing to prevent a developer from considering herself a maintainer for other developers further downstream. But she must now understand that she is in the middle of both an upstream and a downstream dataflow and must adhere to the maintainer and developer contract (see the next section) in this dual role.

Because this dual or mixed-mode role is possible, upstream and downstream is not strictly correlated to being a producer or consumer. You can produce changes with the intent of them going either upstream or downstream.

Maintainer–Developer Interaction

The relationship between a maintainer and a developer is often loose and ill-defined, but there is an implied contract between them. The maintainer publishes branches for the developer to use as her basis. Once published, though, the maintainer has an unspoken obligation not to change the published branches because this would disturb the basis upon which development takes place.

In the opposite direction, the developer, by using the published branches as her basis, ensures that when her changes are sent to the maintainer for integration they apply cleanly without problems, issues, or conflicts.

It may seem as if this makes for an exclusive, lock-step process. Once published, the maintainer can't do anything until the developer sends in changes. And then, after the maintainer applies updates from one developer, the branch will necessarily have changed and thus will have violated the "won't change the branch" contract for some other developers. If this were true then truly distributed, parallel, and independent work could never really take place.

Thankfully, it is not that grim at all! Instead, Git is able to look back through the commit history on the affected branches, determine the merge basis that was used as the starting point for a developer's changes, and apply them even though other changes from other developers may have been incorporated by the maintainer in the meantime.

With multiple developers making independent changes and with all of them being brought together and merged into a common repository, conflicts are still possible. It is up to the maintainer to identify and resolve such problems. The maintainer can either resolve these conflicts directly or reject changes from a developer if they would create conflicts.

Role Duality

There are two basic mechanisms for transferring commits between an upstream and a downstream repository.

The first uses `git push` or `git pull` to directly transfer commits, whereas the second uses `git format-patch` and `git am` to send and receive representations of commits. The method that you use is primarily dictated by agreement within your development team and, to some extent, direct access rights as discussed in Chapter 12.

Using `git format-patch` and `git am` to apply patches achieves the exact same blob and tree object *content* as if the changes had been delivered via a `git push` or incorporated with a `git pull`. However, the actual commit object will be different because the metadata information for the commit will be different between a push or pull and a corresponding application of a patch.

In other words, using push or pull to propagate a change from one repository to another copies that commit exactly, whereas patching copies only the file and directory data exactly. Furthermore, push and pull can propagate merge commits between repositories. Merge commits cannot be sent as patches.

Because it compares and operates on the tree and blob objects, Git is able to understand that two different commits for the same underlying change in two different repositories, or even on different branches within the same repository, really represent the same change. Thus, it is no problem for two different developers to apply the same patch sent via email to two different repositories. As long as the resulting content is the same, Git treats the repositories as having the same content.

Let's see how these roles and dataflows combine to form a duality between upstream and downstream producers and consumers.

Upstream Consumer
> An upstream consumer is a developer upstream from you who accepts your changes either as patch sets or as pull requests. Your patches should be rebased to the consumer's current branch HEAD. Your pull requests should either be directly mergeable or already merged by you in your repository. Merging prior to the pull ensures that conflicts are resolved correctly by you, relieving the upstream consumer of that burden. This upstream consumer role could be a maintainer who turns around and publishes what he has just consumed.

Downstream Consumer
> A downstream consumer is a developer downstream from you who relies on your repository as the basis for work. A downstream consumer wants solid, published topic branches. You shouldn't rebase, modify, or rewrite the history of any published branch.

Upstream Producer/Publisher

An upstream publisher is a person upstream from you who publishes repositories that are the basis for your work. This is likely to be a maintainer with the tacit expectation that he will accept your changes. The upstream publisher's role is to collect changes and publish branches. Again, those published branches should not have their histories altered, given that they are the basis for further downstream development. A maintainer in this role expects developer patches to apply and expects pull requests to merge cleanly.

Downstream Producer/Publisher

A downstream producer is a developer downstream from you who has published changes either as a patch set or as a pull request. The goal of a downstream producer is to have changes accepted into your repository. A downstream producer consumes topic branches from you and wants those branches to remain stable, with no history rewrites or rebases. Downstream producers should regularly fetch updates from upstream and should also regularly merge or rebase development topic branches to ensure they apply to the local upstream branch HEADs. A downstream producer can rebase her own local topic branches at any time, because it doesn't matter to an upstream consumer that it took several iterations for this developer to make a good patch set that has a clean, uncomplicated history.

Working with Multiple Repositories

Your Own Workspace

As the developer of content for a project using Git, you should create your own private copy, or *clone*, of a repository to do your development. This development repository should serve as your own work area where you can make changes without fear of colliding with, interrupting, or otherwise interfering with another developer.

Furthermore, because each Git repository contains a complete copy of the entire project, as well as the entire history of the project, you can feel free to treat your repository as if it is completely and solely yours. In effect, it actually is!

One benefit of this paradigm is that it allows each developer complete control within her working directory area to make changes to any part, or even to the whole system, without worrying about interaction with other development efforts. If you need to change a part, you have the part and can change it in your repository without affecting other developers. Likewise, if you later realize that your work is not useful or relevant, then you can throw it away without affecting anyone else or any other repository.

As with any software development, this is not an endorsement to conduct wild experimentation. Always consider the ramifications of your changes, because ultimately you may need to merge your changes into the master repository. It will then be time to pay the piper, and any arbitrary changes may come back to haunt you.

Where to Start Your Repository

Faced with a wealth of repositories that ultimately contribute to one project, it may seem difficult to determine where you should begin your development. Should your contributions be based on the main repository directly, or perhaps on the repository where other people are focused on some particular feature? Or maybe a stable branch of a release repository somewhere?

Without a clear sense of how Git can access, use, and alter repositories, you may be caught in some form of the "can't get started for fear of picking the wrong starting point" dilemma. Or perhaps you have already started your development in a clone based on some repository you picked but now realize that it isn't the right one. Sure, it's related to the project and may even be a good starting point, but maybe there is some missing feature found in a different repository. It may even be hard to tell until well into your development cycle.

Another frequent starting point dilemma comes from a need for project features that are being actively developed in two different repositories. Neither of them is, by itself, the correct clone basis for your work.

You could just forge ahead with the expectation that your work and the work in the various repositories will all be unified and merged into one master repository. You are certainly welcome to do so, of course. But remember that part of the gain from a distributed development environment is the ability to do concurrent development. Take advantage of the fact that the other published repositories with early versions of their work are available.

Another pitfall comes if you start with a repository that is at the cutting edge of development and find that it is too unstable to support your work, or that it is abandoned in the middle of your work.

Fortunately, Git supports a model where you can essentially pick any arbitrary repository from a project as your starting point, even if it is not the perfect one, and then convert, mutate, or augment that repository until it does contain all the right features.

If you later wanted to separate your changes back out to different respective upstream repositories, you may have to make judicious and meticulous use of separate topic branches and merges to keep it all straight.

On the one hand, you can fetch branches from multiple remote repositories and combine them into your own, yielding the right mix of features that are available elsewhere in existing repositories. On the other hand, you can reset the starting point in your repository back to a known stable point earlier in the history of the project's development.

Converting to a Different Upstream Repository

The first and simplest kind of repository mixing and matching is to switch the basis (usually called the *clone origin*) repository, the one you regard as your origin and with which you synchronize regularly.

For example, suppose you need to work on feature F and you decide to clone your repository from the mainline, M, as shown in Figure 13-1.

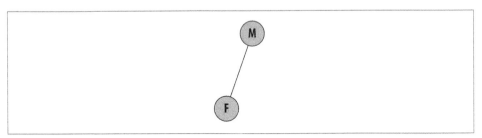

Figure 13-1. Simple clone to develop feature F

You work for a while before learning that there is a better starting point closer to what you would really like, but it is in repository P. One reason you might want to make this sort of change is to gain functionality or feature support that is already in repository P.

Another reason stems from longer term planning. Eventually, the time will come when you need to contribute the development that you have done in repository F back to some upstream repository. Will the maintainer of repository M accept your changes directly? Perhaps not. If you are confident that the maintainer of repository P will accept them, then you should arrange for your patches to be readily applicable to that repository instead.

Presumably, P was once cloned from M, or vice versa, as shown in Figure 13-2. Ultimately, P and M are based on the same repository for the same project at some point in the past.

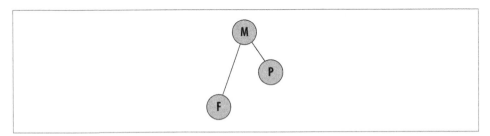

Figure 13-2. Two clones of one repository

The question often asked is whether repository F, originally based on M, can now be converted so that it is based on repository P, as shown in Figure 13-3. This is easy to

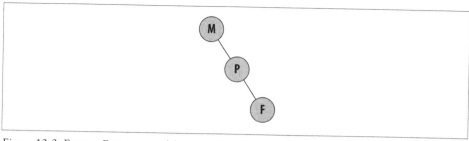

Figure 13-3. Feature F restructured for repository P

do using Git, because it supports a peer-to-peer relationship between repositories and provides the ability to readily rebase branches.

As a practical example, the kernel development for a particular architecture could be done right off of the mainline Linus Kernel repository. But Linus won't take it. If you started working on, say, PowerPC®[3] changes and did not know that, then you would likely have a difficult time getting your changes accepted.

However, the PowerPC architecture is currently maintained by Ben Herrenschmidt; he is responsible for collecting all PowerPC-specific changes and in turn sending them upstream to Linus. To get your changes into the mainline repository, you must go through Ben's repository first. You should therefore arrange to have your patches be directly applicable to his repository instead, and it's never too late to do that.

In a sense, Git knows how to make up the difference from one repository to the next. Part of the peer-to-peer protocol to fetch branches from another repository is an exchange of information stating what changes each repository has or is missing. As a result, Git is able to fetch just the missing or new changes and bring them into your repository.

Git is also able to review the history of the branches and determine where the common ancestors from the different branches are, even if they are brought in from different repositories. If they have a common commit ancestor, then Git can find it and construct a large, unified view of the commit history with all the repository changes represented.

Using Multiple Upstream Repositories

As another example, suppose that the general repository structure looks like Figure 13-4. Here, some mainline repository, M, will ultimately collect all the development for two different features from repositories F1 and F2.

However, you need to develop some super feature, S, that involves using aspects of features found in only F1 and F2. You could wait until F1 is merged into M and then wait for F2 to also be merged into M. That way, you will then have a repository with the

---

3. PowerPC® is a trademark of International Business Machines Corporation in the United States, other countries, or both.

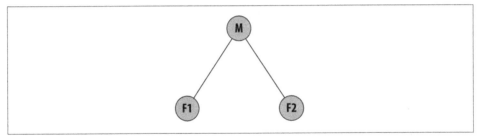

Figure 13-4. Two feature repositories

correct, total basis for your work. But unless the project strictly enforces some project life cycle that requires merges at known intervals, there is no telling how long this process might take.

You might start your repository, S, based off of the features found in F1 or, alternatively, off of F2 (see Figure 13-5). However, with Git it is possible to instead construct a repository, S, that has both F1 and F2 in it; this is shown in Figure 13-6.

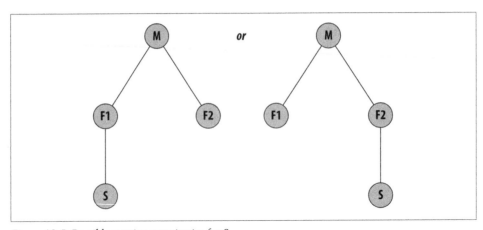

Figure 13-5. Possible starting repositories for S

In these pictures, it is unclear whether repository S is composed of the entirety of F1 and F2 or just some part of each. In fact, Git supports both scenarios. Suppose repository F2 has branches F2A and F2B with features A and B, respectively, as shown in Figure 13-7. If your development needs feature A, but not B, then you can selectively fetch just that F2A branch into your repository S along with whatever part of F1 is also needed.

Again, the structure of the Linux Kernel exhibits this property. Let's say you're working on a new network driver for a new PowerPC board. You will likely have architecture-specific changes for the board that will need code in the PowerPC repository maintained by Ben. Furthermore, you will likely need to use the Networking Development "netdev" repository maintained by Jeff Garzik. Git will readily fetch and make a union repository

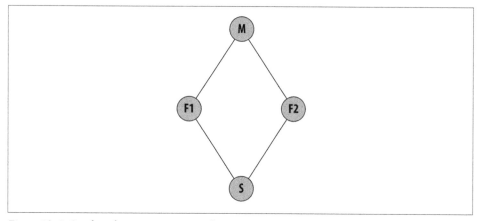

Figure 13-6. Combined starting repository for S

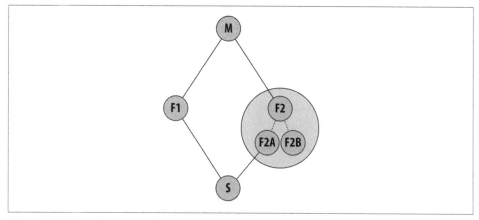

Figure 13-7. Two feature branches in F2

with branches from both Ben's and Jeff's branches. With both basis branches in your repository, you will then be able to merge them and develop them further.

Forking Projects

Anytime you clone a repository, the action can be viewed as *forking* the project. Forking is functionally equivalent to "branching" in some other VCSs, but Git has a separate concept called "branching," so don't call it that. Unlike a branch, a Git fork doesn't exactly have a name. Instead, you simply refer to it by the filesystem directory (or remote server, or URL) into which you cloned.

The term "fork" comes from the idea that when you create a fork, you create two simultaneous paths that the development will follow. It's like a fork in the road of development. As you might imagine, the term "branch" is based on a similar analogy involving trees. There's no inherent difference between the "branching" and "forking" metaphors—the terms simply capture two intents. Conceptually, the difference is that branching usually occurs within a single repository, whereas forking usually occurs at the whole repository level.

Although you *can* fork a project readily with Git, doing so may be more of a social or political choice than a technical one. For public or open source projects, having access to a copy or clone of the entire repository, complete with its history, is both an enabler of and a deterrent to forking.

 GitHub.com, an online Git hosting service, takes this idea to the logical extreme: *everybody's* version is considered a fork, and all the forks are shown together in the same place.

Isn't forking a project bad?

Historically, forking a project was often motivated by perceptions of a power grab, a reluctance to cooperate, or the abandonment of a project. A difficult person at the hub of a centralized project can effectively grind things to a halt. A schism may develop between those "in charge" of a project and those who are not. Often, the only perceived solution is to effectively fork a new project. In such a scenario, it may be difficult to obtain a copy of the history of the project and start over.

Forking is the traditional term for what happens when one developer of an open source project becomes unhappy with the main development effort, takes a copy of the source code, and starts maintaining his own version.

Forking, in this sense, has traditionally been considered a negative thing; it means the unhappy developer couldn't find a way to get what he wanted from the main project. So he goes off and tries to do it better by himself, but now there are *two* projects that are almost the same. Obviously neither one is good enough for everybody, or one of them would be abandoned. So most open source projects make heroic efforts to *avoid* forking.

Forking may or may not be bad. On the one hand, perhaps an alternate view and new leadership is exactly what is needed to revitalize a project. On the other hand, it may simply contribute to strife and confusion on a development effort.

Reconciling forks

In contrast, Git tries to remove the stigma of forking. The real problem with forking a project is not the creation of an alternate development path. Every time a developer downloads or clones a copy of a project and starts hacking on it, she has created an alternative development path, if only temporarily.

In his work on the Linux Kernel, Linus Torvalds eventually realized that forking is only a problem if the forks don't eventually merge back together. Thus, he designed Git to look at forking totally differently: Git *encourages* forking. But Git also makes it easy for anyone to merge two forks whenever they want.

Technically, reconciling a forked project with Git is facilitated by its support for large-scale fetching and importing one repository into another and for extremely easy branch merging.

Although many social issues may remain, fully distributed repositories seem to reduce tensions by lessening the perceived importance of the person at the center of a project. Because an ambitious developer can easily inherit a project and its complete history, he may feel it is enough to know that, if needed, the person at the center could be replaced and development could still continue!

Forking projects at GitHub

Many people in the software community have a dislike for the phrase "forking." But if we investigate why, it is because it usually results in infinitely diverging copies of the software. Our focus should not be on the dislike for the concept of forks, but rather on the quantity of divergence before bringing the two lines of code back together again.

Forking at GitHub typically has a far more positive connotation. Much of the site is built around the premise of short-lived forks. Any drive-by developer can make a copy (fork) of a public repository, make code changes she thinks are appropriate, and then offer them back to the core project owner.

The forks offered back to the core project are called "pull requests." Pull requests afford a visibility to forks and facilitate smart management of these diverging branches. A conversation can be attached to a pull request, thus providing context as to why a request was accepted or returned to sender for additional polish.

Well-maintained projects have the attribute of a frequently maintained pull request queue. Project contributors should process through the pull request queue, either accepting, commenting on, or rejecting all pull requests. This signals a level of care about and active maintenance of the code base and the greater community surrounding the project.

Although GitHub has been intentionally designed to facilitate a good use of forks, it cannot inherently enforce good behavior. The negative form of forking—hostile wrangling of the code base in an isolationist direction—is still possible on GitHub. However, there is a notably low volume of this misbehavior. It can be attributed in large part to the visibility of forks and their potential divergence from the primary code base in the network commit graph.

## CHAPTER 14

Patches

Designed as a peer-to-peer VCS, Git allows development work to be transferred directly and immediately from one repository to another using both a push and a pull model.

Git implements its own transfer protocol to exchange data between repositories. For efficiency (to save time and space), Git's transfer protocol performs a small handshake, determines what commits in the source repository are missing from the target, and finally transfers a binary, compressed form of the commits. The receiving repository incorporates the new commits into its local history, augments its commit graph, and updates its branches and tags as needed.

Chapter 12 mentioned that HTTP can also be used to exchange development between repositories. HTTP is not nearly as efficient as Git's native protocol, but it is just as capable of moving commits to and fro. Both protocols ensure that a transferred commit remains identical in both source and destination repositories.

However, the Git-native and HTTP protocols aren't the only mechanisms for exchanging commits and keeping distributed repositories synchronized. In fact, there are times when using these protocols is infeasible. Drawing on tried-and-true methods from an earlier Unix development era, Git also supports a "patch and apply" operation, where the data exchange typically occurs via email.

Git implements three specific commands to facilitate the exchange of a patch:

- `git format-patch` generates a patch in email form
- `git send-email` sends a Git patch through an Simple Mail Transfer Protocol (SMTP) feed
- `git am` applies a patch found in an email message

The basic use scenario is fairly simple. You and one or more developers start with a clone of a common repository and begin collaborative development. You do some work, make a few commits to your copy of the repository, and eventually decide it's time to convey your changes to your partners. You choose the commits you would like to share and choose with whom to share the work. Because the patches are sent via email, each intended recipient can elect to apply none, some, or all of the patches.

This chapter explains when you might want to use patches and demonstrates how to generate, send, and (if you're a recipient) apply a patch.

Why Use Patches?

Although the Git protocol is much more efficient, there are at least two compelling reasons to undertake the extra effort required by patches: one is technical and the other is sociological.

- In some situations, neither the Git native protocol nor the HTTP protocol can be used to exchange data between repositories in either a push or a pull direction or both.

  For example, a corporate firewall may forbid opening a connection to an external server using Git's protocol or port. Additionally, SSH may not be an option. More-over, even if HTTP is permitted, which is common, you could download reposi-tories and fetch updates but you may not be able to push changes back out. In situations like this, email is the perfect medium for communicating patches.

- One of the great advantages of the peer-to-peer development model is collabora-tion. Patches, especially those sent to a public mailing list, are a means of openly distributing proposed changes for peer review.

  Prior to permanently applying the patches to a repository, other developers can discuss, critique, rework, test, and either approve or veto posted patches. Because the patches represent precise changes, acceptable patches can be directly applied to a repository.

  Even if your development environment allows you the convenience of a direct push or pull exchange, you may still want to employ a "patch email review apply" paradigm to gain the benefits of peer review.

  You might even consider a project development policy whereby each developer's changes must be peer reviewed as patches on a mailing list prior to directly merging them via `git pull` or `git push`. All the benefits of peer review together with the ease of pulling changes directly!

And there are still other reasons to use patches.

In much the same way that you might cherry-pick a commit from one of your own branches and apply it to another branch, using patches allows you to selectively choose commits from another developer's repository without having to fully fetch and merge everything from that repository.

Of course, you could ask the other developer to place the desired commits on a separate branch and then fetch and merge that branch alone, or you could fetch his whole repository and then cherry-pick the desired commits out of the tracking branches. But you might have some reason for *not* wanting to fetch the repository, too.

If you want an occasional or explicit commit—say, an individual bug fix or a particular feature—then applying the attendant patch may be the most direct way to get that specific improvement.

Generating Patches

The `git format-patch` command generates a patch in the form of an email message. It creates one piece of email for each commit you specify. You can specify the commits using any technique discussed in "Identifying Commits" on page 67 of Chapter 6.

Common use cases include:

- A specified number of commits, such as `-2`
- A commit range, such as `master~4..master~2`
- A single commit, often the name of a branch, such as `origin/master`

Although the Git diff machinery lies at the heart of the `git format-patch` command, it differs from `git diff` in two key ways:

- Whereas `git diff` generates one patch with the combined differences of all the selected commits, `git format-patch` generates one email message for each selected commit.
- `git diff` doesn't generate email headers. In addition to the actual diff content, `git format-patch` generates an email message complete with headers that list the commit author, the commit date, and the commit log message associated with the change.

> `git format-patch` and `git log` should seem very similar. As an interesting experiment, compare the output of the following two commands:
> `git format-patch -1` and `git log -p -1 --pretty=email`.

Let's start with a fairly simple example. Suppose you have a repository with just one file in it named *file*. Furthermore, the content of that file is a series of single capitalized letters, A through D. Each letter was introduced into the file, one line at a time, and committed using a log message corresponding to that letter.

```
$ git init
$ echo A > file
$ git add file
$ git commit -mA
$ echo B >> file ; git commit -mB file
$ echo C >> file ; git commit -mC file
$ echo D >> file ; git commit -mD file
```

Thus, the commit history now has four commits.

```
$ git show-branch --more=4 master
[master] D
[master^] C
[master~2] B
[master~3] A
```

The easiest way to generate patches for the most recent *n* commits is to use a *-n* option like this:

```
$ git format-patch -1
0001-D.patch

$ git format-patch -2
0001-C.patch
0002-D.patch

$ git format-patch -3
0001-B.patch
0002-C.patch
0003-D.patch
```

By default, Git generates each patch in its own file with a sequentially numbered name derived from the commit log message. The command outputs the file names as it executes.

You can also specify which commits to format as patches by using a commit range. Suppose you expect other developers to have repositories based on commit B of your repository, and suppose you want to patch their repositories with all the changes you made between B and D.

Based on the previous output of git show-branch, you can see that B has the version name master~2 and that D has the version name master. Specify these names as a commit range in the git format-patch command.

Although you're including three commits in the range (B, C, and D), you end up with two email messages representing two commits: the first contains the diffs between B and C; the second contains the diffs between C and D. See Figure 14-1.

Here is the output of the command:

```
$ git format-patch master~2..master
0001-C.patch
0002-D.patch
```

Each file is a single email, conveniently numbered in the order that it should be subsequently applied. Here is the first patch:

```
$ cat 0001-C.patch
From 69003494a4e72b1ac98935fbb90ecca67677f63b Mon Sep 17 00:00:00 2001
From: Jon Loeliger <jdl@example.com>
Date: Sun, 28 Dec 2008 12:10:35 -0600
Subject: [PATCH] C
```

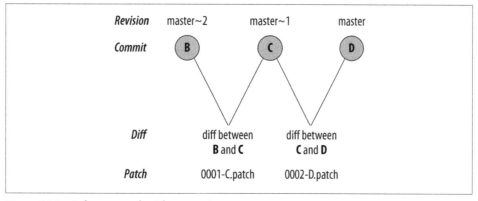

Figure 14-1. git format-patch with a commit range

```
---
 file |    1 +
 1 files changed, 1 insertions(+), 0 deletions(-)

diff --git a/file b/file
index 35d242b..b1e6722 100644
--- a/file
+++ b/file
@@ -1,2 +1,3 @@
 A
 B
+C
--
1.6.0.90.g436ed
```

And here is the second:

```
$ cat 0002-D.patch
From 73ac30e21df1ebefd3b1bca53c5e7a08a5ef9e6f Mon Sep 17 00:00:00 2001
From: Jon Loeliger <jdl@example1.com>
Date: Sun, 28 Dec 2008 12:10:42 -0600
Subject: [PATCH] D

---
 file |    1 +
 1 files changed, 1 insertions(+), 0 deletions(-)

diff --git a/file b/file
index b1e6722..8422d40 100644
--- a/file
+++ b/file
@@ -1,3 +1,4 @@
 A
 B
 C
+D
--
1.6.0.90.g436ed
```

Let's continue the example and make it more complex by adding another branch named alt based on commit B.

While the master developer added individual commits with the lines C and D to the master branch, the alt developer added the commits (and lines) X, Y, and Z to her branch.

```
# Create branch alt at commit B
$ git checkout -b alt e587667

$ echo X >> file ; git commit -mX file
$ echo Y >> file ; git commit -mY file
$ echo Z >> file ; git commit -mZ file
```

The commit graph looks like Figure 14-2.

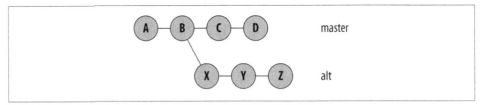

Figure 14-2. Patch graph with alt branch

 You can draw an ASCII graph with all your refs using option --all, like this:

```
$ git log --graph --pretty=oneline --abbrev-commit --all
* 62eb555... Z
* 204a725... Y
* d3b424b... X
| * 73ac30e... D
| * 6900349... C
|/
* e587667... B
* 2702377... A
```

Suppose further that the master developer merged the alt branch at commit Z into master at commit D to form the merge commit E. Finally, he made one more change that added F to the master branch.

```
$ git checkout master
$ git merge alt

# Resolve the conflicts however you'd like
# I used the sequence: A, B, C, D, X, Y, Z

$ git add file
$ git commit -m'All lines'
Created commit a918485: All lines

$ echo F >> file ; git commit -mF file
```

```
Created commit 3a43046: F
 1 files changed, 1 insertions(+), 0 deletions(-)
```

The commit graph now looks like Figure 14-3.

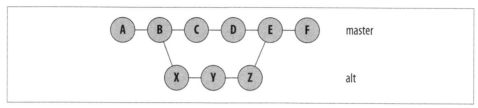

Figure 14-3. History of two branches

A display of the commit branch history looks like this:

```
$ git show-branch --more=10
! [alt] Z
 * [master] F
--
 * [master] F
+* [alt] Z
+* [alt^] Y
+* [alt~2] X
 * [master~2] D
 * [master~3] C
+* [master~4] B
+* [master~5] A
```

Patching can be surprisingly flexible when you have a complicated revision tree. Let's take a look.

You must be careful when specifying a commit range, especially when it covers a merge. In the current example, you might expect that the range D..F would cover the two commits for E and F, and it does. But the commit E contains all the content merged into it from *all* its merged branches.

```
# Format patches D..F
$ git format-patch master~2..master
0001-X.patch
0002-Y.patch
0003-Z.patch
0004-F.patch
```

Remember, a commit range is defined to include all commits leading up to the range *end point* but to exclude all commits that lead up to and including the range *starting point* state. In the case of D..F this means that all the commits contributing to F (every commit in the example graph) are included but, all the commits leading up to and including D (A, B, C, and D) are eliminated. The merge commit itself won't generate a patch.

Issue `git rev-list --no-merges -v` *since..until* to verify the set of commits for which patches will be generated before you actually create your patches.

You can also reference a single commit as a variation of the `git format-patch` commit range. However, Git's interpretation of such as a command is slightly nonintuitive.

Git normally interprets a single commit argument as "all commits that lead up to and contribute to the given commit." In contrast, `git format-patch` treats a single commit parameter as if you had specified the range `commit..HEAD`. It uses your commit as the starting point and takes `HEAD` as the end point. Thus, the patch series generated is implicitly in the context of the current branch checked out.

In our ongoing example, when the `master` branch is checked out and a patch is made specifying the commit `A`, all seven patches are produced:

```
$ git branch
  alt
* master

# From commit A
$ git format-patch master~5
0001-B.patch
0002-C.patch
0003-D.patch
0004-X.patch
0005-Y.patch
```

```
0006-Z.patch
0007-F.patch
```

But when the `alt` branch is checked out and the command specifies the same A commit, only those patches contributing to the tip of the `alt` branch are used:

```
$ git checkout alt
Switched to branch "alt"

$ git branch
* alt
  master

$ git format-patch master~5
0002-B.patch
0003-X.patch
0004-Y.patch
0005-Z.patch
```

Even though commit A is specified, you don't actually get a patch for it. The root commit is somewhat special in that there isn't a previously committed state against which a diff can be computed. Instead, a patch for it is effectively a pure addition of all the initial content.

If you really want to generate patches for every commit including the initial, root commit, up to a named *end-commit*, then use the `--root` option like this:

```
$ git format-patch --root end-commit
```

The initial commit generates a patch as if each file in it was added based on */dev/null*.

```
$ cat 0001-A.patch
From 27023770db3385b23f7631363993f91844dd2ce0 Mon Sep 17 00:00:00 2001
From: Jon Loeliger <jdl@example.com>
Date: Sun, 28 Dec 2008 12:09:45 -0600
Subject: [PATCH] A

---
 file |   1 +
 1 files changed, 1 insertions(+), 0 deletions(-)
 create mode 100644 file

diff --git a/file b/file
new file mode 100644
index 0000000..f70f10e
--- /dev/null
+++ b/file
@@ -0,0 +1 @@
+A
--
1.6.0.90.g436ed
```

Treating a single commit as if you had specified *commit*..HEAD may seem unusual, but this approach has a valuable use in one particular situation. When you specify a *commit* on a branch that's different from the branch you currently have checked out, the command emits patches that are in your current branch but *not* in the named branch. In other words, it generates a set of patches that can bring the other branch in sync with your current branch.

To illustrate this feature, assume you've checked out the master branch:

```
$ git branch
  alt
* master
```

Now you specify the alt branch as the *commit* parameter:

```
$ git format-patch alt
0001-C.patch
0002-D.patch
0003-F.patch
```

The patches for commits C, D, and F are exactly the set of patches in the master branch, but not in the alt branch.

The power of this command, coupled with a single commit parameter, becomes apparent when the named commit is the HEAD ref of a tracking branch from someone else's repository.

For example, if you clone Alice's repository and your master development is based on Alice's master, then you would have a tracking branch named something like alice/ master.

After you have made some commits on your master branch, the command git format-patch alice/master generates the set of patches that you must send her to ensure that her repository has at least all of your master content. She may have *more* changes from other sources in her repository already, but that is not important here. You have isolated the set from your repository (the master branch) that are known not to be in hers.

Thus, git format-patch is specifically designed to create patches for commits that are in your repository in a development branch that are not already present in the upstream repository.

Patches and Topological Sorts

Patches generated by git format-patch are emitted in *topological order*. For a given commit, the patches for all parent commits are generated and emitted before the patch for this commit is emitted. This ensures that a correct ordering of patches is always created, but a correct ordering is not necessarily unique: there may be multiple correct orders for a given commit graph.

Let's see what this means by looking at some of the possible generation orders for patches that could ensure a correct repository if the recipient applies them in order. Example 14-1 shows a few of the possible topological sort orders for the commits of our example graph.

Example 14-1. Some topological sort orders

```
A B C D X Y Z E F

A B X Y Z C D E F

A B C X Y Z D E F

A B X C Y Z D E F

A B X C Y D Z E F
```

Remember, even though patch creation is driven by a topological sort of the selected nodes in the commit graph, only some of those nodes will actually produce patches.

The first ordering in Example 14-1 is the ordering that Git picked for `git format-patch master~5`. Because A is the first commit in the range and no `--root` option was used, there isn't a patch for it. Commit E represents a merge, so no patch is generated for it, either. Thus, the patches are generated in the order B C D X Y Z F.

Whatever patch sequence that Git chooses, it is important to realize that Git has produced a *linearization* of all the selected commits, no matter how complicated or branched the original graph was.

If you are consistently adding headers to the patch email as generated, then you might investigate the configuration options `format.headers`.

Mailing Patches

Once you have generated a patch or a series of patches, the next logical step is to send them to another developer or to a development list for review, with an ultimate goal of it being picked up by a developer or upstream maintainer and applied to another repository.

The formatted patches are generally intended to be sent via email by directly importing them into your *mail user agent* (MUA) or by using Git's `git send-email` command. You are not obliged to use `git send-email`; it is merely a convenience. As you will see in the next section, there are also other tools that use the patch file directly.

Assuming that you want to send a generated patch file to another developer, there are several ways to send the file: you can run `git send-email`, you can point your mailer directly to the patches, or you can include the patches in an email.

Using `git send-email` is straightforward. In this example, the patch *0001-A.patch* is sent to a mail list called `devlist@example.org`:

```
$ git send-email -to devlist@example.org 0001-A.patch
0001-A.patch
Who should the emails appear to be from? [Jon Loeliger <jdl@example.com>]
Emails will be sent from: Jon Loeliger <jdl@example.com>
Message-ID to be used as In-Reply-To for the first email?
(mbox) Adding cc: Jon Loeliger <jdl@example.com> from line \
'From: Jon Loeliger <jdl@example.com>'
OK. Log says:
Sendmail: /usr/sbin/sendmail -i devlist@example.org jdl@example.com
From: Jon Loeliger <jdl@example.com>
To: devlist@example.org
Cc: Jon Loeliger <jdl@example.com>
Subject: [PATCH] A
Date: Mon, 29 Dec 2008 16:43:46 -0600
Message-Id: <1230590626-10792-1-git-send-email-jdl@exmaple.com>
X-Mailer: git-send-email 1.6.0.90.g436ed

Result: OK
```

There are many options to either utilize or work around a myriad of SMTP issues or features. What's critical is ensuring that you know your SMTP server and port. Likely, it is the traditional sendmail program or a valid outbound SMTP host, such as smtp.my-isp.com.

 Don't set up SMTP open relay servers just to send your Git email. Doing so will contribute to spam mail problems.

The git send-email command has many configuration options, which are documented in its manual page.

You may find it convenient to record your special SMTP information in your global configuration file by setting, for example, the value sendemail.smtpserver and sende mail.smtpserverport using commands similar to this:

```
$ git config --global sendemail.smtpserver smtp.my-isp.com
$ git config --global sendemail.smtpserverport 465
```

Depending on your MUA, you may be able to directly import an entire file or directory of patches into a mail folder. If so, this can greatly simplify sending a large or complicated patch series.

Here is an example where a traditional mbox style mail folder is created using format-patch that is then directly imported into mutt, where the message can be addressed and sent.

```
$ git format-patch --stdout master~2..master > mbox
```

```
$ mutt -f mbox
```

```
q:Quit  d:Del  u:Undel  s:Save  m:Mail  r:Reply  g:Group  ?:Help
```

```
1 N   Dec 29 Jon Loeliger        (  15) [PATCH] X
2 N   Dec 29 Jon Loeliger        (  16) [PATCH] Y
3 N   Dec 29 Jon Loeliger        (  16) [PATCH] Z
4 N   Dec 29 Jon Loeliger        (  15) [PATCH] F
```

The latter two mechanisms, using send-email and directly importing a mail folder, are the preferred techniques for sending email, because both are reliable and not prone to messing with the carefully formatted patch contents. You are less likely, for example, to hear a developer complain about a wrapped line if you use one of these techniques.

On the other hand, you may find that you need to directly include a generated patch file into a newly composed email in a MUA such as thunderbird or evolution. In these cases, the risk of disturbing the patch is much greater. Care should be taken to turn off any form of HTML formatting and to send plain ASCII text that has not been allowed to flow or word wrap in any way.

Depending on your recipient's ability to handle mail or contingent on your development list policies, you may or may not want to use an attachment for the patch. In general, inlining is the simpler, more correct approach. It also facilitates an easier patch review. However, if the patch is inlined then some of the headers generated by git format-patch might need to be trimmed, leaving just the From: and Subject: headers in the email body.

If you find yourself frequently including your patches as text files in newly composed emails and are annoyed at having to delete the superfluous headers, you might want to try the following command: git format-patch --pretty=format:%s%n%n%b *commit*. You might also configure that as a Git global alias as described in "Configuring an Alias" on page 30 of Chapter 3.

Regardless of how the patch mail is sent, it should look essentially identical to the original patch file when received, albeit with more and different mail headers.

The similarity of the patch file format before and after transport through the mail system is not an accident. The key to this operating successfully is plain text and preventing any MUA from altering the patch format through such operations as line wrapping. If you can preclude such interdictions, a patch will remain usable irrespective of how many mail transfer agents (MTAs) carry the data.

Use git send-email if your MUA is prone to wrap lines on outbound mail.

There are a host of options and configuration settings to control the generation of email headers for patches. Your project probably has some conventions that you should follow.

If you have a series of patches, you might want to funnel them all to a common directory with the `-o` *directory* option to `git format-patch`. Afterward, you can then use `git send-email` *directory* to send them all at once. In this case, use either `git format-patch --cover-letter` or `git send-email --compose` to write a guiding, introductory cover letter for the entire series.

There are also options to accommodate various social aspects of most development lists. For example, use `--cc` to add alternate recipients, to add or omit each `Signed-off-by:` address as a `Cc:` recipient, or to select how a patch series should be threaded on a list.

Applying Patches

Git has two basic commands that apply patches. The higher level porcelain command, `git am`, is partially implemented in terms of the plumbing command `git apply`.

The command `git apply` is the workhorse of the patch application procedure. It accepts `git diff` or `diff` style outputs and applies it to the files in your current working directory. Though different in some key respects, it performs essentially the same role as Larry Wall's `patch` command.

Because a diff contains only line-by-line edits and no other information (such as author, date, or log message), it cannot perform a commit and log the change in your repository. Thus, when `git apply` is finished, the files in your working directory are left modified. (In special cases, it can use or modify the index as well.)

In contrast, the patches formatted by `git format-patch`, either before or after they have been mailed, contain the extra information necessary to make and record a proper commit in your repository. Although `git am` is configured to accept patches generated by `git format-patch`, it is also able to handle other patches if they follow some basic formatting guidelines.[1] Note that `git am` creates commits on the current branch.

Let's complete the patch generation/mail/apply process example using the same repository from "Generating Patches" on page 265. One developer has constructed a complete patch set, *0001-B.patch* through *0007-F.patch*, and has sent it or otherwise made it available to another developer. The other developer has an early version of the repository and wants to now apply the patch set.

Let's first look at a naïve approach that exhibits common problems that are ultimately impossible to resolve. Then we'll examine a second approach that proves successful.

Here are the patches from the original repository:

---

1. By the time you adhere to the guidelines detailed in the manual page for `git am` (a "From:", a "Subject:", a "Date:", and a patch content delineation), you might as well call it an email message anyway.

```
$ git format-patch -o /tmp/patches master~5
/tmp/patches/0001-B.patch
/tmp/patches/0002-C.patch
/tmp/patches/0003-D.patch
/tmp/patches/0004-X.patch
/tmp/patches/0005-Y.patch
/tmp/patches/0006-Z.patch
/tmp/patches/0007-F.patch
```

These patches could have been received by the second developer via email and stored on disk, or they may have been placed directly in a shared file system.

Let's construct an initial repository as the target for this series of patches. (How this initial repository is constructed is not really important—it may well have been cloned from the initial repository, but it needn't have to be.) The key to long-term success is a moment in time where both repositories are known to have the exact same file content.

Let's reproduce that moment by creating a new repository containing the same file, *file*, with the initial contents A. That is exactly the same repository content as was present at the very beginning of the original repository.

```
$ mkdir /tmp/am
$ cd /tmp/am
$ git init
Initialized empty Git repository in am/.git/

$ echo A >> file
$ git add file
$ git commit -mA
Created initial commit 5108c99: A
 1 files changed, 1 insertions(+), 0 deletions(-)
 create mode 100644 file
```

A direct application of git am shows some problems:

```
$ git am /tmp/patches/*
Applying B
Applying C
Applying D
Applying X
error: patch failed: file:1
error: file: patch does not apply
Patch failed at 0004.
When you have resolved this problem run "git am --resolved".
If you would prefer to skip this patch, instead run "git am --skip".
To restore the original branch and stop patching run "git am --abort".
```

This is a tough failure mode and it might leave you in a bit of a quandary about how to proceed. A good approach in this situation is to look around a bit.

```
$ git diff

$ git show-branch --more=10
[master] D
[master^] C
```

```
[master~2] B
[master~3] A
```

That's pretty much as expected. No file was left dirty in your working directory, and Git successfully applied patches up to and including D.

Often, looking at the patch itself, and the files that are affected by the patch helps clear up the problem. Depending on what version of Git you have installed, either the *.dotest* directory or the *.git/rebase-apply* directory is present when `git am` runs. It contains various contextual information for the entire series of patches and the individual parts (author, log message, etc.) of each patch.

```
# Or .dotest/patch, in earlier Git releases

$ cat .git/rebase-apply/patch
---
 file |    1 +
 1 files changed, 1 insertions(+), 0 deletions(-)

diff --git a/file b/file
index 35d242b..7f9826a 100644
--- a/file
+++ b/file
@@ -1,2 +1,3 @@
 A
 B
+X
--
1.6.0.90.g436ed

$ cat file
A
B
C
D
```

This is a difficult spot. The file has four lines in it, but the patch applies to a version of that same file with just two lines. As the `git am` command output indicated, this patch doesn't actually apply:

```
error: patch failed: file:1
error: file: patch does not apply
Patch failed at 0004.
```

You may know that the ultimate goal is to create a file in which all the letters are in order, but Git is not able to figure that out automatically. There just isn't enough context to determine the right conflict resolution yet.

As with other actual file conflicts, `git am` offers a few suggestions:

```
When you have resolved this problem run "git am --resolved".
If you would prefer to skip this patch, instead run "git am --skip".
To restore the original branch and stop patching run "git am --abort".
```

Unfortunately, there isn't even a file content conflict that can be resolved and resumed in this case.

You might think you could just skip the X patch, as suggested:

```
$ git am --skip
Applying Y
error: patch failed: file:1
error: file: patch does not apply
Patch failed at 0005.
When you have resolved this problem run "git am --resolved".
If you would prefer to skip this patch, instead run "git am --skip".
To restore the original branch and stop patching run "git am --abort".
```

But as with this Y patch, all subsequent patches fail now, too. It's clear that the patch series isn't going to apply cleanly with this approach.

You can try to recover from here, but it's tough without knowing the original branching characteristics that led to the patch series being presented to git am. Recall that the X commit was applied to a new branch that originated at commit B. That means the X patch would apply correctly if it were applied again to that commit state. You can verify this: reset the repository back to just the A commit, clean out the *rebase-apply* directory, apply the B commit using git am /tmp/patches/0002-B.patch, and see that the X commit will apply, too!

```
# Reset back to commit A
$ git reset --hard master~3
HEAD is now at 5108c99 A

# Or .dotest, as needed
$ rm -rf .git/rebase-apply/

$ git am /tmp/patches/0001-B.patch
Applying B

$ git am /tmp/patches/0004-X.patch
Applying X
```

 Cleaning up a failed, botched, or hopeless git am and restoring the original branch can be simplified to just git am --abort.

The success of applying the *0004-X.patch* to the commit B provides a hint on how to proceed. However, you can't really apply patches X, Y, and Z, because then the later patches C, D, and F would not apply. And you don't really want to bother recreating the exact original branch structure even temporarily. Even if you were willing to recreate it, how would you even know what the original branch structure was?

Knowing the basis file to which a diff can be applied is a difficult problem for which Git provides an easy technical solution. If you look closely at a patch or diff file generated by Git, you will see new, extra information that isn't part of a traditional Unix diff summary. The extra information that Git provides for the patch file *0004-X.patch*, is shown in Example 14-2.

Example 14-2. New patch context in 0004-X.patch

```
diff --git a/file b/file
index 35d242b..7f9826a 100644
--- a/file
+++ b/file
```

Just after the `diff --git a/file b/file` line, Git adds the new line `index 35d242b.. 7f9826a 100644`. This information is designed to answer with certainty the following question: "What is the original state to which this patch applies?"

The first number on the `index` line, `35d242b`, is the SHA1 hash of the blob within the Git object store to which this portion of the patch applies. That is, `35d242b` is the file as it exists with just the two lines:

```
$ git show 35d242b
A
B
```

And that is exactly the version of *file* to which this portion of the X patch applies. If that version of the file is in the repository, then Git can apply the patch to it.

This mechanism—having a current version of a file; having an alternate version; and locating the original, base version of a file to which the patch applies—is called a *three-way merge*. Git is able to reconstruct this scenario using the -3 or --3way option to git am.

Let's clean up the failed effort; reset back to the first commit state, A; and try to reapply the patch series:

```
# Get rid of temporary "git am" context, if needed.
$ rm -rf .git/rebase-apply/

# Use "git log" to locate commit A -- it was SHA1 5108c99
# It will be different for you.
$ git reset --hard 5108c99
HEAD is now at 5108c99 A

$ git show-branch --more=10
[master] A
```

Now, using the -3, apply the patch series:

```
$ git am -3 /tmp/patches/*
Applying B
Applying C
Applying D
Applying X
error: patch failed: file:1
error: file: patch does not apply
```

```
Using index info to reconstruct a base tree...
Falling back to patching base and 3-way merge...
Auto-merged file
CONFLICT (content): Merge conflict in file
Failed to merge in the changes.
Patch failed at 0004.
When you have resolved this problem run "git am -3 --resolved".
If you would prefer to skip this patch, instead run "git am -3 --skip".
To restore the original branch and stop patching run "git am -3 --abort".
```

Much better!

Just as before, the simple attempt to patch the file failed but instead of quitting, Git has changed to the three-way merge. This time, Git recognizes it is able to perform the merge, but a conflict remains because overlapping lines were changed in two different ways.

Because Git is not able to correctly resolve this conflict, the `git am -3` is temporarily suspended. It is now up to you to resolve the conflict before resuming the command.

Again, the strategy of looking around can help determine what to do next and how to proceed:

```
$ git status
file: needs merge
# On branch master
# Changed but not updated:
#   (use "git add <file>..." to update what will be committed)
#
#       unmerged:   file
```

As indicated previously, the file *file* still needs to have a merge conflict resolved.

The contents of *file* show the traditional conflict merge markers and must be resolved via an editor:

```
$ cat file
A
B
<<<<<<< HEAD:file
C
D
=======
X
>>>>>>> X:file

# Fix conflicts in "file"
$ emacs file

$ cat file
A
B
C
D
X
```

After resolving the conflict and cleaning up, resume the git am -3:

```
$ git am -3 --resolved
Applying X
No changes - did you forget to use 'git add'?
When you have resolved this problem run "git am -3 --resolved".
If you would prefer to skip this patch, instead run "git am -3 --skip".
To restore the original branch and stop patching run "git am -3 --abort".
```

Did you forget to use git add? Sure did!

```
$ git add file
$ git am -3 --resolved

Applying X
Applying Y
error: patch failed: file:1
error: file: patch does not apply
Using index info to reconstruct a base tree...
Falling back to patching base and 3-way merge...
Auto-merged file
Applying Z
error: patch failed: file:2
error: file: patch does not apply
Using index info to reconstruct a base tree...
Falling back to patching base and 3-way merge...
Auto-merged file
Applying F
```

Finally, success!

```
$ cat file
A
B
C
D
X
Y
Z
F

$ git show-branch --more=10
[master] F
[master^] Z
[master~2] Y
[master~3] X
[master~4] D
[master~5] C
[master~6] B
[master~7] A
```

Applying these patches didn't construct a replica of the branch structure from the original repository. All patches were applied in a linear sequence, and that is reflected in the master branch commit history.

```
# The C commit
$ git log --pretty=fuller -1 1666a7
commit 848f55821c9d725cb7873ab3dc3b52d1bcbf0e93
Author:     Jon Loeliger <jdl@example.com>
AuthorDate: Sun Dec 28 12:10:42 2008 -0600
Commit:     Jon Loeliger <jdl@example.com>
CommitDate: Mon Dec 29 18:46:35 2008 -0600

    C
```

The patch Author and AuthorDate are per the original commit and patch, whereas the data for the committer reflects the actions of applying the patch and committing it to this branch and repository.

Bad Patches

The obligation to create robust, identical content in multiple, distributed repositories around the world—despite the difficulties of today's email systems—is an onerous task. It is no wonder that a perfectly good patch can be trashed by any number of mail-related failures. Ultimately, the onus is on Git to ensure that the complete patch/email/apply cycle can faithfully reconstruct identical content through an unreliable transport mechanism.

Patch failures stem from many areas, many mismatched tools, and many different philosophies. But perhaps the most common failure is simply failing to maintain exact line handling characteristics of the original content. This usually manifests itself as line wrappings due to text being reflowed by either the sender or receiver MUA, or by any of the intermediate MTAs. Luckily, the patch format has internal consistency checks that prevent this type of failure from corrupting a repository.

Patching Versus Merging

Git can handle the situation where applying patches and pulling the same changes have been mixed in one repository. Even though the commit in the receiving repository ultimately differs from the commit in the original repository from which the patch was made, Git can use its ability to compare and match content to sort matters out.

Later, for example, subsequent diffs will show no content changes. The log message and author information will also be the same as they were conveyed in the patch mail, but information such as the date and SHA1 will be different.

Directly fetching and merging a branch with a complex history will yield a different history in the receiving repository than the history that results from a patching sequence. Remember, one of the effects of creating a patch sequence on a complex branch is to topologically sort the graph into a linearized history. Hence, applying it to another repository yields a linearized history that wasn't in the original.

Depending on your development style and your ultimate intent, having the original development history linearized within the receiving repository may or may not be a problem for you and your project. At the very least, you have lost the complete branch history that led to the patch sequence. At best, you simply don't care how you arrived at the patch sequence.

## CHAPTER 15

Hooks

You can use a Git *hook* to run one or more arbitrary scripts whenever a particular event, such as a commit or a patch, occurs in your repository. Typically, an event is broken into several prescribed steps, and you can tie a custom script to each step. When the Git event occurs, the appropriate script is called at the outset of each step.

Hooks belong to and affect a specific repository and are not copied during a clone operation. In other words, hooks you set up in your private repository are not propagated to and do not alter the behavior of the new clone. If for some reason your development process mandates hooks in each coder's personal development repository, arrange to copy the directory *.git/hooks* through some other (nonclone) method.

A hook runs either in the context of your current, local repository or in the context of the remote repository. For example, fetching data into your repository from a remote repository and making a local commit can cause local hooks to run; pushing changes to a remote repository may cause hooks in the remote repository to run.

Most Git hooks fall into one of two categories:

- A *"pre"* hook runs before an action completes. You can use this kind of hook to approve, reject, or adjust a change before it's applied.
- A *"post"* hook runs after an action completes and can be used to trigger notifications (such as email) or to launch additional processing, such as running a build or closing a bug.

As a general rule, if a *pre*-action hook exits with a nonzero status (the convention to indicate failure), the Git action is aborted. In contrast, the exit status of a *post*-action hook is generally ignored because the hook can no longer affect the outcome or completion of the action.

In general, the Git developers advocate using hooks with caution. A hook, they say, should be a method of last resort, to be used only when you can't accomplish the same result in some other way. For example, if you want to specify a particular option each time you make a commit, check out a file, or create a branch, a hook is unnecessary.

You can accomplish the same task with a Git alias (see "Configuring an Alias" on page 30 in Chapter 3) or with shell scripts to augment `git commit`, `git checkout`, and `git branch`, respectively.[1]

At first blush, a hook may seem an appealing and straightforward solution. However, there are several implications of its use.

- A hook changes the behavior of Git. If a hook performs an unusual operation, other developers familiar with Git may run into surprises when using your repository.

- A hook can slow operations that are otherwise fast. For example, developers are often enticed to hook Git to run unit tests before anyone makes a commit, but this makes committing slow. In Git, a commit is supposed to be a fast operation, thus encouraging frequent commits to prevent the loss of data. Making a commit run slowly makes Git less enjoyable.

- A hook script that is buggy can interfere with your work and productivity. The only way to work around a hook is to disable it. In contrast, if you use an alias or shell script instead of a hook, then you can always fall back on the normal Git command wherever that makes sense.

- A repository's collection of hooks is not automatically replicated. Hence, if you install a commit hook in your repository, it won't reliably affect another developer's commits. This is partly for security reasons—a malicious script could easily be smuggled into an otherwise innocuous-looking repository—and partly because Git simply has no mechanism to replicate anything other than blobs, trees, and commits.

Junio's Overview of Hooks

Junio Hamano wrote the following about Git hooks on the Git mailing list (paraphrased from the original).

There are five valid reasons to hook a Git command/operation:

1. To countermand the decision made by the underlying command. The `update` hook and the `pre-commit` hook are two hooks used for this purpose.

2. To manipulate data generated after a command starts to run. Modifying the commit log message in the `commit-msg` hook is an example.

3. To operate on the remote end of a connection, that you access only via the Git protocol. A `post-update` hook that runs `git update-server-info` does this very task.

4. To acquire a lock for mutual exclusion. This is rarely a requirement, but sufficient hooks are available to achieve it.

---

1. As it happens, running a hook at commit time is such a common requirement that a precommit hook exists for that, even though it isn't strictly necessary.

5. To run one of several possible operations, depending on the outcome of the command. The `post-checkout` hook is a notable example.

Each of these five requirements requires at least one hook. You cannot realize a similar result from outside the Git command.

On the other hand, if you always want some action to occur before or after running a Git operation locally, you don't need a hook. For instance, if your postprocessing depends on the effects of a command (item 5 in the list) but the results of the command are plainly observable, then you don't need a hook.

With those "warnings" behind us, we can state that hooks exist for very good reasons and that their use can be incredibly advantageous.

Installing Hooks

Each hook is a script, and the collection of hooks for a particular repository can be found in the *.git/hooks* directory. As already mentioned, Git doesn't replicate hooks between repositories; if you `git clone` or `git fetch` from another repository, you won't inherit that repository's hooks. You have to copy the hook scripts by hand.

Each hook script is named after the event with which it is associated. For example, the hook that runs immediately before a `git commit` operation is named *.git/hooks/ pre-commit*.

A hook script must follow the normal rules for Unix scripts: it must be executable (`chmod a+x .git/hooks/pre-commit`) and must start with a line indicating the language in which the script is written (for example, `#!/bin/bash` or `#!/usr/bin/perl`).

If a particular hook script exists and has the correct name and file permissions, Git uses it automatically.

Example Hooks

Depending on your exact version of Git, you may find some hooks in your repository at the time it's created. Hooks are copied automatically from your Git template directory when you create a new repository. On Debian and Ubuntu, for example, the hooks are copied from */usr/share/git-core/templates/hooks*. Most Git versions include some example hooks that you can use, and these are preinstalled for you in the templates directory.

Here's what you need to know about the example hooks:

- The template hooks probably don't do exactly what you want. You can read them, edit them, and learn from them, but you rarely want to use them as is.
- Even though the hooks are created by default, all the hooks are initially disabled. Depending on your version of Git and your operating system, the hooks are

disabled either by removing the execute bit or by appending *.sample* to the hook file name. Modern versions of Git have executable hooks named with a *.sample* suffix.

- To enable an example hook, you must remove the *.sample* suffix from its filename (`mv .git/hooks/pre-commit.sample .git/hooks/pre-commit`) and set its execute bit, as is apropos (`chmod a+x .git/hooks/pre-commit`).

Originally, each example hook was simply copied into the *.git/hooks/* directory from the template directory with its execute permission removed. You could then enable the hook by setting its execute bit.

That worked fine on systems like Unix and Linux, but didn't work well on Windows. In Windows, file permissions work differently and, unfortunately, files are executable by default. This meant the example hooks were executable by default, causing great confusion among new Git users because all the hooks ran when none should have.

Because of this problem with Windows, newer versions of Git suffix each hook file name with *.sample* so it won't run even if it's executable. To enable the example hooks, you'll have to rename the appropriate scripts yourself.

If you aren't interested in the example hooks, it is perfectly safe to remove them from your repository: `rm .git/hooks/*`. You can always get them back by copying them from their home in the *templates* directory.

 In addition to the template examples, there are more example hooks in Git's *contrib* directory, a portion of the Git source code. The supplemental files may also be installed along with Git on your system. On Debian and Ubuntu, for example, the contributed hooks are installed in */usr/share/doc/git-core/contrib/hooks*.

Creating Your First Hook

To explore how a hook works, let's create a new repository and install a simple hook. First, we create the repository and populate it with a few files:

```
$ mkdir hooktest

$ cd hooktest

$ git init
Initialized empty Git repository in .git/

$ touch a b c

$ git add a b c

$ git commit -m 'added a, b, and c'
Created initial commit 97e9cf8: added a, b, and c
 0 files changed, 0 insertions(+), 0 deletions(-)
```

```
create mode 100644 a
create mode 100644 b
create mode 100644 c
```

Next, let's create a `pre-commit` hook to prevent checking in changes that contain the word "broken." Using your favorite text editor, put the following in a file called *.git/hooks/pre-commit*:

```
#!/bin/bash
echo "Hello, I'm a pre-commit script!" >&2
if git diff --cached | grep '^\+' | grep -q 'broken'; then
        echo "ERROR: Can't commit the word 'broken'" >&2
        exit 1  # reject
fi
exit 0  # accept
```

The script generates a list of all differences about to be checked in, extracts the lines to be *added* (that is, those lines that begin with a + character), and scans those lines for the word "broken."

There are many ways to test for the word "broken," but most of the obvious ones result in subtle problems. I'm not talking about how to "test for the word 'broken'" but rather about how to find the text to be scanned for the word "broken."

For example, you might have tried the test:

```
if git ls-files | xargs grep -q 'broken'; then
```

or, in other words, search for the word "broken," in all files in the repository. But this approach has two problems. If someone else had already committed a file containing the word "broken," then this script would prevent all future commits (until you fix it), even if those commits are totally unrelated. Moreover, the Unix `grep` command has no way of knowing which files will actually be committed; if you add "broken" to file b, make an unrelated change to a, and then run `git commit a`, there's nothing wrong with your commit because you're not trying to commit b. However, a script with this test would reject it anyway.

 If you write a `pre-commit` script that restricts what you're allowed to check in, it's almost certain that you'll need to bypass it someday. You can bypass the `pre-commit` hook either by using the `--no-verify` option to `git commit` or by temporarily disabling your hook.

Now that you've created the `pre-commit` hook, make sure it's executable:

```
$ chmod a+x .git/hooks/pre-commit
```

And now you can test that it works as expected:

```
$ echo "perfectly fine" >a

$ echo "broken" >b
```

```
# Try to commit all files, even a 'broken' one.
$ git commit -m "test commit -a" -a
Hello, I'm a pre-commit script!
ERROR: Can't commit the word 'broken'

# Selectively committing un-broken files works.
$ git commit -m "test only file a" a
Hello, I'm a pre-commit script!
Created commit 4542056: test
1 files changed, 1 insertions(+), 0 deletions(-)

# And committing 'broken' files won't work.
$ git commit -m "test only file b" b
Hello, I'm a pre-commit script!
ERROR: Can't commit the word 'broken'
```

Observe that even when a commit works, the `pre-commit` script still emits "Hello." This would be annoying in a real script, so you should use such messages only while debugging the script. Notice also that, when the commit is rejected, `git commit` doesn't print an error message; the only message is the one produced by the script. To avoid confusing the user, be careful always to print an error message from a "pre" script if it's going to return a nonzero ("reject") exit code.

Given those basics, let's talk about the different hooks you can create.

Available Hooks

As Git evolves, new hooks become available. To discover what hooks are available in your version of Git, run `git help hooks`. Also refer to the Git documentation to find all the command-line parameters as well as the input and output of each hook.

Commit-Related Hooks

When you run `git commit`, Git executes a process like that shown in Figure 15-1.

 None of the commit hooks run for anything other than `git commit`. For example, git rebase, git merge, and git am don't run your commit hooks by default. (Those commands may run other hooks, though.) However, git commit --amend *does* run your commit hooks.

Each hook has its own purpose as follows:

- The `pre-commit` hook gives you the chance to immediately abort a commit if something is wrong with the content being committed. The `pre-commit` hook runs before the user is allowed to edit the commit message, so the user won't enter a commit message only to discover the changes are rejected. You can also use this hook to automatically modify the content of the commit.

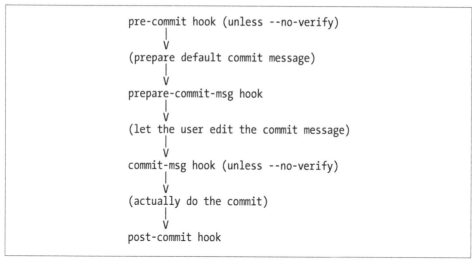

```
              pre-commit hook (unless --no-verify)
                          |
                          V
              (prepare default commit message)
                          |
                          V
              prepare-commit-msg hook
              |
              V
              (let the user edit the commit message)
                          |
                          V
              commit-msg hook (unless --no-verify)
                          |
                          V
              (actually do the commit)
                          |
                          V
              post-commit hook
```

Figure 15-1. Commit hook processing

- `prepare-commit-msg` lets you modify Git's default message before it is shown to the user. For example, you can use this to change the default commit message template.
- The `commit-msg` hook can validate or modify the commit message after the user edits it. For example, you can leverage this hook to check for spelling mistakes or reject messages with lines that exceed a certain maximum length.
- `post-commit` runs after the commit operation has finished. At this point, you can update a log file, send email, or trigger an autobuilder, for instance. Some people use this hook to automatically mark bugs as fixed if, say, the bug number is mentioned in the commit message. In real life, however, the `post-commit` hook is rarely useful, because the repository that you `git commit` in is rarely the one that you share with other people. (The `update` hook is likely more suitable.)

Patch-Related Hooks

When you run `git am`, Git executes a process like that shown in Figure 15-2.

 Despite what you might expect from the names of the hooks shown in Figure 15-2, `git apply` does not run the `applypatch` hooks, only `git am` does. This is because `git apply` doesn't actually commit anything, so there's no reason to run any hooks.

- `applypatch-msg` examines the commit message attached to the patch and determines whether or not it's acceptable. For example, you can choose to reject a patch if it has no `Signed-off-by:` header. You can also modify the commit message at this point if desired.

Figure 15-2. Patch hook processing

- The pre-applypatch hook is somewhat misnamed, because this script actually runs *after* the patch is applied but before committing the result. This makes it exactly analogous to the pre-commit script when doing git commit, even though its name implies otherwise. In fact, many people choose to create a pre-applypatch script that runs pre-commit.

- post-applypatch is analogous to the post-commit script.

Push-Related Hooks

When you run git push, the *receiving end* of Git executes a process like the one shown in Figure 15-3.

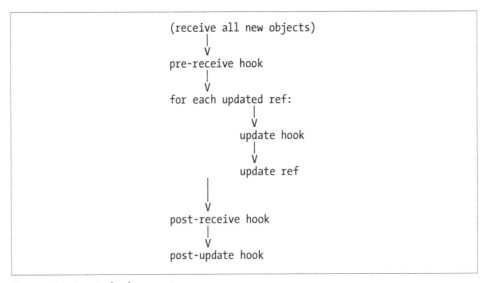

Figure 15-3. Receive hook processing

All push-related hooks run on the receiver, not the sender. Thus, the hook scripts that run are in the *.git/hooks* directory of the receiving repository, not the sending one. Output produced by remote hooks is still shown to the user doing the git push.

As you can see in the diagram, the very first step of git push is to transfer all the missing objects (blobs, trees, and commits) from your local repository to the remote one. There is no need for a hook during this process because all Git objects are identified by their unique SHA1 hash; your hook cannot modify an object because it would change the hash. Furthermore, there's no reason to reject an object, because git gc cleans up anyway if the object turns out to be unneeded.

Instead of manipulating the objects themselves, push-related hooks are called when it's time to update the *refs* (branches and tags).

- pre-receive receives a list of all the refs that are to be updated, including their new and old object pointers. The only thing the prereceive hook can do is accept or reject all the changes at once, which is of limited use. You might consider it a feature, though, because it enforces transactional integrity across branches. Yet, it's not clear why you'd need such a thing; if you don't like that behavior, use the update hook instead.

- The update hook is called exactly once for each ref being updated. The update hook can choose to accept or reject updates to individual branches, without affecting whether other branches are updated or not. Also for each update you can trigger an action such as closing a bug or sending an email acknowledgment. It's usually better to handle such notifications here than in a post-commit hook, because a commit is not really considered "final" until it's been pushed to a shared repository.

- Like the prereceive hook, post-receive receives a list of all the refs that have just been updated. Anything that post-receive can do could also be done by the update hook, but sometimes post-receive is more convenient. For example, if you want to send an update notification email message, post-receive can send just a single notification about all updates instead of a separate email for each update.

- Don't use the post-update hook. It has been superseded by the newer post-receive hook. (post-update knows what branches have changed but not what their old values were; this limited its usefulness.)

Other Local Repository Hooks

Finally, there are a few miscellaneous hooks, and by the time you read this there may be even more. (Again, you can find the list of available hooks quickly with the command `git help hooks`.)

- The `pre-rebase` hook runs when you attempt to rebase a branch. This is useful because it can stop you from accidentally running `git rebase` on a branch that shouldn't be rebased because it's already been published.

- `post-checkout` runs after you check out a branch or an individual file. For example, you can use this to automatically create empty directories (Git doesn't know how to track empty directories) or to set file permissions or Access Control List (ACLs) on checked out files (Git doesn't track ACLs). You might think of using this to modify files after checking them out—for example, to do RCS-style variable substitution—but it's not such a good idea because Git will think the files have been locally modified. For such a task, use smudge/clean filters instead.

- `post-merge` runs after you perform a merge operation. This is rarely used. If your `pre-commit` hook does some sort of change to the repository, you might need to use a `post-merge` script to do something similar.

- `pre-auto-gc` helps `git gc --auto` decide whether or not it's time to clean up. You can make `git gc --auto` skip its `git gc` task by returning nonzero from this script. This will rarely be needed, however.

## CHAPTER 16

Combining Projects

There are many reasons to combine outside projects with your own. A *submodule* is simply a project that forms a part of your own Git repository but also exists independently in its own source control repository. This chapter discusses why developers create submodules and how Git attempts to deal with them.

Earlier in this book, we worked with a repository named *public_html* that we imagine contains your website. If your website relies on an AJAX library such as Prototype or jQuery, then you'll need to have a copy of that library somewhere inside *public_html*. Not only that: you'd like to be able to update that library automatically, see what has changed when you do, and maybe even contribute changes back to the authors. Or perhaps, as Git allows and encourages, you want to make changes and *not* contribute them back but still be able to update your repository to their latest version.

Git does make all these things possible. But here's the bad news: Git's initial support for submodules was unapologetically awful, for the simple reason that none of the Git developers had a need for them. At the time that this book is being written, the situation has only recently started to improve.

In the beginning, there were only two major projects that used Git—Git itself and the Linux Kernel. These projects have two important things in common: they were both originally written by Linus Torvalds, and they both have virtually no dependencies on any outside project. Where they've borrowed code from other projects, they've imported it directly and made it their own. There's no intention of ever trying to merge that code back into someone else's project. Such an occurrence would be rare, and it would be easy enough to generate some diffs by hand and submit them back to the other project.

If your project's submodules are like that, where you import once, leaving the old project behind forever—then you don't need this chapter. You already know enough about Git to simply add a directory full of files.

On the other hand, sometimes things get more complicated. One common situation at many companies is to have a lot of applications that rely on a common utility library or set of libraries. You want each of your applications to be developed, shared, branched, and merged in its own Git repository, either because that's the logical unit of separation, or perhaps because of code ownership issues.

But dividing your applications up this way creates a problem: what about the shared library? Each application relies on a particular version of the shared library, and you need to keep track of exactly which version. If someone upgrades the library by accident to a version that hasn't been tested, they might end up breaking your application. Yet the utility library isn't developed all by itself; usually people are tweaking it to add new features that they need in their own applications. Eventually, they want to share those new features with everybody else writing other applications; that's what a utility library is for.

What can you do? That's what this chapter is about. I discuss several strategies in common use—although some people might not dignify them with that term, preferring to call them "hacks"—and end with the most sophisticated solution, *submodules*.

The Old Solution: Partial Checkouts

A popular feature in many VCSs, including CVS and Subversion, is called a *partial checkout*. With a partial checkout, you choose to retrieve only a particular subdirectory or subdirectories of the repository and work just in there.[1]

If you have a central repository that holds *all* your projects, partial checkouts can be a workable way of handling submodules. Simply put your utility library in one subdirectory and put each application using that library in another directory. When you want to get one application, just check out two subdirectories (the library and the application) instead of checking out all directories: that's a partial checkout.

One benefit of using partial checkouts is that you don't have to download the gigantic, full history of every file. You just download just the files you need for a particular revision of a particular project. You may not even need the full history of just those files; the current version alone may suffice.

This technique was especially popular in an older VCS: CVS. CVS has no conceptual understanding of the whole repository; it only understands the history of individual files. In fact, the history of the files is stored in the file itself. CVS's repository format was so simple that the repository administrator could make copies and use symbolic links between different application repositories. Checking out a copy of each application would then automatically check out a copy of the referenced files. You wouldn't even have to know that the files were shared with other projects.

---

1. In fact, SVN cleverly uses partial checkouts to implement all its branching and tagging features. You just make a copy of your files in a subdirectory and then check out only that subdirectory.

This technique had its idiosyncrasies, but it has worked well on many projects for years. The KDE (K Desktop Environment) project, for example, encourages partial checkouts with their multigigabyte SVN repository.

Unfortunately, this idea isn't compatible with distributed VCSs like Git. With Git, you don't just download the current version of a selected set of files, you download *all* the versions of *all* the files. After all, every Git repository is a complete copy of the repository. Git's current architecture doesn't support partial checkouts well.[2]

As of this writing, the KDE project is considering a switch from SVN to Git, and submodules are their main point of contention. An import of the entire KDE repository into Git is still several gigabytes in size. Every KDE contributor would have to have a copy of all that data, even if they wanted to work on only one application. But you can't just make one repository per application: each application depends on one or more of the KDE core libraries.

For KDE to successfully switch to Git, it needs an alternative to huge, monolithic repositories using simple partial checkouts. For example, one experimental import of KDE into Git separated the code base into roughly 500 separate repositories.[3]

The Obvious Solution: Import the Code into Your Project

Let's revisit one of the options glossed over earlier: why not just import the library into your own project in a subdirectory? Then you can copy in a new set of files if you ever want to update the library.

Depending on your needs, this method can actually work just fine. It has these advantages:

- You never end up with the wrong library version by accident.
- It's extremely simple to explain and understand, and it relies only on everyday Git features.
- It works exactly the same way whether the external library is maintained in Git, some other VCS, or no VCS at all.
- Your application repository is always self-contained, so a `git clone` of your application always includes everything your application needs.
- It's easy to apply application-specific patches to the library in your own repository, even if you don't have commit access to the library's repository.

---

2. Actually, there are some experimental patches that implement partial checkouts in Git. They aren't yet in any released Git version, and may never be. Also, they are only partial *checkouts*, not partial *clones*. You still have to download the entire history even if it doesn't end up in your working tree, and this limits the benefit. Some people are interested in solving that problem, too, but it's extremely complicated—maybe even impossible—to do right.

3. See *http://labs.trolltech.com/blogs/2008/08/29/workflow-and-switching-to-git-part-2-the-tools/*.

- Branching your application also makes a branch of the library, exactly as you'd expect.
- If you use the `subtree` merge strategy (as described in the section "Specialty Merges" on page 143) in your `git pull -s subtree` command, then updating to newer versions of the library is just as easy as updating any other part of your project.

Unfortunately, there are also some disadvantages:

- Each application that imports the same library duplicates that library's files. There's no easy way to share those Git objects between repositories. If KDE did this, for example, and you *did* want to check out the entire project—say, because you're building the KDE distribution packages for Debian or Red Hat—then you would end up downloading the same library files dozens of times.
- If your application makes changes to its copy of the library, then the only way to share those changes is by generating diffs and applying them to the main library's repository. This is OK if you do it rarely, but it's a lot of tedious work if you do it frequently.

For many people and many projects, these disadvantages aren't very serious. You should consider using this technique if you can, because its simplicity often outweighs its disadvantages.

If you're familiar with other VCS, particularly CVS, you may have had some bad experiences that make you want to avoid this method. You should be aware that many of those problems do not arise in Git. For example:

- CVS didn't support file or directory renames, and its features (e.g., "vendor branches") for importing new upstream packages meant it was easy to make mistakes. One common mistake was to forget to delete old files when merging in new versions, which would result in strange inconsistencies. Git doesn't have this problem because importing any package is a simple matter of deleting a directory, recreating it, and using `git add --all`.
- Importing a new module can be a multistep process requiring several commits, and you might make mistakes. In CVS or SVN, such mistakes form a permanent part of the repository's history. This is normally harmless, but making mistakes can unnecessarily bloat the repository when importing huge files. With Git, if you screw up, then you simply throw away the erroneous commits before pushing them to anyone.
- CVS made it hard to follow the history of branches. If you imported upstream version 1.0, then applied some of your own changes, and then wanted to import version 2.0, it was complicated to extract your local changes and re-apply them. Git's improved history management makes this much easier.
- Some VCSs are very slow when checking for changes through a huge number of files. If you import several large packages using this technique, then the everyday

speed impact could cancel out the anticipated productivity gains from including submodules in your repository. Git, however, has been optimized for dealing with tens of thousands of files in one project, so this is unlikely to be a problem.

If you do decide to handle submodules by just importing them directly, there are two ways to proceed: by copying the files manually or by importing the history.

Importing Subprojects by Copying

The most obvious way to import another project's files into your project is by simply copying them. In fact, if the other project isn't stored in a Git repository, this is your only option.

The steps for doing this are exactly as you might expect: delete any files already in that directory, create the set of files you want (e.g., by extracting a tarball or ZIP file containing the library you want to import), and then `git add` them. For example:

```
$ cd myproject.git
$ rm -rf mylib
$ git rm mylib
$ tar -xzf /tmp/mylib-1.0.5.tar.gz
$ mv mylib-1.0.5 mylib
$ git add mylib
$ git commit
```

This method works fine, with the following caveats:

- Only the exact versions of the library you import will appear in your Git history. Compared to our next alternative—including the complete history of the subproject—you might actually find this convenient, because it keeps your log files clean.
- If you make application-specific changes to the library files, then you'll have to re-apply those changes whenever you import a new version. For example, you'll have to manually extract the changes through `git diff` and incorporate them through `git apply` (see Chapter 8 or Chapter 14 for more information). Git won't do this automatically.
- Importing a new version requires you to rerun the full command sequence removing and adding files every time; you can't just `git pull`.

On the other hand, copying is easy to understand and explain to your coworkers.

Importing Subprojects with git pull -s subtree

Another way to import a subproject into yours is by merging the entire history from that subproject. Of course, it works only if the subproject's history is already stored in Git.

This is a bit tricky to set up for the first time; however, once you've done the work, future merges are much easier than with the simple file-copying method. Because Git knows the entire history of the subproject, it knows exactly what needs to happen every time you need to do an update.

Let's say you want to write a new application called myapp and you want to include a copy of the Git source code in a directory called *git*. First, let's create the new repository and make the first commit. (If you already have a myapp project, you can skip this part.)

```
$ cd /tmp
$ mkdir myapp
$ cd myapp

$ git init
Initialized empty Git repository in /tmp/myapp/.git/

$ ls

$ echo hello > hello.txt

$ git add hello.txt

$ git commit -m 'first commit'
Created initial commit 644e0ae: first commit
 1 files changed, 1 insertions(+), 0 deletions(-)
 create mode 100644 hello.txt
```

Next, import the git project from your local copy, assumed to be ~/*git.git*.[4] The first step is just like the one in the previous section: extract a copy of it into a directory called *git*, then commit it.

The following example takes a particular version of the git.git project, denoted by the tag v1.6.0. The command git archive v1.6.0 creates a tar file of all the v1.6.0 files. They are then extracted into the new *git* subdirectory:

```
$ ls
hello.txt

$ mkdir git

$ cd git
$ (cd ~/git.git && git archive v1.6.0) | tar -xf -

$ cd ..

$ ls
git/  hello.txt

$ git add git

$ git commit -m 'imported git v1.6.0'
Created commit 72138f0: imported git v1.6.0
 1440 files changed, 299543 insertions(+), 0 deletions(-)
```

---

4. If you don't have such a repository already, you can clone it from *git://git.kernel.org/pub/scm/git/git.git*.

So far, you've imported the (initial) files by hand, but your myapp project still doesn't know anything about the *history* of its submodule. Now you must inform Git that you have imported v1.6.0, which means you also should have the entire history up to v1.6.0. To do that, use the -s ours merge strategy (from Chapter 9) with your git pull command. Recall that -s ours just means "record that we're doing a merge, but my files are the right files, so don't actually change anything."

Git isn't matching up directories and file contents between your project and the imported project or anything like that. Instead Git is only importing the history and tree pathnames as they are found in the original subproject. We'll have to account for this relocated directory basis later, though.

Simply pulling v1.6.0 doesn't work, which is due to a peculiarity of git pull.

```
$ git pull -s ours ~/git.git v1.6.0
fatal: Couldn't find remote ref v1.6.0
fatal: The remote end hung up unexpectedly
```

This might change in a future version of Git, but for now the problem is handled by explicitly spelling out refs/tags/v1.6.0, as described in "refs and symrefs" on page 68 of Chapter 6:

```
$ git pull -s ours ~/git.git refs/tags/v1.6.0
warning: no common commits
remote: Counting objects: 67034, done.
remote: Compressing objects: 100% (19135/19135), done.
remote: Total 67034 (delta 47938), reused 65706 (delta 46656)
Receiving objects: 100% (67034/67034), 14.33 MiB | 12587 KiB/s, done.
Resolving deltas: 100% (47938/47938), done.
From ~/git.git
 * tag               v1.6.0     -> FETCH_HEAD
Merge made by ours.
```

If all the v1.6.0 files were already committed, then you might think there was no work left to do. On the contrary, Git just imported the *entire history* of git.git up to v1.6.0, so even though the files are the same as before, our repository is now a lot more complete. Just to be sure, let's just check that the merge commit we just created didn't really change any files:

```
$ git diff HEAD^ HEAD
```

You shouldn't get any output from this command, which means the files before and after the merge are exactly the same. Good.

Now let's see what happens if we make some local changes to our subproject and then try to upgrade it later. First, make a simple change:

```
$ cd git
```

```
$ echo 'I am a git contributor!' > contribution.txt
```

```
$ git add contribution.txt
```

```
$ git commit -m 'My first contribution to git'
Created commit 6c9fac5: My first contribution to git
 1 files changed, 1 insertions(+), 0 deletions(-)
 create mode 100644 git/contribution.txt
```

Our version of the Git subproject is now v1.6.0 with an extra patch.

Finally, let's upgrade our Git to version v1.6.0.1 tag but without losing our additional contribution. It's as easy as this:

```
$ git pull -s subtree ~/git.git refs/tags/v1.6.0.1
remote: Counting objects: 179, done.
remote: Compressing objects: 100% (72/72), done.
remote: Total 136 (delta 97), reused 100 (delta 61)
Receiving objects: 100% (136/136), 25.24 KiB, done.
Resolving deltas: 100% (97/97), completed with 40 local objects.
From ~/git.git
 * tag                v1.6.0.1    -> FETCH_HEAD
Merge made by subtree.
```

 Don't forget to specify the -s subtree merge strategy in your pull. The merge might have worked even without -s subtree, because Git knows how to deal with file renames and we do have a lot of renames: all the files from the git.git project have been moved from the root directory of the project into a subdirectory called *git*. The -s subtree flag tells Git to look right away for that situation and deal with it. To be safe, you should always use -s subtree when merging a subproject into a subdirectory (except during the initial import, where we've seen that you should use -s ours).

Was it really that easy? Let's check that the files have been updated correctly. Because all the files in v1.6.0.1 were in the root directory and are now in the *git* directory, we must use some unusual selector syntax with git diff. In this case, what we're saying is: "Tell me the difference between the commit *from* which we merged (i.e., parent #2, which is v1.6.0.1) and what we merged *into*, the HEAD version." Because the latter is in the *git* directory, we have to specify that directory after a colon. The former is in its root directory, so we can omit the colon and default the directory.

The command and its output looks like this:

```
$ git diff HEAD^2 HEAD:git
diff --git a/contribution.txt b/contribution.txt
new file mode 100644
index 0000000..7d8fd26
--- /dev/null
+++ b/contribution.txt
@@ -0,0 +1 @@
+I am a git contributor!
```

It worked! The only difference from v1.6.0.1 is the change we applied earlier.

How did we know it was HEAD^2? After the merge, you can inspect the commit and see which branch HEADs were merged:

```
Merge: 6c9fac5... 5760a6b...
```

As with any merge, those are HEAD^1 and HEAD^2. You should recognize the latter:

```
commit 5760a6b094736e6f59eb32c7abb4cdbb7fca1627
Author: Junio C Hamano <gitster@pobox.com>
Date:   Sun Aug 24 14:47:24 2008 -0700

    GIT 1.6.0.1

    Signed-off-by: Junio C Hamano <gitster@pobox.com>
```

If your situation is a bit more complex, you might need to place your subproject deeper into your repository structure and not right at the top level as shown in this example. For instance, you might instead need *other/projects/git*. Git doesn't automatically keep track of the directory relocation when you imported it. Thus, as before, you would need to spell out the full path to the imported subproject:

```
$ git diff HEAD^2 HEAD:other/projects/git
```

You can also break down our contributions to the *git* directory one commit at a time:

```
$ git log --no-merges HEAD^2..HEAD
commit 6c9fac58bed056c5b06fd70b847f137918b5a895
Author: Jon Loeliger <jdl@example.com>
Date:   Sat Sep 27 22:32:49 2008 -0400

    My first contribution to git

commit 72138f05ba3e6681c73d0585d3d6d5b0ad329b7c
Author: Jon Loeliger <jdl@example.com>
Date:   Sat Sep 27 22:17:49 2008 -0400

    imported git v1.6.0
```

Using -s subtree, you can merge and remerge updates from the main git.git project into your subproject as many times as you want, and it will work just as if you simply had your own fork of the git.git project all by itself.

Submitting Your Changes Upstream

Although you can easily merge history *into* your subproject, taking it out again is much harder. That's because this technique doesn't maintain any history of the subproject. It has only the history of the whole application project, including its subproject.

You could still merge your project's history back into git.git using the -s subtree merge strategy, but the result would be unexpected: you'd end up importing *all* the commits from your entire application project and then recording a deletion of all the files except those in the *git* directory at the point of the final merge.

Although such a merged history would be technically correct, it's just plain wrong to place the history of your entire application into the repository holding the submodule. It would also mean that all the versions of all the files in your application would become a permanent part of the git project. They don't belong there, and it would be a time sink, produce an enormous amount of irrelevant information, and waste a lot of effort. It's the wrong approach.

Instead, you'll have to use alternative methods, such as git format-patch (discussed in Chapter 14). This requires more steps than a simple git pull. Luckily, you only have to approach the problem when contributing changes back to the subproject, not in the much more common case of pulling subproject changes into your application.

The Automated Solution: Checking out Subprojects Using Custom Scripts

After reading the previous section, you might have reasons not to copy the history of your subproject directly into a subdirectory of your application. After all, anyone can see that the two projects are separate: your application depends on the library, but they are obviously two different projects. Merging the two histories together doesn't feel like a clean solution.

There are other ways to do it that you might like better. Let's look at one obvious method: simply git clone the subproject into a subdirectory by hand every time you clone the main project, like this:

```
$ git clone myapp myapp-test
$ cd myapp-test
$ git clone ~/git.git git
$ echo git >.gitignore
```

This method is reminiscent of the partial checkout method in SVN or CVS. Instead of checking out just a few subdirectories of one huge project, you check out two small projects, but the idea is the same.

This method of handling submodules has a few key advantages:

- The submodule doesn't have to be in Git; it can be in any VCS or it can just be a tar or ZIP file from somewhere. Because you're retrieving the files by hand, you can retrieve them from anywhere you want.

- The history of your main project never gets mixed up with the history of your subprojects. The log doesn't become crowded with unrelated commits, and the Git repository itself stays small.

- If you make changes to the subproject, you can contribute them back exactly as if you were working on the subproject by itself, because, in essence, you are.

Of course, there are also some problems that you need to deal with:

- Explaining to other users how to check out all the subprojects can be tedious.

- You need to somehow ensure that you get the *right revision* of each subproject.

- When you switch to a different branch of your main project or when you `git pull` changes from someone else, the subproject isn't updated automatically.
- If you make a change to the subproject, you must remember to `git push` it separately.
- If you don't have rights to contribute back to the subproject (i.e., commit access to its repository), then you may not be able to easily make application-specific changes. (If the subproject is in Git, you can always put a public copy of your changes somewhere, of course.)

In short, cloning subprojects by hand gives you infinite flexibility, but it's easy to over-complicate things or to make mistakes.

If you choose to use this method, the best approach is to standardize it by writing some simple scripts and including them in your repository. For example, you might have a script called `./update-submodules.sh` that clones and/or updates all your submodules automatically.

Depending on how much effort you want to put in, such a script could update your submodules to particular branches or tags or even to particular revisions. You could hard-code commit IDs into the script, for example, and then commit a new version of the script to your main project whenever you want to update your application to a new version of the library. Then, when people check out a particular revision of your application, they can run the script to automatically derive the corresponding version of the library.

You might also think about creating a commit or update hook, using the techniques of Chapter 15, which prevents you from accidentally committing to your main project unless your changes to the subproject are properly committed and pushed.

You can well imagine that, if you want to manage your subprojects this way, then other people do, too. Thus, scripts to standardize and automate this process have already been written. One such script, by Miles Georgi, is called `externals` (or `ext`). You can find it at *http://nopugs.com/ext-tutorial*. Conveniently, `ext` works for any combination of SVN and Git projects and subprojects.

The Native Solution: gitlinks and git submodule

Git contains a command designed to work with submodules called `git submodule`. I saved it for last for two reasons:

- It is much more complicated than simply importing the history of subprojects into your main project's repository.
- It is fundamentally the same as but more restrictive than the script-based solution just discussed.

Even though it sounds like Git submodules should be the natural option, you should consider carefully before using them.

Git's submodule support is evolving fast. The first mention of submodules in Git development history was by Linus Torvalds in April 2007, and there have been numerous changes since then. That makes it something of a moving target, so you should check `git help submodule` in your version of Git to find out if anything has changed since this book was written.

Unfortunately, the `git submodule` command is not very transparent; you won't be able to use it effectively unless you understand exactly how it works. It's a combination of two separate features: so-called gitlinks and the actual `git submodule` command.

Gitlinks

A *gitlink* is a link from a *tree object* to a *commit object*.

Recall from Chapter 4 that each commit object points to a tree object and that each tree object points to a set of blobs and trees, which correspond (respectively) to files and subdirectories. A commit's tree object uniquely identifies the exact set of files, filenames, and permissions attached to that commit. Also recall from "Commit Graphs" on page 74 of Chapter 6, that the commits themselves are connected to each other in a DAG. Each commit object points to zero or more parent commits, and together they describe the history of your project.

But we haven't yet seen a tree object pointing to a commit object. The gitlink is Git's mechanism to indicate a direct reference to another Git repository.

Let's try it out. As in "Importing Subprojects with git pull -s subtree" on page 299, we'll create a `myapp` repository and import the Git source code into it:

```
$ cd /tmp
$ mkdir myapp
$ cd myapp

# Start the new super-project
$ git init
Initialized empty Git repository in /tmp/myapp/.git/

$ echo hello >hello.txt

$ git add hello.txt

$ git commit -m 'first commit'
[master (root-commit)]: created c3d9856: "first commit"
 1 files changed, 1 insertions(+), 0 deletions(-)
 create mode 100644 hello.txt
```

But this time, when we import the git project we'll do so directly; we don't use git archive like we did last time:

```
$ ls
hello.txt

# Copy in a repository clone
$ git clone ~/git.git git
Initialized empty Git repository in /tmp/myapp/git/.git/

$ cd git

# Establish the desired submodule version
$ git checkout v1.6.0
Note: moving to "v1.6.0" which isn't a local branch
If you want to create a new branch from this checkout, you may do so
(now or later) by using -b with the checkout command again. Example:
  git checkout -b <new_branch_name>
HEAD is now at ea02eef... GIT 1.6.0

# Back to the super-project
$ cd ..

$ ls
git/  hello.txt

$ git add git

$ git commit -m 'imported git v1.6.0'
[master]: created b0814ac: "imported git v1.6.0"
 1 files changed, 1 insertions(+), 0 deletions(-)
 create mode 160000 git
```

Because there already exists a directory called *git/.git* (created during the git clone), git add git knows to create a gitlink to it.

 Normally, git add git and git add git/ (with the POSIX-compatible trailing slash indicating that *git* must be a directory) would be equivalent. But that's not true if you want to create a gitlink! In the sequence we just showed, adding a slash to make the command git add git/ won't create a gitlink at all; it will just add all the files in the *git* directory, which is probably not what you want.

Observe how the outcome of the preceding sequence differs from that of the related steps in "Importing Subprojects with git pull -s subtree" on page 299. In that section, the commit changed all the files in the repository. This time, the commit message shows that only *one* file changed. The resulting tree looks like this:

```
$ git ls-tree HEAD
160000 commit ea02eef096d4bfcbb83e76cfab0fcb42dbcad35e    git
100644 blob   ce013625030ba8dba906f756967f9e9ca394464a    hello.txt
```

The *git* subdirectory is of type commit and has mode 160000. That makes it a gitlink.

Git usually treats gitlinks as simple pointer values or references to other repositories. Most Git operations, such as clone, do not dereference the gitlinks and then act on the submodule repository.

For example, if you push your project into another repository, it won't push in the submodule's commit, tree, and blob objects. If you clone your superproject repository, the subproject repository directories will be empty.

In the following example, the *git* subproject directory remains empty after the clone command:

```
$ cd /tmp

$ git clone myapp app2
Initialized empty Git repository in /tmp/app2/.git/

$ cd app2

$ ls
git/  hello.txt

$ ls git

$ du git
4       git
```

Gitlinks have the important feature that they link to objects that are *allowed to be missing* from your repository. After all, they're supposed to be part of some other repository.

It is exactly because the gitlinks are allowed to be missing that this technique even achieves one of the original goals: partial checkouts. You don't have to check out every subproject; you can check out just the ones you need.

So now you know how to create a gitlink and that it's allowed to be missing. But missing objects aren't very useful by themselves. How do you get them back? That's what the git submodule command is for.

The git submodule Command

At the time of this writing, the git submodule command is actually just a 700-line Unix shell script called git-submodule.sh. And if you've read this book all the way through to this point, you now know enough to write that script yourself. Its job is simple: to follow gitlinks and check out the corresponding repositories for you.

First of all, you should be aware that there's no particular magic involved in checking out a submodule's files. In the *app2* directory we just cloned, you could do it yourself:

```
$ cd /tmp/app2

$ git ls-files --stage -- git
160000 ea02eef096d4bfcbb83e76cfab0fcb42dbcad35e 0    git
```

```
$ rmdir git

$ git clone ~/git.git git
Initialized empty Git repository in /tmp/app2/git/.git/

$ cd git

$ git checkout ea02eef
Note: moving to "ea02eef" which isn't a local branch
If you want to create a new branch from this checkout, you may do so
(now or later) by using -b with the checkout command again. Example:
  git checkout -b <new_branch_name>
HEAD is now at ea02eef... GIT 1.6.0
```

The commands you just ran are exactly equivalent to git submodule update. The only difference is that git submodule will do the tedious work such as determining the correct commit ID to check out for you. Unfortunately, it doesn't know how to do this without a bit of help:

```
$ git submodule update
No submodule mapping found in .gitmodules for path 'git'
```

The git submodule command needs to know one important bit of information before it can do anything: where can it find the repository for your submodule? It retrieves that information from a file called *.gitmodules*, which looks like this:

```
[submodule "git"]
        path = git
        url = /home/bob/git.git
```

Using the file is a two-step process. First, create the *.gitmodules* file, either by hand or with git submodule add. Because we created the gitlink using git add earlier, it's too late now for git submodule add, so just create the file by hand:

```
$ cat >.gitmodules <<EOF
[submodule "git"]
        path = git
        url = /home/bob/git.git
EOF
```

> The git submodule add command that performs the same operations is:
>
> ```
> $ git submodule add /home/bob/git.git git
> ```
>
> The git submodule add command will add an entry to the *.gitmodules* and populate a new Git repository with a clone of the added repository.

Next, run git submodule init to copy the settings from the *.gitmodules* file into your *.git/config* file:

```
$ git submodule init
Submodule 'git' (/home/bob/git.git) registered for path 'git'
```

```
$ cat .git/config
[core]
        repositoryformatversion = 0
        filemode = true
        bare = false
        logallrefupdates = true
[remote "origin"]
        url = /tmp/myapp
        fetch = +refs/heads/*:refs/remotes/origin/*
[branch "master"]
        remote = origin
        merge = refs/heads/master
[submodule "git"]
        url = /home/bob/git.git
```

The `git submodule init` command added only the last two lines.

The reason for this step is that you can reconfigure your local submodules to point at a different repository from the one in the official *.gitmodules*. If you make a clone of someone's project that uses submodules, you might want to keep your own copy of the submodules and point your local clone at that. In that case, you wouldn't want to change the module's official location in *.gitmodules*, but you would want `git submodule` to look at your preferred location. So `git submodule init` copies any missing submodule information from *.gitmodules* into *.git/config*, where you can safely edit it. Just find the [submodule] section referring to the submodule you're changing, and edit the URL.

Finally, run `git submodule update` to actually update the files, or if needed, clone the initial subproject repository:

```
# Force a complete new clone by removing what's there
$ rm -rf git

$ git submodule update
Initialized empty Git repository in /tmp/app2/git/.git/
Submodule path 'git': checked out 'ea02eef096d4bfcbb83e76cfab0fcb42dbcad35e'
```

Here `git submodule update` goes to the repository pointed to in your *.git/config*, fetches the commit ID found in `git ls-tree HEAD -- git`, and checks out that revision in the directory specified in *.git/config*.

There are a few other things you need to know:

- When you switch branches or `git pull` someone else's branch, you always need to run `git submodule update` to obtain a matching set of submodules. This isn't automatic because it could cause you to lose work in the submodule by mistake.

- If you switch to another branch and *don't* issue `git submodule update`, Git will think you have deliberately changed your submodule directory to point at a new commit (when really it was the *old* commit you were using before). If you then `git commit -a`, you will accidentally change the gitlink. Be careful!

- You can update an existing gitlink by simply checking out the right version of a submodule, executing `git add` on the submodule directory, and then running `git commit`. You don't use the `git submodule` command for that.
- If you have updated and committed a gitlink on your branch and if you `git pull` or `git merge` another branch that updates the same gitlink *differently*, then Git doesn't know how to represent this as a conflict and will just pick one or the other. You must remember to resolve conflicted gitlinks by yourself.

As you can see, the use of gitlinks and `git submodule` is quite complex. Fundamentally, the gitlink concept can perfectly represent how your submodules relate to your main project, but actually making use of that information is a lot harder than it sounds.

When considering how you want to use submodules in your own project, you need to consider carefully if the complexity is worth it Note that `git submodule` is a standalone command like any other, and it doesn't make the process of maintaining submodules any simpler than, say, writing your own submodule scripts or using the `ext` package described at the end of the previous section. Unless you have a real need for the flexibility that `git submodule` provides, you might consider using one of the simpler methods.

On the other hand, I fully expect that the Git development community will address the shortfalls and issues with the `git submodule` command, to ultimately lead to a technically correct and very usable solution.

## CHAPTER 17

Submodule Best Practices

Submodules are a powerful, but sometimes perceived as complex piece of the Git toolchain. Submodules are, at the highest level, a facility for the composition of Git repositories (Figure 17-1).

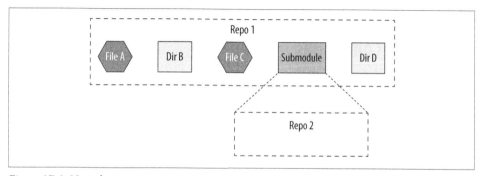

Figure 17-1. Nested repos

But unlike some of their non-Git cousins such as SVN Externals (*http://svnbook.red -bean.com/en/1.5/svn.advanced.externals.html*), they default to offering greater precision, pointing not only at the network address of the nested repository, but also to the commit hash of the nested repository (Figure 17-2).

Because each commit ref has, within a repo, a unique identifier to a specific point in the graph and all parent states that led up to that point, pointing to the ref of another repo records that precise state in the commit history of the parent project.

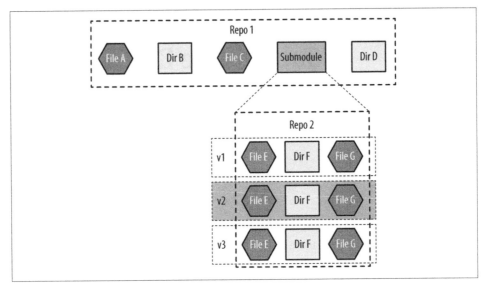

Figure 17-2. Nested repos pointing to precise revision

Submodule Commands

Although the dedicated chapter on submodules provides an exhaustive list of commands, a quick recap of the basic submodule actions is helpful:

`git submodule add` *address localdirectoryname*
> Register a new submodule for this superproject and, optionally, express it in the specified folder name (can be a subfolder path relative to the root of the project).

`git submodule status`
> Summary of the commit ref and dirtiness state of all submodules at this project level.

`git submodule init`
> Use the *.gitmodules* long-term storage of submodule information to update the *.git/config* file used during developer repository actions.

`git submodule update`
> Fetch the submodule contents using the address from *.git/config* and check out the superproject's submodule-recorded ref in a detached `HEAD` state.

`git submodule summary`
> Display a patch of the changes of each submodule's current state as compared to its committed state.

`git submodule foreach` *command*
> Scripts a shell command to be run on each submodule and provides variables for $path, $sha1, and other useful identifiers.

Why Submodules?

The most common driving factor behind the use of submodules is modularization. Submodules provide a componentization of a source code base in the absence of such a modularization at the binary level (DLL, JAR, SO). Solutions such as Maven Multi-module Projects (*http://www.sonatype.com/books/mvnex-book/reference/multimodule .html*) and Gradle Multiproject Builds (*http://www.gradle.org/docs/current/userguide/ multi_project_builds.html*) are well-known Java solutions for componentized binary or semibinary dependency management that don't require the entire source base to be checked out to a monolithic folder. Likewise, the .NET space has Assemblies (*http:// msdn.microsoft.com/en-us/library/hk5f40ct(v=vs.71).aspx*) that allow for binary consumption of subcomponents and plug-ins. Driving the use of submodules in the Objective-C ecosystem is the contrasting sparseness of options for modularity and the inclusion of compiled binaries.

Take, for example, the instructions for the Pull To Refresh (*https://github.com/leah/ PullToRefresh*) functionality that so many iOS apps are leveraging today. The *RE-ADME* suggests that a developer "Copy the files, *PullRefreshTableViewController.h*, *PullRefreshTableViewController.m*, and *arrow.png* into your project." This concept of a nested source in a subdirectory is shown in Figure 17-3.

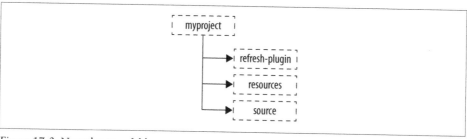

Figure 17-3. Nested source folders

Git submodules facilitate leaving the existing directory structure of a subcomponent intact, provided the separation of components falls along directory fault lines, while enabling precise labeling and version control of each component that contributes to an aggregate project.

Leveraging the appropriate database terminology, submodules can also facilitate the creation of multiple views of different versions of the same plugins or different overlapping sets of plug-ins. More than one superproject can contain the same submodule, and the different superprojects can record a different desired ref of the submodule, thus projecting older and newer views of the composed system, while allowing the submodule developers to continue unimpeded with forward development at no risk to the consuming superprojects.

Submodules Preparation

When considering the use of Git submodules, the first question to ask is if the composition of the code base is ready to accept such a fracture. Submodules are always expressed as subdirectories of the superproject. Submodules cannot blend sets of files into a single directory. Field experience has shown that most systems already have a subdirectory composition, even in a monolithic repository, as the crudest form of modularization. Thus, the translation and extraction of a subfolder (Figure 17-4) to a true submodule is relatively easy and can be implemented by these steps:

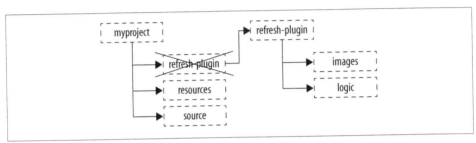

Figure 17-4. Nested source folder extracted

1. Move the subdirectory out of the superproject to be a peer to the superproject directory. If maintaining repository history is important, consider using `git filter-branch` to help extract subdirectory structure.
2. Rename the submodule-to-be directory to more accurately express the nature of the submodule. For example, a *refresh* subdirectory might be renamed to *client-app-refresh-plug-in*.
3. Create a new upstream hosting for the submodule as a first-class project (e.g., create a new project on GitHub to host the extracted code).
4. Initialize the now stand-alone plug-in as a Git repo and push the commit to the newly created project hosting URL.
5. In the superproject, add a Git submodule, pointing to the new submodule project URL.
6. Commit and push the superproject, which will include the newly created *.gitmodules* file.

Why Read Only?

The recommendation for the previous extraction of a subdirectory into a Git submodule advised for it to be cloned via a *read-only address*, which frequently means access through `https://` without a username or `git://`. This recommendation has served many users of submodules very well, making it easier to cope with the complexity that the use of submodules brings about. It offers an enforced separation of activities, pushing work on submodules out into the stand-alone clone of the submodule and sug-gesting that it should first be engineered, tested, and built in an independent way. Then, as a secondary step, the developer switches focus back into the superproject then fetches and checks out the newer revision of the submodule. This step is occasionally lamented as being tedious, but many developers learn to appreciate the precision this offers over the less deterministic approach of having a floating version of the subcomponent (in the style of an SVN External pointing to trunk) always pointing to the latest committed state.

Why Not Read Only?

If the previous recommendation is greatly disliked, it is practical, though more risky, to update the source code directly within the submodules of a superproject, committing, pushing, and checking out from that nested directory. It can be slightly more efficient to use this combined approach, although it foregoes the true separation of implementing versus consuming modes that submodules were meant to bring about.

The greatest risk with this all-in-one working directory approach, even for veteran sub-module users, is the committing of code and the recording of an updated submodule hash in the superproject *without having pushed* the submodule's new commits to a shared network repository. Thus, if the superproject's new commit is pushed, other developers, upon pulling the updated superproject, will find they cannot fully check out the current committed ref because there are inaccessible commits in the unpushed subproject that the superproject is calling for.

Examining the Hashes of Submodule Commits

For developers wanting to examine their project one level deeper than t hey will use it on a daily basis, the recording of a submodule commit ref is a fascinatingly simple thing to observe. The ref of the submodule's commit is stored in the *tree* just as the ref of a subdirectory or blob would be, but with an entry type of *commit* rather than *tree* or *blob*.

```
$ git ls-tree HEAD
100644 blob 0cf8086ddd1ac6c6463405ea9aa46102e0e6eb20  .gitmodules
100644 blob e425f022e79989a5ecb2c8343e697d1e4bf70258  README.txt
040000 tree aaa0af6b82db99c660b169962524e2201ac7079c  resources
040000 tree 42103128ceaebabff8f50cf408903d12e14c21d9  src
160000 commit 47b28b4e89481095f0eefe764eeefafcfa7e5b6c  submodule1
```

A practical use of this tooling output is in the examination of, sometimes from a build automation script, the state of a consumed submodule and comparing it to another known state. `git rev-parse` can be used on a HEAD or labeled build in another phase of automation to capture a known good point of the submodule and then the resultant hash can be compared to the currently preserved ref (state) of the submodule within the superproject.

Credential Reuse

A traditional `git clone user@hostname:pathtorepo` is acceptable for a stand-alone Git repository. However, this is a less desirable address for a `git submodule add URL` command because the username will be saved in the submodule metadata at the superproject repository level. This username will be preserved and unintentionally used by all other repository cloning developers.

In a business where access control to repositories is decided on a per user basis, it would be undesirable to store a specific username as part of the *.gitmodules* recorded address for a submodule. It would be nice if the superproject's username used during cloning was passed along to the submodules cloning operation.

The Git submodule commands know to take the credentials given during the superproject cloning operation and pass them downward (Figure 17-5) to any actions invoked by `--recurse-submodules`. This leaves the *.gitmodules* address free of any usernames and usable by any developer authorized to clone the project.

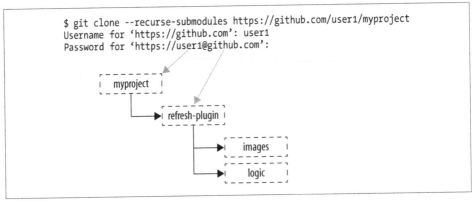

Figure 17-5. Reuse of credentials in submodules

Use Cases

Open Sourcing a Book's Code Samples

One of the most exciting examples of applying submodules was the open sourcing of the *Building and Testing Gradle* book's code examples long before the book itself was put on the market. This allowed for the creation of some early buzz around the book as well as community contributions to and polishing of the examples. Using GitHub as the repository host, the top level book project was closed source, but contained a submodule for the example code in a folder named *examples*. Specific source code files in the *examples* directory were directly referenced by the book prose AsciiDoc files. The book PDF and HTML generation tooling had no idea a Git submodule was used; it was just a regular directory as far as it was concerned. The contributors to the open source examples had no burden on how this code was used in the book. It was an eye-opening experience that other technical authors are encouraged to repeat.

A Plug-in

Frequently in the Objective-C world, but also in the ANSI C and C++ ecosystems, plug-in–like code can be incorporated as a submodule into a superproject without losing the ability to update of a connection to the original add-in author's repository. The traditional *README*-suggested process of copying these files into your project leaves them detached from any historical metadata and subject to a manual copy-and-paste update. This plug-in pattern extends even to noncompiled code such as Emacs Lisp setups (*https://github.com/matthewmccullough/emacs*), and dotfile configurations (*https://github.com/matthewmccullough/dotfiles*) with the inclusion of oh-my-zsh (*https://github.com/robbyrussell/oh-my-zsh*).

A Large Repo

The most contentious use of submodules is for scaling down the size of a repository. Although a practical solution to Git's desire to have relatively small repos (1 to 4GB total) compared to several-hundred-gigabyte SVN repositories, strategic developers should consider solutions that link projects on a binary or Application Programming Interface (API) level rather than at the source level that submodules provide.

Visibility Constraints

A final and unique implementation pattern of submodules is the partitioning of (access control–based) visibility of a composed application. One Git-using development team has cryptographic code that had licensing constraints permitting only a handful of developers to see it. That code was stored as a Git submodule and when the superproject was cloned, the permissions denied the majority of developers from being able to clone that submodule. The build system for this project was carefully constructed to adapt to the missing source of the cryptographic component, outputting a *developer-only* build. The SSH key of the continuous integration server, on the other hand, does have permission to retrieve the cryptography submodule, thus producing the feature-complete builds that customers will ultimately receive.

Multilevel Nesting of Repos

The use of submodules discussed thus far can be extended to another level of recursion. submodules can in turn be superprojects, and thus contain submodules. This proliferated the use of custom automation scripts to recursively apply behavior to every nested submodule. However, that need has been mitigated through recent improvements in submodule support across the Git vocabulary.

Submodules have received renewed attention in the 1.6.x and 1.7.x era of Git, with the addition of `--recurse-submodules` option switch to the majority of the network-enabled

Git commands. As of Git Version 1.7.9.4, this option is supported by the clone, fetch, and pull commands. Furthermore, the convenience of working with nested submodules has been improved with submodule status, submodule update, and submodule for each, all supporting the --recurse option.

Submodules on the Horizon

I've been pleased to see that as submodule tooling support increases, such as the Graphical User Interface (GUI) support for revision updates in Git Tower (*http://www .git-tower.com/files/applicationHelp/pgs/Submodules_ConceptIntroduction.html*), in addition to the hyperlinking of submodules on GitHub (*http://help.github.com/submod ules/*), adoption has also increased (see Figure 17-6). This also parallels the developer community's ever increasing proficiency in Git. As the idea of pointers to specific views of all files at an instant in time becomes more of a pedestrian concept, the use of sub-modules is likely to increase even further.

Figure 17-6. Submodule hyperlinks on GitHub repositories

## CHAPTER 18

Using Git with Subversion Repositories

As you become more and more comfortable with Git, you'll likely find it harder and harder to work without such a capable tool. But sometimes you'll have to do without Git—say, if you work with a team whose source code is managed by some other VCS. (SVN, for example, is popular among open source projects.) Luckily, the Git developers have created numerous plug-ins to import and synchronize source code revisions with other systems.

This chapter demonstrates how to use Git when the rest of your team employs SVN. This chapter also provides guidance if more of your teammates want to make the switch to Git, and it explains what to do if your team wants to drop SVN entirely.

Example: A Shallow Clone of a Single Branch

To begin, let's make a shallow clone of a single SVN branch. Specifically, let's work with the source code of SVN itself (which is guaranteed to be managed with SVN for as long as this book is in print) and a particular set of revisions, 33005 through 33142, from the 1.5.x branch of SVN.

The first step is to clone the SVN repository:

```
$ git svn clone -r33005:33142 \
    http://svn.collab.net/repos/
    svn/branches/1.5.x/ svn.git
```

 In some Git packages, such as those provided by the Debian and Ubuntu Linux distributions, the `git svn` command is an *optional* part of Git. If you type `git svn` and are warned that "svn is not a git-command," try to install the *git-svn* package. (See Chapter 2 for details about installing Git packages.)

The `git svn clone` command is more verbose than the typical `git clone` and is usually slower than running either Git or SVN separately.[1] In this example, however, the initial clone won't be *too* slow, because the working set is but a small portion of the history of a single branch.

Once git svn clone finishes, glance at your new Git repository:

```
$ cd svn.git

$ ls
./              build/          contrib/        HACKING       README        win-tests.py
../             build.conf      COPYING         INSTALL       STATUS        www/
aclocal.m4      CHANGES         doc/            Makefile.in   subversion/
autogen.sh*     COMMITTERS      gen-make.py*    notes/        tools/
BUGS            configure.ac    .git/           packages/     TRANSLATING

$ git branch -a
* master
  git-svn

$ git log -1
commit 05026566123844aa2d65a6896bf7c6e65fc53f7c
Author: hwright <hwright@612f8ebc-c883-4be0-9ee0-a4e9ef946e3a>
Date:   Wed Sep 17 17:45:15 2008 +0000

    Merge r32790, r32796, r32798 from trunk:

    * r32790, r32796, r32798
      Fix issue #2505: make switch continue after deleting locally modified
      directories, as it update and merge do.
      Notes:
        r32796 updates the docstring.
        r32798 is an obvious fix.
      Justification:
        Small fix (with test).  User requests.
      Votes:
        +1: danielsh, zhakov, cmpilato


    git-svn-id: http://svn.collab.net/repos/svn/branches/
            1.5.x@33142 612f8ebc-c883-4be0-9ee0-a4e9ef946e3a

$ git log --pretty=oneline --abbrev-commit
0502656... Merge r32790, r32796, r32798 from trunk:
77a44ab... Cast some votes, approving changes.
de50536... Add r33136 to the r33137 group.
96d6de4... Recommend r33137 for backport to 1.5.x.
e2d810c... * STATUS: Nominate r32771 and vote for r32968, r32975.
23e5373... * subversion/po/ko.po: Korean translation updated (no
                        fuzzy left; applied from trunk of r33034)
92902fa... * subversion/po/ko.po: Merged translation from trunk r32990
4e7f79a... Per the proposal in
```

1. The git svn command is sluggish because it isn't highly optimized. SVN support in Git has fewer users and developers than plain Git or plain SVN. Additionally, git svn simply has more work to do. Git downloads the repository's history, not just the most recent version, whereas the SVN protocol is optimized for downloading just one version at a time.

```
            http://svn.haxx.se/dev/archive-2008-08/0148.shtml,
            Add release stream openness indications to the
            STATUS files on our various release branches.
    f9eae83... Merge r31546 from trunk:
```

There are a few things to observe:

- You can now manipulate all the imported commits directly with Git, ignoring the SVN server. Only `git svn` commands talk to the server; other Git commands such as `git blame`, `git log`, and `git diff` are as fast as always and function even when you're not online. This offline feature is a major reason developers prefer to use `git svn` instead of SVN.

- The working directory lacks *.svn* directories, but it does have the familiar *.git* directory. Normally, when you check out a SVN project, each subdirectory contains a *.svn* directory for bookkeeping. However, `git svn` does its bookkeeping in the *.git* directory, as Git always does. The `git svn` command does use an extra directory called *.git/svn*, which is described momentarily.

- Even though you checked out a branch named `1.5.x`, the local branch has the standard Git name `master`. Nonetheless, it still corresponds to the `1.5.x` branch, revision 33142. The local repository also has a remote ref called `git-svn`, which is the parent of the local `master` branch.

- The author's name and email address in `git log` is atypical for Git. For example, the author is listed as `hwright` instead of the author's real name, Hyrum Wright. Moreover, his email address a string of hex digits. Unfortunately, SVN doesn't store an author's full name or email address. Instead, it stores only the author's login, which in this case is `hwright`. However, because Git wants the extra information, `git svn` fabricates it. The string of hex digits is the unique ID of the SVN repository. With it, Git can uniquely identify *this* particular `hwright` user on this particular server by using his generated email address.

 If you know the proper name and email address of every developer in your SVN project, you can specify the `--authors-file` option to use a list of known identities instead of a set of manufactured ones. However, this is optional and matters only if you care about the aesthetics of your logs. Most developers don't. Run the command `git help svn` for more information.

 User identification differs between SVN and Git. Every SVN user must have a login on the central repository server to make a commit. Login names must be unique and thus are suitable for identification in SVN.

Git, on the other hand, does not require a server. In Git's case, the user's email address is the only reliable, easily understood, and globally unique string.

- SVN users don't typically write one-line summaries in commit messages, as Git users do, so the one line format from `git log` produces rather ugly results. There's not much you can do about this, but you might ask or encourage your SVN colleagues to adopt the one-line summary voluntarily. After all, a one-line summary is helpful in any VCS.

- There's an extra line in each commit message, prefixed with `git-svn-id`. This line is used by `git svn` to keep track of where the commit came from. In this case, the commit came from *http://svn.collab.net/repos/svn/branches/1.5.x*, as of revision 33142, and the server unique ID is the same one used to generate Hyrum's fake email address.

- `git svn` created a new commit ID number (0502656...) for each commit. If you used exactly the same Git software and command-line options as those shown here, then the commit numbers you see on your local system should likewise be identical. That's appropriate, because your local commits are the same commits from the same remote repository. This detail is critical in certain `git svn` work flows, as you'll see shortly.

  It's also fragile. If you use different `git svn clone` options, even just cloning a different revision sequence, then *all* your commit IDs will change.

Making Your Changes in Git

Now that you have a Git repository of SVN source code, the next thing to do is make a change:

```
$ echo 'I am now a subversion developer!' >hello.txt
$ git add hello.txt
$ git commit -m 'My first subversion commit'
```

Congratulations, you've contributed your first change to the SVN source code!

Well, not really. You've *committed* your first change to the SVN source code. In plain SVN, where every commit is stored in the central repository, committing a change and sharing it with everyone is the same thing. In Git, however, a commit is just an object in your local repository until you push the change to someone else. And `git svn` doesn't change that.

Alas, if you want to contribute your changes back, the usual Git operation doesn't work:

```
$ git push origin master
fatal: 'origin': unable to chdir or not a git archive
fatal: The remote end hung up unexpectedly
```

In other words: you didn't create a Git remote called `origin`, so the command doesn't make any sense. (For more about defining remotes, see Chapter 12.) In fact, a Git remote won't solve this problem. If you want to commit back to SVN, you must use `git svn dcommit`.[2]

```
$ git svn dcommit
Committing to http://svn.collab.net/repos/svn/branches/1.5.x ...
Authentication realm: <http://svn.collab.net:80> Subversion Committers
Password for 'bob':
```

If you actually had commit access to the central SVN source code repository (only a few people in the world have this privilege), you would enter your password at the prompt and `git svn` would do its magic. But then things would become even more confusing, because you're trying to commit to a revision that isn't the latest one.

Let's examine what to do about this next.

Fetching Before Committing

Recall that SVN keeps a linear, sequential view of history. If your local copy has an older version from the SVN repository (it does) and you've made a commit to that old version (you did), then there's no way to send it back to the server. SVN simply has no way of creating a new branch at an earlier point in the history of a project.

However, you did create a fork in the history, as a Git commit always does. That leaves two possibilities:

1. The history was intentionally forked. You want to keep both parts of the history, merge them together, and commit the merge to SVN.

2. The fork wasn't intentional and it would be better to linearize it and then commit.

Does this sound familiar? It's similar to the choice between merging and rebasing discussed in "rebase Versus merge" on page 174 of Chapter 10. The former option corresponds to `git merge`, and the latter is akin to `git rebase`.

The good news here is that, once again, Git offers both options. The bad news is that SVN is going lose some part of your history no matter which option is chosen.

To continue, fetch the latest revisions from SVN:[3]

```
$ git svn fetch
    M       STATUS
    M       build.conf
    M       COMMITTERS
r33143 = 152840fb7ec59d642362b2de5d8f98ba87d58a87 (git-svn)
    M       STATUS
r33193 = 13fc53806d777e3035f26ff5d1eedd5d1b157317 (git-svn)
```

---

2. Why "dcommit" instead of "commit"? The original `git svn commit` command was destructive and poorly designed, and it should be eschewed. However, rather than break backward compatibility, the `git svn` developers decided to add a new command, `dcommit`. The old `commit` command is now better known as `set-tree`, but don't use that command, either.

3. Your local repository will definitely be missing revisions, because only a subset of all revisions was cloned at the start. You'll probably see more new revisions than those shown here, because SVN developers are still working on the `1.5.x` branch.

```
     M      STATUS
  r33194 = d70041fd576337b1d0e605d7f4eb2feb8ce08f86 (git-svn)
```

You can interpret the previous log messages as follows:

- The M means a file was modified.
- r33143 is the SVN revision number of a change.
- 152840f... is the corresponding Git commit ID generated by git svn.
- git-svn is the name of the remote ref that's been updated with the new commit.

Let's look at what's going on:

```
$ git log --pretty=oneline --abbrev-commit --left-right master...git-svn
<2e5f71c... My first subversion commit
>d70041f... * STATUS: Added note to r33173.
>13fc538... * STATUS: Nominate r33173 for backport.
>152840f... Merge r31203 from trunk:
```

In plain English, the left branch (master) has one new commit and the right branch (git-svn) has three new commits. (You'll likely see different output when you run the command because this output was captured during production of the book.) The --left-right option and the symmetric difference operator (...) are discussed in "git log with conflicts" on page 132 of Chapter 9 and in "Commit Ranges" on page 78 of Chapter 6, respectively.

Before you can commit back to SVN, you need one branch with all the commits in one place. Additionally, any new commits must be relative to the current state of the git-svn branch because that's all SVN knows how to do.

Committing Through git svn rebase

The most obvious way to add your changes is to rebase them on top of the git-svn branch:

```
$ git checkout master

# Rebase current master branch on the upstream git-svn branch
$ git rebase git-svn
First, rewinding head to replay your work on top of it...
Applying: My first subversion commit

$ git log --pretty=oneline --abbrev-commit --left-right master...git-svn
<0c4c620... My first subversion commit
```

A shortcut for git svn fetch followed by git rebase git-svn is simply git svn rebase. The latter command automatically deduces that your branch is based on the one called git-svn, fetches that from SVN, and rebases your branch onto it. Furthermore, when git svn dcommit notices that your SVN branch is out of date, it doesn't just give up; it automatically calls git svn rebase first.

If you always want to rebase instead of merging, `git svn rebase` is a great time saver. But if you don't like rewriting history by default, you must *be very careful not to dcommit until you've done `git svn fetch` and `git merge` manually.*

If you're just using Git as a convenient way to access your SVN history, then rebasing is fine—just as `git rebase` is a perfectly fine way to rearrange a set of patches you're working on—as long as you've never pushed those patches to anyone else. But rebasing with `git svn` faces all the same drawbacks as rebasing in general.

If you rebase your patches before committing them to SVN, make sure you understand the following:

- Don't create local branches and `git merge` them. As mentioned in "rebase Versus merge" on page 174 of Chapter 10, rebasing confuses `git merge`. With plain Git, you can choose not to rebase any branch that another branch is based on, but with `git svn` you don't have that option. *All* your branches are based on the `git-svn` branch, and that's the one that all other branches need to be based on.

- Don't let anyone pull from or clone your repository; let them use `git svn` to create their own Git repository instead. Because pulling one repository into another always causes a merge, it won't work, and for the same reason that `git merge` won't work when you've rebased your repository.

- Rebase and dcommit frequently. Remember, an SVN user does the equivalent of a `git push` every time she makes a commit, and that's still the best way to keep things under control when your history has to stay linear.

- Don't forget that, when you rebase a series of patches onto another branch, the intermediate versions created by the patches never really existed and were never really tested. You are essentially rewriting history and, indeed, that's what it is. If later you try to use `git bisect` or `git blame` (or `svn blame` in SVN) to determine when a problem was introduced, you won't have a true view of what happened.

Do these warnings make `git svn rebase` sound dangerous? Good. Every variation of `git rebase` is treacherous. However, if you follow the rules and don't try anything fancy, you'll be OK.

Now let's try something fancy.

Pushing, Pulling, Branching, and Merging with git svn

Rebasing all the time is fine if you simply want to use Git as a glorified SVN repository mirror. Even that by itself is a great step forward: you get to work offline; you get faster `log`, `blame`, and `diff` operations; and you don't annoy your coworkers who are perfectly happy using SVN. Nobody even has to know you're using Git.

But what if you want to do a little more than that? Maybe one of your coworkers wants to collaborate with you on a new feature using Git. Or perhaps you want to work on a few topic branches at a time and wait on committing them back to SVN until you're sure they're ready. Most of all, maybe you find SVN's merging features tedious and you want to use Git's much more advanced capabilities.

If you use `git svn rebase`, you can't really do any of those things. The good news is that if you avoid using rebase, `git svn` *will* let you do it all.

There's only one catch: your fancy, nonlinear history won't ever be in SVN. Your SVN-using coworkers will see the results of your hard work in the form of an occasional squashed merge commit (see "Squash Merges" on page 147 in Chapter 9), but they won't be able to see exactly how you got there.

If that's going to be a problem, you should probably skip the rest of this chapter. But if your coworkers don't care—most developers don't look at others' histories, anyway—or if you want to use it to prod your coworkers to try out Git, then what's described next is a much more powerful way to use `git svn`.

Keeping Your Commit IDs Straight

Recall from Chapter 10 that a rebase is disruptive because it generates entirely new commits that represent the same changes. The new commits have new commit IDs, and when you merge one branch with one of the new commits into another branch that had one of the old commits, Git has no way of knowing you're applying the same change twice. The result is duplicate entries in `git log` and sometimes a merge conflict.

With plain Git, preventing such situations is easy: avoid `git cherry-pick` and `git rebase` and the problems won't occur at all. Or use the commands carefully, and issues will occur only in controlled situations.

With `git svn`, however, there's one more potential source of problems, and it's not as easy to avoid. The problem is that the Git commit objects created by your `git svn` are not always the same as the ones produced by other people's `git svn`, and you can't do anything about it. For example:

- If you have a different version of Git than someone else, your `git svn` might generate different commits than your coworker. (The Git developers try very hard to avoid this, but it can happen.)
- If you use the `--authors-file` option to remap author names or apply various other `git svn` options that change its behavior, all the commit IDs will be different.
- If you use a SVN URI that's different from someone else working in the SVN repository (e.g., if you access an anonymous SVN repository but someone else uses an authenticated method to access the same repository), then your `git-svn-id` lines will be different; this changes the commit message, which changes the SHA1 of the commit, which changes the commit ID.

- If you fetch only a subset of SVN revisions by using the `-r` option to `git svn clone` (as in the first example in this chapter) and someone else fetches a different subset, then the history will be different and so the commit IDs will be different.

- If you use `git merge` and then `git svn dcommit` the results, the new commit will look different to you from the same commit that other people retrieve through `git svn fetch` because only your copy of `git svn` knows the true history of that commit. (Remember that, on its way into SVN, the history information is lost, so even Git users retrieving from SVN can't get that history back again.)

With all those caveats, it might sound like trying to coordinate between `git svn` users is almost impossible. But there's one simple trick you can use to avoid all these problems: make sure there's *only one* Git repository, the "gatekeeper," which uses `git svn fetch` or `git svn dcommit`.

Using this trick has several advantages:

- Because only one repository ever interfaces with SVN, there will never be a problem with incompatible commit IDs, because every commit is created only once.

- Your Git-using coworkers will never have to learn how to use `git svn`.

- Because all Git users are just using plain Git, they can collaborate with each other, using any Git workflow, without worrying about SVN.

- It's faster to convert a new user from SVN to Git because a `git clone` operation is much faster than downloading every single revision from SVN, one at a time.

- If your entire team eventually converts to Git, then you can simply unplug the SVN server one day and nobody will know the difference.

But there's one main disadvantage: you end up with a bottleneck between the Git world and the SVN world. Everything must go through a single Git repository, which is probably administered by a small number of people.

At first, compared to a completely distributed Git setup, requiring a centrally managed `git svn` repository may seem like a step backward. But you already have a central SVN repository, so this doesn't make matters any worse.

Let's look at setting up that central gatekeeper repository.

Cloning All the Branches

Earlier, when you set up a personal `git svn` repository, the procedure cloned just a few revisions of a single branch. That's good enough for one person who wants to do some work offline, but if an entire team is to share the same repository then you can't make assumptions about what parts are needed and what parts are not. You want all the branches, all the tags, and all the revisions of each branch.

Because this is such a common requirement, Git has an option to perform a complete clone. Let's clone the SVN source code again, but this time doing all the branches:

```
# All on one line
$ git svn clone --stdlayout --prefix=svn/
    -r33005:33142 http://svn.collab.net/repos/svn svn-all.git
```

 The best way to produce a gatekeeper repository is to leave out the -r option entirely. But if you did that here, it would take hours or even days to complete. As of this writing, the SVN source code contains tens of thousands of revisions, and git svn would have to download each one individually over the Internet. If you're following along with this example, keep the -r option. But if you're setting up a Git repository for your own SVN project, leave it out.

Notice the new options:

- --stdlayout tells git svn that the repository branches are set up in the standard SVN way, with the /trunk, /branches, and /tags subdirectories corresponding (respectivel) to mainline development, branches, and tags. If your repository is laid out differently then you can try the --trunk, --branches, and --tags options instead, or edit *.git/config* to set the *refspec* option by hand. Type git help svn for more information.

- --prefix=svn/ creates all the remote refs with the prefix svn/, allowing you to refer to individual branches as svn/trunk and svn/1.5.x. Without this option, your SVN remote refs wouldn't have any prefix at all, making it easy to confuse them with local branches.

git svn should churn for a while. When it's all over, the results look like this:

```
$ cd svn-all.git
$ git branch -a -v | cut -c1-60
* master              0502656 Merge r32790, r32796, r32798
  svn/1.0.x           19e69aa Merge the 1.0.x-issue-2751 br
  svn/1.1.x           e20a6ce Per the proposal in http://sv
  svn/1.2.x           70a5c8a Per the proposal in http://sv
  svn/1.3.x           32f8c36 * STATUS: Leave a breadcrumb
  svn/1.4.x           23ecb32 Per the proposal in http://sv
  svn/1.5.x           0502656 Merge r32790, r32796, r32798
  svn/1.5.x-issue2489 2bbe257 On the 1.5.x-issue2489 branch
  svn/explore-wc      798f467 On the explore-wg branch:
  svn/file-externals  4c6e642 On the file externals branch.
  svn/ignore-mergeinfo e3d51f1 On the ignore-mergeinfo branc
  svn/ignore-prop-mods 7790729 On the ignore-prop-mods branc
  svn/svnpatch-diff   918b5ba On the 'svnpatch-diff' branch
  svn/tree-conflicts  79f44eb On the tree-conflicts branch,
  svn/trunk           ae47f26 Remove YADFC (yet another dep
```

The local master branch has automatically been created, but it isn't what you might expect. It's pointing at the same commit as the svn/1.5.x branch, not the svn/trunk branch. Why? The most recent commit in the range specified with -r belonged to the svn/1.5.x branch. (But don't count on this behavior; it's likely to change in a future version of git svn.) Instead, let's fix it up to point at the trunk:

```
$ git reset --hard svn/trunk
HEAD is now at ae47f26 Remove YADFC (yet another deprecated function call).

$ git branch -a -v | cut -c1-60
* master                    ae47f26 Remove YADFC (yet another dep
  svn/1.0.x                 19e69aa Merge the 1.0.x-issue-2751 br
  svn/1.1.x                 e20a6ce Per the proposal in http://sv
  svn/1.2.x                 70a5c8a Per the proposal in http://sv
  svn/1.3.x                 32f8c36 * STATUS: Leave a breadcrumb
  svn/1.4.x                 23ecb32 Per the proposal in http://sv
  svn/1.5.x                 0502656 Merge r32790, r32796, r32798
  svn/1.5.x-issue2489       2bbe257 On the 1.5.x-issue2489 branch
  svn/explore-wc            798f467 On the explore-wg branch:
  svn/file-externals        4c6e642 On the file externals branch.
  svn/ignore-mergeinfo      e3d51f1 On the ignore-mergeinfo branc
  svn/ignore-prop-mods      7790729 On the ignore-prop-mods branc
  svn/svnpatch-diff         918b5ba On the 'svnpatch-diff' branch
  svn/tree-conflicts        79f44eb On the tree-conflicts branch,
  svn/trunk                 ae47f26 Remove YADFC (yet another dep
```

Sharing Your Repository

After importing your complete git svn gatekeeper repository from SVN, you need to publish it. You do that in the same way you would set up any bare repository (see Chapter 12), but with one trick: the SVN branches that git svn creates are actually remote refs, not branches. The usual technique doesn't quite work:

```
$ cd ..

$ mkdir svn-bare.git

$ cd svn-bare.git

$ git init --bare
Initialized empty Git repository in /tmp/svn-bare/

$ cd ..

$ cd svn-all.git

$ git push --all ../svn-bare.git
Counting objects: 2331, done.
Compressing objects: 100% (1684/1684), done.
Writing objects: 100% (2331/2331), 7.05 MiB | 7536 KiB/s, done.
Total 2331 (delta 827), reused 1656 (delta 616)
To ../svn-bare
 * [new branch]      master -> master
```

You're almost there. With `git push` you copied the `master` branch but none of the `svn/` branches. To make things work properly, modify the `git push` command by telling it explicitly to copy those branches:

```
$ git push ../svn-bare.git 'refs/remotes/svn/*:refs/heads/svn/*'
Counting objects: 6423, done.
Compressing objects: 100% (1559/1559), done.
Writing objects: 100% (5377/5377), 8.01 MiB, done.
Total 5377 (delta 3856), reused 5167 (delta 3697)
To ../svn-bare
 * [new branch]      svn/1.0.x -> svn/1.0.x
 * [new branch]      svn/1.1.x -> svn/1.1.x
 * [new branch]      svn/1.2.x -> svn/1.2.x
 * [new branch]      svn/1.3.x -> svn/1.3.x
 * [new branch]      svn/1.4.x -> svn/1.4.x
 * [new branch]      svn/1.5.x -> svn/1.5.x
 * [new branch]      svn/1.5.x-issue2489 ->  svn/1.5.x-issue2489
 * [new branch]      svn/explore-wc -> svn/explore-wc
 * [new branch]      svn/file-externals -> svn/file-externals
 * [new branch]      svn/ignore-mergeinfo -> svn/ignore-mergeinfo
 * [new branch]      svn/ignore-prop-mods -> svn/ignore-prop-mods
 * [new branch]      svn/svnpatch-diff -> svn/svnpatch-diff
 * [new branch]      svn/tree-conflicts -> svn/tree-conflicts
 * [new branch]      svn/trunk -> svn/trunk
```

This takes the `svn/` refs, which are considered remote refs, from the local repository and copies them to the remote repository, where they are considered heads (i.e., local branches).[4]

Once the enhanced `git push` is done, your repository is ready. Tell your coworkers to go ahead and clone your `svn-bare.git` repository. They can then push, pull, branch, and merge among themselves without a problem.

Merging Back into Subversion

Eventually, you and your team will want to push changes from Git back into SVN. As before, you'll do this using `git svn dcommit`, but you need not rebase first. Instead, you can first `git merge` or `git pull` the changes into a branch in the `svn/` hierarchy and then dcommit only the single new merged commit.

For instance, suppose that your changes are in a branch called `new-feature` and that you want to dcommit it into `svn/trunk`. Here's what to do:

```
$ git checkout svn/trunk
Note: moving to "svn/trunk" which isn't a local branch
If you want to create a new branch from this checkout, you may do so
(now or later) by using -b with the checkout command again. Example:
  git checkout -b <new_branch_name>
HEAD is now at ae47f26... Remove YADFC (yet another deprecated function call).
```

---

4. If you think this sounds convoluted, you're right. Eventually, `git svn` may offer a way to simply create local branches instead of remote refs, so that `git push --all` will work as expected.

```
$ git merge --no-ff new-feature
Merge made by recursive.
 hello.txt |    1 +
 1 files changed, 1 insertions(+), 0 deletions(-)
 create mode 100644 hello.txt

$ git svn dcommit
```

There are three surprising things here:

- Rather than checking out your local branch, `new-feature`, and merging in `svn/trunk`, you *must* do it the other way around. Normally, merging works fine in either direction, but `git svn` won't work if you do it the other way.
- You merge using the `--no-ff` option, which ensures there will always be a merge commit (even though sometimes a merge commit might seem unnecessary).
- You do the whole operation on a disconnected `HEAD`, which sounds dangerous.

You absolutely must do all three surprising things, or the operation won't work reliably.

How dcommit handles merges

To understand why it's necessary to dcommit in such a strange way, consider carefully how dcommit works.

First, dcommit figures out the SVN branch to commit to by looking at the `git-svn-id` of commits in the history.

 If you're nervous about which branch dcommit will pick, you can use `git svn dcommit -n` to try a harmless dry run.

If your team has been doing fancy things—which is, after all, the point of this section —then there might be merges and cherry-picked patches on your `new-feature` branch, and some of those merges might have `git-svn-id` lines from branches other than the one to which you want to commit.

To resolve the ambiguity, `git svn` looks at only the left side of every merge, in the same way that `git log --first-parent` does. That's why merging from `svn/trunk` into `new-feature` doesn't work: `svn/trunk` would end up on the right, not the left, and `git svn` wouldn't see it. Worse, it would think your branch was based on an older version of the SVN branch and so would try to automatically `git svn rebase` it for you, making a terrible mess.

The same reasoning explains why `--no-ff` is necessary. If you check out the `new-feature` branch and `git merge svn/trunk`, then check out the `svn/trunk` branch and `git merge new-feature` without the `--no-ff` option, Git will do a fast-forward rather

---

than a merge. This is efficient, but results in svn/trunk being on the right side, with the same problem as before.

Finally, after it figures all this out, git svn dcommit needs to create one new commit in SVN corresponding to your merge commit. When that's done, it must add a git-svn-id line to the commit message, which means *the commit ID changes*, so it's not the same commit anymore.

The new merge commit ends up in the real svn/trunk branch, and the merge commit you created earlier (on the detached HEAD) is now redundant. In fact, it's worse than redundant. Using it for anything else eventually results in conflicts. So, just forget about that commit. If you haven't put it on a branch in the first place, it's that much easier to forget.

Miscellaneous Notes on Working with Subversion

There are a few more things that you might want to know when you're using git svn.

svn:ignore Versus .gitignore

In any VCS, you need to be able to specify files that you want the system to ignore, such as backup files, compiled executables, and so on.

In SVN, this is done by setting the svn:ignore property on a directory. In Git, you create a file called *.gitignore*, as explained in "The .gitignore File" on page 58 of Chapter 5.

Conveniently, git svn provides an easy way to map from svn:ignore to *.gitignore*. There are two approaches to consider:

- git svn create-ignore automatically creates *.gitignore* files to match the svn:ignore properties. You can then commit them, if you'd like.
- git svn show-ignore finds all the svn:ignore properties in your whole project and prints the entire list. You can capture the command's output and put it in your *.git/info/exclude* file.

Which technique you choose depends on how covert your git svn usage is. If you don't want to commit the *.gitignore* files into your repository, thus making them show up for your SVN-using coworkers, then use the exclude file. Otherwise, *.gitignore* is usually the way to go, because it's automatically shared by everyone else using Git on that project.

Reconstructing the git-svn Cache

The git svn command stores extra housekeeping information in the *.git/svn* directory. This information is used, for example, to quickly detect whether a particular SVN revision has already been downloaded and so doesn't need to be downloaded again. It also contains all the same `git-svn-id` information that shows up in imported commit messages.

If that's the case, then why do the `git-svn-id` lines exist at all? The reason is that, because the lines are added to the commit object and the content of a commit object determines its ID, it follows that the commit ID changes after sending it through `git svn dcommit`, and changing the commit IDs can make future Git merging painful unless you follow the careful steps listed earlier. But if Git just omitted the `git-svn-id` lines, then the commit IDs wouldn't have to change and `git svn` would still work fine. Right?

Yes, except for one important detail. The *.git/svn* directory isn't cloned with your Git repository. An important part of Git's security design is that only blob, tree, and commit objects are ever shared. Hence, the `git-svn-id` lines need to be part of a commit object, and anyone with a clone of your repository will get all the information they need to reconstruct the *.git/svn* directory. This has two advantages:

1. If you accidentally lose your gatekeeper repository or break something, or if you disappear and there's nobody to maintain your repository, then anyone with a clone of your repository can set up a new one.

2. If `git-svn` has a bug and corrupts its *.git/svn* directory, you can regenerate it whenever you want.

You can try out regenerating the cache information whenever you want by moving the *.git/svn* directory out of the way. Try this:

```
$ cd svn-all.git
$ mv .git/svn /tmp/git-svn-backup
$ git svn fetch -r33005:33142
```

Here, `git svn` regenerates its cache and fetches the requested objects. (As before, you would normally leave off the `-r` option to avoid downloading thousands of commits, but this is just an example.)

## CHAPTER 19

Advanced Manipulations

Using git filter-branch

The command `git filter-branch` is a generic branch processing command that allows you to arbitrarily rewrite the commits of a branch using custom commands that operate on different objects within the repository. Some filters work on commits, some filters on tree objects and directory structures, and others provide environmental manipulation opportunity.

Does that sound useful and yet dangerous?

Good.

As you might suspect, with great power comes great responsibility.[1] The power and purpose of `filter-branch` is also the source of my warning: it has the potential to rewrite the entire repository's commit history. Executing this command on a repository that has already been published for others to clone and use will likely cause them endless grief later. As with all rebasing operations, commit history will change. After this command, you should consider any repositories cloned from it earlier as obsolete.

With that warning about rewriting repository history behind us, let's find out what the command can do, when and why it might be useful, and how to use it responsibly.

The `filter-branch` command runs a series of filters on one or more branches within your repository. Each filter can have its own custom filtering command. You don't have to run them all, or even more than one. But they are designed and sequenced so that earlier filters can affect the behavior of later filters. The `subdirectory-filter` runs as a precommit-processing selection filter, and the `tag-name-filter` runs as a postcommit-processing step,

---

1. François-Marie Arouet, of course!

To help you get a clearer picture of what is happening during the filtering process, it might help to know that as of version 1.7.9, git filter-branch is a shell script.[2] Except for the commit-filter, each *command* is evaluated in a shell (sh) context using eval.

Here is a brief description of each filter and the order in which they run:

env-filter *command*

> The env-filter can be used to create or alter the shell environment settings prior to running the subsequent filters and committing the newly rewritten objects. Of note, changing variables such as GIT_AUTHOR_NAME, GIT_AUTHOR_EMAIL, GIT_COMMIT TER_NAME, and GIT_COMMITTER_EMAIL may be useful. The *command* should likely both set and export environment variables.

tree-filter *command*

> The tree-filter allows you to modify the contents of a directory that will be captured by a tree object. You can use this filter to remove files from or add files to the repository retroactively. This filter checks out the branch at each commit during the filtering. Be aware that the *.gitignore* file is not effective during this filter.

index-filter *command*

> The index-filter is used to alter the contents of the index prior to making a commit. Throughout the filtering process, the index of each commit is made available without checking out the corresponding files into a working directory. Thus, this filter is similar to the tree-filter but faster if you don't actually need the file contents during the filter. You should study the low-level git update-index command.

parent-filter *command*

> The parent-filter allows you to restructure the parent relationship of every commit. For a given commit, you specify its new parent or parents. To use this properly, you should study the low-level git commit-tree command.

msg-filter *command*

> Just prior to actually making a newly filtered commit, the msg-filter allows you to edit the commit message. The *command* should accept the old message on stdin and write the new message on stdout.

commit-filter *command*

> Normally during the filtering pipeline, git commit-tree will be used to perform the commit. However, this filter gives you control over this step yourself. Your *command* will be called with the new (possibly rewritten) *tree-obj* and a list of (possibly rewritten) -p *parent-obj* parameters. The (possibly rewritten) commit message will be on stdin. You should likely still use git commit-tree, but there are also a few convenience functions provided environmentally as well: map, skip_com mit, git_commit_non_empty_tree, and die. The git filter-branch manual page has details for each of these functions.

---

2. Due to the scripting context for each filter, it's likely to stay that way, too.

`tag-name-filter` *command*

> If your repository has any tags, you should probably use `tag-name-filter` to rewrite existing tags to reference the newly created corresponding commits. By default, the old tags will remain, but you can use `cat` as the filter to obtain direct new-for-old mappings of your tags. Although simply mapping tags to reference the new, corresponding commits is certainly possible, maintaining a *signed* tag is not. Remember that the whole point of signing a tag was to maintain a cryptographically secure indicator of the repository at a certain point in its history. That just went out the window here, right? So all those signatures on signed tags will be removed from the corresponding new tags.

`subdirectory-filter` *command*

> The `subdirectory-filter` can be used to limit the rewriting of history to only those commits that affect a specific directory. That is, after filtering, the new repository will contain *only* the named directory at its root.

After a `git filter-branch` completes, the original references comprising the entire old commit history are available as new refs in *refs/original*. Naturally, this implies that the *refs/original* directory must be empty at the start of the filtering operation. After verifying that you obtained the filtered history you desired, and the original commit history is no longer needed, carefully remove the *.git/refs/original* refs. (Or, if you want to be fully Git compliant and Git friendly, you can even use the command `git update-ref -d refs/original/`*branch* for each *branch* you filtered.) If you do not remove this directory, you will continue to have the entirety of both the old and new content within your repository. The old refs will linger and prevent garbage collection (see "Garbage Collection" on page 368) from trimming out the otherwise obsolete commits.[3] If you don't want to explicitly remove this directory, you can also clone away from it. That is, make a clone of the repository, leaving these original refs behind and not cloning them into a new repository. Think of it as a natural checkpoint backup.

There are several reasons that best practices with `git filter-branch` suggest you should always operate on a newly cloned repository. For starters, `git filter-branch` flat-out requires that the operation to begin with a clean working directory. Because the `git filter-branch` modifies your original repository in place, it is often described as being a "destructive" operation. Because the command has many steps, options, and subtleties, running the command can be quite tricky and often difficult to get right on the first attempt. Saving the original repository is just prudent computing.

Examples Using git filter-branch

Now that we know what `git filter-branch` can do, let's look at a few cases where it can be used productively. One of the most useful situations occurs when you have just

---

3. But also see the section called "Checklist for Shrinking a Repository" from the `git-filter-branch` manual page.

created a repository full of commit history and want to clean it up or do a large-scale alteration on it prior to making it available for cloning and general use by others.

Using git filter-branch to expunge a file

A common use for `git filter-branch` is to completely remove a file from the entire history of a repository. Remember, Git maintains the complete history of every file within the repository. Thus, simply deleting a file with `git rm` will not remove it from older history. One can always go back to earlier commits and retrieve the file.

However, by using `git filter-branch`, a file can be removed from any and every commit in the repository, making it appear as if it was never there in the first place.

Let's work on an example repository that contains personal notes after reading various books. The notes are stored in files named after the works.

```
$ cd BookNotes

$ ls
1984  Animal_Farm  Nightfall  Readme  Snow_Crash

$ git log --pretty=oneline --abbrev-commit
ffd358c Read Asimov's 'Nightfall'.
4df8f74 Read a few classics.
8d3f5a9 Read 'Snow Crash'
3ed7354 Collect some notes about books.
```

And the classics from the third commit 4df8f74 are:

```
$ git show 4df8f74
commit 4df8f74b786b31b6043c44df59d7d13ee2b4b298
Author: Jon Loeliger <jdl@example.com>
Date:   Sat Jan 14 12:57:35 2012 -0600

    Read a few classics.

        - Animal Farm by George Orwell
        - 1984 by George Orwell

diff --git a/1984 b/1984
new file mode 100644
index 0000000..84a2da2
--- /dev/null
+++ b/1984
@@ -0,0 +1 @@
+George Orwell is disturbed.
diff --git a/Animal_Farm b/Animal_Farm
new file mode 100644
index 0000000..e1fcda1
--- /dev/null
+++ b/Animal_Farm
@@ -0,0 +1 @@
+Animal Farm was interesting.
```

Suppose for some history-revising reason we have decided to remove any record of George Orwell's *1984* from the repository. If you don't care about the old commit history, simply issuing a `git rm 1984` would suffice. But to be thoroughly Orwellian, it must be removed from the complete history of the repository. It must never have existed.

Of all the filters listed previously, the likeliest candidates for this operation are the `tree-filter` and `index-filter`. Because this is a small repository and the operation we want to do, namely, remove one file, is pretty simple and direct, we'll use the `tree-filter`.

As advised earlier, start with a clean clone, just in case.

```
$ cd ..
$ git clone BookNotes BookNotes.revised
Cloning into 'BookNotes.revised'...
done.
$ cd BookNotes.revised

$ git filter-branch --tree-filter 'rm 1984' master
Rewrite 3ed7354c2c8ae2678122512b26d591a9ed61663e (1/4)
    rm: cannot remove `1984': No such file or directory
tree filter failed: rm 1984

$ ls
1984  Animal_Farm  Nightfall  Readme  Snow_Crash
```

Clearly that didn't go well and something failed. The file is still in the repository.

Let's think a little about what Git is doing here. Git will iterate over each commit in the `master` branch, starting with the very first commit, establish the context (index, files, directories, etc.) of that commit, and then try to remove the file *1984*.

Git tells you which commit it was modifying when the command failed. Commit `3ed7354` is the first of 4 commits.

```
Rewrite 3ed7354c2c8ae2678122512b26d591a9ed61663e (1/4)
```

But recall that the file *1984* was introduced in the third commit, `4df8f74`, and not the first. That means that for the first two commits, `3ed7354` and `8d3f5a9`, the *1984* file was not yet in the repository or any of its managed files. That in turn means that when establishing the filtering context of those first two commits, a simple `rm 1984` shell command within the top-level directory will fail for lack of a file to remove. It's exactly as if you had typed `rm snizzle-frotz` in a directory with no *snizzle-frotz* file in it.

```
$ cd /tmp
$ rm snizzle-frotz
rm: cannot remove `snizzle-frotz': No such file or directory
```

The trick is to realize that when removing a file, you don't care whether the file is actually present or not. So just force the removal and ignore nonexistent files using the `-f` or `--force` option:

```
$ cd /tmp
$ rm -f snizzle-frotz
$
```

OK, back to the *BookNotes.revised* repository:

```
$ cd BookNotes.revised
$ git filter-branch --tree-filter 'rm -f 1984' master
Rewrite ffd358c675a1c6d36114e10a92d93fdc1ee84629 (4/4)
Ref 'refs/heads/master' was rewritten
```

As a side note, Git really scrolls through all the commits, stating which one it is presently rewriting, but only the last one shows up on your screen, as just shown. If you are a bit more clever, perhaps by piping that output through less, you can see that it actually prints each commit processed:

```
Rewrite 3ed7354c2c8ae2678122512b26d591a9ed61663e (1/4)
Rewrite 8d3f5a96b18f9795a1bb41295e5a9d2d4eb414b4 (2/4)
Rewrite 4df8f74b786b31b6043c44df59d7d13ee2b4b298 (3/4)
Rewrite ffd358c675a1c6d36114e10a92d93fdc1ee84629 (4/4)
```

But it worked this time:

```
$ ls
Animal_Farm  Nightfall  Readme  Snow_Crash
```

The *1984* file is now gone!

 For the terminally curious, the corresponding command using index-filter would be something like this:

```
$ git filter-branch --index-filter \
  'git rm --cached --ignore-unmatch 1984' master
```

Let's look at the new commit log:

```
$ git log --pretty=oneline --abbrev-commit
ad1000b Read Asimov's 'Nightfall'.
7298fc5 Read a few classics.
8d3f5a9 Read 'Snow Crash'
3ed7354 Collect some notes about books.
```

Notice how each commit starting with the original third commit (4df8f74 and ffd358c) now has different SHA1 values (7298fc5 and ad1000b), whereas the earlier commits (3ed7354 and 8d3f5a9) remain unchanged.

During the filtering and rewriting process, Git creates and maintains this mapping between old and new commit values and makes it available to you as the map convenience function. If for some reason you need to convert from an old commit SHA1 to the corresponding new SHA1, you can do so using this mapping from within your filter *command* command.

Let's investigate a bit more, though.

```
$ git show 7298fc5
commit 7298fc55d1496c7e70909f3ebce238d447d07951
Author: Jon Loeliger <jdl@example.com>
Date:   Sat Jan 14 12:57:35 2012 -0600

    Read a few classics.

        - Animal Farm by George Orwell
        - 1984 by George Orwell

diff --git a/Animal_Farm b/Animal_Farm
new file mode 100644
index 0000000..e1fcda1
--- /dev/null
+++ b/Animal_Farm
@@ -0,0 +1 @@
+Animal Farm was interesting.
```

Indeed the commit that first introduced *1984* no longer does so! That means the file was never introduced in the first place. It is not just gone from the top commit; it is not just gone from any commit reachable from the master branch; it never existed on this branch.

But doesn't it bother you that the commit message itself still mentions the 1984 book? Let's fix that in the next section!

Using filter-branch to edit a commit message

Here's the problem we're solving: some commit message needs to be revised. In the previous section, we saw how to remove a file from the complete history of a repository. However, the commit message that *used* to introduce it still alludes to it:

```
$ git log -1 7298fc55
commit 7298fc55d1496c7e70909f3ebce238d447d07951
Author: Jon Loeliger <jdl@example.com>
Date:   Sat Jan 14 12:57:35 2012 -0600

    Read a few classics.

        - Animal Farm by George Orwell
        - 1984 by George Orwell
```

That last line has to go!

This is the perfect use case for the --msg-filter filter. Your filter command should accept the old text of a commit message on stdin and write its revised text on stdout. That is, your filter should be a classic stdin-to-stdout edit filter. Typically, it will be something like sed, although it can be as complex as needed.

In our case, we'll want to delete that last 1984 line. We'll also want to touch up the previous sentence to just talk about one book rather than a "a few." A sed command to do these edits looks like this:

```
sed -e "/1984/d" -e "s/few classics/classic/"
```

Put that together with the `--msg-filter` option. Be careful with your line breaks on input here. It should be all one line, or use the single quote as a command input continuation technique.

```
$ git filter-branch --msg-filter '
    sed -e "/1984/d" -e "s/few classics/classic/"' master
Rewrite ad1000b936acf7dbe4a29da6706cb759efded1ae (4/4)
Ref 'refs/heads/master' was rewritten
```

Let's check:

```
$ git log --pretty=oneline --abbrev-commit
bf7351c Read Asimov's 'Nightfall.'
f28e55d Read a classic.
8d3f5a9 Read 'Snow Crash'
3ed7354 Collect some notes about books.
```

We can already see that the log message from commit f28e55d has been singularized by our sed script. Good. Looking again at the whole message:

```
$ git log -1 f28e55d
commit f28e55dc8bbdee555a3f7778ba8355db9ab4c4a1
Author: Jon Loeliger <jdl@example.com>
Date:   Sat Jan 14 12:57:35 2012 -0600

    Read a classic.

    - Animal Farm by George Orwell
```

Now it is truly as if it never existed in this repository! And we've always been at war with Eastasia.

One cautionary note about the filtering process: make sure that you are both operating on the items you *want* to change, and that you are operating on only those items!

For example, the sed command from the previous `--msg-filter` example appears to change precisely the one commit message we wanted to adjust. However, be aware that same sed script is applied to every commit message in the history. If there were other, perhaps incidental occurrences of the string 1984 in other commit messages, they would also have been deleted because our script was not very discriminating. Subsequently, you may have to write a more detailed sed command or a more clever script.

filter-branch Pitfalls

It is important to understand a brutal consequence of the name of this Git command: it is filter-*branch*. At its core, the `git filter-branch` command is designed to operate on just one branch or ref. However, it *can* operate on many branches or refs.

In many cases, you want to have it operate on *all* branches so as to obtain a repository-wide coverage. In these cases, you will need the `--` `--all` tacked onto the end of the command.

```
$ git filter-branch --index-filter \
"git rm --cached -f --ignore-unmatch '*.jpeg'" \
-- --all
```

Similarly, you almost certainly want to translate any tag refs from a prefiltered state into the new postfiltered repository. That means adding `--tag-name-filter cat` is also quite common:

```
$ git filter-branch --index-filter \
"git rm --cached -f --ignore-unmatch '*.jpeg'" \
--tag-name-filter cat \
-- --all
```

 How about this one? You used `--tree-filter` or `--index-filter` to remove a file from a repository, but did that file get moved or have its name changed at some point in its history? You can use a command like this to find out:

```
$ git log --name-only --follow --all -- file
```

If other names for that file exist, you might want to delete those versions as well.

How I Learned to Love git rev-list

One day, I received this piece of email:

> Jon,
>
> I'm trying to figure out how to do a date-based check out from a Git repository into an empty working directory. Unfortunately, winding my way through the Git manual pages makes me feel like I'm playing "Adventure."
>
> Eric

Indeed. Let's see if we can navigate some of those twisty passages.

Date-Based Checkout

It might seem that a command like `git checkout master@{Jan 1, 2011}` should work. However, that command is really using the `reflog` (See "The Stash" on page 181) to resolve the date-based reference for the `master` ref. There are lots of ways this innocent looking construct might fail: your repository may not have the reflog enabled, you may not have manipulated the `master` ref during that time period, or the reflog may have already expired refs from that time period. Even more subtly, that construct may not give you your expected answer. It requests the reflog to resolve where your `master` was at the given time as you manipulated the branch, and not according to the branch's commit time line. They may be related, especially if you developed and committed that history in this repository, but they don't have to be.

Ultimately, this approach can be a misleading dead-end. Using the reflog *might* get what you want. But it can also fail, and it isn't a reliable method.

Instead, you should use the `git rev-list` command. It is the general purpose workhorse whose job is to combine a multitude of options, sort through a complex commit history of many branches, intuit potentially vague user specifications, limit search spaces, and ultimately locate selected commits from within the repository history. It then emits one or more SHA1 IDs for use by other tools. Think of `git rev-list` and its myriad options as a commit database front-end query tool for your repository.

In this case, the goal is fairly simple: find the one commit in a repository that existed immediately before a given date on a given branch and then check it out.

Let's use the actual Git source repository because it has a fairly extensive and explorable history. First, we'll use `rev-list` to find that SHA1. The `-n 1` option limits the output from the command to just one commit ID.

Here, we try to locate just the last `master` commit of 2011 from the Git source repository:

```
$ git clone git://github.com/gitster/git.git
Cloning into 'git'...
remote: Counting objects: 126850, done.
remote: Compressing objects: 100% (41033/41033), done.
remote: Total 126850 (delta 93115), reused 117003 (delta 84141)
Receiving objects: 100% (126850/126850), 27.56 MiB | 1.03 MiB/s, done.
Resolving deltas: 100% (93115/93115), done.

$ cd git
$ git rev-list -n 1 --before="Jan 1, 2012 00:00:00" master
0eddcbf1612ed044de586777b233caf8016c6e70
```

Having identified the commit, you may use it, tag it, reference it, or even check it out. But as the checkout note reminds you, you are on a detached HEAD.

```
$ git checkout 0eddcb
Note: checking out '0eddcb'.

You are in 'detached HEAD' state. You can look around, make experimental
changes and commit them, and you can discard any commits you make in this
state without impacting any branches by performing another checkout.

If you want to create a new branch to retain commits you create, you may
do so (now or later) by using -b with the checkout command again. Example:

  git checkout -b new_branch_name

HEAD is now at 0eddcbf... Add MYMETA.json to perl/.gitignore
```

But is that really the right commit?

```
$ git log -1 --pretty=fuller
commit 0eddcbf1612ed044de586777b233caf8016c6e70
Author:     Jack Nagel <jacknagel@gmail.com>
AuthorDate: Wed Dec 28 22:42:05 2011 -0600
Commit:     Junio C Hamano <gitster@pobox.com>
```

```
CommitDate: Thu Dec 29 13:08:47 2011 -0800

Add MYMETA.json to perl/.gitignore
...
```

The `rev-list` date selection uses the `CommitDate` field, not the `AuthorDate` field. So it looks like the last commit of 2011 in the Git repository happened on December 29, 2011.

Date-based checkout cautions

A few words of caution are in order, though. Git's date handling is implemented using a function called `approxidate()`. Not that dates are inherently approximate, but rather that Git's interpretation of what you meant are approximated, usually due to insufficient details or precision.

```
$ git rev-list -n 1 --before="Jan 1, 2012 00:00:00" master
0eddcbf1612ed044de586777b233caf8016c6e70

$ git rev-list -n 1 --before="Jan 1, 2012" master
5c951ef47bf2e34dbde58bda88d430937657d2aa
```

I typed those two commands at 11:05 A.M. local time. For lack of a specified *time* in the second command, Git assumed I meant "at this time on Jan 1, 2012." Subsequently, 11 more hours of leeway were available in which to match commits.

```
$ git log -1 --pretty=fuller 5c951ef
commit 5c951ef47bf2e34dbde58bda88d430937657d2aa
Author:     Clemens Buchacher <drizzd@aon.at>
AuthorDate: Sat Dec 31 12:50:56 2011 +0100
Commit:     Junio C Hamano <gitster@pobox.com>
CommitDate: Sun Jan 1 01:18:53 2012 -0800

Documentation: read-tree --prefix works with existing subtrees
...
```

This commit happened an hour and 18 minutes into the new year; well within the 11 hours past midnight that I accidentally specified in my second command.

Git's Date Parsing

So does Git's date parsing behavior even make sense? Probably.

Git is trying to intuit the intended meaning behind vaguely specified time requests. For example, how should **yesterday** be interpreted? As the previous 24-hour period? As the absolute time period midnight-to-midnight of the previous calendar date? As some vague notion of yesterday's business working hours? Git happens to use the first interpretation: the 24 hours prior to the current time. Generalizing now, any date used as a starting or ending point in Git uses the current time, and if a date is specified without a time, the current time is used as the demarcation, which is where the notion of "the current time" comes in. If you wanted to be more precise about just exactly *when* yesterday, you could have said something like **yesterday noon**, or **5pm yesterday**.

One more caution about date-based checkout. Although you may get a valid answer to your query for a specific commit, that same question at some later date may yield a different answer. For example, consider a repository with several lines of development happening on different branches. As previously, when you request the commit --before *date* on a given branch, you get an answer for the branch as it exists just then. At some later point in time, however, new commits from other branches might be merged into your branch, altering the notion of which commit might satisfy your search conditions. In the previous January 1, 2012 example, someone might merge in a commit from another branch that is closer to midnight December 31, 2011 than December 29, 2011 at 13:08:47.

Retrieve Old Version of a File

Sometimes in the course of software archeology, you simply want to retrieve an old version of a file from the repository history. It seems overkill to use the techniques of a date-based checkout as described in "Date-Based Checkout" on page 345 because that causes a complete change in your working directory state for every directory and file just to get one file. In fact, it is even likely that you want to keep your current working directory state but replace the current version of just one file by reverting it to an earlier version.

The first step is to identify a commit that contains the desired version of the file. The direct approach is to use an explicit branch, tag, or ref already known to have the correct version. In the absence of that information, some searching has to be done. And when searching the commit history, you should think about using some `rev-list` techniques to identify commits that have the desired file. As previously seen, dates can be used to select interesting commits. Git also allows the search to be restricted to a particular file or set of files. Git calls this approach "path limiting." It provides the ultimate guide to possible previous commits that might contain different versions of a file, or as Git calls them, paths.

Again, let's explore Git's source repository itself to see what previous versions of, say, *date.c* are available.

```
$ git clone git://github.com/gitster/git.git
Cloning into 'git'...
remote: Counting objects: 126850, done.
remote: Compressing objects: 100% (41033/41033), done.
remote: Total 126850 (delta 93115), reused 117003 (delta 84141)
Receiving objects: 100% (126850/126850), 27.56 MiB | 1.03 MiB/s, done.
Resolving deltas: 100% (93115/93115), done.

$ git rev-list master -- date.c
ee646eb48f9a7fc6c225facf2b7449a8a65ef8f2
f1e9c548ce45005521892af0299696204ece286b
...
89967023da94c0d874713284869e1924797d30bb
ecee9d9e793c7573cf3730fb9746527a0a7e94e7
```

Uh, yeah, something like 60-odd lines of SHA1 commit IDs. Fun! But what does it all mean? And how do you use it?

Because I didn't specify the -n 1 option, all matching commit IDs have been generated and printed. The default is to emit them in reverse chronological order. So this means commit ee646e contains the most recent version of the file *date.c*, and ecee9d9 contains the oldest version. In fact, looking at commit ecee9d9 shows the file being introduced into the repository for the first time.

```
$ git show --stat ecee9d9 --pretty=short
commit ecee9d9e793c7573cf3730fb9746527a0a7e94e7
Author: Edgar Toernig <froese@gmx.de>

[PATCH] Do date parsing by hand...

 Makefile      |   4 +-
 cache.h       |   3 +
 commit-tree.c |  27 +--------
 date.c        | 184 ++++++++++++++++++++++++++++++++++++++++++++++++++++++++++++
 4 files changed, 191 insertions(+), 27 deletions(-)
```

Where you go from here to find your desired commit is kind of sketchy. You could do git log operations on randomly selected SHA1 values from that rev-list list output. Or you could binary search the time stamps on commits from that list. Earlier we used the -n 1 to select the most recent. It's really hard to say what trick might work in your selection process to identify the precise commit that contains the version of a file that is interesting to you.

But once you *have* identified one of those commits, how do you use it? What does that version of *date.c* look like? What if we wanted to retrieve it in place?

There are three slightly different approaches you can use to get that version of a file. The first form directly checks out the named version and overwrites the existing version in your working directory.

```
$ git checkout ecee9d9 date.c
```

 If you want to get the version of a file from a commit and you don't know its SHA1, but you do happen to know some text from its commit log message, you can use this searching technique to obtain it:

```
$ git checkout :/"Fix PR-1705" main.c
```

The youngest commit found is used.

In two other very similar commands, Git accepts the form *commit:path* to name the desired file (i.e., path) as it existed at the time the commit happened, and writes the specified version of the file to be written to stdout. What you do with that output is up to you, though. You could pipe the output to other commands or create files:

```
$ git show ecee9d9:date.c > date.c-oldest
```

Or:

```
$ git cat-file -p 89967:date.c > date.c-first-change
```

The difference between these two forms is a bit esoteric. The former filters the output file through any applicable text conversion filters, whereas the latter is a more basic, plumbing command and does not. Differences might show up between these two commands when manipulating binaries, when `textconv` filters are set up, or possibly during some newline handling transformations. If you want the raw data, use the `cat -p` form. If you want the transformed version as it would be when checked out or added to the repository, use the `show` form.

These are exactly the same mechanisms you would use to obtain versions of a file as it appears in another branch:

```
$ git checkout dev date.c
```

```
$ git show dev:date.c > date.c-dev
```

Or even earlier on the same branch:

```
$ git checkout HEAD~2:date.c
```

Interactive Hunk Staging

Although a bit of an ominous moniker, interactive hunk staging is nevertheless an incredibly powerful tool that can be used to simplify and organize your development into concise and easily understood commits. If anyone has ever asked you to split your patch up or make single-concept patches, chances are good that this section is for you!

Unless you are a super coder, and both think and develop in concise patches, your day-to-day development probably resembles mine: a little scattered, perhaps over-extended, and likely containing several intertwined ideas all mixed up as they occurred to you. One coding thought leads to another and pretty soon you fixed the original bug, stumbled onto another (but fixed it!), and then added a new easy feature while you were there. Oh, and, you fixed those two typos as well.

And, if you, like I do, appreciate having someone review your changes to important code before you ask for it to be accepted upstream, chances are good that having all of those different, unrelated changes will not make for a logical presentation of a single patch. Indeed, some open source projects insist that submitted patches contain separate self-contained fixes. That is, a patch shouldn't serve multiple purposes in one shot. Instead, each idea should stand alone and should be presentable as a well-defined, simple patch that is just large enough to do the job and nothing more. If more than one idea needs to be upstreamed, more than one patch, perhaps in a sequence, will be needed. Common wisdom suggests that these sorts of patches and patch sequences lead to very solid reviews, quick turnaround, and easy acceptance into the mainline upstream development.

So how do these perfect patch sequences come about? Although I strive for a development style that facilitates simple patches, I'm not always successful. Nevertheless, Git provides some tools to help formulate good patches. One of those tools is the ability to interactively select and commit pieces, or "hunks," of a patch, leaving the rest to be committed in a later patch. Ultimately, you will want to create a new sequence of smaller commits that still sum up to your original work.

What Git won't do for you is decide which conceptual pieces of a patch belong together and which do not. You have to be able to discern the meaning and grouping of hunks that make logical sense together. Sometimes those hunks are all in one file, but sometimes they are in multiple files. Collectively, all the conceptually related hunks must be selected and staged together as part of one commit.

Furthermore, you must ensure that your selection of hunks still meets any external requirements. For example, if you are writing source code that must be compiled, you will likely want to ensure that the code base continues to be compilable after each commit. Thus, you must ensure that your patch breakup, when reassembled in smaller parts, still compiles at each commit within the new sequence. Git can't do that for you; that's the part where you have to think. Sorry.

Staging hunks interactively is as easy as adding the -p option to the git add command!

```
$ git add -p file.c
```

Interactive hunk staging looks pretty easy, and it is. But we should probably still have a mental model in mind of what Git is doing with our patches. Remember way back in Chapter 5, I explained how Git maintains the index as a staging area that accumulates your changes prior to committing them. That's still happening. But instead of gathering the changes an entire file at a time, Git is picking apart the changes you have made in your working copy of a file, and allowing you to select which individual part or parts to stage in the index, waiting to be committed.

Let's suppose we're developing a program to print out a histogram of white-space–separated words found in a file. The very first version of this program is the "Hello, World!" program that proves things are starting out on the right compilation track. Here's *main.c*:

```
#include <stdio.h>

int main(int argc, char **argv)
{
    /*
     * Print a histogram of words found in a file.
     * "Words" are any whitespace separated characters.
     * Words are listed in no particular order.
     * FIXME: Implementation needed still!
     */
    printf("Histogram of words\n");
}
```

Add a *Makefile* and *.gitignore*, and put it all in a new repository:

```
$ mkdir /tmp/histogram
# cd /tmp/histogram
$ git init
Initialized empty Git repository in /tmp/histogram/.git/
$ git add main.c Makefile .gitignore

$ git commit -m "Initial histogram program."
[master (root-commit) 42300e7] Initial histogram program.
 3 files changed, 18 insertions(+), 0 deletions(-)
 create mode 100644 .gitignore
 create mode 100644 Makefile
 create mode 100644 main.c
```

Let's do some miscellaneous development until *main.c* looks like this:

```
#include <stdio.h>
#include <stdlib.h>

struct htentry {
    char *item;
    int count;
    struct htentry *next;
};

struct htentry ht_table[256];

void ht_init(void)
{
    /* FIXME: details */
}

int main(int argc, char **argv)
{
    FILE *f;

    f = fopen(argv[1], "r");
    if (f == 0)
        exit(-1);

    /*
     * Print a histogram of words found in a file.
     * "Words" are any whitespace separated characters.
     * Words are listed in no particular order.
     * FIXME: Implementation needed still!
     */
    printf("Histogram of words\n");

    ht_init();
}
```

Notice that this development effort has introduced two conceptually different changes: the hash table structure and storage, and the beginnings of the file reading operation. In a perfect world, these two concepts would be introduced into the program with two separate patches. It will take us a couple of steps to get there, but Git will help us split these changes properly.

Git, along with most of the Free World, considers a hunk to be any series of lines from a `diff` command that are delineated by a line that looks something like this:

```
@@ -1,7 +1,27 @@
```

or this:

```
@@ -9,4 +29,6 @@ int main(int argc, char **argv)
```

In this case, git diff shows two hunks:

```
$ git diff
diff --git a/main.c b/main.c
index 9243ccf..b07f5dd 100644
--- a/main.c
+++ b/main.c
@@ -1,7 +1,27 @@
 #include <stdio.h>
+#include <stdlib.h>
+
+struct htentry {
+       char *item;
+       int count;
+       struct htentry *next;
+};
+
+struct htentry ht_table[256];
+
+void ht_init(void)
+{
+       /* FIXME: details */
+}

 int main(int argc, char **argv)
 {
+       FILE *f;
+
+       f = fopen(argv[1], "r");
+       if (f == 0)
+               exit(-1);
+
    /*
     * Print a histogram of words found in a file.
     * "Words" are any whitespace separated characters.
@@ -9,4 +29,6 @@ int main(int argc, char **argv)
     * FIXME: Implementation needed still!
     */
    printf("Histogram of words\n");
+
+       ht_init();
 }
```

The first hunk starts with the line @@ -1,7 +1,27 @@ and finishes at the start of the second hunk: @@ -9,4 +29,6 @@ int main(int argc, char **argv).

When interactively staging hunks with git add -p, Git offers a choice for each hunk in turn: do you want to stage it?

But let's look at our patch a bit more closely and consider the need to break up the pieces so that conceptually related parts are all gathered up and staged at the same time. That means we'd like to stage all the hash table parts together in one patch, and then stage all the file operations in a second patch. Unfortunately, it looks like the first hunk has *both* hash table and file operation pieces in one hunk! That means, for the purposes of the first commit (i.e., the hash table pieces), we want to both stage it and not stage it. Or more precisely, we want to stage *part* of the hunk. If Git only asks us about the first and second hunks, we are in trouble.

But, not to worry! The hunk staging will allow us to *split* a hunk. Any place where a contiguous sequence of added and deleted lines identified by a plus or minus in the first column is broken up by original context text, a split operation may be performed.

Let's see how this works by starting with a git add -p main.c command:

```
$ git add -p
diff --git a/main.c b/main.c
index 4809266..c60b800 100644
--- a/main.c
+++ b/main.c
@@ -1,7 +1,27 @@
 #include <stdio.h>
+#include <stdlib.h>
+
+struct htentry {
+    char *item;
+    int count;
+    struct htentry *next;
+};
+
+struct htentry ht_table[256];
+
+void ht_init(void)
+{
+    /* FIXME: details */
+}

 int main(int argc, char **argv)
 {
+    FILE *f;
+
+    f = fopen(argv[1], "r");
+    if (f == 0)
+        exit(-1);
+
     /*
      * Print a histogram of words found in a file.
```

```
                * "Words" are any whitespace separated characters.
        Stage this hunk [y,n,q,a,d,/,j,J,g,s,e,?]?
```

After reviewing this hunk and seeing both the hash table and file operation related changes there, you realize you need to both stage and not stage this hunk. That is your clue to answer **s**, for split, to the question.

```
        Stage this hunk [y,n,q,a,d,/,j,J,g,s,e,?]? s
        Split into 2 hunks.
        @@ -1,4 +1,18 @@
         #include <stdio.h>
        +#include <stdlib.h>
        +
        +struct htentry {
        +    char *item;
        +    int count;
        +    struct htentry *next;
        +};
        +
        +struct htentry ht_table[256];
        +
        +void ht_init(void)
        +{
        +    /* FIXME: details */
        +}

         int main(int argc, char **argv)
         {
        Stage this hunk [y,n,q,a,d,/,j,J,g,e,?]?
```

Excellent. We want this hunk staged.

```
        Stage this hunk [y,n,q,a,d,/,j,J,g,s,e,?]? y
```

And immediately next up:

```
        @@ -2,6 +16,12 @@

         int main(int argc, char **argv)
         {
        +    FILE *f;
        +
        +    f = fopen(argv[1], "r");
        +    if (f == 0)
        +        exit(-1);
        +
             /*
              * Print a histogram of words found in a file.
              * "Words" are any whitespace separated characters.
        Stage this hunk [y,n,q,a,d,/,K,j,J,g,e,?]?
```

But not that one.

```
        Stage this hunk [y,n,q,a,d,/,j,J,g,s,e,?]? n
```

And finally, Git offers to stage the last hunk. We want it, too.

```
@@ -9,4 +29,6 @@ int main(int argc, char **argv)
        * FIXME: Implementation needed still!
        */
       printf("Histogram of words\n");
+
+     ht_init();
 }
Stage this hunk [y,n,q,a,d,/,j,J,g,s,e,?]? y
```

Let's review. Originally, there were two hunks. But we wanted only part of the first hunk and all of the second. So when Git offered us the first hunk we had to split it into two subhunks. We then staged the first subhunk, and not the second subhunk. We then staged the entire original second hunk.

Verifying that the staged pieces look correct is easy:

```
$ git diff --staged
diff --git a/main.c b/main.c
index 4809266..8a95bb0 100644
--- a/main.c
+++ b/main.c
@@ -1,4 +1,18 @@
 #include <stdio.h>
+#include <stdlib.h>
+
+struct htentry {
+       char *item;
+       int count;
+       struct htentry *next;
+};
+
+struct htentry ht_table[256];
+
+void ht_init(void)
+{
+       /* FIXME: details */
+}

 int main(int argc, char **argv)
 {
@@ -9,4 +23,6 @@ int main(int argc, char **argv)
        * FIXME: Implementation needed still!
        */
       printf("Histogram of words\n");
+
+     ht_init();
 }
```

That looks good, so you can go ahead and commit it. Don't worry that there are lingering differences remaining in the file *main.c*. That's by design because it is the *next* patch! Oh, and don't use the filename with this next git commit command because that would use the entire file and not the just the staged parts.

```
$ git commit -m "Introduce a Hash Table."
[master 66a212c] Introduce a Hash Table.
 1 files changed, 16 insertions(+), 0 deletions(-)

$ git diff
diff --git a/main.c b/main.c
index 8a95bb0..c60b800 100644
--- a/main.c
+++ b/main.c
@@ -16,6 +16,12 @@ void ht_init(void)

 int main(int argc, char **argv)
 {
+        FILE *f;
+
+        f = fopen(argv[1], "r");
+        if (f == 0)
+                exit(-1);
+
     /*
      * Print a histogram of words found in a file.
      * "Words" are any whitespace separated characters.
```

And with that, just add and commit the remaining change because it is the total material for the file operations patch.

```
$ git add main.c
$ git commit -m "Open the word source file."
[master e649d27] Open the word source file.
 1 files changed, 6 insertions(+), 0 deletions(-)
```

A glance at the commit history shows two new commits:

```
$ git log --graph --oneline
* e649d27 Open the word source file.
* 66a212c Introduce a Hash Table.
* 3ba81f7 Initial histogram program.
```

And that is a happy patch sequence!

As usual, there are a few caveats and extenuating circumstances. For instance, what about that sneaky line:

```
#include <stdlib.h>
```

Doesn't it really belong with the file operation patch and not the hash table patch? Yep. You got me. It does.

That's a bit trickier to handle. But let's do it anyway. We'll have to use the e option. First, reset to the first commit and leave all those changes in your working tree so we can do it all over again.

```
$ git reset 3ba81f7
Unstaged changes after reset:
M     main.c
```

Do the `git add -p` again, and split the first patch just like before. But this time, instead of answering y to the first subhunk staging request, answer **e** and request to edit the patch:

```
$ git add -p
diff --git a/main.c b/main.c
index 4809266..c60b800 100644
--- a/main.c
+++ b/main.c
@@ -1,7 +1,27 @@
 #include <stdio.h>
+#include <stdlib.h>
+
+struct htentry {
+    char *item;
+    int count;
+    struct htentry *next;
+};
+
+struct htentry ht_table[256];
+
+void ht_init(void)
+{
+    /* FIXME: details */
+}

 int main(int argc, char **argv)
 {
+    FILE *f;
+
+    f = fopen(argv[1], "r");
+    if (f == 0)
+        exit(-1);
+
     /*
      * Print a histogram of words found in a file.
      * "Words" are any whitespace separated characters.
Stage this hunk [y,n,q,a,d,/,j,J,g,s,e,?]? s
Split into 2 hunks.
@@ -1,4 +1,18 @@
 #include <stdio.h>
+#include <stdlib.h>
+
+struct htentry {
+    char *item;
+    int count;
+    struct htentry *next;
+};
+
+struct htentry ht_table[256];
+
+void ht_init(void)
+{
+    /* FIXME: details */
+}
```

```
    int main(int argc, char **argv)
    {
Stage this hunk [y,n,q,a,d,/,j,J,g,e,?]? e
```

You will be placed in your favorite editor[4] and allowed the chance to manually edit the patch. Read the comment at the bottom of the editor buffer. Carefully delete that one `#include <stdlib.h>` line. Don't disturb the context lines, and don't mess with the line counts. Git, and most any patch program, will lose its mind if you mess with the context lines. However, my editor updates the line counts automatically.

In this case, because the `#include` line was removed, it will be swept up in the remainder of the patches that get formed. This effectively introduces it at the correct time in the patch with the other file operation changes.

It is kind of tricky here, but Git now assumes that when you exit your editor, the patch that is left in your editor should be applied and its effects staged. So it offers you the *following* hunk and lets you choose its disposition. Be careful.

Because Git has moved on to the file operation changes, don't stage those changes yet, but do pick up the last hash table change:

```
@@ -2,6 +16,12 @@

 int main(int argc, char **argv)
 {
+    FILE *f;
+
+    f = fopen(argv[1], "r");
+    if (f == 0)
+        exit(-1);
+
     /*
      * Print a histogram of words found in a file.
      * "Words" are any whitespace separated characters.
Stage this hunk [y,n,q,a,d,/,K,j,J,g,e,?]? n
@@ -9,4 +29,6 @@ int main(int argc, char **argv)
      * FIXME: Implementation needed still!
      */
     printf("Histogram of words\n");
+
+    ht_init();
 }
Stage this hunk [y,n,q,a,d,/,K,g,e,?]? y
```

The separation can be verified, noting that the `#include <stdlib.h>` line has been correctly associated with the file operations now:

```
$ git diff
diff --git a/main.c b/main.c
index 3e77315..c60b800 100644
--- a/main.c
```

---

4. emacs, right?

```
+++ b/main.c
@@ -1,4 +1,5 @@
 #include <stdio.h>
+#include <stdlib.h>

 struct htentry {
     char *item;
@@ -15,6 +16,12 @@ void ht_init(void)

 int main(int argc, char **argv)
 {
+        FILE *f;
+
+        f = fopen(argv[1], "r");
+        if (f == 0)
+                exit(-1);
+
     /*
      * Print a histogram of words found in a file.
      * "Words" are any whitespace separated characters.
```

As before, wrap up with a `git commit` for the hash table patch, then stage and commit the remaining file operation pieces.

I've only touched on the essential responses to the "Stage this hunk?" question. In fact, even more options than those listed in its prompt (i.e., [y,n,q,a,d,/,K,g,e,?]) are available. There are options to delay the fate of a hunk and then revisit it when prompted again later.

Furthermore, although this example only had two hunks in one file, the staging operation generalizes too many hunks, possibly split, in many files. Pulling together changes across multiple files can be a simple process of applying `git add -p` to each file that has a hunk needing to be staged.

However, there is another, outer level to the whole interactive hunk staging process that can be invoked using the `git add -i` command. It can be a bit cryptic, but its purpose is to allow you to select which paths (i.e., files) to stage in the index. As a sub-option, you may then select the `patch` option for your chosen paths. This enters the previously described per file staging mechanism.

Recovering a Lost Commit

Occasionally, an ill-timed `git reset` command or an accidental branch deletion leaves you wishing you hadn't lost the development it represented, and wishing you could recover it somehow. The usual approach to recovering such work is to inspect your reflog as shown in Chapter 11. Sometimes the reflog isn't available, perhaps because it has been turned off (e.g., `core.logAllRefUpdates = false`), because you are manipulating a bare repository directly, or perhaps because the reflog has simply expired. For whatever reason, sometimes the reflog cannot help recover a lost commit.

The git fsck Command

Although not foolproof, Git provides the command `git fsck` to help locate lost data. The word "fsck" is an old abbreviation for "file system check." Although this command does not check your filesystem, it does have many characteristics and algorithms that are quite similar to a traditional filesystem check, and results in some of the same output data as well.

Understanding how `git fsck` works is predicated on a good understanding of Git's data structures as described in Chapter 4. Normally, every object in the Git repository, whether it is a blob, tree, commit, or tag, is connected to another object and anchored to a branch name, tag name, or some other symbolic ref such as a reflog name.

However, various commands and manipulations can leave objects in the object store that are not linked into the complete data structure somehow. These objects are called "unreachable" or "dangling." They are unreachable because a traversal of the full data structure that starts from every named ref and follows every tag, commit, commit parent, and tree object reference will never encounter the lost object. In a sense, it is out there dangling on its own.

But traversing the ref-based commit graph isn't the only way to walk every object in the database! Consider simply listing the objects in your object store using `ls` directly:

```
$ cd path/to/some/repo
$ ls -R .git/objects/
.git/objects/:
25  3b  73  82  info  pack

.git/objects/25:
7cc5642cb1a054f08cc83f2d943e56fd3ebe99

.git/objects/3b:
d1f0e29744a1f32b08d5650e62e2e62afb177c

.git/objects/73:
8d05ac5663972e2dcf4b473e04b3d1f19ba674

.git/objects/82:
b5fee28277349b6d46beff5fdf6a7152347ba0

.git/objects/info:

.git/objects/pack:
```

In this simple example, the set of objects in the repository has been listed without doing a traversal of the refs and commits.

By carefully comparing the total set of objects with those reachable via a traversal of the ref-based commit graph, you can determine all of the unreferenced objects. From the previous example, the second object listed turns out to be an unreferenced blob (i.e., file):

```
$ git fsck
Checking object directories: 100% (256/256), done.
dangling blob 3bd1f0e29744a1f32b08d5650e62e2e62afb177c
```

Let's follow an example that shows how a lost commit can occur, and see how git fsck can recover it. First, construct a simple, new repository with a single simple file in it.

```
$ mkdir /tmp/lost
$ cd /tmp/lost
$ git init
Initialized empty Git repository in /tmp/lost/.git/
$ echo "foo" >> file
$ git add file
$ git commit -m "Add some foo"
[master (root-commit) 1adf46e] Add some foo
 1 files changed, 1 insertions(+), 0 deletions(-)
 create mode 100644 file

$ git fsck
Checking object directories: 100% (256/256), done.

$ ls -R .git/objects/
.git/objects/:
25  4a  f8  info  pack

.git/objects/25:
7cc5642cb1a054f08cc83f2d943e56fd3ebe99

.git/objects/4a:
1c03029e7407c0afe9fc0320b3258e188b115e

.git/objects/f8:
5b097ee0f77c5f4dc1868037acbffe59b0e93e

.git/objects/info:

.git/objects/pack:
```

Notice that there are only three objects and none of them are dangling. In fact, starting from the master ref, which is the f85b097ee commit object, the traversal points to the tree object 4a1c0302 and then the blob 257cc564.

 The command git cat-file -t *object-id* can be used to determine an object's type.

Now let's make a second commit, and then hard reset back to the first commit:

```
$ echo bar >> file
$ git commit -m "Add some bar" file
[master 11e0dc9] Add some bar
 1 files changed, 1 insertions(+), 0 deletions(-)
```

And now the "accident" that causes us to lose a commit:

```
$ git commit -m "Add some bar" file
[master 11e0dc9] Add some bar
 1 files changed, 1 insertions(+), 0 deletions(-)

$ git reset --hard HEAD^
HEAD is now at f85b097 Add some foo

$ git fsck
Checking object directories: 100% (256/256), done.
```

But wait! `git fsck` doesn't report any dangling object. It doesn't seem to be lost after all. This is exactly what the reflog is designed to do: prevent you from accidentally losing commits. (See "The Reflog" on page 189.)

So let's try again after brutally eliminating the reflog:

```
# Not recommended; this is for purposes of exposition only!
$ rm -rf .git/logs
$ git fsck
Checking object directories: 100% (256/256), done.
dangling commit 11e0dc9c11d8f650711b48c4a5707edf5c8a02fe

$ ls -R .git/objects/
.git/objects/:
11   25   3b   41   4a   f8   info   pack

.git/objects/11:
e0dc9c11d8f650711b48c4a5707edf5c8a02fe

.git/objects/25:
7cc5642cb1a054f08cc83f2d943e56fd3ebe99

.git/objects/3b:
d1f0e29744a1f32b08d5650e62e2e62afb177c

.git/objects/41:
31fe4d33cd85da805ac9a6697c2251c913881c

.git/objects/4a:
1c03029e7407c0afe9fc0320b3258e188b115e

.git/objects/f8:
5b097ee0f77c5f4dc1868037acbffe59b0e93e

.git/objects/info:

.git/objects/pack:
```

You can use the `git fsck --no-reflog` command to find dangling objects as if the reflog were not available to reference commits. That is, objects that are only reachable from the reflog will be considered unreachable.

Now we can see that only the reflog was referencing the second commit `11e0dc9c` in which the "bar" content was added.

But how would we even know what that dangling commit is?

```
$ git show 11e0dc9c
commit 11e0dc9c11d8f650711b48c4a5707edf5c8a02fe
Author: Jon Loeliger <jdl@example.com>
Date:   Sun Feb 10 11:59:59 2012 -0600

    Add some bar

diff --git a/file b/file
index 257cc56..3bd1f0e 100644
--- a/file
+++ b/file
@@ -1 +1,2 @@
 foo
+bar

# The "index" line above named blob 3bd1f0e

$ git show 3bd1f0e
foo
bar
```

Note that the blob `3bd1f0e` is not considered dangling because it is actually referenced by the commit `11e0dc9c`, even though the commit itself is unreferenced.

Sometimes, though, `git fsck` will find blobs that are unreferenced. Remember, every time you `git add` a file to the index, its blob is added to the object store. If you subsequently change that content and re-add it, no commit will have captured the intermediate blob that was added to the object store. Thus, it will be unreferenced.

```
$ echo baz >> file
$ git add file
$ git fsck
Checking object directories: 100% (256/256), done.
dangling commit 11e0dc9c11d8f650711b48c4a5707edf5c8a02fe

$ echo quux >> file
$ git add file
$ git fsck
Checking object directories: 100% (256/256), done.
dangling blob 0c071e1d07528f124e31f1b6c71348ec13f21a7a
dangling commit 11e0dc9c11d8f650711b48c4a5707edf5c8a02fe
```

The reason the first `git fsck` didn't show a dangling blob was because that blob was still referenced directly by the index. Only after the content associated with the pathname *file* was changed again and re-added did that blob become dangling.

```
$ git show 0c071e1d
foo
baz
```

If you find you have a very cluttered `git fsck` report consisting entirely of unnecessary blobs and commits and want to clean it up, consider running garbage collection as described in "Garbage Collection" on page 368.

Reconnecting a Lost Commit

Although using `git fsck` is a handy way to discover the SHA1 of lost commits and blobs, I mentioned the reflog earlier as another mechanism. In fact, you could cut and paste it from some lingering line of output found by scrolling back over your terminal output log. Ultimately, it doesn't matter how you discover the SHA1 of a lost blob or commit. The question remains, once you know it, how do you reconnect it or otherwise incorporate it into your project?

By definition, blobs are nameless file content. All you really have to do to reestablish a blob is place that content into a file and `git add` it again. As I showed in the previous section, `git show` can be used on the blob SHA1 to obtain the full object content. Just redirect that to your desired file:

```
$ git show 0c071e1d > file2
```

On the other hand, reconnecting a commit might depend on what you want to do with it. The simple example from the previous section is only one commit. But it could equally well have been the first commit in an entire sequence of commits that was lost. Maybe even an entire branch was accidentally lost! Consequently, a usual practice would reintroduce a lost commit as a branch.

Here, the previously lost commit that introduced the bar content, `11e0dc9c`, is re-introduced on the new branch called `recovered`:

```
$ git branch recovered 11e0dc9c
$ git show-branch
* [master] Add some foo
 ! [recovered] Add some bar
--
 + [recovered] Add some bar
*+ [master] Add some foo
```

From there it can manipulated (kept as is, merged, etc.) as you wish.

## CHAPTER 20

Tips, Tricks, and Techniques

With a plethora of commands and options, Git provides a rich resource for performing varied and powerful changes to a repository. Sometimes, though, the actual means for accomplishing some particular task are a bit elusive. Sometimes, the purpose of a particular command and option isn't really clear or becomes lost in a technical description.

This chapter provides a collection of various tips, tricks, and techniques that highlight Git's ability to do interesting transformations.

Interactive Rebase with a Dirty Working Directory

Frequently, when developing a multicommit change sequence on a local branch, I realize that I need to make an additional modification to some commit I've already made earlier in the sequence. Rather than scribbling a note about it on the side and coming back to it later, I will immediately edit and introduce that change directly into a new commit with a reminder note in the commit log entry that it should be squashed into a previous commit.

When I eventually get around to cleaning up my commit sequence, and want to use `git rebase -i`, I am often midstride and find myself with a dirty working directory. In this case, Git will refuse to do the rebase.

```
$ git show-branch --more=10
[master] Tinker bar
[master^] Squash into 'More foo and bar'
[master~2] Modify bar
[master~3] More foo and bar
[master~4] Initial foo and bar.

$ git rebase -i master~4
Cannot rebase: You have unstaged changes.
Please commit or stash them.
```

As suggested, clean out your dirty working directory with `git stash` first!

```
$ git stash
Saved working directory and index state WIP on master: ed6e906 Tinker bar
HEAD is now at ed6e906 Tinker bar

$ git rebase -i master~4

# In the editor, move master^ next to master~3
# and mark it for squashing.
pick 1a4be28 More foo and bar
squash 6195b3d Squash into 'more foo and bar'
pick 488b893 Modify bar
pick ed6e906 Tinker bar

[detached HEAD e3c46b8] More foo and bar with additional stuff.
 2 files changed, 2 insertions(+), 1 deletions(-)
Successfully rebased and updated refs/heads/master.
```

Naturally, you will want to recover your working directory changes now:

```
$ git stash pop
# On branch master
# Changes not staged for commit:
#   (use "git add <file>..." to update what will be committed)
#   (use "git checkout -- <file>..." to discard changes in working directory)
#
#       modified:   foo
#
no changes added to commit (use "git add" and/or "git commit -a")
Dropped refs/stash@{0} (71b4655668e49ce88686fc9eda8432430b276470)
```

Remove Left-Over Editor Files

Because the git filter-branch command really drives a shell operation, either the
--index-filter *command* or the --tree-filter *command* can use normal shell wild card
matching in its *command*. That can be handy when you accidentally add, say, temporary
editor files on first creating your repository.

```
$ git filter-branch --tree-filter 'rm -f *~' -- --all
```

That command will remove all files matching the *~ pattern from -- --all refs in one
command.

Garbage Collection

In "The git fsck Command" on page 361, which I expanded on the concept of reach-
ability was first introduced in Chapter 4. In those sections, I explained how the Git
object store and its commit graph might leave unreferenced or dangling objects within
the object store. I also gave a few examples how some commands might leave these
unreferenced objects in your repository.

Having dangling commits or unreachable objects is not necessarily bad. You may have moved away from a particular commit intentionally or added a file blob and then changed it again before actually committing it. The problem, however, is that over a long period, manipulating the repository can be messy and leave many unreferenced objects in your object store.

Historically, within the computer science industry, such unreferenced objects are cleaned up by an algorithm called "garbage collection." It is the job of the `git gc` command to perform periodic garbage collection and keep your repository object stores neat and tidy.

This is neat, tidy, and small. Git's garbage collection has one other very important task: optimizing the size of the repository by locating unpacked objects (loose objects) and creating pack files for them.

So when does garbage collection happen, and how often? Is it automatic or is it something that needs to be done manually? When it runs does it remove everything it can? Pack everything it can?

All good questions and, as usual, the answers are all, "It depends."

For starters, Git runs garbage collection automatically at strategic times. At other times, you should run `git gc` directly by hand.

Git runs garbage collection automatically:

- If there are too many loose objects in the repository
- When a push to a remote repository happens
- After some commands that might introduce many loose objects
- When some commands such as `git reflog expire` explicitly request it

And finally, garbage collection occurs when you explicitly request it using the `git gc` command. But when should that be? There's no solid answer to this question, but there is some good advice and best practice.

You should consider running `git gc` manually in a few situations:

- If you have just completed a `git filter-branch`. Recall that `filter-branch` rewrites many commits, introduces new ones, and leaves the old ones on a `ref` that should be removed when you are satisfied with the results. All those dead objects (that are no longer referenced since you just removed the one `ref` pointing to them) should be removed via garbage collection.
- After some commands that might introduce many loose objects. This might be a large rebase effort, for example.

And on the flip side, when should you be wary of garbage collection?

- If there are orphaned refs that you might want to recover
- In the context of `git rerere` and you do not need to save the resolutions forever

- In the context of only tags and branches being sufficient to cause Git to retain a commit permanently
- In the context of FETCH_HEAD retrievals (URL-direct retrievals via git fetch) because they are immediately subject to garbage collection

Git doesn't spontaneously jump to life and carry out garbage collection of its own free will, not even automatically. Instead, what happens is that certain commands that you run cause Git to then consider running garbage collection and packing. But just because you run those commands and Git runs git gc doesn't mean that Git *acts* on this trigger. Instead, Git takes that opportunity to inspect a whole series of configuration parameters that guide the inner workings of both the removal of unreferenced objects and the creation of pack files. Some of the more important git config parameters include:

gc.auto
> The number of loose objects allowed to exist in a repository before garbage collection causes them to be packed. The default is 6700.

gc.autopacklimit
> The number of pack files that may exist in a repository before pack files are themselves repacked into larger, more efficient pack files. The default is 50.

gc.pruneexpire
> The period of time unreachable objects may linger in an object store. The default is two weeks.

gc.reflogexpire
> The git reflog expire command will remove reflog entries older than this time period. The default is 90 days.

gc.reflogexpireunreachable
> The git reflog expire command will remove reflog entries older than this time period only if they are unreachable from the current branch. The default is 30 days.

Most of the garbage collection config parameters have a value that means either "do it now" or "never do it."

Split a Repository

You can use Git's filter-branch to split a repository or to extract subdirectories. And in this case, we mean split a repository and maintain the history that lead to this point. (If you don't care about the development and commit history and want to split a repository, just clone the repository and remove the parts from each that you don't want!) This approach preserves the appropriate development and commit history.

For example, let's say you had a repository with four top-level directories named part1, part2, part3, and part4, and you wanted to split the top-level directory part4 into its own repository.

For starters, you should work in a clone of the original repository and remove all of the origin remote references. This will ensure that you don't destroy the original repository, nor will you think you can push or fetch changes from your original via a lingering remote reference.

Then, use the --subdirectory-filter option like this:

```
$ git filter-branch --subdirectory-filter part4 HEAD
```

However, there are likely some extenuating circumstances that will cause you to want to extend that command to allow for incidental and tricky situations. Do you have tags and want them reflected in the new part4 repository too? If so, add the --tag-name-filter cat option. Might a commit end up empty due to its inapplicability to this subsection of the original repository? Almost certainly, so add the --prune-empty too. Are you interested in only the one current branch indicated by HEAD? Almost certainly not. Instead, you might want to cover all branches from the original repository. In that case, you'll want to use -- --all in place of the final HEAD parameter.

The revised command now looks like this:

```
$ git filter-branch --tag-name-filter cat \
--subdirectory-filter part4 -- --all
```

Naturally, you will want to verify the contents are as expected and then expire your reflog, remove the original refs, and do garbage collection on the new repository.

Finally, you might (or might not) need to return to your original repository and perform a different git filter-branch to remove part4 from it, too!

Tips for Recovering Commits

Time is the enemy of lost commits. Eventually, Git's garbage collection will run and clean out any dangling or unreferenced commits and blobs. Garbage collection will eventually retire reflog refs as well. At that point, lost commits are lost and git fsck will no longer be able to find them. If you know you are slow to realize a commit has been lost, you may want to adjust the default timeouts for reflog expiration and retiring unreferenced commits during garbage collection.

```
# default is 90 days
$ git config --global gc.reflogExpire "6 months"

# default is 30 days
$ git config --global gc.reflogExpireUnreachable "60 days"

# default is 2 weeks
$ git config --global gc.pruneexpire="1 month"
```

Sometimes, using a graphical tool such as gitk or viewing a log graph can help find and establish necessary context for interpreting and understanding the reflog and other dangling or orphaned commits.

Here are two aliases that you might add to your global *.gitconfig*:

```
$ git config --global \
    alias.orphank=!gitk --all `git reflog | cut -c1-7`&
$ git config --global \
    alias.orphanl=!git log --pretty=oneline --abbrev-commit \
    --graph --decorate `git reflog | cut -c1-7`
```

Subversion Conversion Tips

General Advice

Maintaining an SVN repository and a Git repository in parallel is a lot of work, especially if subsequent new commits to the SVN repository are allowed. Make absolutely sure that you need to do this before you commit to this workflow. By far the easiest approach is to do the SVN to Git conversion once, making the SVN repository inaccessible when the conversion has been completed.

Plan on doing all of your importing, converting, and cleaning up once up front before ever publishing the first Git version of your repository. There are several steps in a well-planned conversion that you really should do before anyone else has a chance to clone the first version of your Git repository. For example, all of your global changes, such as directory renaming, author and email address cleanup, large file removal, branch fiddling, tag construction, etc., will be significantly more difficult for both you and your downstream consumers if they happen after they have cloned the conversion repository.

Do you really want to remove all the SVN commit identifiers from your Git commit logs? Just because recipes exist to do so and someone shows you how, doesn't mean you should. It's your call.

After doing a conversion, the metadata in the *.git* directory for the SVN conversion is lost upon cloning or pushing to a Git repository. Make sure you are done.

If you can, ensure that you have a good author and email mapping file prior to doing your import. Having to fix them up later with `git filter-branch` is just extra pain.

If creating and maintaining parallel SVN and Git repositories seems complicated, and you find you still must use both, using GitHub's Subversion Bridge (see "Subversion Bridge" on page 407) is an easy alternative that meets this requirement.

Remove a Trunk After an SVN Import

Often, after creating a new repository from an SVN import, you are left with a top-level directory such as *trunk* that you don't really want in your Git repository.

```
$ cd OldSVNStuff
```

```
$ ls -R .
.:
trunk

./trunk:
Recipes  Stuff  Things

./trunk/Recipes:
Chicken_Pot_Pie  Ice_Cream

./trunk/Stuff:
Note_to_self

./trunk/Things:
Movie_List
```

There is no real reason to keep *trunk*. You can use Git's `filter-branch` to remove it:

```
$ git filter-branch --subdirectory-filter trunk HEAD
Rewrite b6b4781ee814cbb6fc6a01a91c8d0654ec78fbe1 (1/1)
Ref 'refs/heads/master' was rewritten

$ ls
Recipes  Stuff  Things
```

Everything under *trunk* will be hoisted up one level and the directory *trunk* will be eliminated.

Removing SVN Commit IDs

First, run `git filter-branch --msg-filter` using a `sed` script to match and delete the SVN commit IDs from your Git log messages.

```
# From the git-filter-branch manual page
$ git filter-branch --msg-filter 'sed -e "/^git-svn-id:/d"'
```

Toss the reflog or else it will have lingering references:

```
$ git reflog expire --verbose --expire=0 --all
```

Remember that after a `git filter-branch` command, Git leaves the old, original branch refs in *refs/original/*. You should remove them and take the garbage out with prejudice:

```
# Careful...
$ rm -rf .git/refs/original

$ git reflog expire --verbose --expire=0 --all
$ git gc --prune=0
$ git repack -ad
```

Alternatively, clone away from it:

```
$ cd /tmp/somewhere/else/
$ git clone file:///home/jdl/stuff/converted.git
```

Remember to use a `file:///` URL, because a normal, direct file reference will hard link the files rather than copy them; that won't be effective.

Manipulating Branches from Two Repositories

I am occasionally asked the question, "How do I compare two branches from different repositories?" It is sometimes asked with slight variations as well: "How do I tell whether my commits from my repository have been merged into a branch in some other repository?" Or sometimes something like, "What does the `devel` branch in this remote repository have that isn't in my repository?"

These are all fundamentally the same question in that they aim to resolve or compare branches from two different repositories. Developers are sometimes thrown off by the fact that the branches they wish to compare are in two or more different repositories, and that those repositories might also be remote or located on another server.

In order for these questions to make sense at all, the developer must know that, at some point back in time during the earlier development of these repositories, they must have had some common ancestor and were derived from a common basis. Without such a relationship, it makes little to no sense to even ask how two branches might compare to each other. That means that Git should be able to discover the commit graph and branch history of both repositories and be able to relate them.

The key technique for solving all these questions, then, is to realize that Git can compare branches only within one local repository. Thus, you need to have all the branches from all the repositories colocated in one repository. Usually, this is a simple matter of adding a new `remote` for each of the *other* repositories containing a needed branch, and then `fetching` from it.

Once the branches are all in one repository, use any of the usual `diff` or comparison commands on those branches as needed.

Recovering from an Upstream Rebase

Sometimes, when working in a distributed environment where you don't necessarily control the upstream repository from which you derived your current development clone, the upstream version of the branch on which you have developed your work will undergo a non–fast-forward change or a rebase. That change destroys the basis of your branch, and prevents you from directly sending your changes upstream.

Unfortunately, Git doesn't provide a way for an upstream repository maintainer to state how its branches will be treated. That is, there is no flag that says "this branch will be rebased at will," or "don't expect this branch to fast-forward." You, the downstream developer, just have to know, intuit its intended behavior, or ask the upstream maintainer. For the most part, other than that, branches are expected to fast-forward and not be rebased.

Sure, that can be bad. I've explained before how changing published history is bad. Nevertheless, it happens sometimes. Furthermore, there are some very good development models that even encourage the occasional rebasing of a branch during the normal course of development. (For an example, see how the pu, or proposed updates branches, of the Git repository itself are handled.)

So when it happens, what do you do? How do you recover so that your work *can* be sent upstream again?

First, ask yourself whether the rebased branch is really the right branch on which you should have been basing your work in the first place. Branches are often intended to be read only. For example, maybe a collection of branches are being gathered and merged together for testing purposes into a read only branch, but are otherwise available individually and should form the basis of development work. In this case, you likely shouldn't have been developing on the merged collection branch. (The Linux next branches tend to operate like this.)

Depending on the extent of the rebase that occurred upstream, you may get off easily and be able to recover with a simple `git pull --rebase`. Give it a try; if it works, you win. But I wouldn't count on it. You should be prepared to recover an ensuing mess with a judicious use of `reflog`.

The real, more reliable approach is to methodically transfer your developed and orphaned commit sequence from your now defunct branch to the new upstream branch. The basic sequence is to:

- Rename your old upstream branch. It is important to do this before you fetch because it allows a clean fetch of the new upstream history. Try something like: `git branch save-origin-master origin/master`.
- Fetch from upstream to recover the current upstream content. A simple `git fetch` should be sufficient.
- Rebase your commits from the renamed branch onto the new upstream branch using commands like `cherry-pick` or `rebase`. This should be the command: `git rebase --onto origin/master save-origin-master master`.
- Clean up and remove the temporary branch. Try using the command `git branch -D save-origin-master`.

It seems easy enough, but the key can often be in locating the point back in the history of the upstream branch where the original history and the new history begin to diverge. It's possible that everything between that point and your first commit isn't needed at all; that is, the rewritten commit history changes nothing that intersects with your work. In this case, you win because a rebase should happen readily. On the other hand, it is also possible that the rewritten history touches the same ground that you were developing. In this case, you likely have a tough rebase road ahead of you and will need to fully understand the semantic meanings of the original and changed histories in order to figure out how to resolve your desired development changes.

Make Your Own Git Command

Here's a neat little trick to make your own Git command that looks like every other git *command*.

First, write your command or script using a name that begins with the prefix `git-`. Place it in your *~/bin* directory or some other place that is found on your shell PATH.

Suppose you wanted a script that checked to see if you were in the top level of your Git repository. Let's call it `git-top-check`, like this:

```
#!/bin/sh
# git-top-check -- Is this the top level directory of a Git repo?

if [ -d ".git" ]; then
    echo "This is a top level Git development repository."
    exit 0
fi

echo "This is not a top level Git development repository."
exit -1
```

If you now place that script in the file *~/bin/git-top-check* and make it executable, you can use it like this:

```
$ cd ~/Repos/git
$ git top-check
This is a top level Git development repository.

$ cd /etc
$ git top-check
This is not a top level Git development repository.
```

Quick Overview of Changes

If you need to keep a repository up to date by continually fetching from an upstream source, you may find yourself frequently asking a question similar to, "So, what changed in the last week?"

The answer to your wonderment might be the `git whatchanged` command. Like many commands, it accepts a plethora of options centered around `git rev-parse` for selecting commits, and formatting options typical of, say, `git log` such as the `--pretty=` options.

Notably, you might want the `--since=` option.

```
# The Git source repository
$ cd ~/Repos/git
$ git whatchanged --since="three days ago" --oneline
745950c p4000: use -3000 when promising -3000
:100755 100755 d6e505c... 7e00c9d... M  t/perf/p4000-diff-algorithms.sh
42e52e3 Update draft release notes to 1.7.10
:100644 100644 ae446e0... a8fd0ac... M  Documentation/RelNotes/1.7.10.txt
561ae06 perf: export some important test-lib variables
```

```
:100755 100755 f8dd536... cf8e1ef... M  t/perf/p0000-perf-lib-sanity.sh
:100644 100644 bcc0131... 5580c22... M  t/perf/perf-lib.sh
1cbc324 perf: load test-lib-functions from the correct directory
:100755 100755 2ca4aac... f8dd536... M  t/perf/p0000-perf-lib-sanity.sh
:100644 100644 2a5e1f3... bcc0131... M  t/perf/perf-lib.sh
```

That's dense. But we did ask for --oneline! So the commit log has been summarized in single lines like this:

```
561ae06 perf: export some important test-lib variables
```

And each of those are followed by the list of files that changed with each commit:

```
:100755 100755 f8dd536... cf8e1ef... M  t/perf/p0000-perf-lib-sanity.sh
:100644 100644 bcc0131... 5580c22... M  t/perf/perf-lib.sh
```

That's file mode bits, before and after the commit, the SHA1s of each blob before and after the commit, a status letter (M here means modified content or mode bits), and finally the path of the blob that changed.

Although the previous example defaulted the branch reference to master, you could pick anything of interest, or explicitly request the set of changes that were just fetched:

```
$ git whatchanged ORIG_HEAD..HEAD
```

You can also limit the output to the set of changes that affect a named file:

```
$ cd /usr/src/linux
$ git pull

$ git whatchanged ORIG_HEAD..HEAD --oneline Makefile
fde7d90 Linux 3.3-rc7
:100644 100644 66d13c9... 56d4817... M  Makefile
192cfd5 Linux 3.3-rc6
:100644 100644 b61a963... 66d13c9... M  Makefile
```

The workhorse behind this output is git diff-tree. Grab yourself a caffeinated beverage prior to reading that manual page.

Cleaning Up

Everyone enjoys a clean and tidy directory structure now and then! To help you achieve repository directory nirvana, the git clean command may be used to remove untracked files from your working tree.

Why bother? Perhaps cleaning is part of an iterative build process that reuses the same directory for repeated builds but needs to have generated files cleaned out each time. (Think make clean.)

By default, git clean just removes all files that are *not* under version control from the current directory and down through your directory structure. Untracked directories are considered slightly more valuable than plain files and are left in place unless you supply the -d option.

Furthermore, for the purposes of this command, Git uses a slightly more conservative concept of under version control. Specifically, the manual page uses the phrase "files that are unknown to Git" for a good reason: even files that are mentioned in the *.gitignore* and *.git/info/exclude* files are actually known to Git. They represent files that are not version controlled, but Git does *know* about them. And because those files are called out in the *.gitignore* files, they must have some known (to you) behavior that shouldn't be disturbed by Git. So Git won't clean out the ignored files unless you explicitly request it with the -x option.

Naturally, the -X option causes the inverse behavior: namely, only files explicitly ignored by Git are removed. So choose the files that are important to you carefully.

If you are skittish, do a --dry-run first.

Using git-grep to Search a Repository

You may recall from "Using Pickaxe" on page 88 that I introduced the pickaxe option (spelled -S*string*) for the git log command, and then in "git diff with Path Limiting" on page 117, I showed it in use with the git diff command. It searches back through a branch's history of commit changes for commits that introduce or remove occurrences of a given string or regular expression.

Another command that can be used to search a repository is git grep. Rather than searching each commit's changes to a branch, the git grep command searches the content of files within a repository. Because git grep is really a generic Swiss Army knife with a multitude of options, it is more accurate to say that git grep searches for text patterns in tracked blobs (i.e., files) of the work tree, blobs cached in the index, or blobs in specified trees. By default, it just searches the tracked files of the working tree.

Thus, pickaxe can be used to search a series of commit differences, whereas git grep can be used to search the repository tree at a specific point in that history.

Want to do some ego surfing in a repository? Sure you do. Let's go get the Git source repository and find out![1]

```
$ cd /tmp
$ git clone git://github.com/gitster/git.git

Cloning into 'git'...
remote: Counting objects: 129630, done.
remote: Compressing objects: 100% (42078/42078), done.
Receiving objects: 100% (129630/129630), 28.51 MiB | 1.20 MiB/s, done.
remote: Total 129630 (delta 95231), reused 119366 (delta 85847)
Resolving deltas: 100% (95231/95231), done.

$ cd git
```

---

1. I both elided an obsolete name reference, and shortened the actual output lines for this example. Oh, and apparently I'm a closet Git artist!

```
$ git grep -i loeliger
Documentation/gitcore-tutorial.txt:Here is an ASCII art by Jon Loeliger
Documentation/revisions.txt:Here is an illustration, by Jon Loeliger.
Documentation/user-manual.txt:Here is an ASCII art by Jon Loeliger

$ git grep jdl
Documentation/technical/pack-heuristics.txt:  <jdl> What is a "thin" pack?
```

Ever wonder where the documentation for the `git-grep` command itself is located? What files in the *git.git* even mention git-grep by name? Do you even know where it is located? Here's how you can find out:

```
# Still in the /tmp/git repository

$ git grep -l git-grep
.gitignore
Documentation/RelNotes/1.5.3.6.txt
Documentation/RelNotes/1.5.3.8.txt
Documentation/RelNotes/1.6.3.txt
Documentation/git-grep.txt
Documentation/gitweb.conf.txt
Documentation/pt_BR/gittutorial.txt
Makefile
command-list.txt
configure.ac
gitweb/gitweb.perl
t/README
t/perf/p7810-grep.sh
```

A few things to note here: `git-grep` supports many of the normal command line options to the traditional `grep` tool, such as `-i` for case insensitive searches, `-l` for a list of just the matching file names, `-w` for word matching, etc. Using the `--` separator option, you can limit the paths or directories that Git will search. To limit the search to the occurrence within the *Documentation/* directory, do something like this:

```
# Still in the /tmp/git repository

$ git grep -l git-grep -- Documentation
Documentation/RelNotes/1.5.3.6.txt
Documentation/RelNotes/1.5.3.8.txt
Documentation/RelNotes/1.6.3.txt
Documentation/git-grep.txt
Documentation/gitweb.conf.txt
Documentation/pt_BR/gittutorial.txt
```

Using the `--untracked` option, you can also search for patterns in untracked (but not ignored) files that have neither been added to the cache nor committed as part of the repository history. This option may come in handy if you are developing some feature and have started adding new files but haven't yet committed them. A default `git grep` wouldn't search there, even though your past experience with the traditional `grep` command might lead you to believe that all files in your working directory (and possibly its subdirectories) would otherwise be searched.

So why even bother introducing the `git grep` in the first place? Isn't the traditional shell tool sufficient? Yes and no.

There are several benefits to building the `git grep` command directly into the Git tool-set. First, speed and simplicity. Git doesn't have to completely check out a branch in order to do the search; it can operate directly on the objects from the object store. You don't have to write some script to check out a commit from way back in time, then search those files, then restore your original checked out state. Second, Git can offer enhanced features and options by being an integrated tool. Notably, it offers searches that are limited to tracked files, untracked files, files cached in the index, ignored or excluded files, variations on searching snapshots from the repository history, and repository-specific pathspec limiters.

Updating and Deleting refs

Way back in "refs and symrefs" on page 68, I introduced the concept of a ref and mentioned Git also had several symbolic refs that it maintained. By now, you should be familiar with branches as refs, how they are maintained under the *.git* directory, and that the symbolic refs are also maintained there. Somewhere in there a bunch of SHA1 values exist, get updated, shuffled around, deleted, and referenced by other refs.

Occasionally, it is nice or even necessary to directly change or delete a ref. If you know exactly what you are doing, you could manipulate all of those files by hand. But if you don't do it correctly, it is easy to mess things up.

To ensure that the basic ref manipulations are done properly, Git supplies the command `git update-ref`. This command understands all of the nuances of refs, symbolic refs, branches, SHA1 values, logging changes, the reflog, etc. If you need to directly change a ref's value, you should use a command like:

```
$ git update-ref someref SHA1
```

where *someref* is the name of a branch or ref to be updated to the new value, *SHA1*. Furthermore, if you want to delete a ref, the proper way to do so is:

```
$ git update-ref -d someref
```

Of course, the normal branch operations might be more appropriate, but if you find yourself directly changing a ref, using `git update-ref` ensures that all of the bookkeeping for Git's infrastructure is done properly, too.

Following Files that Moved

If, over the history of a file, it is moved from one place to another within your repository directory structure, Git will usually only trace back over its history using its current name.

To see the complete history of the file, even across moves, use the `--follow` as well. For example, the following command shows the commit log for a file currently named *file*, but includes the log for its prior names as well:

```
$ git log --follow file
```

Add the `--name-only` option to have Git also state the name of that file as it changes:

```
$ git log --follow --name-only file
```

In the following example, file *a* is first added in the directory *foo* and then moved to directory *bar*:

```
$ git init
$ mkdir foo
$ touch foo/a
$ git add foo/a
$ git commit -m "First a in foo" foo/a
$ mkdir bar
$ git mv foo/a bar/a
$ git commit -m "Move foo/a to bar/a"
```

At this point, a simple `git log bar/b` will show only the commit that created file *bar/a*, but adding option `--follow` will trace back through its name changes, too:

```
$ git log --oneline bar/a
6a4115b Move foo/a to bar/a

$ git log --oneline --follow bar/a
6a4115b Move foo/a to bar/a
1862781 First a in foo
```

If you want to use its original name, you have to work harder because only the current name of the file, *bar/a*, is able to be referenced normally. Adding option `--` and then any of its current or former names will work. And adding `--all` will produce a comprehensive search as if all refs were searched, too.

```
$ git log --oneline foo/a
fatal: ambiguous argument 'foo/a': unknown revision or path not in the
        working tree.
Use '--' to separate paths from revisions

$ git log --oneline -- foo/a
6a4115b Move foo/a to bar/a
1862781 First a in foo
```

Keep, But Don't Track, This File

A common developer problem, described here by Bart Massey, arises with *Makefiles* and other configuration files: the version that the developer works with locally may be customized in ways that are not intended to be visible upstream. For example, I commonly change my *Makefile* `CFLAGS` from `-Wall -g -O2` to `-Wall -g -pg` during development. Of course, I also change the *Makefile* in ways that should be visible upstream, such as adding new targets.

I could maintain a separate local development branch, which differs only in the *Makefile*. Whenever I make a change, I could merge back to `master` and push upstream. I'd have to do an interactive merge in order to omit my custom `CFLAGS` (while maybe merging other changes). This seems hard and error prone.

Another solution would be to implement some form of *Makefile* snippet that provided local overrides for certain variable settings. But this approach is highly specific where an otherwise general problem remains.

It turns out that `git update-index --assume-unchanged Makefile` will leave the *Makefile* in the repository, but will cause Git to assume that subsequent changes to the working copy are not to be tracked. Thus, I can commit the version with the `CFLAGS` I want published, mark the *Makefile* with `--assume-unchanged`, and edit the `CFLAGS` to correspond to my development version. Now, subsequent pushes and commits will ignore the *Makefile*. Indeed, `git add Makefile` will report an error when the *Makefile* is marked `--assume-unchanged`.

When I want to make a published change to my *Makefile*, I can proceed via:

```
$ git update-index --no-assume-unchanged Makefile
$ git add -p Makefile

#  [add the Makefile changes I want published]
$ git commit
$ git update-index --assume-unchanged Makefile
$ git push
```

This work flow does require that I remember to perform the previous steps when I want a *Makefile* change published. But that is relatively infrequent. Further, initially forgetting carries a low price tag: I can always do it later.

Have You Been Here Before?

Ever have that feeling you've worked through a complex merge or rebase over and over again? Are you getting tired of it yet? Do you wish there was some way to automate it?

I thought so. And so did the Git developers!

Git has a feature named rerere that automates the chore of solving the same merge or rebase conflicts repeatedly. The seemingly alliterative name is a shortening of reuse recorded resolution. Sometimes long development cycles that use a branch to hold a line of development that undergoes many development iterations before finally being merged into a mainline development will have to be rebased or moved through the same set of conflicts and resolutions many times.

To enable and use the `git rerere` command, you must first set the Boolean `rerere.enabled` option to true.

```
$ git config --global rerere.enabled true
```

Once enabled, this feature records the right and left side of a merge conflict in the *.git/rr-cache directory* and, if resolved, also records the manual resolution to that conflict. If the same conflict is seen again, the automatic resolution engages and preemptively solves the conflict.

When rerere is enabled and participates in a merge, it will prevent autocommitting of the merge, giving the opportunity to review the automatic conflict resolution before making it a part of the commit history.

Rerere has only one prominent shortcoming: the nonportability of the *.rr-cache* directory. Conflict and resolution recording happens on a per clone basis and is not transmitted in push or pull operations.

## CHAPTER 21

Git and GitHub

Although the other chapters of this book have focused on the Git command line tool, the years since the 2005 inception of Git have allowed and fostered the growth of a community of tools around it. Those tools number in the hundreds and take on many forms, from desktop GUIs like SmartGit (*http://syneveo.com/smartgit*) to disk backup tools like SparkleShare (*http://sparkleshare.org*). But out of this ocean of Git tooling, one stands at the forefront of the mind of many developers and even nondevelopers: GitHub (*http://github.com*).

This website, shown in Figure 21-1, introduced the phrase that seemed dismissible just a few years ago, but now feels like the way many of us should consider working: social coding. This model of social coding was first applied to open source, but the last two years have seen this idea of code as a point of geographically distributed collaboration grow even in the closed source enterprise. Let's take a look at what GitHub has to offer.

Repo for Public Code

Statistics indicate that the first interaction that many developers have with Git is in cloning a repository from GitHub. This is the original function of GitHub. It offers an interface to repositories over the `git://`, `https://`, and `git+ssh://` protocols. Accounts are free for open source projects and all accounts can create unlimited publicly accessible repositories. This has greatly fostered the adoption of Git within the open source community for languages from JavaScript to ClojureScript.

Creating an account begins with opening *http://github.com* in your web browser and clicking the Sign Up link shown in Figure 21-2.

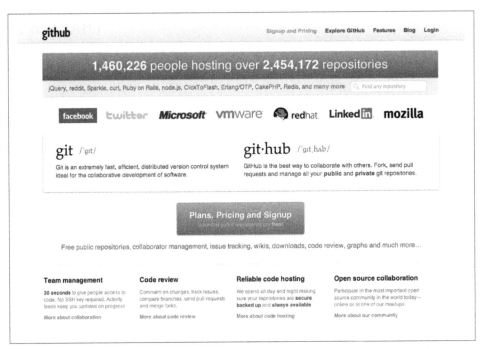

Figure 21-1. GitHub homepage

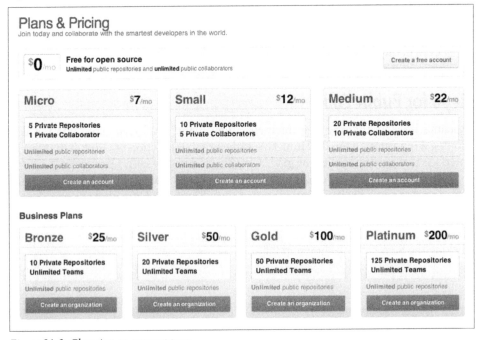

Figure 21-2. Choosing an account type

GitHub has four types of account and plan combinations: free personal, paid personal, free organization and paid organization. A personal account is a pre-requisite for joining as an organization. Be thoughtful in your choice of username because only one rename action is allowed per account by default (Figure 21-3). Multiple email addresses can be associated with a single username and can be changed at any time. Thus, the username is the most permanent part of the sign up information.

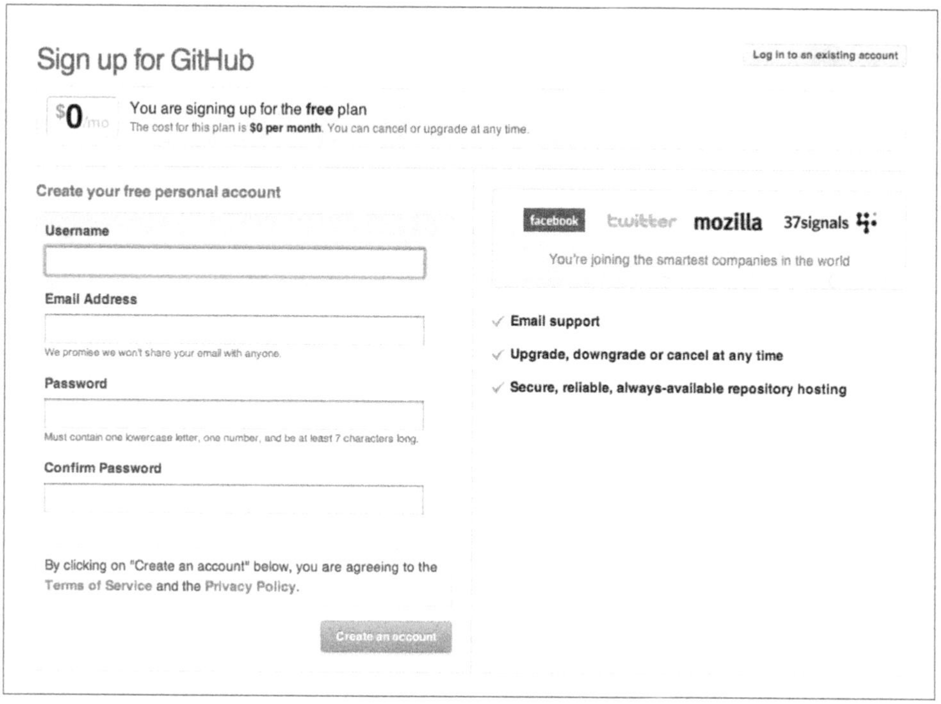

Figure 21-3. Free personal account

At the conclusion (Figure 21-4) of creating a free personal account, which is the most common type, users are directed to the GitHub help pages, which offer tutorials on setting up a few necessary configuration parameters of the developer desktop installation of Git.

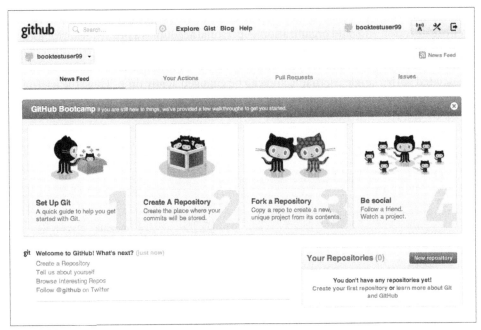

Figure 21-4. Account creation complete

Creating a GitHub Repository

New Repository Information

Once you've created an account, creating a repository is as easy as clicking on the New Repository button on the top-most toolbar, visible at all times once logged in, or by navigating directly to the New Repository page by typing *http://github .com/new*.

The only required data is the name of the repository, but an optional description of the project's objectives and the URL of its home page signal attentiveness of the maintainers (Figure 21-5).

Next, the repository must be given its initial content. There are two distinct approaches based on whether or not you have existing commits to preserve.

README Seeding (Option 1)

If the first step in working with the project was to create the GitHub repository before writing any code, you'll want to create a placeholder file as the first commit. During the new repository creation on the GitHub site, you are presented with choices to optionally seed the repository with an initial *README* file and a *.gitignore* file. Projects use this *README* text file to describe the intent of the project.

The project is then ready to be cloned with the command `git clone url`, after which new code can begin to be locally added and committed.

Adding a Remote (Option 2)

If you already have a local Git repository with commits, you can connect the GitHub address to the existing local repo. You do this by adding the GitHub URL (a Git remote) to an existing local Git repository with the `git remote add url` command.

Pushing the Local Contents to GitHub

Once one of the two options has been followed to connect the local repository to the remote repository, the contents of the local repo can be pushed to GitHub. This is done with the `git push remote branch` command. If the branch has never been published before, the more specific invocation `git push -u origin master` is appropriate, in which `-u` tells Git to track the pushed branch, push it to the `ori gin` remote, and to push just the `master` branch.

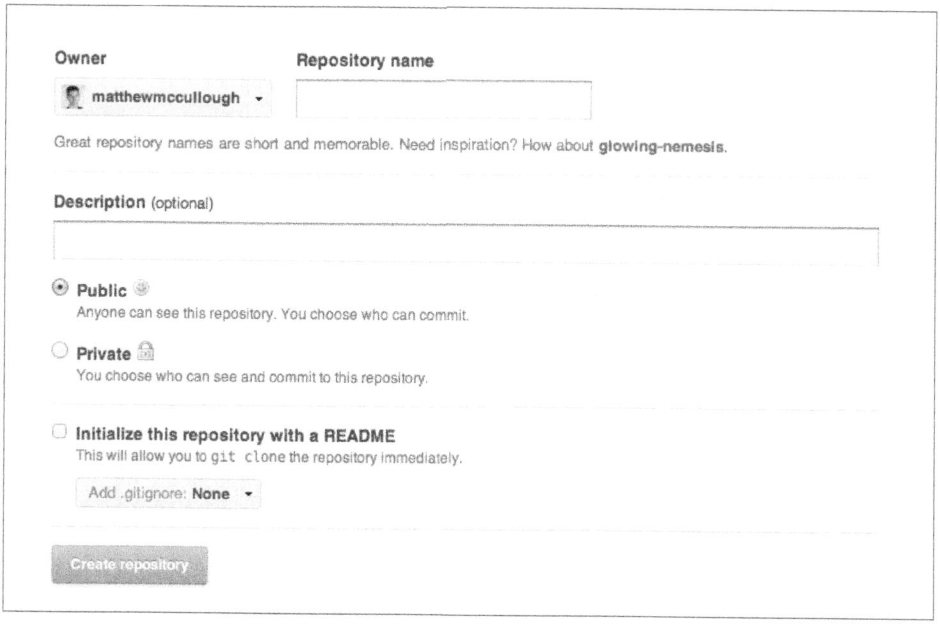

Figure 21-5. Creating a public repo

Once the connection with the upstream (GitHub) server is established with one of the previous techniques, further code changes can be easily pushed with additional `git push` calls. This exhibits a core benefit of a centrally accessible Git repository host, even in a very distributed worker–focused tool such as Git: the ability to see the changes that all members of the project have completed and pushed (Figure 21-6), even if they are offline.

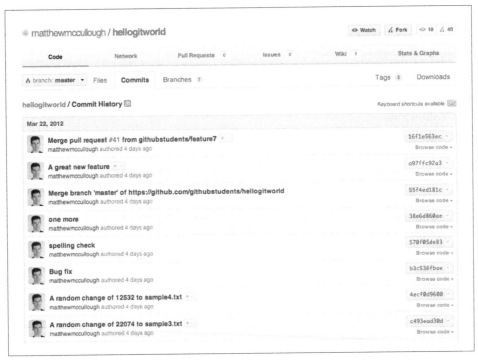

Figure 21-6. Commit history on GitHub

Social Coding on Open Source

GitHub can be minimally thought of as a place to host open source projects. However, the pedestrian concept of repository hosting isn't new and has been well pioneered by forges such as SourceForge and Google Code, among many others, each with their own user interface strengths. The extended idea of a forge with organizational policies, licenses, and commit rights through meritocracy was furthered by The Apache Foundation, Codehaus, and The Eclipse Foundation.

But GitHub took a different approach to extending the mere concept of a forge with community contributions (Figure 21-7). GitHub offers social aspects of the Web, as seen on Twitter, Facebook, and other social networks, mapped onto the previously considered solitary activity of programming. With the concepts of *watching* other users that seem to be making interesting contributions, repository *forks* to permit anyone to copy a project, *pull requests* to signal project owners that another programmer has an interesting set of code to potentially merge in, and *line-level comments* on commits to allow simple iterative refinement to contributions, GitHub has made coding a social activity. In the process, a vast amount of open source has benefited from a much wider range of contributors than were afforded in the days of patch files attached to bug tickets.

Figure 21-7. Social coding

Watchers

The simplest of the social coding features to be found on GitHub is *watching*, which begins with the press of the Watch button as shown in Figure 21-8. Watching, a concept similar to that of Twitter followers or Facebook friends, signals interest in a GitHub user, organization, or particular project.

Figure 21-8. Watch button

The watcher count can often be a signal of the usefulness of an open source project. The GitHub explore page allows for site-wide searching or browsing based on repository follower count (Figure 21-9). When combined with a particular programming language search, watcher count data can yield useful public domain code examples.

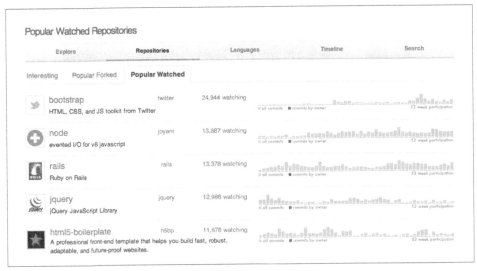

Figure 21-9. Explore and search watcher count

News Feed

Besides the technical high-five that watching a user, organization, or repository provides, it also shapes the content of your personalized news feed as shown in Figure 21-10. This news feed reports the interesting activities of the user repositories and organizations that you're watching.

News feeds are offered both as a web page that you can view on the GitHub.com site, as well as an RSS feed for consumption in the reader application of your choosing.

Forks

The next idea that GitHub popularized, so much so that the phrase has spread to other domains, is personal forks of projects (Figure 21-11). The term forking has commonly carried a negative connotation. In the coding landscape of yesteryear, forking often meant an aggressive parting of ways with the primary copy of the project with the intent of taking the program in a different direction.

GitHub's idea of forking is a positive one that enables a greater number of contributors to make a greater number of contributions in a controlled and highly visible way. Forking is the democratic ability of *any* potential contributor to get a personal copy of a project's code. This personal copy (a fork in GitHub parlance) can then be changed at will without any explicit permission from the original author. This does not pose any risk to the core project because the changes are happening in the forked repository, not the original repository.

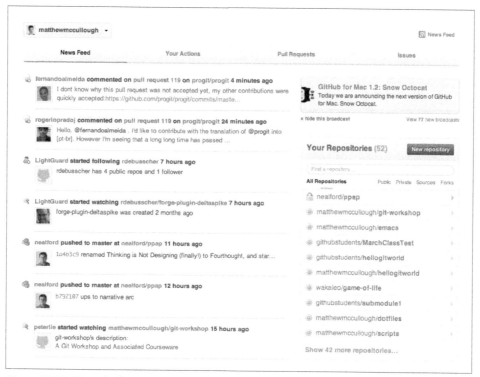

Figure 21-10. News feed

Figure 21-11. Fork button

This is the inverse of the protected core concept of an Apache or Eclipse project, where patches are submitted as file attachments to bug reports. A primary benefit of this model is the transparency and public visibility of the community contributions (Figure 21-12), even before they are submitted back to the core project for discussion and potential incorporation.

The network graph, shown in Figure 21-12, displays the relation of the core project's branches and commits to those of other branches and commits, including repository forks. This provides a high level overview of the community's activity on this project and whether a given fork is diverging significantly from the core project. This allows

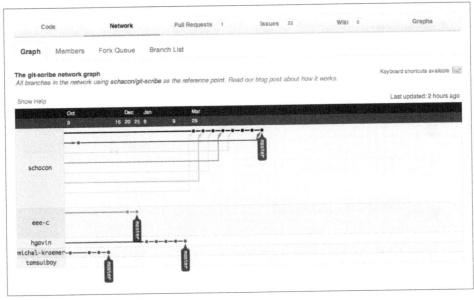

Figure 21-12. Network graph

for a thoughtful review of the divergent community contributions and if they are beneficial to merge back into the core, even in the absence of a pull request.

Several years of observing community behavior with the concept of forks shows that a greater number of fringe users of a project decide to actually submit fixes and small improvements because the ceremony of doing so is extremely low. Many consumers of open source that have worked in both the old patches-attached-to-bugs model and the new fork-and pull-request approach say that the barrier to making contributions in the old model was the disproportionate time required to prepare the patch compared to the time it took to make the actual fix to the code.

Creating Pull Requests

Forking is the enabling step of creating a personal copy of a project, but the real value for the core project lies in the second action, formally called a pull request. Pull requests allow any user with a commit that she feels makes a useful contribution to the project to announce that contribution to the core project owners.

Once a contributor has finished coding a feature, committed that new code to a well-named branch, and pushed that new branch to a fork, it can be turned into a pull request. A pull request can be accurately but minimally described as a *list of topically focused commits*. Pull requests are most commonly based on the entire contents of a topic branch, but can be adjusted to a more narrow range of commits when less than the full branch is ready for offering as a contribution to the release branch. When the newly pushed branch has been selected from the branch selector drop-down control, the context-sensitive Pull Request button, shown in Figure 21-13, is pressed to initiate the assembly of the pull request announcement.

Figure 21-13. Pull request button

The default behavior of a pull request is to include all of the commits on the current topic branch. However, in cases that call for it, a specific range of commits, as well as the source and target branch, can be manually altered as shown in Figure 21-14.

Figure 21-14. Pull request ranges

With the pull request now created, it is up to the core project owners to review, evaluate, comment on, and potentially merge in these changes. Conceptually, this is often compared to the code review process of Crucible and Gerrit. However, it is GitHub's opinion that this process works well—it strikes the perfect balance of being lightweight, yet sufficient for a thorough code review. It also automates the most burdensome step of incorporating new code, merging it in, which can in most cases be done from the GitHub site on a Pull Request page via a mere button click.

Managing Pull Requests

A successful project on GitHub has a queue of Pull Requests (Figure 21-15) to manage. Anyone that is a collaborator on this core instance of the project can manage and process pull requests. It is useful to note that pull requests do not necessarily have to come from forks. Disciplined contributors that have the collaborator privilege on the core project may still decide to use pull requests as a means of soliciting code feedback before merging it in.

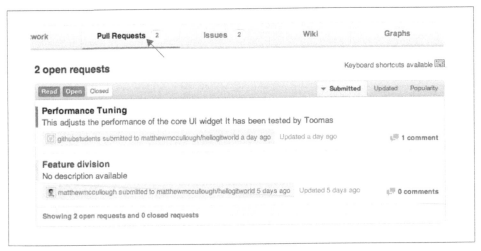

Figure 21-15. Project pull request queue

Pull requests are such an important part of the GitHub ecosystem that each user has his own custom dashboard to display pull requests across all the projects he is associated with as a contributor (Figure 21-16).

Figure 21-16. System-wide pull request queue

Part of the concept behind pull requests is turning a typically binary accept/deny operation into a conversation. That conversation happens with comments on pull requests or comments on specific commits (Figure 21-17). Comments can be of an instructive nature, indicating that the proposed solution still needs work. If the contributor then makes further commits on the topic branch that is part of the pull request, those commits, when pushed, show up sequentially in the pull request thread.

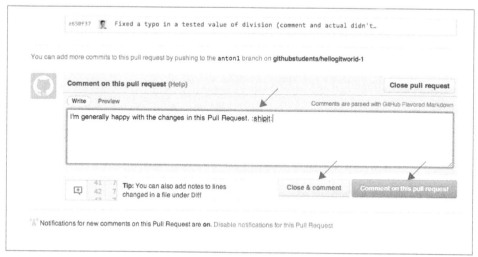

Figure 21-17. Pull request comments

Comments can be made at one of three levels of precision: pull request, commit, or line of code. The line-level comments (Figure 21-18) are the most useful for technical adjustments, offering the reviewer an ability to precisely suggest a more preferred way of coding the same logic to the author.

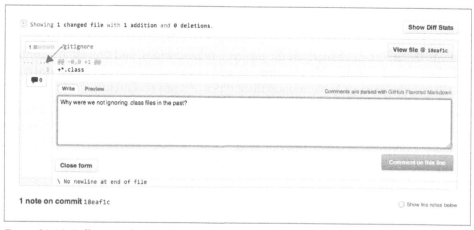

Figure 21-18. Pull request line level commit comments

When the solution in the pull request is sufficiently polished and ready to be merged in, typically to the master branch, it can be done in one of several ways. The most innovative and time-saving approach is to use the automatic merge button on the GitHub web user interface (Figure 21-19). This performs a real Git commit, just as if it had been done from the command line, minus the ceremony of locally downloading and merging the code and pushing the result back up to GitHub.

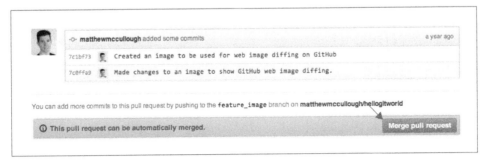

Figure 21-19. Pull request automatic merges

It is natural to think of pull requests as an activity that is done at the end of working on a feature, bug fix, or other contribution. However, pull requests can be effectively used at the beginning of a concept too. It is becoming ever more common to see pull requests initiated with a mere mockup JPEG image or quick text file outline of the objectives of the topic branch, followed by solicitation of team feedback via the pull request comment approaches given previously. The contributors to the topic branch continue to push their changes to GitHub and the pull request is automatically updated in conversation style with links to the latest commits.

Notifications

A social system like GitHub needs a strong notification mechanism to announce potentially important changes on the projects, organizations, and users that a contributor has elected to watch. Notifications, as you might reasonably guess, are driven by watches of the previously mentioned three types of items on GitHub.

The summary of all notifications that pertain to you are centrally located on a notifications page that is reachable by an icon in the top level navigation, as shown in Figure 21-20.

Figure 21-20. Notifications button

This list of pertinent notifications is iconified based on the source of the event. It has icons for repository- user- and organization-level activities. A summary of each activity is provided and hyperlinked to the details of the event, as shown in Figure 21-21.

Figure 21-21. Notifications list

Notifications can be toggled on and off on a per repository basis by a hyperlink at the bottom of the repository's page (Figure 21-22).

System-wide options for notifications are performed under the user's administration settings. The type of events to be notified about, as well as whether these should be routed solely to the web page or additionally to the user's email address are all controlled through this page, as shown in Figure 21-23.

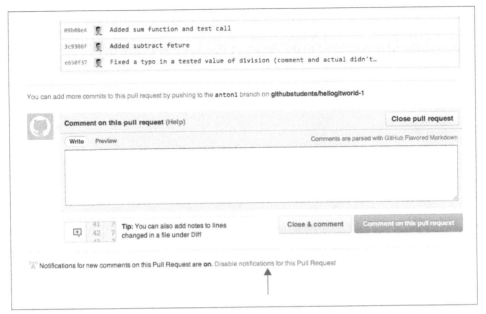

Figure 21-22. *Notifications repository toggle*

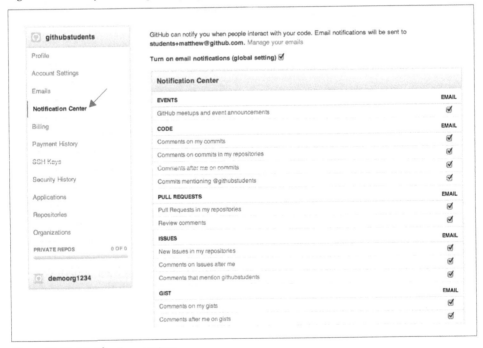

Figure 21-23. *Notifications settings*

Finding Users, Projects, and Code

GitHub certainly is keen on hosting and facilitating collaboration on open source projects. However, the greater portion of the open source community is focused on finding and using open source libraries. This discovery is facilitated by the GitHub Explore page (Figure 21-24). The opening Explore page provides a curated set of repositories that are exhibiting statistical trends, making them likely to be of interest to the greater open source community.

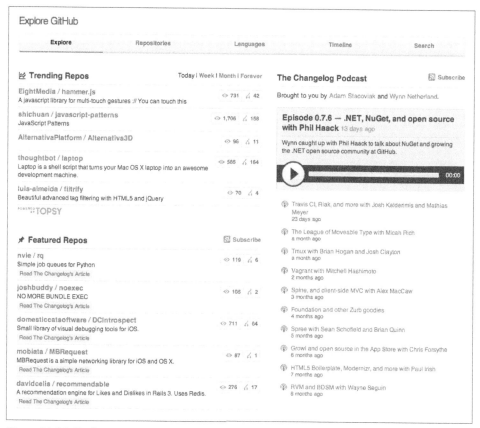

Figure 21-24. Explore

If your focus is to find a code example in a particular programming language, then the Advanced Search page is what you are looking for, as shown in Figure 21-25. Available criteria for user, popularity, repository name, and programming language allow for highly targeted searches.

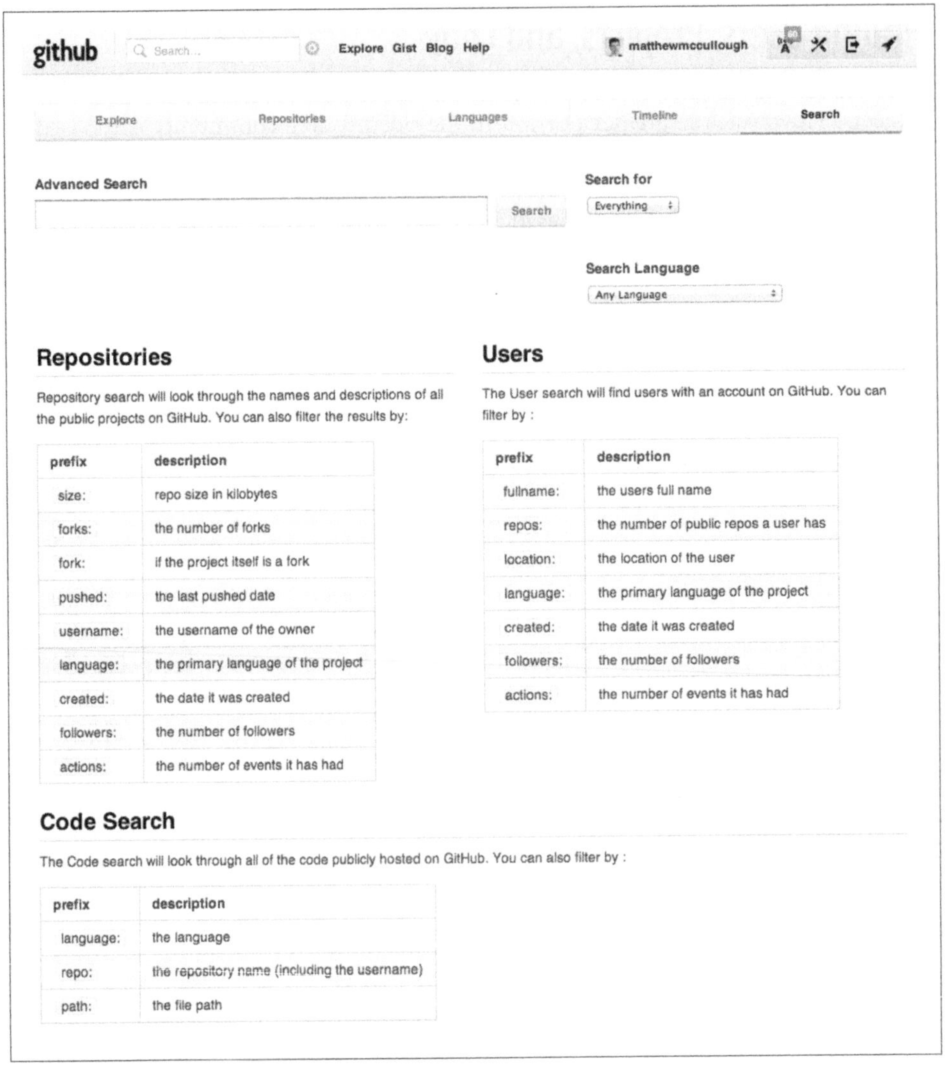

github | Search... | Explore Gist Blog Help | matthewmccullough

Explore | Repositories | Languages | Timeline | **Search**

Advanced Search

[   ] Search

Search for

Everything ⬍

Search Language

Any Language ⬍

Repositories

Repository search will look through the names and descriptions of all the public projects on GitHub. You can also filter the results by:

prefix	description
size:	repo size in kilobytes
forks:	the number of forks
fork:	if the project itself is a fork
pushed:	the last pushed date
username:	the username of the owner
language:	the primary language of the project
created:	the date it was created
followers:	the number of followers
actions:	the number of events it has had

Users

The User search will find users with an account on GitHub. You can filter by :

prefix	description
fullname:	the users full name
repos:	the number of public repos a user has
location:	the location of the user
language:	the primary language of the project
created:	the date it was created
followers:	the number of followers
actions:	the number of events it has had

Code Search

The Code search will look through all of the code publicly hosted on GitHub. You can also filter by :

prefix	description
language:	the language
repo:	the repository name (including the username)
path:	the file path

Figure 21-25. Site search

Wikis

Updating a wiki previously meant editing a page in a browser. This was a very volatile form of editing with minimal version control. Changes could be lost at the slightest browser refresh.

With a simple Markdown (*http://daringfireball/markdown*) syntax, wikis are first-class Git repos that sit alongside their project. GitHub wikis (Figure 21-26) permit commits, comments, merging, rebasing, and all the features that Git users have come to enjoy, but that wiki users previously have not had at their disposal.

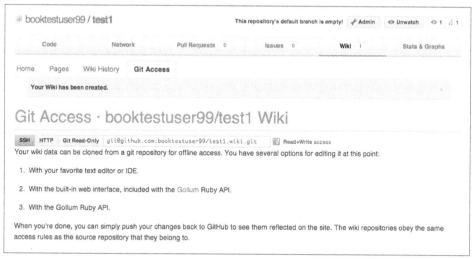

Figure 21-26. GitHub wikis

But just because you can edit the wiki via a Git repository cloned to your local machine doesn't mean giving up the convenience of the in-browser editing approach (Figure 21-27). The in-browser editor is also writing back to the underlying Git repo so users can trace the author and reasoning history of all page edits.

GitHub Pages (Git for Websites)

If the wiki page idea sounded attractive, what about having Git-tracked Markdown files as the foundation of a tool for publishing entire websites? GitHub pages based on Jekyll (*https://github.com/mojombo/jekyll*) provide exactly that, and can even be mapped to a Domain Name System (DNS) CNAME record as content for a subdomain or primary domain name (Figure 21-28).

Octopress (*http://octopress.org*) (Figure 21-29) is gaining traction as a mashup of Jekyll and GitHub pages, making it easier than ever to publish dynamic content in a static way. The security vulnerabilities and the growing set of attack vectors on dynamically generated sites using live databases and just-in-time compilation has pushed a large number of individuals back to statically served content. But that doesn't mean giving up dynamic site generation, it just means relocating the dynamic processing to authoring time rather than its traditional location at the time of page requests with technologies like JavaServer Pages (JSPs) and PHP: Hypertext Preprocessor (PHP).

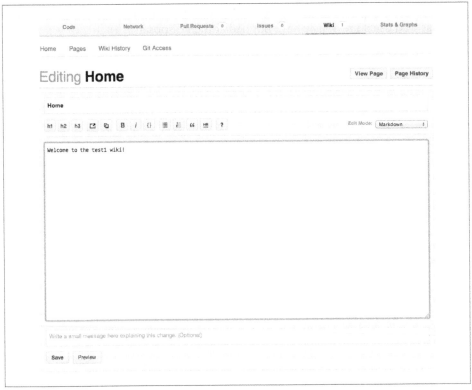

Figure 21-27. GitHub in-browser editing of wikis

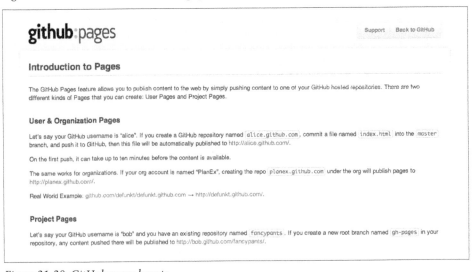

Figure 21-28. GitHub pages how to

Figure 21-29. Octopress home page

In-Page Code Editor

Traditionally, coding is done on the desktop in the user's text editor of choice. But for a small fix this seems like a burdensome ceremony of pulling the code, editing the code, committing the code, and pushing the code. For something as simple as a spelling correction in an error message, GitHub supports in-browser code editing, as shown in Figure 21-30.

The in-browser editor is based on Mozilla's Ace (*http://ace.ajax.org/*) JavaScript–based control. This is the same control used by the Cloud9 IDE and Beanstalk. This control, shown in Figure 21-31, supports line numbering, syntax highlighting, and space and tab formatting. Code changes become as simple as browsing to the source file on GitHub, clicking Edit this file, and committing the change with your commit message entered directly below the in-browser editor. Small fixes have never been so easy.

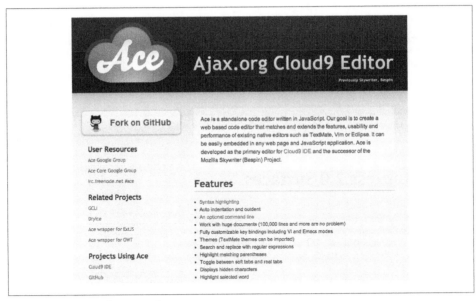

Figure 21-30. Ace in-browser editor

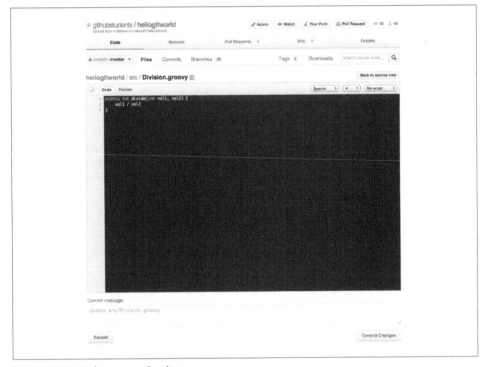

Figure 21-31. In-browser code editing

Subversion Bridge

Although GitHub certainly believes that Git is the VCS of the future, there is also an understanding that SVN will be with us for quite some time. GitHub supports that dual existence in two ways.

Traditionally, Git users have kept their repository in SVN and used `git-svn` to bridge the two technologies. However, this approach means that only the lower fidelity SVN metadata can be kept for commits, excluding the ever useful Git Author and Git Committer fields, as well as the Git parent commit refs.

GitHub makes the opposite bridge possible, without the aid of any client-side conversion software. Every Git repository at GitHub is also dynamically converted at request-time to be served as an SVN repository at exactly the same HTTPS URL used for Git cloning, as shown in action in Figure 21-32. This is a complex dynamic conversion, unique to Git repositories served from GitHub. This bridge facilitates continued SVN use in a cautious and stepwise conversion to an eventual sole use of Git. This server-side bridge (Figure 21-33) permits not just commit GUIs, but other SVN-connected legacy tools to work with a Git-based repository of commits. The Git default branch, typically `master`, is automatically mapped to `trunk` in the SVN interface, showing forethought of even mapping to the idioms of the SVN realm.

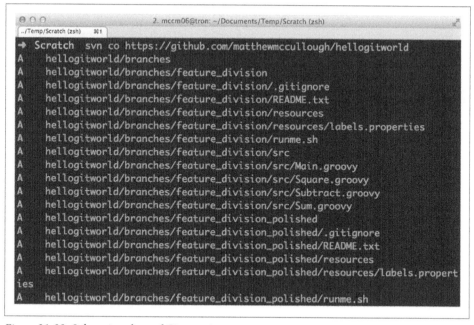

Figure 21-32. Subversion clone of Git repository

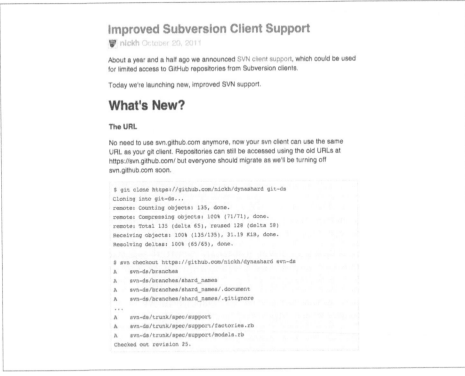

Figure 21-33. Git-SVN bridge

Tags Automatically Becoming Archives

When an open source project wants to create a compressed archive of the project on GitHub, there's an easy shortcut: just tag the desired revision of code. Git tags are automatically converted into TGZ and ZIP compressed archives available from the Tags page as shown in Figure 21-34.

Figure 21-34. Tags as archives

Organizations

Up until now, this book has primarily discussed interactions of smaller quantities of GitHub users, acting in a relatively independent fashion. However, the attraction of Git has spread to more cohesive groups, small businesses, and enterprises. GitHub has an Organizations (Figure 21-35) set of features to serve those groups well.

Figure 21-35. Organization selector

GitHub Organizations provide ownership of repositories at a higher level than mere user accounts. In support of that, there is an additional security construct: Teams. Teams are a grouping mechanism for users that associates with a certain permission level and a set of repositories. The three permission levels are pull only, pull+push, and pull+push+administration as shown in Figure 21-36.

Figure 21-36. Organization permissions

REST API

Having a web application is a great starting point, but GitHub has a rich community of developers that are eager to use true services, not just page scraping, to build the next layer of useful features. To facilitate the community construction of supporting tools, GitHub has built a full Application Programming Interface (API). GitHub's API has evolved in three major eras, and the current *v3* of the API (*http://developer.github .com/v3/*), as it is known, offers almost all UI-accessible features in an equivalent API form. In some cases, advanced services are offered though the API that aren't even part of the GitHub UI yet.

An example shown in Example 21-1 makes a call to the API to get the organizations that a user belongs to. The response, as are all responses from the GitHub API, are given in JavaScript Object Notation (JSON) format. Note that the avatar_url is really one long string value that has been split here for typography reasons.

Example 21-1. Calling the GitHub API

```
curl https://api.github.com/users/matthewmccullough/orgs

[
  {
    "avatar_url": "https://secure.gravatar.com/avatar/11f43e3d3b15205be70289ddedfe2de7
        ?d=https://a248.e.akamai.net/assets.github.com
        %2Fimages%2Fgravatars%2Fgravatar-orgs.png",
    "login": "gradleware",
    "url": "https://api.github.com/orgs/gradleware",
    "id": 386945
  },
  {
    "avatar_url": "https://secure.gravatar.com/avatar/61024896f291303615bcd4f7a0dcfb74
        ?d=https://a248.e.akamai.net/assets.github.com
        %2Fimages%2Fgravatars%2Fgravatar-orgs.png",
    "login": "github",
    "url": "https://api.github.com/orgs/github",
    "id": 9919
  }
]
```

The gamut of GitHub operations are exposed through the RESTful API and are well-documented on the GitHub API site, as shown in Figure 21-37. But what is more idea enabling than just calling out for a list of users, repositories, or files is the ability to use

Figure 21-37. GitHub REST API

the open standard for authorization, OAUTH, to request and gain the ability to act on behalf of a GitHub user. This opens up the possibility of querying and manipulating private repository contents, using repositories as storage containers for versioned artifacts beyond source code, and building applications that can abstract themselves from the difficulty of building a version control persistence layer.

Social Coding on Closed Source

Though the first idea that comes to mind with a collaborative development model like GitHub is open source, nearly all of the benefits described can be derived even inside the offices of a company. Businesses should take full advantage of the talents of all developers in their employ, even if they aren't currently assigned to a given project. Pull requests, in combination with organizations and pull only teams, enable gated contributions by any authorized employee, but with the safety net of a code review by core project collaborators.

Eventual Open Sourcing

Although open source is often thought of as being open from birth, an increasing number of projects are being open sourced after a certain amount of maturity is achieved or after a certain development milestone is reached. This eventual open sourcing benefits from the history having been kept in Git and the repository being maintained on GitHub. The fully preserved context of "why is this line of code the way it is?" is available from the Git commit history. The actual act of converting the repo to gain the full benefit of GitHub's social coding aspects is as simple as a Boolean toggle on the repository's admin page, as shown in Figure 21-38.

Figure 21-38. Public and private repo toggle

Coding Models

The choice of Git as the VCS of a development team and, more specifically, the choice of GitHub as the repository host, facilitates dozens of unique usage patterns. Three of these usage styles are briefly described.

The centralized model, shown in Figure 21-39, while still offering the local commit insulation that isn't afforded by true centralized systems like SVN, is the simplest, but least interesting of the models. It is an easy first step because developers push their local commits frequently so as to simulate the "everything is on the central server" state that was enforced by their version control tool of yesteryear. Although this can be a viable starting pattern with Git, it is a mere stepping stone toward unique and valuable leveraging of the distributed and collaborative model Git and GitHub have to offer.

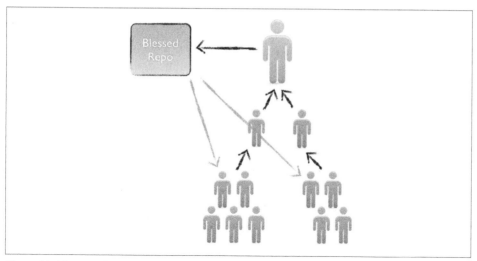

Figure 21-40. Linux lieutenant and commander model

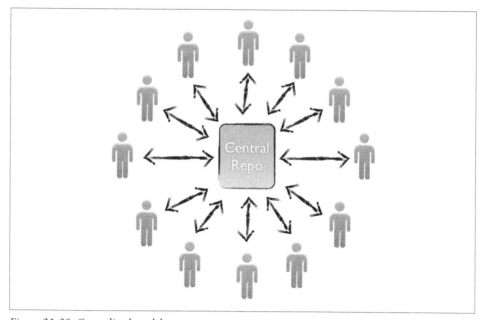

Figure 21-39. Centralized model

Next up is the lieutenant and commander model shown in Figure 21-40. You'll recognize it as very similar to that enabled by pull request facilities of GitHub. It is important to note that Git projects in the absence of GitHub have a means of implementing this model through emails and links passed around, but always with greater apparent friction and ceremony than real pull requests.

Lastly, for companies that are leveraging open source, want to donate back their bug fixes, but keep the innovations in-house, an arbitrator for the two repositories can be established. This arbitrator, as shown in Figure 21-41, picks and chooses which commits are cherry-picked and pushed back into the public domain to the open source version of the project. This is being done today on well-known entities such as RedHat's JBoss Server.

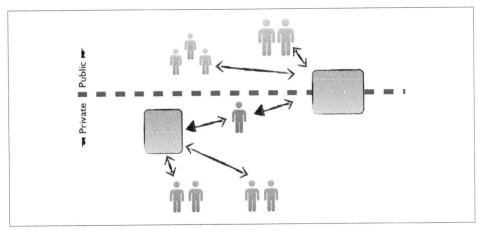

Figure 21-41. Partial open sourcing model

GitHub Enterprise

All of this may sound very attractive, but your business may be governed by requirements or even laws that prohibit the storage of code on the public Internet, no matter how secure the offering. The solution for this is GitHub Enterprise, whose home page is shown in Figure 21-42. It offers the same public GitHub experience as described in so many of the sections previously, but is delivered as a virtual machine image (shown in VirtualBox in Figure 21-43) for on-premise hosting. Additionally, GitHub Enterprise is compatible with Exchange Server Lightweight Directory Access Protocol (LDAP) and Central Authentication Service (CAS) user authentication that many enterprises already have in place.

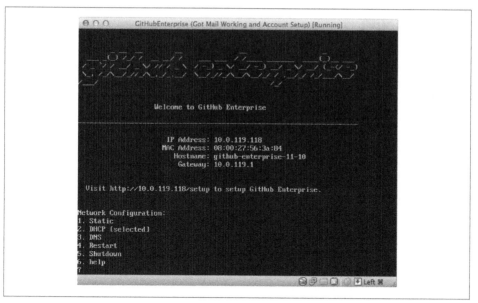

Figure 21-43. GitHub Enterprise in VirtualBox

Figure 21-42. GitHub Enterprise home page

GitHub in Sum

Git is a developer tool that has shaken the very foundations of CVS, SVN, Perforce, and ClearCase installations by showing that high performance, collaborative, and distributed version control can be found in an open source solution. Offset by only a short delay from Git's own development, GitHub has equally shown that a sharp web application can reduce tool burden, facilitate quicker fixes, allow a greater number of contributors to further a project, and most importantly, turn the act of coding into a truly social activity.

Index

Symbols

! (exclamation point), for inverted pattern, 59
(pound sign)
    for comments, 127
    in .gitmore file, 59
$GIT_DIR variable, 68
' (quotes), for ref as single word, 193
* (asterisk)
    branch name restrictions and, 91
    globbing, 59
    in git show-branch output, 95
+ (plus sign)
    in diff, 107, 131
    in git show-branch output, 95
    in refspec, 202
    and location for split operation, 354
    when viewing commit differences, 26
+++ (triple plus signs), in diff, 107
- (minus sign)
    in diff, 107, 131
    in git show-branch output, 95
    and location for split operation, 354
-- (double dash) operand separator, 21
--- (triple minus signs)
    in diff, 107
. (dot)
    branch name restrictions and, 91
    for current directory, 22
.. (double period)
    for commit range, 78
    in git diff command, 115
... (triple period), symmetric difference, 82, 117, 230

/ (slash character), trailing, for directory name, 59, 91, 307
-3 or --3way option
    for git am command, 280
: (colon)
    branch name restrictions and, 91
    in refspec, 202
< (left), for git log --left-right display, 133
<<<<<<<
    as merge markers, 129, 146
    in diff output, 126
> (right), for git log --left-right display, 133
>>>>>>>
    as merge markers, 129, 146
    in diff output, 126
? (question mark), branch name restrictions and, 91
@ (at sign)
    in reflog, 160, 190
    in stash entry names, 184, 187
[ ] (square brackets), in git show-branch output, 95
^ (caret), 69–71
    branch name restrictions and, 91
    for branch name, 95
~ (tilde), 69–71
    branch name restrictions and, 91

A

-a option
    for git branch command, 211
    for git diff command, 112
--abbrev-commit option, for git log command, 73, 124, 187, 323

We'd like to hear your suggestions for improving our indexes. Send email to *index@oreilly.com.*

descendant node, in commit graph, 75
detached HEAD branches, 84, 102–103, 229
developer, 251
    adding new to authoritative repository, 210–212
    interaction with maintainer, 252
development
    distributed, 248–250
        position in project, 250–254
        recovering from upstream rebase, 374–375
    manipulating history, 152
development branch, 90, 199
development projects, within distributed environment history, 249
development repository, 196
    clone of repository as, 210
    push into, 233
didactic realistic history, 152
diff program, 26, 416
    (see also git diff command)
    -r option, 108
differences
    in commits, viewing, 26
    between files, 36
    symmetric, 82
diffs, 107–120
    of merge commit, 136
    Subversion vs. Git, 119
digest, 42
directed acyclic graph (DAG), 75
directories
    for Git revision information, 22
    impact of selecting new current branch, 97
    slash character (/) trailing in name for, 59
    structure cleanup, 377–378
dirty state
    of index, 61
    resetting loss of, 137
    tree objects, 185
    of working directory, 122
        interactive rebase with, 367–368
DISPLAY environment variable, 86
distributed development, 248–250
    position in project, 250–254
        upstream and downstream flows, 250–254, 251
    recovering from upstream rebase, 374–375
    VCS with, 2

distributed repository structure, 244–245
distributed version control system (DVCS), 121
diverged history of repository, 219
documentation
    complete build of, 13
    for git subcommands, 20
    for git-grep command, 379
    online for Git, 20
dot (see . (dot))
.dotest directory, 278
dotfile configurations, 319
double period (..)
    for commit range, 78
    in git diff command, 115
downstream consumer, 253
downstream flows, 251
downstream producer/publisher, 254
downstream repository, mechanisms for transferrring commits, 253–254
--dry-run option, for git commit command, 185, 188
dynamic commit history, 248

E

editing
    commit message, 338
        with git filter-branch, 343–344
    meta-information on commit, 167
editor
    for commit log message, 30, 54
    opening during git commit, 23
    for remote repository configuration, 226
    template message for merge, 127
editor files, removing left-over, 368
Emacs Lisp setups, 319
email address, in Git configuration, 24
email, for patch, 264, 265
emerge command (Gentoo), 10
empty directories, creating, 294
env-filter, 338
environment variables
    DISPLAY, 86
    GIT_AUTHOR_EMAIL, 24
    GIT_AUTHOR_NAME, 24
    GIT_EDITOR, 23
error messages, 23
    branch 'bug/pr-3' is not an ancestor of your current HEAD, 103

Objective-C ecosystem, submodules, 315
objects, unreachable, 369
Octopress, 403
octopus strategy for merge, 142
octothorp (#)
    for comments, 127
    in .gitmore file, 59
oh-my-zsh, 319
--onto option, for git rebase command, 169,
        248
open source libraries, finding and using, 401
open source, social coding on, 390
open sourcing, eventual, 411
openssl library, 12
operating system, xi
options for Git, listing, 19
origin remote, 206–208
origin, for clone, 198
origin/HEAD ref, 211
ORIG_HEAD, 69
--ours option, for git diff command, 131
ours strategy merges, 143

P

-p option
    for git add command, 351, 354
    for git cat-file command, 46
    for git log command, 73, 132, 133
Pacific Northwest-based operating system, 29
pack files, 33, 36
packages for Git install, 9
    verifying up-to-date, 11
Packard, Keith, 247
parent commits, 70, 136
parent repository, 251
parent-filter, 338
partial checkouts, 296–297
partial open source model for GitHub
        development, 414
password, for remote hosting machine, 237
patch command, 276
patch-related hooks, 291–292
patches, 263–284
    applying, 276–284
    bad, 283
    commands for exchange, 263
    generating, 265–273
    guidelines for, 350
    mailing, 273–276

reasons for use, 264–265
and topological sorts, 272–273
verifying set of commits for, 270
vs. merges, 283
path limiting, git diff command with, 117–119
pathname, vs. content, 35
patterns, .gitignore and filenames, 58
peer repository, 251
peer review, "patch email review apply"
        paradigm for, 264
peer-to-peer backup, 250
peer-to-peer repository model , 5, 232, 244,
        256, 263
performance
    hook impact, 286
    of VCS, 2
period (see . (dot))
periods (...), symmetric difference, 82, 117,
        230
personal account in GitHub, 387
PHP: Hypertext Preprocessor (PHP), 403
physical data layout, in Git, 35
pickaxe, 88
plug-ins, submodules for, 319
plus sign (+)
    in diff, 107, 131
    in git show-branch output, 95
    in refspec, 202
    and location for split operation, 354
    when viewing commit differences, 26
plus signs (+++), in diff, 107
ports, default
    for Git, 202
    for inetd service, 238
post hook, 285
post-applypatch hook, 292
post-checkout hook, 287, 294
post-commit hook, 291
post-merge hook, 294
post-receive hook, 293
post-update hook, 286, 293
post-update script, 240
pound sign (#)
    for comments, 127
    in .gitmore file, 59
PowerPC architecture, 257
pre hook, 285
pre-applypatch hook, 292
pre-auto-gc hook, 294

About the Authors

Jon Loeliger is a freelance software engineer who contributes to Open Source projects such as Linux, U-Boot, and Git. He has given tutorial presentations on Git at many conferences, including *Linux World*, and has written several papers on Git for *Linux Magazine*. In prior lives, Jon has spent a number of years developing highly optimizing compilers, router protocols, Linux porting, and the occasional game. Jon holds degrees in computer science from Purdue University. In his spare time, he is a home winemaker.

Matthew McCullough, Vice President of Training for GitHub.com, is an energetic 15-year veteran of enterprise software development, a world-traveling open source educator, and co-founder of a US consultancy. All of these activities provide him avenues of sharing success stories of leveraging Git and GitHub. Matthew is a contributing author to the Gradle and Jenkins O'Reilly books and creator of the Git Master Class series for O'Reilly. Matthew regularly speaks on the No Fluff Just Stuff conference tour, is the author of the *DZone Git RefCard*, and is president of the Denver Open Source Users Group.

Colophon

The animal on the cover of *Version Control with Git* is a long-eared bat. It is a fairly large bat that is common and widespread throughout Great Britain and Ireland. It can also be found in Japan. Often seen in colonies of 50 to a 100 or more, it lives in open woodlands, as well as parks and gardens and in spaces under houses and church roofs. It also hibernates in caves, where it is more solitary in habit.

The long-eared bat is a medium-size bat with a broad wingspan of about 25 cm. Its ears are very long and have a very distinctive fold—their inner edges meet each other on the top of the head, and their outer edges end just behind the angle of the mouth. When the bat sleeps, it folds its ears under its wings. During flight, the ears are pointing forward. Its fur is long, fluffy, and silky, extending a short way onto the surface of its wings. It is dusky brown in color on top and light or dirty brown in color below. Juveniles are pale grey, lacking the brown tinges of the adults. Their diet consists of flies, moths, and beetles. It glides among foliage, frequently hovering to scour for insects. When traveling to another tree, its flight is swift, strong, and close to the ground.

Long-eared bats breed in autumn and spring. Pregnant females form nursery colonies of 100 or more in early summer, and the single young or twins are born in June and July. Bats are the only true flying mammals. Contrary to popular misconception, they are not blind—many can actually see very well. All British bats use echolocation to orient themselves at night; they emit bursts of sound that are of such high frequencies they are beyond the human range of hearing and are therefore called "ultrasound." The bats then listen to and interpret the echoes bounced back from objects around them (including prey), which allows them to build a "sound-picture" of their surroundings.

Like all bats, this species is vulnerable to a number of threats, including the loss of roost sites, as hollow trees are often cut down if thought unsafe. Pesticide use has devastating effects, causing severe declines in insect abundance and contaminating food with potentially fatal toxins. Insecticides applied to timbers inside buildings where roosts occur are a particular danger—the initial treatment can wipe out whole colonies (spraying timber where bats are roosting is now illegal), but the effects of these chemicals can be lethal to bats for up to 20 years. In Britain, under the Wildlife and Countryside Act, it is illegal to intentionally kill, injure, take, or sell a bat; to possess a live bat or part of a bat; and to intentionally, recklessly damage, obstruct, or destroy access to bat roosts. Under the conservation regulations, it is an offense to damage or destroy breeding sites or resting places. Offenders can be charged up to 5,000 pounds per bat affected and be sentenced to six months imprisonment.

The cover image is from Lydekker's. The cover font is Adobe ITC Garamond. The text font is Linotype Birka; the heading font is Adobe Myriad Condensed; and the code font is LucasFont's TheSansMonoCondensed.

Have it your way.

Get even more for your money.

Join the O'Reilly Community, and register the O'Reilly books you own. It's free, and you'll get:

- $4.99 ebook upgrade offer
- 40% upgrade offer on O'Reilly print books
- Membership discounts on books and events
- Free lifetime updates to ebooks and videos
- Multiple ebook formats, DRM FREE
- Participation in the O'Reilly community
- Newsletters
- Account management
- 100% Satisfaction Guarantee

Signing up is easy:

1. **Go to: oreilly.com/go/register**
2. **Create an O'Reilly login.**
3. **Provide your address.**
4. **Register your books.**

Note: English-language books only

To order books online:
oreilly.com/store

For questions about products or an order:
orders@oreilly.com

To sign up to get topic-specific email announcements and/or news about upcoming books, conferences, special offers, and new technologies:
elists@oreilly.com

For technical questions about book content:
booktech@oreilly.com

To submit new book proposals to our editors:
proposals@oreilly.com

O'Reilly books are available in multiple DRM-free ebook formats. For more information:
oreilly.com/ebooks

O'REILLY®

Spreading the knowledge of innovators   oreilly.com

CPSIA information can be obtained at www.ICGtesting.com
Printed in the USA
BVOW102246190613

323766BV00010B/197/P